ECHOES OF THE PEARL

ECHOES OF THE PEARL

The Evolution of Uganda's Popular
Music, 1880–1980

ROBERT BWIRE

KIIRA RIVER PRESS

ATLANTA, GEORGIA

2026

Published by
Kiira River Press
Atlanta, Georgia

First edition, 2026

ISBN: 979-8-9952481-0-1
Printed in the United States of America

For the musicians of Uganda, whose voices shaped a
nation's sound; may your melodies carry the
wind, and your echoes never fade

Contents

Introduction

The music begins before the dancers reach the floor. A trumpet sends out a bright call, followed by the languid cry of a saxophone. Guitars ripple beneath the horns, weaving melodies above the steady pulse of drums and maracas. In the half-lit hall, the rhythm gathers momentum, and the murmur of conversation gives way to movement. It is a Saturday night in Kampala in the early 1960s.

Outside, the city rests quietly across its seven hills, but inside the dance halls the night has only begun. Men in sharply pressed suits guide their partners onto the floor. The women wear elegant dresses, some trimmed with beads that shimmer beneath the colored lights. Perfume mingles with cigarette smoke and the faint sweetness of beer as couples take their places. The first dances are formal: Waltz, Tango, and Foxtrot. Pairs glide across the polished floor with deliberate grace, counting their steps as they move in slow arcs beneath the bandstand. At the edges of the hall, groups of young men watch and wait for their moment of courage, rehearsing in their minds the simple question that will carry them onto the floor.

But as the night deepens, something shifts. The guitars grow more playful. The rhythm section leans forward. A Lingala melody floats above the instruments and suddenly the careful geometry of ballroom dancing dissolves. Bodies loosen. Couples draw closer. The dancers no longer count their steps but surrender to the pulse. It is rumba time.

From Leopoldville across the Congo River came a sound that felt strangely familiar to Ugandan ears. The rhythm carried echoes of older

Central African traditions even as its guitars and harmonies bore the marks of long journeys across the Atlantic and back again. By the middle of the twentieth century, Congolese rumba had become one of Africa's most irresistible musical languages, and in Kampala it spread like wildfire. At nightclubs such as Susana in Nakulabye, New Life in Mengo, or the White Nile in Kibuye, the bands commanded the room. Trumpets flashed above the crowd. Saxophones crooned with effortless charm. Guitars traced melodies that seemed to spiral endlessly into the night.

Some evenings the stage might feature performers such as Israel Magembe, Ecklas Kawalya, Margaret Nakibuuka, Bonnie Kyambadde, or Fred Kanyike. On others, singers like Hadija Namale or Mary Nattima held the room spellbound with voices that floated above the orchestra. Each song pulled the dancers back to the floor again and again. For many Ugandans of the era, these evenings were more than entertainment. They were encounters with a changing world. Village rhythms met brass band traditions learned in mission schools. Church harmonies mingled with Cuban recordings broadcast on Radio Uganda. Congolese guitar styles intertwined with local languages and melodies. On the dance floor these influences blended into something new. They became the sound of modern Uganda.

The history of Ugandan music is therefore a story of encounter, adaptation, and creativity. Across generations, musicians absorbed influences from distant places while remaining deeply rooted in local traditions. The resulting musical culture was neither purely indigenous nor simply imported. It was syncretic, a blending of forms, rhythms, and ideas that produced new sounds reflecting the realities of a changing society.

This book traces that story across roughly a century, from the late nineteenth century to the close of the 1970s. The narrative begins in the final decades of the Buganda kingdom before colonial rule, when early observers recorded the central role of music in court ceremonies and daily life. It follows the introduction of gramophones and recording technology, and the emergence of dance ensembles in Kampala and other towns.

By the middle of the twentieth century, Uganda's musical landscape had expanded dramatically. Radio broadcasts carried songs across the country. Recording studios preserved the voices of emerging artists. Nightclubs and social halls brought musicians and audiences together in vibrant urban settings. The sounds of Congolese rumba, Cuban son, Western ballroom styles, and local traditions intertwined, giving rise to new bands, new songs, and new audiences. The musicians who shaped this era created a body of work that still endures today. Their music captured the optimism of independence, the vitality of urban life, and the resilience of cultural traditions that adapted to new circumstances without losing their essence.

A history such as this one could never be written without the generosity of the musicians and witnesses who carried these recollections across the decades. Many of the artists who animated Uganda's musical life in the 1960s and 1970s spoke about their experiences with remarkable openness, allowing that era to be reconstructed with clarity and depth. Hadija Namale spoke with warmth and enthusiasm about the music of her youth, and our collaboration eventually led her back into the recording studio, where she revisited two of her beloved classics, Johnny and Bossa, recording them anew with Ziwuuna Band. Louise Bagenda generously shared her time and photographs from the period, helping to illuminate the faces behind the music. Frank Mbalire has walked this long journey of research with me for many years, offering guidance and encouragement along the way. Andrew "Andy" Kyambadde, David Jingo, who despite ailing health remained eager to recount his experiences, Simon Berunga, and John Sentamu all contributed valuable perspectives and connections.

Moses Matovu continues to lead the Afrigo Band, ensuring that the distinctive rumba sound, endogo semadongo, still enchants Ugandans across generations and sustains Kampala's enduring love affair with rumba. I am particularly grateful for his generosity. During a busy rehearsal period at his studios in Kibuli, he graciously stepped away to grant us an interview, reflecting on his long and storied career. William Mujwala, during one of our conversations, burst unexpectedly into song, reminding me that the spirit of the stage still lived strongly within him. The late Sammy Kasule shared many stories of his life as a young musician in Uganda, recounting them with humor even when recalling the painful episode in which he was tortured by soldiers who had falsely accused him. We spoke only a few days before his passing in Amsterdam, and I remain grateful for the candor and warmth he brought to our conversations.

I am also indebted to Engineer Henry Wassanyi Serukenya for his thoughtful reflections; to Martin Munyenga of the Democratic Republic of Congo, mentor to many musicians and a quiet force behind the success of Susana nightclub; and to the elegant Congolese dancer Suismann N'goy, whose artistry elevated dance culture in Kampala's clubs. Both Munyenga and N'goy made Uganda their home, and their perspectives helped me better understand the role and influence of Congolese musicians in the Ugandan music scene. I also remember with gratitude the late Grace Nsubuga Lukomwa of Afrigo who, unsolicited, reached out to me and offered his recollections.

Researching Ugandan music presents particular challenges. Many of the central figures of the era, among them Ecklas Kawalya, Fred Kanyike, Peterson T. Mutebi and Elly Wamala, had already passed away by the time this project began more than a decade ago. Interviews with surviving musicians provided rare firsthand accounts, but memory is inevitably fragile, and printed sources are often difficult to obtain. Over decades of political upheaval and regime change, archives have not always been preserved with the care they deserve. Documents have sometimes been lost or scattered, and even newspapers could become objects of suspicion if they mentioned leaders who had fallen from power.

For this reason, the assistance of my sister Restituta Kagguma Nabwire and my niece Vivian Nalubowa proved indispensable. Despite demanding professional responsibilities, they devoted countless hours traversing the country to conduct interviews and comb through newspapers and magazines preserved at the Makerere University Library and the Uganda National Records Centre and Archives in Wandegeya. Access was sometimes denied, but they persevered and ultimately assembled a remarkable collection of articles dating back to the 1950s. Without their determination and dedication, much of the documentary foundation of this book would not exist.

The Dutch journalist and author Michiel van Oosterhout also played a vital role in the development of this project. His book The Soul of Uganda Through Song: An Alternative History Book provided valuable guidance, and he kindly read and critiqued an early draft of this manuscript. Michiel also shared materials from his extensive archive and allowed me to acquire a significant number of shellac and vinyl recordings that he had collected over many years. Over time I became an avid collector myself. Since beginning this pursuit, I have assembled more than two thousand shellac and vinyl recordings of Ugandan music. The pages that follow reference more than 950 unique songs, ranging from traditional repertoire and early recordings to the rumba-influenced popular music that flourished from the 1960s through the early 1980s.

Listening to these recordings was essential to understanding the music itself. Uganda's earliest commercial recordings date to 1930, when the German recording engineer Heinrich Lampe, working with Columbia Records, recorded roughly sixty tracks of Ugandan secular and Christian songs. Among them were Gowa's Omugeni Agenda, Blandina's Kamungolo, and Mundu Tesaga's Ngolo and Aziraya. Hearing these recordings provided a rare window into the beginnings of Uganda's recorded musical history.

Other individuals contributed generously to this journey. Michael Kiefer of California shared rare recordings from his remarkable collection after what began as a friendly rivalry over a record auction on eBay. Andrew J. Eisenberg made available important materials from his own collection, The Andrew Eisenberg Collection of East African Commercial Sound Recordings. The late General Ali Fadhul shared recollections of the Rwenzori band, while the Francis brothers of the African Record Center in Brooklyn provided invaluable information about Fred Kanyike's Rwenzori International during its New York tour in the mid-1970s. Harry Kasigwa encouraged this project from its early inception and introduced me to several key collaborators. My friend Joseph Kabugo of Kiteezi, Kampala, devoted time to tracking down recordings and interviewing musicians whose stories might otherwise have been lost.

My children, Annelore and Thomas Bwire, read the manuscript with care and offered feedback that sharpened both the writing and my thinking. Thomas deserves a particular note of gratitude: his guitar playing, weaving through Dr. Nico's Congolese rumba riffs during our evenings together, stirred something deep in me and became an unexpected but constant reminder of the beauty of rumba grooves — propelling me forward whenever the work felt long. I am also grateful to Hazel Brinkley, who gifted me with a Rhino Boys shellac she had won through what I understand was a spirited and competitive bidding contest on eBay. That record arrived as a true act of generosity.

Many others offered pieces of the larger puzzle. Johnson Brick Mutalya in Jinja provided information about the musician Aloziyo Nnyago. Edward Kabuye shared recollections of his father Charles Sonko and his aunt Frida Sonko. Jamie Candelaria-Greene offered a rare glimpse into Charles Sonko's years in Nairobi. While serving there with the Peace Corps, she came to know Sonko personally and even recorded a duet with him, preserving a small but memorable moment of his musical journey. Charles Chuza recounted aspects of his father Joseph Chuza Kabasele's life in Uganda and also shared recollections of the musicians who would later form the City Five Band, including the Ugandan musician Charles Ssenkatuka. Susan Batuuka shared family photographs and introduced me to Robina Nalwoga, the muse of Hanny Sensuwa's song Robina. John Luggya provided valuable information about the Mengo African Orchestra led by his father John Bosa. Sarah Mdigos-Mukasa shared recollections of her father Livingstone Ngadha Mdigos who was part of the musical circle surrounding Eva Nanyonga.

Patrick "Hadiba" Bwire assisted with organizing interviews and logistics, while Teopister Agutu helped track down elusive information by reaching out to individuals who might hold fragments of the story. My friend Dr. Geraldine Tibayungwa Magara accompanied me on much of this journey, listening to many of the recordings and offering thoughtful observations along the way. Mama Domitula Aoko and Mama Anne Nekesa shared vivid recollections of the dance halls of the 1960s, reminding me that a painting hanging in my parents' home in Banda, Bukooli, had once been a gift from Kamulu, the proprietor of the New Life clubs in Mengo and Bugembe.

All these voices, recollections, recordings, and fragments of history have helped reconstruct a musical past that might otherwise have faded into silence. The chapters that follow trace the evolution of Ugandan music across a century of change. They explore the musical life of the Buganda court, the impact of missionary and colonial influences, the emergence of recording technology, and the vibrant popular music scene that flourished in Kampala's dance halls and nightclubs. Along the way they follow the musicians, bands, and songs that carried Ugandan music from royal courtyards to modern stages. The echoes of that history continue to shape Uganda's musical landscape today.

CHAPTER 1

Ekitongole Ekigowa: Band, Faith, and Forgotten Legacy

Tucked behind an unassuming red brick low-rise building on Bombo Road, midway between Kampala's bustling City Square and the historic Makerere University, Club Obligato once stood as a cherished venue. Every Saturday evening, this iconic spot played host to Afrigo Band, Uganda's oldest and most beloved local band. Founded in 1975, Afrigo remained a musical mainstay for more than five decades, led by the soft-spoken but immensely talented Moses Matovu, a saxophonist, vocalist and songwriter. Their performances consistently drew large, enthusiastic crowds eager to revel in the band's signature sound.

Afrigo's music was deeply influenced by Congolese rumba, known locally as *la rumba Congolaise* or Congolese guitar music, a genre that had taken root in Uganda during the late 1950s. One balmy December evening, the atmosphere at Club Obligato was electric. Moses Matovu, dressed in white baggy pants, a floral short-sleeved shirt and a stylish porkpie hat, confidently took the stage with his bandmates. The club was packed with excited revelers, all prepared for a night of dancing and celebration. With a wide grin, Matovu waved to the crowd and playfully tested his saxophone, which drew a chorus of cheers. It was time for Afrigo.

Without delay, the band launched into their distinctive vibrant sound, opening with their signature song Afrigo Batuuse II (Afrigo Has Arrived II), a 1988 composition by Deo Mukungu. The crowd joined in, singing along to the self-praising anthem that celebrated Afrigo's universal appeal across generations and social divides. The song's lyrics extolled the band's magnetic charm, proclaiming that even the spirits of the dead rose, and ancestors rejoiced when Afrigo's sound reverberated. As the song progressed, the initial lyrical verses gave way to a more relaxed, danceable section. The music shifted into a lively blend of drums, playful lead guitar, a pulsing rhythm and the hypnotic thrum of a deep bass line. On the dance floor, generations blended seamlessly as baby boomers, Generation Z and everyone in between moved in unison to the music, their hips swaying and voices uniting in harmony. Outside, the constant hum of traffic on Bombo Road was drowned out by the joyous celebration within. The air in the club, filled with the soothing melodies of Afrigo's music, provided a welcome escape from the stresses of city life. Cold beer bottles of Bell, Club and Nile Special, their dewy glass catching the soft glow of the lights, circled endlessly among the patrons. The beer flowed without pause, as effortlessly as the great Nile winds its way north, timeless and unbothered.

On stage, the musicians, whose ages ranged from their twenties to their seventies, stood on a simple elevated platform without the need for flashy lights or video screens. The absence of high-tech frills did nothing to diminish the spirit of the night. Fans had come purely for the music, affectionately known as *endongo semadongo*, the beat of all beats.

As the night wore on, Afrigo took the crowd on a beguiling tour of its legendary music catalogue, performing some of its most iconic hits such as Speed (also known as Speed Controller), Jim, Mundeke (Leave Me Alone!) and Oswadde Nnyo (Great Shame On You). The revelers were then treated to a brilliantly arranged medley of classic 1960s Ugandan rumba hits. The medley included unforgettable tunes like Juma Odundo's Bambi Suza Onkyaye (Oh Dear Suza, You Have Spurned Me), which had been erroneously titled Babisuza Okyaye on the record; Fred Kanyike's Nonya Lukia (Looking For Lukia); Fred Masagazi's Kaawa Takyadda (Eve Won't

Come Back); Philly Lutaaya's Empisa Zo (Your Mores); Simon Berunga and Mary Nattima's Nanyonga (a female name); and B. K. Stephen's Nkwagale Ntya (How Should I Love You?).

As the nearly five-hour musical marathon neared its end, Afrigo delivered a powerful rendition of Baluti, originally composed by the legendary Congolese musician Verckys Kiamuangana Mateta. The song served as a fitting homage to one of the great figures of Congolese rumba. During that performance, Moses Matovu, affectionately nicknamed "Moise" by his fans, truly shone. Widely regarded as Uganda's most celebrated saxophonist, Matovu's saxophone on Baluti ignited the stage with fiery, electrifying notes. His playing was both hypnotic and conversational, leaving the crowd in awe of his musical prowess. The energy in the room reached a fever pitch, and the audience erupted into ecstatic cheers. For Afrigo's fans, a live performance was more than just a concert; it was a spiritual experience. The atmosphere was filled with infectious energy and shared joy, as music served as a universal language that united people from all walks of life. In that sacred space, strangers and friends came together, bound by the rhythms of music and dance, as they roistered into the wee hours of the morning.

Ugandans have always had a deep connection with music. Even the earliest visitors to the country, including the first Europeans, took note of the people's exuberant love for music. Captain Charles Chaille Long, an American soldier serving with the Egyptian Army, remarked during his visit to Uganda in the latter half of the nineteenth century: "Uganda is a land of music and musicians. It possesses a great variety of native musical instruments, such as the drum, horn, rattles, bells, flute, harp, etc." Alfred Tucker, the British Anglican bishop of Uganda from 1899 to 1908, also observed Uganda's deep connection with music. He once remarked, "Every little goatherd has his flute. Almost every other man who walks along the road is playing on a reed flageolet. If he is carrying a burden on his head, it makes no difference; he tries to make his load lighter with music. Harps, beautifully made, are twanged on all roads... In a word, the sound of music of some kind or another is in your ears from morn till dewy eve." Tucker's reflection paints a vivid picture of the omnipresence of music in the daily life of Ugandans at the time. Music was not a mere pastime, but a fundamental part of existence. It accompanied people from dawn to dusk, in labor and in leisure. Whether it was the plaintive notes of a flute played by a young goatherd or the vibrant plucking of a harp, music provided rhythm and meaning to life's routines, easing burdens and lifting spirits.

This deep-rooted tradition of musical expression has carried forward across generations, evolving and blending with outside influences over time. Just as Afrigo Band fuses traditional Ugandan sounds with Congolese rumba, the music of Uganda has always been a living, breathing entity, constantly adapting while preserving its core identity. The vibrant music scene of today, represented by the enduring popularity of bands like Afrigo, is a testament to this rich musical heritage. From the earliest accounts of European visitors to the modern-day celebrations at Club Obligato, one thing remains clear: music in Uganda is more than just entertainment. It is a vital, inescapable part of the cultural landscape, a force that brings people together and provides solace in both good times and bad times.

But when did Uganda's music evolve from traditional instruments such as the bowl lyre, drums, notched flute, tube fiddles, animal horns, and xylophones to the syncretic styles that incorporate Western instrumentation and shape today's popular music?

The earliest evidence of Ugandan musicians adopting Western instruments dates to the royal court of Kabaka (King) Mutesa I during the latter half of the 1870s. Mutesa, who ruled the Buganda Kingdom from 1856 to 1884, presided over a powerful and centralized kingdom to the north and west of Lake Victoria. The modern Ugandan state takes its name from this historic kingdom, and Mutesa's court, which was then located on Kampala's Rubaga Hill, was renowned for its artistic and musical sophistication.

Mutesa's court boasted a professional band of highly skilled musicians who performed with an impressive array of instruments. Drums, in particular, came in various sizes and shapes, with some so large they reached the player's waist. These drummers created intricate and mesmerizing rhythms. There were also musicians who expertly played the antelope horns and the *ndere*, or reed flute. The *madinda*, a twelve-keyed xylophone, produced enchanting melodies, often played by two musicians seated opposite each other, engaging in a delicate musical dialogue. The *nnanga*, or bow harp, and the *ndongo*, or bowl lyre, added further layers to the music's rich texture, while the *nsaasi*, or gourd shakers, injected a vibrant energy into the ensemble's sound. The singers, the finest in the land, wove these elements together, narrating stories of great wars, love, and current affairs. They were particularly adept at composing and performing songs that showered the Kabaka and his most powerful chiefs with lavish praise.

The Reverend Charles Wilson, an Evangelical Anglican missionary from the Church Missionary Society (CMS), arrived at Kabaka Mutesa I's court in July 1877. He was deeply moved by the court's musical grandeur and was especially struck by one particular song, a composition that celebrated the invincible character and power of the Buganda monarch. For Wilson, this was not just music; it was a reflection of the Buganda Kingdom's might and its ruler's near-mythical status:

> Thy feet are hammers
> Great is the fear of thee
> Great is thy peace
> Son of the forest
> Great is thy wrath
> Great is thy power

The kings of Buganda were patrons of the arts, offering favors to musicians who pleased them. However, serving as a court musician in pre-colonial Buganda came with significant risks. Despite their honored status, these musicians were vulnerable to the unpredictable and often violent whims of the kings. They were not spared the cruel juggernaut of the monarchs' capricious behavior. Kabaka Mutesa I, for instance, was a brutal and ruthless ruler who terrorized his subjects and wreaked havoc on neighboring territories.

One story of Mutesa's cruelty involved a royal drummer who had the misfortune of offending the sensitivities of a princess. The princess had stumbled upon him bathing naked in the king's pond. This was the very pond that, in the 1880s, would be excavated and expanded by Mutesa's son and successor, Mwanga, to become the largest man-made lake in Uganda. Shocked by the sight of the naked musician, the princess ran off screaming and reported the drummer to the royal guards. Enraged by this unintended offense, Mutesa ordered his chief executioner to cut off the drummer's ears. It was a harsh punishment for a seemingly innocent encounter, but such acts of violence were not uncommon under Mutesa's reign.

Another tragic tale is that of Mayanja, a tall and distinguished man who served as Kabaka Mutesa I's chief harp player. Mayanja was always at the king's side, ready to perform whenever Mutesa desired to hear the harp's melodies or songs that praised his might and invincibility. However, one day Mayanja left the palace to visit his friend Kawekwa, an influential chief in Busabala, a parish south of Kampala on the shores of Lake Victoria. He remained there for a year and a half, much longer than the king would have allowed. When Mayanja finally returned to the palace, he was met with the wrath of Mutesa. Furious over the harpist's long absence, the king gave the chilling order: "Take him away, take him away. Put out both his eyes. I will teach him how to stay here in future; he shall no longer see the road to Busabala, lest I lose him entirely." The horrific punishment was carried out, and Mayanja was blinded.

Kabaka Mwanga, who succeeded Mutesa I after his death, was no less ruthless. Mwanga's reign (1884–1888, and 1889–1897) was marked by similar acts of cruelty. One account claims that Mwanga had the eyes of a royal lyre player gouged out after a lackluster performance. While the veracity of this particular event is debatable, with some historians suggesting it may be a confused retelling of Mayanja's story, the legacy of violence against musicians in the royal court is undeniable. These seemingly random acts of cruelty against musicians in pre-colonial times foreshadowed even more egregious acts of violence in the post-independence era. As Uganda transitioned into a new political landscape, musicians would once again find themselves at the mercy of powerful rulers.

Surprisingly, both the blinded harp and lyre players survived the harrowing mutilation and continued to serve as musicians in the royal court well into the early twentieth century. Despite his mutilation, Mayanja remained steadfastly loyal to the king who had inflicted such grievous harm. In an extraordinary display of resilience, he picked up the harp once more and continued to create beautiful music, providing lavish entertainment in the palace. He even composed a song in honor of the Christian faith, repeating the following words as he played:

> God is in heaven, it is a beautiful place.
> You all of you take hold of religion and you will go there

The early Christian missionaries who heard Mayanja's music were unimpressed. To them, he was a pagan, an animist, whose songs lacked the spiritual virtues of Christian sanctity. Despite their dismissal, Mayanja later converted to Christianity, taking the name James upon his baptism. As James Mayanja, he became a tutor to the renowned Temusewo Mukasa, who would go on to be known as the "last great harp player" of Buganda. Mukasa, in turn, passed on his knowledge to another prominent and revered musician, Evaristo Muyinda, who mastered the intricate art of playing the *enanga*, the traditional Ugandan harp.

At the time when Kabaka Mutesa I was mutilating the royal musicians, Uganda was largely isolated from the outside world, its interior undiscovered by European explorers and relatively untouched by Arab traders. Nonetheless, parts of the region had long been the subject of fantastical speculation and legend. Ancient Arab geographers spoke of Jebel Qamar, the green or lunar mountain, which they believed overshadowed the headwaters of the Nile. Likewise, the origins of the Nile fascinated the ancient Greeks. In the first century AD, a Greek trader named Diogenes claimed to have marched inland from Rhapta, a coastal city in East Africa, to the snowy Mountains of the Moon, whose melting snow, he said, fed the great lakes that gave rise to the Nile. These mythical Mountains of the Moon are now widely believed to be the Rwenzori Mountains in western

Uganda. While it is doubtful that Diogenes ever ventured deep into the heart of Central Africa to reach the Rwenzori Mountains, his tales are part of the long history of curiosity about Uganda's interior. Despite its relative isolation, Uganda would not remain hidden for long. The forces of international commerce, foreign evangelization, and colonial conquest that characterized the nineteenth century soon arrived, altering the course of the country's history.

Arab and Swahili traders from the island of Zanzibar arrived in the Buganda Kingdom around the 1840s, bringing with them not only the Islamic religion but also a lucrative trading network. They introduced goods such as guns, gunpowder, soap, brandy, and gin, which were exchanged for ivory, otter skins, and slaves. Kabaka Mutesa I welcomed the Zanzibari traders and settled them on the foothills of Natete Hill, on the outskirts of Kampala. What was once a nondescript hamlet swiftly transformed into a bustling trading post, with caravans arriving and departing regularly. Natete began to exude a sense of cosmopolitanism as it grew. Among the banana plantations and lush fields of beans, sweet potatoes, and coffee, local men and women dressed in flowing barkcloth and cotton robes moved about, engaging in commerce and daily life. The once quiet village became a hub of activity and exchange, marking the beginning of a more outward-looking Buganda.

Between 1862 and 1890, a handful of European explorers, adventurers, and Christian missionaries visited Uganda following John Speke's discovery of the source of the Nile at Jinja in 1862. Among them was Henry Morton Stanley, the Welsh journalist and adventurer, who visited Kabaka Mutesa's court in 1875 for a 12-day stay. Stanley saw the potential of Christianity to rival Islam, which had already established deep roots in Buganda. Inspired by his observations, Stanley wrote a letter that was published in London's *Daily Telegraph*, urging Christian missionaries of the "white race" to come to Uganda. He described the country as a "promising field for a [Christian] mission," one that stood out among "all the pagan world." Stanley declared that the "field and harvest" in Uganda were "ripe for the sickle of civilization." Encouraged by Stanley's appeal, the first white Christian missionaries arrived in Buganda in June 1877. Reverend C. T. Wilson and Lieutenant Shergold Smith came to Mutesa's court, bringing with them the seeds of Christian evangelism that would shape the religious landscape of the region for years to come.

At Mutesa's court, both the Zanzibari traders and European visitors worked tirelessly to win the favor of the king, who was adept at playing them against each other. Gifts became a crucial tool in currying favor with the Kabaka. After all, everyone is a friend to a man who gives gifts. One notable Zanzibari trader, Khamis Bin Abdullah, arrived at Mutesa's court around 1867. He soon won the king's affection by lavishing him with extravagant offerings, including gold-embroidered jackets, fine white shirts, crimson slippers, swords, silk sashes, daggers, and even a revolving rifle. Among the gifts that held Mutesa's total attention was the music box, an invention from the Swiss town of Sainte-Croix in 1811, which introduced a fascinating new sound to the royal court. Both the Zanzibari traders and European visitors brought music boxes as gifts, further endearing themselves to the Kabaka. In 1874, Charles Chaillé-Long, an American colonel in the Egyptian army and emissary of Colonel Charles George Gordon, a British general appointed by Khedive Ismail Pasha as governor of the Sudanese province of Equatoria, presented Mutesa with a music box. The box played popular tunes of the time, including "Dixie," "Tramp, Tramp, Tramp," and "Johnny Comes Marching Home."

When Alexander Mackay of the Church Missionary Society arrived in Buganda in November 1878 to join Reverend C. T. Wilson, he also brought gifts for Mutesa. Among them was a music box that played The Heavens Are Telling from Joseph Haydn's masterpiece The Creation. In 1881, Arab traders in Natete further endeared themselves to the king by presenting him with a plated revolver and two additional music boxes.

Mutesa also developed a keen interest in Western musical instruments, particularly those carried by the military escorts and marching bands that accompanied European emissaries. British ethnomusicologist Klaus Wachsmann, who would later become curator of the Uganda Museum in the 1940s, speculated that Western music first reached Ugandan ears during

Speke's expedition. Wachsmann suggested that the expedition included a bugler and that the bugle call marked the introduction of Western music to the people of Uganda. Instruments like bugles, cymbals, and steel drums from Europe caught the king's eye, especially those brought by visitors such as Chaillé-Long and the French explorer Ernest Linant de Bellefonds. Determined to acquire these instruments for his own collection, Mutesa began purchasing bugles, cymbals, and European-style drums from his foreign visitors.

The king's fascination with these instruments did not stop at acquisition. Mutesa employed skilled artisans to replicate various items of European manufacture, including guns. These smiths, under his instruction, also began fabricating European musical instruments, expanding the king's growing collection and adding a new dimension to the music of his court.

The Western musical instruments and music boxes were a novelty throughout the kingdom of Buganda. Alexander Mackay often delighted in playing his music box for the locals, who were intrigued and fascinated, especially when he played God Save the Queen. Alongside the mesmerizing foreign tunes from the music boxes and the marching bands that accompanied foreign expeditions into Buganda, there were also the fascinating stories brought by the Zanzibari traders. These traders regaled the Buganda court with tales of the glamour and opulence of their sultan, weaving fabulous narratives about the sultan's military band.

Sultan Sayyid Barghash bin Said Al-Busaid of Zanzibar, who reigned from 1870 to 1888, had established a grand marching band early in his rule. This band was composed of over thirty Goan musicians from India and was at one time conducted by a German bandmaster. The sultan's band regularly performed in Stone Town's public square in front of the House of Wonders. The performances were part of the sultan's efforts to transform the Zanzibari waterfront into a cultural spectacle. Kabaka Mutesa, ever keen to emulate foreign grandeur, soon developed a desire to establish a band modeled after the sultan's marching band. With the European instruments he had acquired, he envisioned a similar display of musical prowess at his own court. And there was one man in Buganda who could help him realize this dream: Toli.

Toli, a native of Madagascar, had originally come to Uganda as part of Khamis Bin Abdullah's trading expedition. He had served as Abdullah's private cook but chose to remain in Buganda when Abdullah returned to Zanzibar. Over time, Toli became an important and trusted adviser to both Mutesa I and his successor, Kabaka Mwanga, advising them on civil and military matters alike. His influence extended beyond court politics. Toli even led Mutesa's army in various military campaigns in the Busoga and Toro regions of Uganda. Toli's knowledge of foreign customs and his trusted position in the Buganda court made him the ideal person to assist Mutesa in creating the European-style band that the Kabaka envisioned. With his guidance, Mutesa hoped to replicate the musical splendor of Zanzibar's sultanate, adding a new dimension to the cultural life of Buganda.

Toli was a well-traveled and worldly man for his time. As a cabin boy aboard a French ship, he had sailed to Marseilles and likely to other European ports as well. His experiences abroad made him familiar with European customs, and he presumably spoke a number of European languages. These linguistic abilities made Toli an invaluable asset at Mutesa's court, where such knowledge was rare. Skilled in many trades, Toli's reputation extended beyond the palace. Despite the intense rivalry between Islam and Christianity in Buganda during that period, even European Christian missionaries turned to Toli, a Muslim, for his high-quality carpentry work. Toli is also credited with advising Kabaka Mutesa I to welcome the first Catholic missionaries, despite objections from Alexander Mackay, the Scottish Presbyterian missionary affiliated with the Church Missionary Society, a British Anglican mission. Alongside Mathew Kisule, also known as Fundi, and missionary Alexander Mackay, Toli was recognized as one of the preeminent blacksmiths in Buganda, unmatched in the task of repairing guns for the Kabaka's army.

What further set Toli apart was his musical ability. He had been trained to play European kettledrums and bugle. He may have played other Western instruments as well. It was to Toli, this fascinating figure of late nineteenth-century Uganda, that Mutesa entrusted the task of forming a

European-style brass band. Mutesa selected a group of young men from among the palace pages and sent them to Toli, who trained them to play European steel drums, cymbals, and bugles. In Toli's compound, located in the Arab quarters on the slopes of Natete Hill, Uganda's first European-style band began to take shape during the 1870s.

Among Toli's pupils, one young man stood out. Andrew Kaggwa, a squint-eyed, quick-witted youth of slight build, had been captured as a slave during a raid on the neighboring Bunyoro Kingdom. He proved to be an exceptionally fast learner, becoming an accomplished bugler and drummer. Mutesa, impressed by his skill, appointed Andrew Kaggwa as the Master Drummer and later chief bandmaster of the newly formed brass band. Kaggwa was placed in charge of a group of about twenty-five musicians.

Religious sectarianism was a defining feature of the time, and Kaggwa, who had converted from Islam to Roman Catholicism, recruited other young men who, like him, were recent Catholic converts. This shared faith fostered a strong camaraderie and esprit de corps among the bandsmen. Notable members of the band included James Buzabaliawo, who served as Kaggwa's second-in-command, as well as Leo Kyagwogera, Adolphus Mukasa Ludigo, and Pontian Ngodwe. The band performed at festive occasions and was called upon to play whenever foreign guests visited the royal palace. Initially, the ensemble was named *Ekitongole Ekijaasi* (Military Unit), though it was not a military unit but rather a group of musicians who could march, play drums, blow trumpets, and present arms. Through this band, Mutesa succeeded in merging the grandeur of European musical traditions with the vibrant cultural life of his court. The band's joyous music filled Kabaka Mutesa I with pride. In recognition of Andrew Kaggwa's leadership of Ekitongole Ekijaasi, Mutesa allocated him land in Lungujja, a suburb of Kampala, where Kaggwa built his home.

When Kabaka Mwanga ascended the throne in 1884 following his father Mutesa's death, Andrew Kaggwa was reappointed as the bandleader. Kaggwa was a favorite of the new Kabaka, having often accompanied Mwanga on fishing and hunting trips when Mwanga was still a prince. Mwanga, recognizing Kaggwa's value, created a new royal title tied to music and immediately bestowed it upon the bandleader of Ekitongole Ekijaasi. As with all royal positions in Buganda, the title came with a large tract of land, this time located on Kiwatule Hill on the outskirts of Kampala. Kaggwa became the first holder of the new title, *Mugowa*, a position equivalent to Bandmaster-General, which carried with it the command of the entire militia from which the royal bandsmen were drawn.

The bandsmen were eventually relocated from Natete to an area near Kaggwa's land on Kiwatule Hill. The band's new encampment became known as Kigowa, a name still in use today. The band also changed its name from Ekitongole Ekijaasi to *Ekitongole Ekigowa* — the Goan Unit. Both *Kigowa* and *Mugowa* are derived from the Swahili word *Ki-Goa*, reflecting Kabaka Mwanga's association of the new band's music with that of the Goan musicians in Sultan Sayyid Barghash bin Said Al-Busaid's palace in Zanzibar.

It is likely that the musicians of Ekitongole Ekigowa primarily rehearsed and performed military marching music, drawing inspiration from the musicians who accompanied explorers and adventurers to Buganda. However, given the creativity and improvisational talent of these young musicians, it is equally plausible that they created original musical arrangements. Unfortunately, the specific pieces they rehearsed and performed have been lost to history. However, Andrew Kaggwa and several of his fellow band members are still remembered in Uganda today, though not for their pioneering roles as royal musicians or for their mastery of Western instruments. Their legacy, as we will see, took on a far more significant and tragic dimension in the years to come.

During his reign, Mutesa I had tolerated the Christian missionaries he had invited to his kingdom. Although Mutesa never embraced Christianity himself, he did not hinder the missionaries from spreading their message. European missionaries were eager to evangelize Ugandans, and they found a receptive audience. Henry Morton Stanley (born John Rowland), the Welsh-American explorer, had described the country as a "harvest ripe for the sickle of civilization," and indeed, missionaries were free to gather, preach the gospel, and baptize thousands. In contrast, Kabaka Mwanga, who succeeded Mutesa in 1884, viewed the missionaries and their teachings with deep suspicion. To Mwanga, Christianity posed not only a threat to his political power but also a challenge to long-established cultural and social norms.

Christian converts, emboldened by their newfound faith, began questioning the king's secular authority and the traditional religious practices that had long underpinned the kingdom's social structure, coherence, and identity. Among these converts were several prominent officials, including Andrew Kaggwa, Mwanga's trusted Bandmaster-General. Thus, an inevitable confrontation between Mwanga and the Christian converts loomed. By January 1885, Mwanga's anger at the insolence of the Christian converts at his court had reached a breaking point. What followed was a brutal persecution of Christians throughout the kingdom. Converts were rounded up, condemned, and many were sentenced to death. Some of Mwanga's Christian officials were castrated, with two of them dying from the injuries. The persecution reached its gruesome peak on June 3, 1886, at Namugongo, where thirty-two recent Christian converts were burned to death.

Andrew Kaggwa, who had first encountered Catholic teachings while receiving music instruction from Toli at Natete, did not escape Mwanga's wrath. On the afternoon of May 26, 1886, in present-day Munyonyo, a suburb of Kampala where Kabaka Mwanga kept a lakeside retreat, Kaggwa was arrested under Mwanga's orders. Despite his personal reluctance and the misgivings he felt about persecuting his Bandmaster-General and long-time companion, Mwanga was urged on by his prime minister, Mukasa. Mukasa viewed Andrew Kaggwa as a political rival, aware of rumors that Mwanga had been considering Kaggwa for the position of prime minister, a move that would have displaced Mukasa, who belonged to an older generation of chiefs.

Kaggwa's arrest marked the end of his life. In a final act of cruelty, the arresting party severed his arm before beheading him. Other members of Ekitongole Ekigowa who perished during the Christian persecution included James Buzabaliawo, Adolphus Mukasa Ludigo, and Pontian

Ngodwe. By the time the brutal killings came to an end in January 1887, a total of 23 Anglican and 22 Catholic converts had been put to death for refusing to renounce their faith. The majority were burned alive between May 25 and June 3, 1886. These early Ugandan Christians are now known worldwide as the Uganda Martyrs, or the Blessed Martyrs of Uganda.

In June 1920, Andrew Kaggwa, James Buzabaliawo, Adolphus Mukasa Ludigo, Pontian Ngodwe, and the other Catholic converts killed by Kabaka Mwanga were beatified by the Catholic Church. In 1964, Pope Paul VI canonized them, making them the first Black African saints in the Roman Catholic Church. Most of the 25 original members of Ekitongole Ekigowa survived the horrific killings. When some semblance of peace returned, several surviving band members resumed their musical duties, continuing the tradition established by Toli, the Madagascan who had originally put the band together. When Rev. R. H. Walker and Gordon of the Church Missionary Society visited Kabaka Mwanga's palace at Mengo in 1888, they described the scene upon entering the royal court: "The band now struck up. It consisted of a big drum, two kettledrums, a bugle, and several horns and trumpets formed from the long-necked gourds of the country."

However, the stability of Mwanga's reign was short-lived. The religious wars that erupted between 1888 and 1893 resulted in new socio-political alignments, and the king's band gradually faded into obscurity. With his throne under threat from religious rivals and political adversaries, Mwanga had little time to focus on his band of musicians. Western instruments like bugles, trumpets, and kettledrums became an afterthought as Mwanga fought for survival.

Mwanga was deposed twice before being permanently exiled by the British to the Seychelles in 1898. His one-year-old son, Daudi Chwa, ascended to the throne in 1896. Under Chwa's reign, the royal appetite for Western music diminished. When the American journalist and travel writer Frank Carpenter visited the young Kabaka Chwa in 1908, he noted that the bugles and kettledrums were no longer in use. Instead, Kabaka Chwa's court boasted an impressive orchestra of musicians playing indigenous instruments. Pipes and drums filled the air, a return to traditional

Buganda music. The music of Andrew Kaggwa and his fellow bandmates gradually faded from the collective memory. Despite their pioneering work in introducing Western instruments to Buganda, the martyred members of Ekitongole Ekigowa would be remembered not for their contributions to music but rather as the forefathers of the Christian faith in Uganda. Their legacy as martyrs overshadowed their roles as musicians, and they became symbols of devotion and sacrifice.

This legacy was further cemented when Pope Paul VI visited Uganda in 1969. In honor of the occasion, the Uganda Roman Catholic Church commissioned the renowned musician Elly Wamala to compose a song welcoming the pontiff to the country. The resulting piece, titled Welcome Pope Paul, was recorded on the Serenade label and backed by The Jambos, the resident band of the Apolo Hotel, the grandest hotel in Uganda at the time. Wamala's composition was a calypso-inspired arrangement, featuring his vibrant tenor delivering a cheerful and catchy melody. The song's jubilant tone was enhanced by the prominent horn section, which dovetailed seamlessly with Wamala's vocals.

Frank Mbalire, who made his mark on the Ugandan music scene in the early 1970s with Peterson T. Mutebi's The Tames Band, composed and recorded a Christian pop song titled Ekyasa Simuzanyo (A Century Is Not a Small Feat). The song was commissioned by the Roman Catholic Church, commemorating the church's centenary celebrations in Uganda in 1979. Ekyasa Simuzanyo was released on the church's own Centenary Special label. It paid tribute to the courage of the Christian martyrs and the resilience of Christianity in Uganda at a time when the faith was fighting for its survival.

Uganda, by the mid-1970s, was in the grip of Idi Amin's brutal dictatorship. Having seized power from President Milton Obote in January 1971, Amin embarked on a systematic dismantling of the country's institutions, ushering in a reign of terror marked by unprecedented violence. Although Christians were still allowed to practice their faith under Amin, they lived in constant fear and suspicion of his intentions. Many felt that the regime unfairly targeted and marginalized them. Rumors swirled that Amin intended to force every Ugandan to convert to Islam, if necessary, through coercion. Amin's actions seemed to fuel these fears. In February 1974, Uganda was admitted as a Muslim state during the Islamic Summit Conference in Lahore, Pakistan, further stoking anxieties among the Christian population. Prominent Christian leaders, both secular and religious, were singled out for persecution and often executed. One of the most notable victims was Rev. Clement Kiggundu, a respected Catholic leader and editor of *Munno*, a Catholic newspaper, who was murdered in 1974.

Tragedy struck again in February 1977 when Janani Luwum, the Anglican Archbishop of the Church of Uganda, along with two Christian cabinet ministers, was shot to death. The government claimed the three men had died in a car accident, but few believed the official narrative. Amin showed little remorse, coldly stating, "The accident was indeed a punishment of God because God does not want people to carry out activities to make others suffer or even be killed." In March 1978, as preparations for the centenary celebrations of the Roman Catholic Church in Uganda reached their peak, tragedy struck once again. Raphael Amooti Ssebuggwao, the president of the Uganda Industrial Court and a prominent figure in the Catholic community, was gunned down outside his home. His murder was widely believed to have been carried out by agents of the State Research Bureau (SRB), Amin's feared secret police, responsible for the deaths of thousands of Ugandans during his reign of terror.

Ssebuggwao had been closely involved in the preparations for the centenary celebrations, representing the laity in this momentous occasion for the Catholic Church in Uganda. His assassination sent shockwaves through the community, deepening the sense of fear and oppression under Amin's regime. The murder of such a prominent Catholic leader just months before the centenary year highlighted the precarious position of Christians in Uganda during this dark period, further fueling the sense of uncertainty that hung over the celebrations. Despite these challenges, the Roman Catholic Church pressed on with its preparations, determined to honor the resilience of its faithful and the sacrifices of the Uganda Martyrs, whose legacy had become even more poignant in the face of the violence that gripped the country.

Joseph Bukenya, familiarly known as *mzee* Bukenya, was the owner of a Kampala band based in the Ntinda suburb of Kampala during the 1960s. In a subtle nod to the legacy of Ekitongole Ekigowa, the band of musicians who had both pioneered Christianity in Uganda and laid the groundwork for the country's vibrant music scene, Bukenya named his own band Buye Kigowa Galimasani, better known by its acronym, BKG Jazz Band. By choosing this name, Bukenya paid tribute to the memory of the nineteenth-century musicians who had embraced Western instruments and experimented with a new musical form. Their contributions to Uganda's musical history, however, have remained largely overlooked.

Andrew Kaggwa, who had played a key role in this early musical experimentation, is still not widely recognized for his pioneering work in musical syncretism. His efforts to blend traditional Ugandan music with Western instruments during the reigns of Mutesa I and Mwanga have received little formal acknowledgment. Even the Catholic Church, which venerates him as a martyr and a champion of the faith, has tended to emphasize his religious legacy over his musical innovations. Today, Andrew Kaggwa is remembered by the Roman Catholic Church in Uganda as the patron saint of catechists, families, and teachers.

As the country's socio-political and cultural landscape evolved at the turn of the twentieth century, new Ugandan musicians began to emerge, influenced by the rapidly changing demographic profile. The British had declared Uganda a British Protectorate and consolidated political power, exerting control over society and its resources. Believing that indigenous Ugandans shunned hard work and organized labor, the British brought in Indian laborers, many of whom were indentured workers recruited to construct the Uganda Railway, linking the Port of Mombasa in Kenya to Uganda's interior. This interaction between non-indigenous and indigenous cultures had a significant impact on the way Ugandans created and consumed music.

British colonialism introduced new cultural dynamics, including the rise of exclusive social clubs for both Europeans and Indians. These clubs were racially segregated, barring indigenous Black Ugandans from membership. The Entebbe Goan Institute, which later became the Goan Recreational Institute, opened in 1905, followed by the Goan Institute of Kampala in 1921. Meanwhile, the European community established its own social hub in 1911 with the founding of Top Club, which later became Kampala Club on Nakasero Hill.

Like other European clubs in British colonies, Kampala Club was the focal point of social life for the European elite in Uganda. It was here that British colonial administrators and other Europeans would retreat after work, sinking into armchairs with whisky-sodas in hand to read the latest newspapers, exchange gossip, and maintain the illusion of permanence in their foreign enclave. Music was ever-present at both the Goan and European clubs, where it played a central role in the social activities of the time.

Even before the outbreak of World War II, the Goan club had a dance orchestra that occasionally staged live performances. By the 1950s and 1960s, the Goan community in Uganda had fostered a vibrant music scene, producing successful bands such as the Melody Makers, Bennett Dias and the Diatones, Rhythm Kings Orchestra, The Drifters, and Nobby and His Band, to name a few.

While membership to these social clubs was off-limits to Black Ugandans, they were nevertheless present in the clubs, employed in various low-level or menial jobs. Through their proximity to the social activities of the clubs, many Ugandans were introduced to foreign music and dance. One can easily imagine Ugandans working at Kampala Club or the Victoria Nyanza Sailing Club, a sister European club in the eastern town of Jinja, listening to Duke Ellington's lively Washington Wobble or Jimmie Rodgers' Blue Yodel songs, with the twang of a guitar blaring from the club's gramophone.

By and large, Christian missionaries and British colonial administrators showed little respect or appreciation for Ugandan traditional music. For the missionaries, as Terrence Ranger pointed out, "European music represented a world of order in contrast to the inexplicable monotony and sudden passions of African drumming; musical ability was taken as a sign, a promise of potential civilization."

The European missionaries established schools and implemented curricula that prioritized European music over indigenous traditions. Ugandans were encouraged to learn, admire, and sing English songs or to compose native songs in the European tradition. When Mary Hall, a British traveler, visited King's College Budo, a Ugandan boarding school at the beginning of the twentieth century, she approvingly noted that the students were "taught class-singing, and it was a pretty sight to see them ... holding in their hands the *Royal Songster* ... with King Edward's portrait on the front." J. M. Duncan, an English adviser in music to the Native Anglican Church in Uganda during the 1920s, observed: "From the first, it has been the policy of the Church Mission Society in Uganda to teach its converts English tunes ... African native melodies cannot be converted to Christian uses ... it would be difficult to dissociate native vocal music from the undesirable words to which it is nearly always set." Duncan went so far as to suggest that the folk music of Central Africa "did not seem capable of evolution."

In contrast, years later, the renowned ethnomusicologist Hugh Tracey reached a different conclusion after listening to Ugandan indigenous music. Following a performance by a Soga musician on a traditional stringed instrument, he remarked that he had "no doubt at all that the music played by David to King Solomon on his harp must have sounded far more like modern Ugandan music than any European tune." Ugandan musicians had long played harps and lyres. Similar instruments are depicted in ancient Egyptian tombs, underscoring the deep historical roots of the region's musical traditions.

Despite their colonial attitudes, Christian missionary institutions, churches, and schools inadvertently contributed significantly to shaping Uganda's syncretic music. As Prof. Mitchel Strumpf, a renowned ethnomusicologist, noted in his essay "Early Studies of the Music of East Africa," "Catholic, Anglican, and Lutheran Church hymn singing in many areas of East Africa greatly affected the tonality, instrumentation, and structure of the music traditions of East Africa." The introduction of music notation and the tonic-solfa system, used in churches and schools from the late 1800s, had a lasting influence on East African music.

In 1895, a group of Mill Hill Fathers, a Catholic society of apostolic life, landed at the port of Mombasa and began their mission in Uganda. This marked the beginning of a long collaborative effort to evangelize Ugandans, train catechists and priests, and provide education and health care. The Mill Hill Missionaries undertook many initiatives, including the establishment of a brass band. This band was first formed at their headquarters in Nsambya, a Kampala suburb, around 1908, and later another was established at Namilyango, a parish east of Kampala. The brass bands aimed to introduce young people to Western culture while also evangelizing and integrating them into the Catholic faith. The tradition of the Catholic brass band continued for decades and, by the 1980s and 1990s, was represented by Father Wijnard Huijs, a Mill Hill missionary in Kamuli town in eastern Uganda. It was from this band, Kamuli Youth Brass, that Moses Nakintije Ssekibogo, better known as Mowzey Radio, one of Uganda's most notable musicians of the twenty-first century, emerged.

Of course, not all Europeans were comfortable with British cultural imperialism. One notable exception was Klaus Wachsmann, a keen ethnomusicologist who arrived in Uganda in 1937 as a guest of the Church Missionary Society. Wachsmann dedicated himself to extensively recording indigenous Ugandan folk songs and studying the rich musical traditions of the country. Thanks to his work among the many tribes of Uganda, the Uganda Museum now boasts a beautiful collection of traditional musical instruments, preserving a vital aspect of the country's cultural heritage.

Another important influence on the development and mainstreaming of neo-traditional Ugandan music was the military. Captain Lugard, one of the early British administrators, based his garrison of Sudanese mercenaries atop Old Kampala Hill. Every morning, a bugler would sound the reveille to wake the soldiers. The crisp tune of the British army's "Fall in" call also echoed through the town, waking up the locals. In response, the townspeople created a playful ditty to the tune of the reveille: *Kaape, Kaape, Kaperere, yazimba enyumba e'Kampala.* The song, which loosely translates to "The captain (Lugard) built a house in Kampala," is likely one of the earliest examples of a neo-traditional Ugandan song with wide popularity. The word *Kapere* was a local adaptation of "captain," and the jingle became part of the town's daily life.

In 1902, the British colonial administration established the King's African Rifles (KAR), a multi-battalion regiment that recruited soldiers from across Britain's East African colonies. The 4th KAR battalion, based in Bombo town, was primarily Ugandan and had its own drum and bugle band composed of Ugandan musicians. In 1918, the capabilities of the battalion's band were expanded with the acquisition of additional musical instruments from the Catholic mission in Nsambya, Kampala. Sergeant Venable of the South Staffs Regiment was assigned to train the Ugandan bandsmen, and after nine months of rigorous instruction, the band was ready for its debut.

The band's first major performance came at the end of 1919, when they welcomed returning battalions for demobilization after World War I. Their performance was a spectacle, exhibiting the successful integration of Western instruments with local musical traditions. The band's popularity grew because of this event, and the outbreak of World War II further accelerated the spread of neo-traditional music styles. Ugandan servicemen, deployed overseas as part of the KAR, brought with them a blend of Western instrumentation and local sounds, contributing to the evolution and popularization of these hybrid musical forms.

CHAPTER 2

Beneath the Gramophone Horn: Uganda's Earliest Recordings

From the late 1890s, the nascent years of British colonial rule, until the eve of World War II in 1939, Ugandan folk songs reigned as the dominant form of entertainment. This vibrant musical landscape, however, existed in a complex relationship with the encroaching colonial presence. While European missionaries and colonial administrators often dismissed traditional folk music as "primitive" or "heathen," a contrasting perspective emerged from Western ethnomusicologists who were mesmerized by Uganda's rich and diverse musical heritage.

A pioneering figure in this early documentation was Harry Johnston, the British government's Special Commissioner to Uganda from 1899 to 1901. Johnston's 1901 field recordings, made using a bulky and revolutionary cylinder phonograph, represent what is likely the first recorded instance of Ugandan music, and indeed, the first sound recording ever made in East Africa. These fragile wax cylinders captured fleeting snippets of local musical expression, including a melody played on flutes and a man performing a praise song. The phonograph itself, a technological marvel beyond the grasp of most Ugandans, sparked particular fascination in Semei Kakungulu, a prominent local general instrumental in expanding

British influence in eastern and northeastern Uganda during the 1890s. Kakungulu, deeply impressed by the machine's ability to "capture sound," ordered a phonograph from England. However, the British colonial administration, perhaps wary of Kakungulu's growing influence or viewing the purchase as an extravagant indulgence, disapproved. Whether Kakungulu ever received his coveted phonograph remains a historical enigma, and sadly, no wax cylinders from his collection, if they existed, have survived.

The first three decades of the twentieth century saw limited progress in recording Ugandan music. This changed dramatically in 1930, following the groundbreaking success of Tanzanian musician Siti binti Saad and her *taarab* band, who became the first East African artists to record on gramophone discs. Recognizing the potential of the Ugandan market, the Columbia Gramophone Company, in partnership with its local agent, the Uganda Bookshop, ventured to Kampala to record local talent.

Established in 1927 by the Church Missionary Society (CMS), the Uganda Bookshop served as a conduit for Christian literature and evangelism, reflecting the close ties between colonial commerce and religious expansion. Ironically, this institution, which had often viewed Ugandan "tribal" music with disdain, found itself playing a crucial role in preserving these very sounds for posterity.

In 1930, Heinrich Lampe, a German mastering and recording engineer working with Columbia, recorded approximately 60 tracks of Ugandan secular folk and Christian songs. An experienced field engineer, Heinrich was well accustomed to recording in remote locations off the beaten path. This groundbreaking effort culminated in the production of forty-two 78 rpm records on Columbia's Odeon label, comprising thirty-seven discs of secular folk songs and five of Africanized Christian hymns. The Christian hymns were performed by members of the esteemed choir of St. Paul's Cathedral Namirembe, the heart of the Native Anglican Church, commonly known as the Protestant Church of Uganda. These hymns were adaptations of traditional English ecclesiastical music, translated and performed in the local Luganda language, with titles like Mwana Wange (My Child), Katonda Lwe Lwazi Lwaffe (God Is Our Rock), and Lero Lwa

Sanyu Nyo (Today Is a Joyful Day). Notably, the recordings conspicuously lacked any representation from the Catholic songbook, a reflection of the intense rivalry between Protestant and Catholic missions.

Given the Protestant affiliation of the Uganda Bookshop, the exclusion of Catholic choirs, despite their established musical prowess, is understandable. The Catholic seminary at Bukalasa, for example, boasted a formidable choir trained in the Western tradition and had introduced Gregorian chant to Uganda with a midnight mass in 1906. The Catholic missionary headquarters in Nsambya also housed a brass band. Had these Catholic musical groups been included, the recordings would have offered a more comprehensive snapshot of Uganda's evolving musical landscape.

The 1930 Odeon recordings, manufactured in Germany and bearing the series number 242200, marked the first time Ugandan music became commercially available. The Uganda Bookshop, demonstrating remarkable marketing acumen, aggressively promoted these records, distributing flyers titled *Amayinja Ge Nyimba Mu Luganda – Records of Songs in Luganda* in towns across the country. These flyers represent the earliest documented instance of mass commercial advertising and marketing in Uganda. The Uganda Bookshop also leveraged its extensive network of approximately 20 branches in major urban centers to distribute and market the Odeon records.

The public's response to the secular folksong records was overwhelmingly positive, with the initial batch selling out rapidly. However, the Christian hymns, while undoubtedly reverent and technically impressive, failed to resonate with the wider public, resulting in disappointing sales. This disparity highlighted the enduring popularity of traditional Ugandan folk music and the complex interplay between cultural preservation and commercial success in the early colonial era.

The selection of Christian hymns for the 1930 Odeon recordings was notably authorized by British missionary John Murray Duncan, a man of profound musical passion and equally profound cultural biases. A fervent devotee of European classical music, Duncan had served several curacies in England before his interest was piqued by the work of Church Missionary Society (CMS) missionaries in Uganda. Following his retirement from pastoral duties, he embarked on a journey up the Nile and arrived in Kampala in March 1927. Duncan was immediately riveted by the architectural grandeur of St. Paul's Cathedral Namirembe, perched majestically atop one of Kampala's original seven hills and overlooking the vast expanse of Lake Victoria. Upon entering, he was equally impressed by the cathedral's exceptional acoustics, which he deemed comparable to, if not superior to, those of London's St. Paul's. However, he perceived a crucial deficiency: the absence of an organ. Driven by his vision, Duncan spearheaded a successful campaign to install a magnificent organ in 1931.

As *maestro di cappella*, he assumed the responsibility of training the cathedral choir, rigorously instructing the Ugandan choirboys in the intricacies of European classical singing. Under his exacting tutelage, the choir achieved remarkable renditions of masterpieces by composers such as Giovanni Palestrina, William Byrd, Henry Purcell, Johann Sebastian Bach, George Frideric Handel, and Wolfgang Amadeus Mozart.

Among Duncan's most gifted pupils was Eriya Paulo Lwasampijja Kayizzi, the son of a Ugandan Anglican minister, who possessed an exceptional natural aptitude for music. Duncan personally taught Kayizzi to play the organ, leading him to become the cathedral's sub-organist and the first Ugandan to master the instrument. Notably, Kayizzi's lineage was deeply intertwined with Buganda's royal family, as he was the brother of Queen Irene Drusilla Namaganda, the mother of Kabaka Mutesa II. With Duncan's endorsement, Kayizzi delivered breathtaking performances of challenging pieces like Bach's *Fugue in G Minor* and Mozart's *Fantasia in F Minor*, earning the admiration of European audiences in Uganda. His intense concentration on the sheet music, the graceful dexterity of his feet on the pedals reminiscent of the traditional *Baakisimba* dance, and the effortless fluidity of his fingers across the organ's manuals solidified his reputation as Uganda's preeminent organist for decades. At the time, the only Ugandan who came close to Kayizzi's virtuosity was Mr. Yuda Nyondo of Mbarara High School, organist at St. James Cathedral at Ruharo Hill in Mbarara.

Despite his unwavering dedication to imparting European church music to Ugandans, Duncan harbored a deeply troubling disdain for traditional Ugandan folk music. As an anonymous writer noted in his 1936 obituary in *The Musical Times*, Duncan firmly believed that "the missionary's first task was to teach the Native the European alphabet, thus giving him access to the noblest thought in the world," and that the second task was "to teach him the European musical scale, whereby he has access to noble thought expressed in sound." British historian David Somervell, who spent time with Duncan in Uganda during the 1930s, further illuminated Duncan's unwavering conviction in *The Musical Times* (May 1935), noting his "rejection of the native musical idiom and of all attempts to build upon it."

Duncan's efforts to suppress traditional Ugandan music, however, proved futile. Ironically, the very church choirs he established became incubators for some of Uganda's most influential secular neo-traditional musicians, who drew inspiration from and enriched the native musical idiom. This lineage includes luminaries such as Polycarp Kakooza, who began recording shortly after World War II; Israel Magembe of the popular Kampala City Six band in the 1960s; Jimmy Katumba of The Ebonies, whose hit Twalina Omukwano Ne Gufa (We Had a Love That Died) resonated deeply in the late 1970s; and Moses Matovu, the charismatic frontman of Afrigo, a band that continues to define Ugandan music. In a particularly revealing passage from the journal, *The Musical Times* (August 1935), Duncan declared that the "Baganda have no use for their folk-song, and to me it is so hideous as to be the negation of music." Despite his vehement condemnation of Ugandan traditional music, Duncan's meticulously crafted choir hymns, recorded by Heinrich Lampe in 1930, failed to capture the public imagination.

At the time of the Odeon recordings, Kayizzi was serving as a government clerk, while also working as an assistant choirmaster at Namirembe Cathedral. He had also learned to play the pianoforte under Duncan's tutelage. Kayizzi's moment of recognition would come later. Two decades afterward, ethnomusicologist Hugh Tracey recorded the Namirembe Cathedral choir. Under Kayizzi's direction, the choir's brilliance was undeniable. Kayizzi's masterful command of European Renaissance church music, executed with both delicacy and authority, stood as a testament to his exceptional talent. His achievements as a conductor and organist garnered him respect not only within Uganda but also among international observers of African music, highlighting the enduring legacy of a man trained by a missionary who had little respect for the music of his homeland.

No one captured the sheer excitement surrounding Uganda's first commercial discs of traditional folk music quite like Yakobo Kabi Kasumba. A man of remarkable distinction, Kasumba was a decorated Ugandan World War I veteran and one of more than 17,000 Ugandan soldiers who served in the 4th Battalion of the King's African Rifles (KAR). This battalion proved to be an effective fighting force, achieving notable success against German troops in East Africa. After the war, Kasumba rose to prominence as an influential chief in Nakaseke, central Uganda. In 1966, reflecting on a life shaped by colonial education and military service, he shared vivid memories of the gramophone's arrival in Uganda in an interview with *The People* newspaper, offering a compelling portrait of a society on the verge of a musical awakening.

Kasumba's trajectory was emblematic of a particular stratum of Ugandan society emerging under British colonial rule. Born at the turn of the twentieth century, he belonged to a generation of Ugandans whose lives were considerably shaped by British imperial ambitions. He was a graduate of King's College Budo, an elite institution established by British colonial administrators to instill Christian British values and cultivate a class of loyal, educated Africans who could serve as intermediaries between the colonial government and the local population. The ethos of the school emphasized discipline, Anglican morality, and an appreciation of Western customs, all of which Kasumba absorbed as he prepared for a career in colonial service.

His subsequent enlistment in the African Native Medical Corps during World War I further endeared him to the British establishment. The war had presented a paradoxical opportunity for many African soldiers. While they served under an often harsh colonial system, military service also provided them with a degree of respectability, financial stability, and exposure to foreign cultures. Kasumba, like many of his compatriots, returned to Uganda with a heightened sense of modernity, eager to translate his experiences into professional and social advancement.

After the war, he transitioned into the field of education, teaching at Mengo Central School in Kampala, where he became known for his strict discipline and commitment to excellence. His reputation soon caught the attention of the Protectorate administration, which recruited him into its ranks. In his new role as an administrator, he was entrusted with various responsibilities that reflected the complexities of colonial governance in a rapidly urbanizing Kampala. Among his more challenging assignments was the task of ridding the city of sex workers, a mission that required frequent, unannounced inspections of bars and brothels suspected of harboring them. Kasumba was both feared and respected for his unwavering enforcement of the law. He earned the moniker *Omukulu we kibuga*, *"The City Boss,"* a title that underscored his power within the colonial bureaucracy and the authoritarian measures often required to maintain order in Kampala.

While the gramophone had made its presence felt in Uganda in the early 1900s, it remained an object of fascination and exclusivity. It was largely confined to European households and a handful of Indian merchants who had settled in East Africa. It was not until 1928 that Kasumba first became aware of its existence, an encounter that left him both perplexed and intrigued. The idea that a machine could reproduce the human voice with such clarity seemed almost otherworldly. Determined to own one, he resolved to save up for the device. This endeavor required considerable financial commitment.

At the time, the social hierarchy in Uganda was rigid. As one of the few Ugandan teachers educated in the British tradition, Kasumba occupied a rarefied space within the emerging African middle class. His status afforded him access to luxuries that were beyond the reach of the average Ugandan. In 1931, he finally made his way to the Kampala branch of the Uganda Bookshop, a hub of European literature and imported goods. There, he invested a significant sum, equivalent to approximately $1,750 in today's currency, to purchase a Columbia wind-up gramophone. It was a statement purchase that marked his ascent into a world of modernity and cultural sophistication.

Recognizing the significance of Kasumba's acquisition, the Uganda Bookshop, which served as the local agent for the Columbia Gramophone Company, gifted him two free Odeon discs of Ugandan folk songs. This was both a gesture of goodwill and a clever marketing strategy. Kasumba, as a well-connected figure, would undoubtedly attract interest to the newly available recordings. Indeed, he became the first Black Ugandan in Kampala, and quite possibly in the entire country, to own a wind-up gramophone. It was an achievement that transformed him into an overnight sensation.

His home in Kibuye, one of the lively native neighborhoods that sat on the fringe of Kampala at the time, became a pilgrimage site for the curious and the skeptical alike. Crowds gathered daily, forming long, patient queues outside his residence, eager to witness this technological marvel in action. Each evening, Kasumba would prepare for his informal demonstrations, positioning the gramophone at the center of his modest but well-furnished living room. With practiced precision, he would crank the handle, set the heavy disc in motion, and release the needle onto the groove. As the sound emerged, crisp, resonant, and uncannily lifelike, the audience would gasp in astonishment. Many who heard the gramophone for the first time struggled to comprehend how a machine could replicate human voices with such fidelity. "Kasumba has an instrument that sings exactly like a human being!" they would murmur in awe, reinforcing the notion that the gramophone was not just an object of entertainment but something almost supernatural.

For a society accustomed to live musical performances, whether in royal courts, church choirs, or village gatherings, the idea that sound could be preserved and played back at will was nothing short of revolutionary. Kasumba's acquisition of the gramophone was more than a personal indulgence. It was a powerful symbol of changing times. As an educated African navigating the contradictions of colonial rule, he embraced modernity while remaining deeply connected to his cultural heritage. The gramophone, in this context, represented both his alignment with the colonial elite and his role as a conduit for the dissemination of Ugandan music.

More broadly, Kasumba's experience highlighted the transformative power of recorded sound in African societies. The ability to capture and reproduce music altered the way people engaged with their own traditions, creating new opportunities for preservation and innovation. By bringing the gramophone into his home, Kasumba unwittingly became a pioneer in the popularization of recorded Ugandan music, helping to shape the listening habits of a generation. His story, though centered on a single machine, speaks to a much larger historical narrative in which technology, status, and cultural identity were in constant negotiation. In his later years, reflecting on his first encounter with the gramophone, Kasumba would often remark, "It was then that I knew the world would never be the same again." And indeed, for Uganda's musical landscape, it never was.

One of the Odeon discs gifted to Kasumba by the Uganda Bookshop featured two particularly spirited folk songs: Sabasaja Tumukiriza (We Accept Your Majesty) and Sabasaja Mwana Wa Nabijano (Your Majesty, Son of Nabijano). These vibrant recordings, pulsating with infectious energy and accompanied by the distinctive sounds of the endongo (bowl-lyre) and ndingidi (single-string tube fiddle), were performed by none other than Ekibina kya Badongo ba Ssabasajja Kabaka (His Majesty the King's Music Ensemble). Leading this esteemed courtly ensemble was John Kasirye, a highly regarded musician who had dedicated many years of service to the Kabaka's court. (Interestingly, the Odeon disc misspelled Kasirye's name as "Kasirie," a testament to the challenges of transliteration and documentation in this early era of recording.)

The significance of these songs extended beyond their musical value. They were deeply embedded in the political fabric of Buganda. Both tracks paid homage to the reigning Kabaka of Buganda, Daudi Chwa, who had ascended to the throne under extraordinary and turbulent circumstances.

Daudi Chwa was the son of Kabaka Mwanga II, who had been deposed by the British and exiled in July 1897. In a strategic move designed to maintain control while placating the Baganda aristocracy, the British installed the one-year-old Daudi Chwa as the new king. Though nominally the ruler, Chwa's reign in his early years was effectively governed by the powerful Lukiiko (Buganda's parliament) and British colonial officials. The political undercurrents of these recordings reflect the enduring power of the *Kabakaship*, even under colonial rule, and serve as a sonic affirmation of loyalty to Buganda's monarchy during an era of profound transformation.

Kasumba's gramophone, along with his curated collection of recordings, became his passport to the highest echelons of Buganda society. His reputation as a gramophone owner and cultural enthusiast preceded him, and before long, he and his machine were invited to the Lubiri (royal palace) to entertain the Kabaka and his courtiers. This royal summons was more than just an honor. It was a tribute to Kasumba's growing social standing and his ability to navigate elite circles. His shared educational background with Daudi Chwa, as both were alumni of King's College Budo, likely facilitated this privileged connection.

Kasumba's role as a musical emissary extended beyond the palace walls. He became a sought-after guest in the homes of Buganda's royals and aristocrats, where his Columbia-brand gramophone was the centerpiece of elite gatherings. Whether playing records for chiefs, Ugandan colonial administrators, or wealthy merchants, Kasumba dazzled audiences with the enchanting sounds from his machine. His ability to bridge modern technology with traditional music elevated his status and earned him the moniker "The Gramophone King."

The 1930 Odeon recordings of traditional folk songs provide a fascinating glimpse into Uganda's diverse musical landscape during this period. They unveiled an array of musical ensembles and styles, bringing to prominence some of the era's most celebrated folk musicians. Among these was Ekibina kya Bazinyi na Bayimbi be Busega (The Music Ensemble of Busega Dancers and Singers), who contributed several notable tracks to the collection. This group was led by the enigmatic musician Gowa, a masterful performer known for his deep, resonant voice and evocative compositions.

One of Gowa's most poignant recordings from the 1930 sessions was Omugeni Agenda (The Visitor Departs). This melancholic song explored themes of impermanence, mortality, and the transience of human relationships. Accompanied by intricate drumming and an expressive vocal delivery, the track captured the emotional weight of bidding farewell to loved ones. The lyrics, which list names of individuals the protagonist is leaving behind, added a layer of intimacy and personal resonance to the song. Within Buganda's oral tradition, such farewell songs were often sung during funerals or long journeys, reinforcing Omugeni Agenda's significance as both a cultural artifact and an emotional touchstone.

On the flip side of Omugeni Agenda was Kamungolo, a lively and infectious tune performed by the talented female singer Blandina. This track, characterized by vibrant drumming and an exuberant chorus, became one of the most celebrated recordings of the 1930 series. Of all the early folk recordings, Kamungolo stands out for its enduring legacy. Decades later, it was revived and reinterpreted by renowned Ugandan musicians such as Albert Bisase Ssempeke and Kinobe, and today it remains a staple in primary school music education across central Uganda.

Scholars and folklorists have debated the deeper meaning behind Kamungolo. Some believe it to be an ancient song rooted in Buganda's spiritual and mythical traditions. In his 2012 article *Kusamira: Singing Rituals of Wellness in Central Uganda*, published in the journal *African*, Peter Hoesing suggests that the figure of Kamungolo represents an ancestor whose "bag full of ritual accoutrements symbolized the careful containment of indigenous spiritual knowledge." While this interpretation provides a valuable lens through which to understand the song's possible historical function, its lyrics also hint at alternative readings.

In Blandina's rendition, Kamungolo emerges as an allegory for political authority and affluence. One particularly striking line references a man casually entering his car in 1930s Uganda, an unmistakable symbol of status and modernity at the time. This suggests that Kamungolo may have also functioned as a satire or social commentary, highlighting the intersection of wealth, power, and colonial influence. The very name Kamungolo itself may be a linguistic play on the words "come" and "go," frequently used by British colonial officers and Christian missionaries when issuing orders to Ugandan servants. This theory adds another layer of subtext, subtly illuminating the hierarchical and often demeaning relationships that existed between colonial administrators and the local population.

However, the song's complexity and playfulness resist a singular interpretation. Blandina's lyrics seamlessly weave together references to divine wonders, romantic love, and admiration for a member of Buganda's royal family. A particularly intriguing verse mentions one of Kabaka Mutesa I's sons residing in Kibuli, a neighborhood in Kampala that later became a center of Islamic scholarship and influence. This blending of spiritual, political, and personal themes reflects the dynamic cultural landscape of early twentieth-century Buganda, where Christian conversion, traditional belief systems, and colonial modernity coexisted in a delicate and ever-evolving balance.

Gowa and Blandina contributed to other notable recordings in the 1930 sessions. Gowa's Kawulu (The Bachelor) explored the joys and perils of singlehood, while Blandina's Galimuwagula (It Will Force Its Way Through) was an animated commentary on perseverance and destiny. Both songs, driven by the rhythmic pulse of drums and the expressive vocal stylings of their performers, reinforced the power of recorded sound as a vehicle for storytelling and cultural transmission.

The name "Gowa" itself remains a subject of intrigue. It was likely a nickname, possibly connected to the Busega-Natete area, based on the name of his ensemble, Ekibina kya Bazinyi na Bayimbi be Busega. Natete held historical significance as the home of Uganda's first musical group to adopt European-style instruments, Ekitongole Ekigowa, also known as the Goan Unit. This raises the possibility that Gowa was either a former member of this pioneering group or a successor who carried forward its musical traditions. Alternatively, his moniker may have been an homage to St. Andrew Kaggwa's Ekitongole Ekigowa, the Catholic musical unit that blended indigenous and Western influences in its compositions and performances.

The 1930 Odeon recordings brought to life a diverse pool of musical talent, including lesser-known groups that deserve recognition for their contributions to Uganda's early recorded music history. One such group was Ekibina kya Badongo (The Ensemble of Musicians), consisting of Crespo Mukwaya, Eresa Nkunyingi, and their companions. They recorded two spirited and lively folk songs, Alimuntuti and Akasozi Kyengera (Kyengera Hill), both driven by the characteristic sounds of the endongo and ndingidi.

Another noteworthy contribution came from Abisage, who was listed as "Abisajin" on the disc, and her ensemble Ekibina kya Bayimbi ba JKMB Kazimili (The Music Ensemble of JKMB Kazimili), who performed the enchanting song Mukuyege. The flip side of Mukuyege featured Minuro by Mundu Tesaga, performed with Ekibina kya Abalunyanja ba Gabunga (The Music Ensemble of Gabunga's Sailors). In another instance of misspelling, Odeon recorded the group's name as Kibina kya Abalunyunya ba Gabunga. The name of the ensemble carries historical weight. "Gabunga" was the title given to the admiral of the Buganda King's canoe fleet, who also served as the head of the *mmamba* (lungfish) clan, the largest of Buganda's fifty-two clans.

The name "Mundu Tesaga," which translates to "Gun-jokes-not," is almost certainly a nickname, suggesting courage and possibly a military background. He may have been a soldier or a veteran of World War I. In his evocative canoe songs Ngolo (Bogey) and Aziraya (He Who Sounds the Alarm), Mundu Tesaga chose a stripped-down, a cappella approach, foregoing instrumental accompaniment. His powerful vocals, delivered in the distinct dialect of the Ssese Islands, resonate with a haunting quality. The Ssese archipelago, composed of eighty-four islands in Lake Victoria, is renowned for its serene beauty. Mundu Tesaga's striking solo performance of Ngolo, punctuated only by a hypnotic "ay, ay" refrain, conjures vivid imagery: well-built young men, their bodies glistening with sweat, rhythmically rowing canoes across the vast lake under the scorching afternoon sun. Between his verses and the chorus, one can almost hear the distant roar of waves, adding atmosphere and emotional depth to the scene.

The forty-two Odeon records released in 1930 held the distinction of being the only commercial representation of Ugandan music on disc for nearly a decade. This interruption in recording activity was largely due to the global economic downturn triggered by the Great Depression. Beginning in 1929 and persisting until 1933, the Depression caused a sharp decline in economic activity across the world, impacting numerous industries.

The recording industry was especially affected. As demand for non-essential goods like records collapsed, production and distribution declined dramatically. In British colonies across Africa, the effects of the Depression were intensified by economies that were designed to serve the needs of the colonial powers. With falling demand for African exports such as coffee, cotton, and minerals, local economies contracted. This led to widespread unemployment and a sharp drop in household income. At the same time, colonial governments slashed public spending, limiting funds for cultural programs and activities, including musical ventures.

The Depression forced a restructuring of the recording industry itself. As competition intensified in a shrinking market, the Gramophone Company and Columbia International Ltd. merged in 1931 to form EMI (Electric and Musical Industries Ltd). This newly formed conglomerate came to dominate the music record market in most British and French colonies, bringing under its umbrella iconic labels such as HMV (His Master's Voice), Odeon, Columbia, Pathé, Parlophone, and Zonophone. This consolidation of power further limited opportunities for smaller, independent recording ventures, particularly in the colonies. The confluence of these global economic forces and the restructuring of the recording industry created a challenging environment for further recording efforts in Uganda. It would take the outbreak of World War II and its aftermath to usher in a new era of musical recording and innovation in the country.

Despite the interruption caused by the Great Depression and World War II, Ugandan music remained a vibrant part of social life. Even as recording activities were temporarily halted, Ugandan society was undergoing significant change, shaped by colonial rule, war, and a shifting labor market. More Ugandans moved from rural villages to urban centers, seeking employment in factories, tea plantations, and coffee estates established by the colonial administration to support a Western-style industrial economy. This migration contributed to the expansion of towns such as Entebbe, Kampala, Jinja, Mbale, Fort Portal, Lira, and Tororo, creating new markets and audiences for music.

The relative affluence of these wage earners enabled them to acquire gramophones, opening up a world of musical possibilities. Through outlets like the Uganda Bookshop, they were exposed to a diverse array of global sounds, including American fox trots, Argentinian tangos, Afro-Caribbean rumbas, Cuban cha-cha, European waltzes, Hawaiian steel guitar music, and the swinging rhythms of African-American jazz and blues. This influx of international music broadened musical horizons and influenced the development of Ugandan popular music.

EMI, the recording industry giant, resumed its East African recording activities in 1937, releasing music on the Columbia label in the EO series. However, the outbreak of World War II soon disrupted these efforts, putting a temporary hold on further recordings. Following the war, recording activities picked up again in the late 1940s, with new releases appearing on EMI's Columbia EO series and the MA series on the His Master's Voice (HMV) label. During this period, traditional folk music ensembles remained prominent in recorded music, demonstrating their continued popularity.

Among the notable folk musicians of this era were Elizabeth Nkomommo Namale, affectionately known as Namale of Salama, and her cousin, Malyamu Namale, known as Namale of Kasangati. Her name was unfortunately misspelled as "Muliamu" on some of the discs. Both Namales were highly respected in the Ugandan music scene. Their songs explored themes of battles and conquest, the complexities of love, mythology, and, like many of their contemporaries, praised their sovereign, the Kabaka. Their first recordings were released on the Columbia label in the late 1930s, marking their entry into the world of recorded music.

Interestingly, Elizabeth and Malyamu often shared the same disc, with one appearing on the "A" side and the other on the "B" side. This practice, evident in at least two recordings on the Columbia label, highlights the close relationship between these two talented musicians and their shared prominence in the folk music scene. For example, on Columbia EO 473, Elizabeth and her group, Namale and Party, recorded the joyous song Wananda, while Malyamu and her ensemble, Malyamu and Party, performed Bwendimuta on the flip side.

Elizabeth Namale, considerably younger than her cousin Malyamu, enjoyed a distinguished career and became a regular performer at Sir Edward Mutesa's palace in the 1950s and early 1960s. Her talent and artistry left a lasting impression on those who encountered her music. The renowned Ugandan poet and academic Austin Bukenya, who knew Elizabeth personally in the 1960s and even invited her to live in his home, spoke highly of her musical abilities. By then, she had retired from public performances and was likely in her late sixties. Bukenya fondly recalled, "What I particularly liked about her was the air of quiet tranquility, which was reflected in the perfectly controlled pitch, volume, and timbre of her voice." This description captures the essence of Elizabeth's musical style, characterized by its grace, emotional depth, and technical mastery.

Elizabeth Namale's early recordings on the Columbia label included the evocative Salambwa Lya Wamala (The Gaboon Viper of Wamala). In this song, she appears to draw inspiration from the mythical legend of the Chwezi, a group believed to have held political sway over much of the interlacustrine region of East Africa, including central Uganda, during the fourteenth or fifteenth century. The Chwezi were revered as demigods, and their spiritual legacy continues to this day in a cult that worships them. According to legend, during the reign of their last king, Wamala, the Chwezi mysteriously vanished into the depths of the lake that now bears his name. He is still venerated as a water deity, his story intertwined with the history and mythology of the region. Malyamu Namale also made significant contributions to recorded music, with popular songs on the Columbia label such as Omugenyi Yafuta Ngombe (The Guest Blew the

Trumpet), which was listed on the label as Omugenyiyafuwangobe, and Nange Nditukayo (I Too Will Get There).

Between 1937 and the late 1950s, as the 78-rpm era drew to a close, a distinct naming convention emerged among Ugandan folk music ensembles. Many groups adopted the practice of appending "and Party" to the lead singer's name. This trend is reflected in the Columbia label releases, which featured ensembles such as Sauda and Party, Amisi and Party, Arajabu and Party, Ayeni and Party, Nusula Nakibule and Party, Kotida and Party, Galabuzi and Party, and numerous others. This naming pattern not only highlighted the lead singer but also emphasized the collaborative nature of these musical groups.

This period also saw the return of some folk musicians who had previously recorded on the Odeon label. Abisage, for instance, reappeared on the Columbia label as Abisage and Party, performing the heartfelt song Ndimuwa Ente (I Will Gift a Cow), which was incorrectly listed on the label as Ndimuwaente. Similarly, Kazimili, who had previously recorded on the Odeon label with his group Kibina kya Bayimbi ba JKMB Kazimili, reemerged as Kazmiri and Party, displaying his continued dedication to his musical craft.

These recordings from the 1930s and 1950s offer a valuable window into the evolving traditions of Ugandan folk music. They highlight the sustained popularity of traditional musical styles, the emergence of new recording conventions, and the ongoing contributions of both established and emerging artists.

The late 1930s marked a transformative period in Ugandan music, with artists and ensembles experimenting with a unique fusion of traditional and Western styles. Among the pioneering groups of this era was Ivan and Co., led by Ivan Mukasa, a musician whose passion for English choral traditions helped shape a new musical landscape in Uganda. Ivan Mukasa hailed from Bunamwaya, a village south of Natete, and attended King's College Budo, a prestigious institution where he sang in the school choir, performing hymns and English folk songs. Inspired by these influences, he formed Ivan and Co. in 1937, a group composed mostly of fellow Budo alumni and church choir members.

Their approach was novel. They retained the melodies of English choral compositions but adapted the lyrics into vernacular languages, a practice that dazzled audiences in Kampala. Performing at weddings and beer parties across Kampala's local neighborhoods, Ivan and Co. gained recognition for their harmonized European-style singing. Their growing popularity eventually gave rise to the Mengo African Orchestra, also known as the Budonians, an influential ensemble that played a key role in shaping Uganda's evolving musical identity. Under Ivan and Co., they recorded notable tracks such as Ya Ye Yi Yo Yu, an alphabet rhyme, and Eda Waliwo Omuwala (Once There Was a Girl) on the Columbia label.

Another significant force in Uganda's early syncretic music was the Ham Mukasa family. Ham Mukasa (1870–1956), a son of a chief and an influential political figure, was a modest musician known for his ability to play the Kiganda lute, xylophone, and other traditional instruments. In an obituary published in the *Uganda Journal*, Catherine Sebuliba, the first Black Ugandan to work as a typist, reflected on Mukasa's musical abilities, writing, "Ham Mukasa was an average musician, with a good voice and the ability to play the Kiganda lute, xylophone, and other instruments. When in good spirits, he would sing Kiganda, Kisoga, or Kisese songs, accompanying himself on various instruments. He also wrote his own lyrics to fit the music."

Mukasa's daughters, Jeanne Katalina (also known as Catherine Nanjjobe) and Alexandria, inherited his musical talents. Educated at Gayaza High School, they were trained in harmonious singing and European contrapuntal compositions, mastering both hymns and secular music. Gayaza's choir was widely praised for its performances, particularly its rendition of Orlando di Lasso's motet Adoramus Te. Spurred by their father, the Mukasa girls made recordings for Columbia and HMV in the late 1930s, just prior to World War II. Their work is significant because it provides some of the earliest documented instances of guitar usage in recorded Ugandan music.

Performing as the Ham Mukasa Family, they produced patriotic and religious songs such as Tusanyukide Omutanda (We Celebrate His Majesty) and Olunaku Lwali Lumu (Once Upon a Time). Under their individual stage names, Jeanne Katalina (misspelled as "Kaslina" on record labels) and Alexandria recorded Kiriyo Mutoto Kirya, a playful rhyming song, and Bampitire Omwana (Call My Baby). Alexandria also recorded solo under the name Miss Alexandrea Mukasa and Party, producing tracks like Okwagala Okwekitalo (Great Love), Kambatendere Kitange (Let Me Praise My Father), and Wololo Walala (Jubilation), all on the HMV label. These self-composed guitar songs reflected the Mukasa girls' deep Christian faith and the centrality of God in their lives. Other musically talented Mukasa siblings included Rebecca Mulira and Edward Galabuzi Mukasa. Edward even pursued musical studies in London and Paris. The flip side of Wololo Walala featured Olusozi Manyangwa (Manyangwa Hill), performed by Asanasiyo Kironde. This HMV disc featuring both Alexandria Mukasa and Asanasiyo Kironde is more than a musical collaboration. It symbolizes the union of two powerful Ugandan families, their histories intertwined with the complex narrative of colonial Uganda. Jeanne Katalina, Alexandria's sister, was the wife of Michael Ernest Kawalya-Kaggwa, the younger brother of Asanasiyo Kironde.

Asanasiyo Kironde and Michael Ernest Kawalya-Kaggwa were the sons of Sir Apollo Kaggwa, a towering figure in Buganda's political history. Sir Apollo was one of the kingdom's longest-serving prime ministers and played a key role in shaping Uganda's colonial administration. As *Katikkiro* (prime minister) from 1890 to 1926, Kaggwa was instrumental in negotiating the 1900 Buganda Agreement, which formalized British rule in Buganda and apportioned vast tracts of land to chiefs and landowners. The agreement resulted in forty percent of the Buganda Kingdom's land, about eight thousand square miles, being divided among one thousand chiefs and private landowners.

Prior to this agreement, the land belonged to the king, who would occasionally grant land to favored chiefs. As a result of the agreement, Apollo Kaggwa acquired roughly one hundred square miles of land, and

Ham Mukasa secured a substantial estate. This land deal left ordinary people in Buganda resentful, as they were relegated to landless sharecropping. The anger over the greed of the chiefs and the injustices of the British colonial administration fueled widespread discontent.

In response, an anonymous musician composed the song Buto Dene, a satirical jingle that mocked those perceived to have betrayed the people, including Apollo Kaggwa and Ham Mukasa. The song's lyrics were sharp and biting: *Buto dene bangenze Entebbe okutunda abana* (The pot-bellied have gone to Entebbe to sell the children), encapsulating the anger of the landless peasantry.

But there was a noble side to Apollo Kaggwa. He was also a champion of modern education, administrative reforms, and Western-style governance, which significantly influenced Buganda's elite class. However, his role in these land reforms made him a polarizing figure. He was celebrated by some for his vision but criticized by others who saw him as complicit in entrenching inequalities.

Throughout Uganda's history, music has served as a powerful medium for political and social critique. From the satirical Buto Dene to the songs reflecting tensions between Apollo Kaggwa and his rival Stanislaus Mugwanya, musicians have used their craft to expose corruption, injustice, and the shifting tides of power. One such song captured a moment of high drama on the floor of the Buganda Lukiiko, where tensions between Sir Apollo Kaggwa and Stanislaus Mugwanya erupted in unforgettable fashion. The confrontation began when Kaggwa, in a fit of anger, lunged forward and tore the speaking notes from Mugwanya's hands. Stunned but unyielding, Mugwanya sprang to his feet, seized Kaggwa by the lapels, and shook him violently in front of the assembled chiefs and notables. Gasps echoed through the chamber as aides from both sides rushed in, turning the scene into a full-blown scuffle. The clash was the talk of the kingdom, but it was in song that it was immortalized: *Kanjogere byenalaba, Katikkiro yamega Mugwanya, Ekyabalwanyisa z'empapula* (Let me speak of what I saw, the Katikkiro grabbed Mugwanya because of the papers).

The descendants of Sir Apollo Kaggwa made profound contributions to Uganda's social, cultural, and political development during a time of dramatic national transformation. By the time Jeanne Katalina began recording her music, she had been married for years to Michael Ernest Kawalya-Kaggwa, who became Katikkiro of Buganda in 1945. Like his father before him, he was a leading figure in Buganda's traditional leadership, but his tenure also reflected a broader shift toward modern governance. He played a key role in persuading the British colonial administration to introduce foundational infrastructure, including hydroelectric power, piped water, a sewerage system for Kampala, and a national postal service. These efforts laid the groundwork for a more urban and connected Uganda.

Katalina herself became the first Ugandan woman to obtain a driving license, marking a symbolic step forward for Ugandan women in public life. Their son, Michael Hamilton Kawalya-Kaggwa, became a barrister and ran KK Wholesalers, one of the few large and successful Black-owned businesses in Uganda at the time. His wife, Olive Amelia Kaggwa, of Ghanaian Ga and British descent, stood out in a society where interracial marriages were still rare. Their union was seen as both socially bold and culturally significant. The couple lived with flair and distinction, owning two private planes. However, their prominence came with risk. In January 1971, Idi Amin seized power and declared himself president. It was rumored that Amin had shown romantic interest in Olive, which she reportedly rebuffed. That September, Michael Hamilton was found dead in his ivory-colored convertible Mercedes Benz, having been shot and then burned.

Another prominent figure from the Kaggwa lineage was Apollo Kironde, the son of Asanasiyo Kironde and Bulandina. He pursued his education at Fort Hare University in South Africa, where he became proficient in guitar, though the flute held a special place in his heart. After completing his studies, he returned to Uganda and taught history and music at his alma mater, King's College Budo, from 1945 to 1949. With his students, he recorded four Negro spirituals under the name Kironde & Party on the Jambo label in 1950, including Gwine To Ride Up In De

Chariot with I Got A Robe on the flip side, and Couldn't Hear Nobody Pray paired with Down By The Riverside. Influenced by Western choral traditions, these recordings reflected the musical path pursued by many elite Ugandans in the mid-twentieth century.

After his time at Budo, Kironde studied law in England and was called to the Bar at Middle Temple. Returning to Uganda, he emerged as a strong advocate for national development, lobbying for the establishment of Mulago Hospital and championing the construction of the National Theatre in Kampala. At independence, he was appointed Uganda's first ambassador to the United Nations, representing the country with distinction on the global stage. Under Amin, he later served as Minister of Tourism and then as Minister of Planning and Economic Development. Like many others, he benefited from the 1972 expulsion of Ugandans of Indian ancestry, acquiring the Mercedes Benz dealership from DT Dobie, which had been operated by former British Army officer David Theodore Dobie, and reestablishing it as Action Motors. Kironde's family left a lasting legacy beyond politics and business. In 1968, his daughter Katiti Kironde became the first Black model to appear on the cover of the prestigious Glamour magazine, breaking racial barriers and offering a powerful celebration of Black beauty.

In 1939, a landmark recording emerged from Uganda, capturing the burgeoning fusion of indigenous musical traditions with Western influences. This defining moment in the nation's musical evolution was marked by a shellac disc released under the prestigious Columbia label, featuring two favorite songs at the time: Omwana Akaba (The Baby Is Crying) and Buli Woda Olaba (Every Turn, You See). The creators of this groundbreaking record were Ernest Ssempebwa, Joshua Luyimbazi Zaake, and Emmanuel Lumu. All were alumni of King's College Budo and crafted music defined by the warm, resonant tones of acoustic guitars. Their work exemplified the emerging syncretic sound that was beginning to shape Ugandan popular music.

Rather than simply imitating Western styles, they blended traditional Ugandan melodies and lyrical themes with the instrumentation and structural elements of Western folk and early popular music. This sophisticated fusion balanced the familiar with the innovative, ensuring the music remained both accessible and engaging to a wide audience. Their approach captured the nation's imagination and marked the beginning of a new era in artistic expression, expanding the reach of Ugandan guitar music.

Omwana Akaba was a poignant love song, a reinterpretation of a traditional children's lullaby transformed into a romantic ballad. The trio used the metaphor of an inconsolable crying baby in need of a seasoned babysitter to mirror their own yearning for love. These "babysitters," as they were affectionately called, were not literal caregivers but the women they admired: Mary, Dora, and Lydia. These young women, celebrated for their beauty and intellect, attended the leading girls' schools of the time: Gayaza High School, Stella Maris College in Nsube, and King's College Budo.

The lyrics reflected the social and romantic ideals of the era, where education and refinement were prized alongside traditional beauty. One memorable verse praised a young woman from Nsube, highlighting her "European" stride, her central-parted hairstyle, and her elegance, ending with a promise of marriage. This blend of traditional courtship and modern admiration offered a window into the evolving social dynamics of pre-independence Uganda.

The reverse side, Buli Woda Olaba, continued the theme of romantic admiration. It painted a vivid portrait of the women who populated the musicians' daily lives. The lyrics described beautiful women seen on buses and bicycles, playing pianos, and attending colleges. They were praised for their "godly" teeth, intricately styled hair, necklaces lined in symmetrical rows, and long, slender noses, which were associated with pastoralist heritage and ideals of beauty.

Musically, the songs were lively and uplifting, subtly infused with the rhythmic sensibilities of American folk and bluegrass. This careful blend of diverse influences gave the music a fresh appeal and invited listeners to imagine a future shaped by harmony, hope, and youthful exuberance in a rapidly modernizing urban world. What makes this recording especially remarkable is that the three musicians did not pursue careers in music. Instead, they used their talents in service of their nation. Ernest Ssempebwa became the Private Secretary to Sir Edward Frederick Mutesa II, the Kabaka of Buganda, in 1942. He later dedicated his life to education and rose to become Deputy Headteacher of King's College Budo, helping to shape future generations. Joshua Luyimbazi Zaake, a central figure in Uganda's path to independence, moved from education into politics. He became Uganda's first post-independence Minister of Education and played a foundational role in shaping the country's educational system. Dr. Emmanuel Lumu, a respected physician, also played a key role in Uganda's early independence. He became the first post-independence Minister of Health and was instrumental in building the national health infrastructure that continues to serve the country. In February 2019, he was honored by family and friends at his Bakuli residence as he celebrated his 103rd birthday, a testament to a life of long-standing public service and quiet musical legacy.

The outbreak of World War II temporarily dampened and paralyzed the budding Ugandan music recording industry, as many promising young musicians were drafted into the King's African Rifles to fight for the British Empire in distant lands like Burma. Even as the war raged on, with its machine guns and bombs claiming the lives of many young Ugandans, British colonial administrators in Uganda continued to maintain a busy social calendar. The English-language newspaper *Uganda Herald* regularly featured stories about lively concerts, dinner parties with the Governor, and other social events. Elite Ugandans, eager to imitate British customs, kept the war at a distance.

In 1943, Uganda's first "nightclubs" opened, catering to the Black Ugandan elite. These clubs were filled with revelers who drank and danced to Western music blaring from gramophones. Ballroom dancing and the fox-trot were especially popular. In 1944, the Buganda Cultural Society was founded, with its home in the Budonian Club (later known as the Mengo Social Center) in Kisenyi-Mengo, just a mile from the Lubiri, the king's palace. Chaired by Ms. Yunia Kisosonkole, the society aimed to promote social cohesion among the urban Ugandan elite, offering a welcoming venue and free evening lessons in Western dance styles. The colonial state was highly stratified, and Black Ugandans were largely excluded from European and Indian social clubs, which continued to thrive in the city.

Around 1944, live performances by Ugandan musicians accompanied by banjo, mandolin, and guitars began appearing in these "nightclubs." They mostly played covers of popular Western and African songs. Some of these "nightclubs" were located in the homes of ordinary people living in Kampala's local townships, such as Kibuye, Nakulabye, Bwaise, Mengo, and Natete.

Returning World War II veterans added further momentum to this creative evolution. Having spent time abroad, they brought back expanded musical perspectives and a drive to explore new possibilities. Their exposure to diverse global sounds during their military service inspired an experimental spirit that began to reshape Uganda's music scene. These veterans, along with local folk musicians and emerging innovators, pushed the boundaries of performance and composition in new directions. Together, these artists helped lay the foundation for a dynamic and evolving musical tradition. The blend of heritage and modernity they embraced continued to shape Ugandan music in the years that followed, offering future generations a model for creativity rooted in both history and transformation.

CHAPTER 3

From Burma to Busega: Veterans, Big Bands, and a New Sound

The aftermath of World War II ushered in a transformative era for Uganda, with returning veterans acting as pivotal conduits for the dissemination of Western-style music and dance. Among these veterans, Sergeant-Major Robert H. Kakembo stood out as a particularly influential figure. His dedication to this cultural exchange stemmed from a unique blend of personal experience and intellectual curiosity. Kakembo's background was distinguished. A product of Uganda's elite educational institutions, King's College Budo and Makerere College, he possessed a sophisticated worldview that was further broadened by his wartime experiences. In 1939, he was conscripted into the King's African Rifles (KAR), joining over 77,000 Ugandan soldiers who served the British Empire across diverse theaters of war. This global exposure profoundly altered Kakembo's perspective, extending far beyond the confines of military duty.

His insights were captured in the influential booklet *An African Soldier Speaks*, a testament to his intellectual engagement with the war. This work served as a powerful platform for advocating for veterans' rights, including improved services, economic development, and increased political participation. Kakembo's analysis went beyond mere grievances. He recognized the war's paradoxical role as a catalyst for personal and cultural growth. He astutely observed that, "in spite of its many drawbacks, [war] is the best practical school one can ever go to. No university rivals the war as a teacher of sociology and geography. The war is a great molder of character." This perspective highlighted the war's capacity to transform soldiers into cosmopolitan individuals, exposed to a multitude of cultures and perspectives.

The practical benefits of military service extended beyond intellectual growth. KAR troops acquired valuable skills and, for many, experienced a standard of living that surpassed their pre-war circumstances. Kakembo documented the soldiers' evolving tastes and lifestyles, noting their adaptation to new norms: the practicality of boots, the expectation of regular, nutritious meals, and the introduction of tea and coffee as daily staples. Furthermore, the army provided opportunities for literacy, fostering a new-found appreciation for newspapers and other printed materials. Soldiers like Kakembo, deployed to Burma (Myanmar), had access to publications such as *HESHIMA*, and they also engaged with the wider world through wireless broadcasts, cinema, and live music.

The power of music as a morale booster and cultural bridge was vividly illustrated by the No. 1 East African Entertainment Unit. Led by British officers Captain John Gower and Captain Peter Colmore, the unit featured the celebrated band The Rhino Boys, under the direction of Captain Jeff Seabrook. This ensemble, composed of talented East African musicians recruited for their proficiency with Western instruments, offered a diverse repertoire that included rumbas, tangos, and waltzes. The band's instrumentation included guitars, mandolins, violins, a harmonium, drums, maracas, trumpets, saxophones, and accordions, creating a dynamic and immersive musical experience.

In March 1944, The Rhino Boys embarked on an extraordinary tour, beginning at the Kenyan port of Mombasa. They covered more than 60,500 miles and delivered 350 performances to Allied troops across nine nations, including Ethiopia, Ceylon (Sri Lanka), India, Madagascar, and Burma. In Burma, they performed for the 11th East African Division of the KAR, which had been deployed to relieve the 23rd Indian Infantry Division in the summer of 1944. Often playing within earshot of the frontlines, the band offered a crucial source of entertainment and respite. Their repertoire spanned original compositions and popular hits of the era, including Al Jolson's I'm Down In Honolulu Looking Them Over, Roger Edens' Minnie From Trinidad, and Gene Autry's Deep In The Heart Of Texas. Notably, their time in Madagascar led to the incorporation of popular French songs, further enriching their musical offerings, which also included traditional military marches.

This exposure to a wide range of musical styles and cultures had a lasting impact on the soldiers. Upon their return to Uganda, veterans such as Kakembo became key figures in the country's evolving music scene. They introduced new instruments and styles and adapted them to local traditions, fostering a rich fusion that would define Ugandan popular music in the post-war era. Through informal gatherings, performances, and mentorship, these veterans helped lay the groundwork for a vibrant music industry that bridged indigenous and Western influences. The post-war period marked the beginning of a cultural renaissance in Uganda, with returning soldiers acting as both preservers of tradition and pioneers of modernity.

Robert Kakembo's time in Burma, particularly his exposure to The Rhino Boys' lush performances, left an indelible mark on his worldview. The band's music, along with the broader experiences of military life, convinced him that demobilized soldiers would no longer tolerate a return to the same old dull conditions of their pre-war existence. The army had broadened their horizons, instilled new expectations, and cultivated a sense of entitlement to a better future. Upon his return to Kampala, Kakembo was driven by a profound sense of purpose. He was determined to translate his wartime insights into tangible change for his fellow veterans and for Ugandan society more broadly.

His natural leadership qualities propelled him to the chairmanship of the Uganda Veterans Association, where he immediately confronted the formidable challenge of securing adequate compensation for returning soldiers. The colonial administration, however, displayed a marked indifference to the welfare of these men who had risked their lives in service of the British Empire. Officials argued that the responsibility for veteran care lay with African tribal authorities, reflecting a dismissive attitude that disregarded the soldiers' contributions. Kakembo, undeterred, embarked on a relentless campaign of disciplined advocacy. His persistence and strategic approach gradually forced the colonial government to acknowledge its obligations, ultimately leading to improved welfare provisions for Ugandan veterans, surpassing those offered in neighboring Kenya and Tanzania.

Kakembo's vision extended beyond immediate veteran concerns. He recognized the transformative potential of the cultural exposure gained by Ugandan soldiers abroad and believed it should be harnessed to enrich Ugandan society. He envisioned the establishment of entertainment centers across the country, serving as hubs for both education and recreation. These centers would introduce ordinary Ugandans to the vibrant sounds of Western-style music and provide instruction in popular dances such as the fox-trot, quickstep, and rumba. Kakembo sought to cultivate a more cosmopolitan and culturally dynamic Uganda, bridging the gap between traditional life and the modern world.

His vision resonated strongly with a circle of influential Ugandans, primarily drawn from the Buganda aristocracy. Among his most ardent supporters was Pumla Ngozwana Kisosonkole, a South African woman married to Buganda aristocrat Christopher Ssekuuma Kisosonkole. As a member of the Buganda Cultural Society, an organization dedicated to promoting Western-style music and dance, she provided crucial support for Kakembo's initiatives. Kakembo, himself an accomplished guitarist and multi-instrumentalist, became deeply involved in the Buganda Cultural Society, lending his expertise to organizing and promoting Ugandan music groups. He also championed the creation of local bands capable of performing rumbas, tangos, and waltzes, encouraging Ugandan musicians to develop their own unique interpretations of these styles.

Two prominent members of the Buganda Cultural Society, Eridadi Mulira and Joseph "Jolly Joe" Kiwanuka, were particularly inspired by

Kakembo's vision. Mulira, a refined and diplomatic politician, was married to Rebecca Mulira, a respected musician from the influential Ham Mukasa musical and political dynasty. Kiwanuka, an outspoken and entrepreneurial businessman, wielded significant influence as the editor of the *Uganda Express*, an English-language weekly, and the *Uganda Post*, a tri-weekly Luganda paper. Both publications, with their substantial readership, served as vital platforms for shaping public discourse on cultural and political issues. Like Kakembo, both Mulira and Kiwanuka were alumni of King's College Budo. They shared a common educational foundation and a commitment to Uganda's progress. Recognizing the immense talent of Ugandan musicians, they provided the crucial financial backing needed to realize Kakembo's dream of establishing a local band that would cater to the tastes of the Black elite with Western-style music. Kakembo, with his deep musical knowledge, took on the responsibility of training aspiring musicians, ensuring they met the exacting standards of their discerning audiences.

The task of leading this pioneering band fell to Joshua Serunkuma, another Budo alumnus and a fellow World War II veteran. Serunkuma, a gifted polyglot fluent in Swahili, English, and Luganda, had served in the King's African Rifles as a translator, facilitating communication between British officers and East and Central African troops. Before the war, Serunkuma and his siblings, John Bosa, Festo Kiguli, and their younger sister Miriam Ssempa (née Nabalende), were members of the popular musical act Ivan & Co., which had been founded by Ivan Mukasa. With the financial support of Jolly Joe Kiwanuka and Eridadi Mulira, Serunkuma was able to assemble a group of exceptionally talented musicians. The band was initially formed in late 1945 as the Bukesa Orchestra, named after the Kampala neighborhood where they first rehearsed. At the time, Bukesa was a flat-topped hill of slum dwellings, contiguous with Nakulabye to the south and Makerere Hill to the north, offering a spectacular view of Namirembe Cathedral in the distance. By August 1946, the ensemble had evolved and rebranded itself as the Mengo African Orchestra. This new name became associated with the modern music movement emerging in Uganda at the time.

The Mengo African Orchestra was a grand ensemble that often featured more than fourteen musicians. Their instrumentation was a rich array of European instruments, including guitars, banjos, a resonant double bass, brassy trumpets, smooth saxophones, melodic accordions, rhythmic drums, the percussive marimba, a warm harmonium, and vibrant maracas. Beyond their musical skill, the band was renowned for its distinctive and coordinated style. They were a visual spectacle that matched their sonic sophistication. The musicians frequently appeared in crisp white shirts, tailored black trousers, and elegant bow ties. At times, they opted for bold striped jackets and matching ties. Their appearance reinforced their identity not only as musicians but also as cultural trendsetters. Their fashion sensibility was as influential as their music, with young men across Kampala eagerly adopting their sartorial choices.

Shortly after the orchestra's formation, Joshua Serunkuma, its initial leader, was appointed to a prominent administrative position as a *gombolola* (sub-county) chief. This new role, demanding significant time and attention, necessitated a shift in leadership. The mantle of the Mengo African Orchestra's direction then passed to his younger brother, John Bosa. A musical prodigy, Bosa had distinguished himself early on, earning a scholarship to King's College Budo through his exceptional vocal talent. His voice, marked by a distinctive gravelly timbre, held a unique power, delighting listeners with its depth and character. Bosa infused the band with his artistic energy, serving as both lead vocalist and principal songwriter. His musical contributions extended beyond his vocal prowess, as he also skillfully played the maracas, adding a vital rhythmic layer to the orchestra's performances.

The composition of the Mengo African Orchestra reflected the interconnectedness of Uganda's emerging elite. A significant proportion of its members were either alumni of King's College Budo or veterans of the King's African Rifles (KAR). In addition to the siblings John Bosa and Joshua Serunkuma, the band included their brother Aloni Kiguli, who contributed vocals and the rhythmic strumming of the banjo, and their teenage sister, Miriam Ssempa, a vocalist of impressive range and the orchestra's sole female member. The ensemble's roster evolved over its lifespan, spanning from the 1940s to the mid-1950s, and included a constellation of talented musicians. Ivan Mukasa, a veteran of the pre-war group Ivan & Co., lent his vocal talents, while Mudido and Sekinemye mastered the evocative sounds of the Hawaiian guitar. Kalinimi Mpagi and Sevume Salongo, also known as Sevume of Bunamwaya mu Ngobe, were not only accomplished vocalists but also virtuosos of the harmonium and accordion. Shem Sepuya anchored the rhythm with his steady double bass, and Nelson Gonzabato, an ex-KAR serviceman and former member of the Rhino Boys, joined the orchestra in the 1950s, adding his expertise on the banjo. A foundational member was Joseph Chuza Kabasele, a Congolese-born drummer and another veteran of the Rhino Boys, whose rhythmic innovation would later propel his own *soukous* bands, Orchestra Les Noir and City Five Band, to immense popularity in the 1960s and 1970s. Other notable musicians who graced the ranks of this legendary orchestra included Robert Kakembo, Lameka Kamanyi, Luwemba, Mponye, Yeko Mukasa, and Abraham Waligo, who would later ascend to the position of Uganda's Prime Minister from August 1985 to January 1986.

The Mengo African Orchestra drew heavily from popular Western musical styles that resonated with Uganda's small but influential elite, crafting a repertoire ideally suited for ballroom dances such as the waltz, foxtrot, and quickstep. These dances, deeply cherished by the elite, were central to their social gatherings, offering elegance, structure, and a sense of cosmopolitan refinement. During public appearances, young men and women from the Buganda Cultural Society brought these dances to life with graceful precision and polished flair, offering a vivid, moving portrait of the cultural fusion embodied by the band's music. Many of these dancers, often drawn from prominent aristocratic families, became central figures in Kampala's social scene and played a vital role in preserving and popularizing these refined dance forms within elite circles.

While the band conducted its regular musical rehearsals at John Bosa's residence in Busega, near Natete township, their ballroom dance rehearsals were held at Mr. Mukamba's elegant and spacious home in the verdant Lungujja suburb of Kampala. The leading ballroom dance instructors included Rebecca Mulira, Mr. Kamanyi and his wife, Yunia Kisosonkole, and Pumla Ngozwana Kisosonkole. Among the dancers, two figures stood out for their exceptional skill and charisma: Kate "Keti" Kalanzi Kanjogolo, who radiated glamour, and the tall, graceful Ms. Namazzi, the daughter of the esteemed chief Andereya Luwandagga from the Buluri region of Buganda. Dressed in flowing white skirts and gleaming shoes, these dancers tantalized audiences with their intricate footwork and boundless energy, becoming celebrated social icons in Kampala and beyond. John Bosa, the orchestra's bandleader, was particularly smitten with Ms. Namazzi and eventually married the slender and delicate beauty.

Despite their dedication to music, the members of the Mengo African Orchestra were not full-time musicians. John Bosa, for example, held a position as a clerk at the Uganda Bookshop Printing Press on Balintuma Road, while Abraham Waligo was a student at King's College Budo. Aloni Kiguli balanced his musical pursuits with a deep commitment to advancing soccer in the Buganda Kingdom. He successfully lobbied the Kabaka to establish the Buganda Clan Soccer League, a tournament that continues to this day as one of the country's longest-running sporting events. Their dedication was driven by a genuine love of music, and their amateur status did nothing to diminish their popularity. Their performances, typically held on Saturdays at the Mengo Social Center and occasionally at the Blue Gardens, were consistently sold out, drawing enthusiastic crowds who reveled in the orchestra's vibrant and polished performances.

The Blue Gardens, owned by Kampala businessman Mr. Kawoya, was a sanctuary nestled within the Kibuye neighborhood of Kampala. Also known as Mengo Blue Gardens, or simply Ewa'Kawoya (Kawoya's), it was more than just a nightclub; it was a crucible of Ugandan identity. Its walls echoed both the aspirations and the anxieties of a nation on the cusp of change. In 1961, the venue changed hands from Kawoya to Jolly Joe Kiwanuka, who renamed it the White Nile Club. By the mid-1960s, Kiwanuka sold it to Mr. Joseph Ssalongo Kyeyune, who retained the White Nile name. For the Black Ugandan elite, it was a vital social hub, where prominent politicians, business leaders, and intellectuals gathered after long days of work to debate politics and strategize for an independent Uganda. At the time, Black Ugandans were unwelcome at European and Indian clubs, so places like Blue Gardens provided a crucial space for socializing and networking. When Jolly Joe acquired the club, he transformed it from a social club into a fully-fledged nightclub. Under his proprietorship, White Nile became one of the premier entertainment spots in Kampala, attracting musicians, dancers, and socialites from across East Africa.

The Mengo African Orchestra also enjoyed a close relationship with the Kabaka's palace. Edward Frederick Walugembe Mutesa II, the king of Buganda, was a patron of the band. It was not uncommon to see the king riding his horse from his Mengo Lubiri (palace) to the nearby Mengo Social Center to attend their performances. For the young musicians, playing before the Kabaka was a lifelong memory. Many of the orchestra's members, including John Bosa, had shared classrooms with Mutesa II at King's College Budo. Bosa had even served as the Kabaka's valet de chambre during their schooldays, a detail that underscored the social intimacy between the musicians and Buganda's aristocracy. Later, after his studies at Magdalene College, Cambridge, Mutesa returned home more committed than ever to blending tradition with the best of the Western world. Ballroom dancing, at which the Kabaka was a graceful dancer, became a favored pastime of the royal court, and the Mengo African Orchestra often found itself invited to perform at private palace festivities such as birthday celebrations, receptions, and national ceremonies.

Despite their popularity among the elite, the orchestra's Westernized music was unfamiliar to the general population, largely due to the absence of a national radio broadcaster. This limited their reach to a relatively small class of wealthy and educated Ugandans who could afford gramophones.

However, the band made concerted efforts to broaden their audience by touring and playing at venues outside Kampala. Their live performances often combined "modern" Western-style music with traditional folk music, which still had strong appeal among the masses. This blending of styles played a crucial role in bridging the gap between Western musical influences and indigenous Ugandan traditions.

Traditional folk musicians like Sekinomu and Elizabeth Nkomommo Namale (also known as Namale of Salama) made guest appearances at Mengo African Orchestra shows, adding a local flavor to their performances. Both Sekinomu and Namale were megastars, revered in Buganda and beyond. Namale, a statuesque woman standing around 5'6", was arguably the leading female traditional folk singer in Buganda at the time. She was also a superb dancer of the Baakisimba, a traditional dance of the Baganda people. Sekinomu, on the other hand, was a master of the endigindi, a one-stringed fiddle. Known for his playful and gruff voice, Sekinomu's compositions were usually filled with naughty improvisations, double entendre, and irreverent humor that often embarrassed and delighted fans in equal measure.

In 1945, Sekinomu recorded his first songs on the Columbia label, including Ekyalema Nakato (The Thing That Defeated Nakato) and Wireless, the latter recounting the introduction of the first wireless service in Uganda. One of Sekinomu's biggest hits was Kayanda, a popular song about an immigrant domestic worker who expands his duties to include an affair with the lady of the house. His song Ekyalema Nakato has been further analyzed by Ugandan academic Professor Samuel Kasule, who translated the title as Nakato's Challenge, adding depth to Sekinomu's playful but socially aware lyrics. Professor Kasule points out that Ekyalema Nakato was inspired by a scandalous historical event that left Buganda's elders reeling.

In November 1939, Buganda's king, Daudi Chwa, passed away, leaving behind his relatively young widow, Drusilla Irene Namaganda. Their son, Mutesa II, ascended to the throne, and Drusilla assumed the role of Queen Mother. However, just two years later, she revealed she was expecting a child with a commoner, Mr. Peter Kigozi. This revelation outraged the kingdom's establishment. According to Buganda's traditions and culture, a Queen Mother could not have an affair, let alone remarry, which was deemed unthinkable.

Samuel Wamala, the kingdom's prime minister, condemned Drusilla's actions as an "abominable and shameful disease." The ensuing political and cultural turmoil must have left Drusilla shocked and disillusioned, especially since the criticism came from people she considered friends, including Wamala himself. Undeterred, she fought back against the Buganda establishment, rallying her son and the British colonial administration to her cause. With the Kabaka's approval, she married Peter Kigozi in April 1941. What followed was a highly publicized court case, described by Professor Nakanyike Musisi as an intense legal battle in which "custom, identity, class, gender, power, and space became contested and redefined." The case, which became infamous as the Case of the Abominable Act, was heatedly debated in both private and public spheres, as well as in courtrooms. The Buganda government warned that unless the Queen Mother was convicted, riots would break out across the kingdom. In June 1941, after a dramatic court case, Namaganda and Kigozi were convicted of violating Buganda's customs. Kigozi was exiled for four years, forbidden to come within forty miles of Mengo (Kampala), while the Queen Mother was officially dethroned and stripped of all state benefits.

Sekinomu responded to this controversy with his characteristic bluntness in Ekyalema Nakato, a "multilayered text" that narrated the encounter between Mulinnyabigo, an allegedly promiscuous man, and his mistress, Nakato. Mulinnyabigo and Nakato are widely believed to represent Peter Kigozi and Queen Mother Drusilla Namaganda. Through the song's widespread popularity and underlying social critique, Sekinomu solidified his standing as both an entertainer and a sharp cultural commentator.

A slight modification of Professor Kasule's translation of Ekyalema Nakato, rich with innuendos and double entendre, gives us the following lyrics:

Hmm, they say, to fall in love with a 'barefooted lover' is
like playing the children's game of *nkuyo*.
As soon as the cock crows at dawn, he calls out for a
journey or dreams of one.
My love, wake up and let's go, it's dawn, time to work.
Yeah, see how he raises the stick at you as if herding cattle.
Ah, he splits the journey into two parts, as if sharing out meat.
Yeah, it's true, he envies you as he watches you
disappear over the horizon.
My dear, people like courting popularity.
Isn't it senseless?

Kasule notes that the "stick" in the lyrics is a reference to male genitals, and the phrase "splits the journey into two parts" refers to the thrusting movements during lovemaking. Sekinomu's performance of Ekyalema Nakato was notorious for its ability to "burn down the house," thrilling audiences with its raw, unfiltered take on the events surrounding the Queen Mother's affair.

When the Mengo African Orchestra, then performing as the Bukesa Music Club, staged a show at Jinja's Town Talkies cinema hall on May 1, 1946, Sekinomu and a traditional folk music ensemble, listed as the Native Music Party, were among the main acts. The program for that Wednesday night was a simple one-page guide listing the songs in order of performance, with Luganda titles translated into English.

The Mengo African Orchestra performed the following Luganda songs: Ndikuwa (I Will Give You), Omwana Akaba (The Child Cries), Kijujulu Kyange (My Young Beauty or, in urban slang, "Youngen"), and Ekitibwa Kya Buganda (The Pride of Buganda). Ekitibwa Kya Buganda, co-written by John Bosa and Polycarp Kibuuka Kakooza, was eventually adopted as the Buganda Kingdom anthem. Kakooza, a seasoned piano player, went on to record Omubaka Omwepanzi (The Boastful Emissary) and Buganda Yaffe (Our Buganda) on the Columbia label.

Omwana Akaba, a slow waltz sung by Bosa, was one of the band's most popular songs, though it was originally composed by Ernest Ssempebwa, Joshua Luyimbazi, and Emmanuel Lumu, and released on the Columbia label. It was considered one of the greatest Ugandan guitar songs of the time. The orchestra also performed English songs, including Everybody and D.C. Valley. The vocalist Sevume Salongo, accompanying himself on the harmonium, sang Bring Back and Oh Si-Se. Bring Back was the orchestra's take on the traditional Scottish folk song My Bonnie Lies Over the Ocean, which was hugely popular in Uganda in the 1940s and continues to be a favorite, especially among primary school pupils. In fact, during this time, the name "Bonnie" became quite common for Ugandan boys, one of whom, Bonnie Steven Kyambadde (also known as B. K. Steven or B. K. Steven, a name he adopted to distinguish himself from another popular musician, Andrew Kyambadde), would go on to become a prominent music star in the 1960s.

The Native Music Party performed Luganda songs including Kiwanataka (The Valley), Empologoma (The Lion, one of the forty titles and names given to the King of Buganda), Ekyalema Nakato, and Abaseveni (The Seventh). Abaseveni was the name given to the soldiers of the King's African Rifles, specifically those of the 7th (Uganda Territorial Force) Battalion. Sekinomu held a special place in the program, commanding the stage with a solo performance, accompanying himself on his beloved endigindi. He sang Uganda Basi (Uganda Buses), Talinanyiniye (Does Not Belong to No One), and performed solo versions of Kiwanataka and Abaseveni, which had been performed earlier by the full traditional folk ensemble.

On August 1, 1946, the Mengo African Orchestra returned to Jinja, this time performing at Gill's Opera House, a cinema theatre owned by one of Jinja's wealthiest men, Mr. Indar Singh Gill. Affectionately known by locals as Bwana Kubwa (Big Man), Gill's company, Sikh Saw Mills & Ginners, Jinja Ltd., was Uganda's first plywood and veneer mill. Following the expulsion of Ugandans of Indian descent by Idi Amin, the mill was renamed Kira Saw Mills. The Opera House, located on Lubas Road, was one of Jinja's most iconic buildings of the 1940s. In its prime, its white-washed façade, symmetrical lines, and tall arched windows conveyed a sense of modern elegance. The entrance, marked by a proud frontage with decorative pillars and a parapet, opened into a spacious interior of high ceilings, polished concrete floors, and a balcony that overlooked the stage. To concertgoers, the building seemed to glow in the evenings, its walls reflecting the anticipation of a town eager for music and film.

Over the decades, the venue changed with the times. It first became Deluxe Cinema, then Alka Cinema, and by the 1970s it was renamed Dingos Cinema. By 2025, the building stood in a state of total disrepair, a haunting relic of the city's cultural golden age. Its façade had grown weathered and scarred, its windows broken or sealed, its plaster peeling in long patches. Small market stalls clustered around its base, and the shouts of traders and customers had replaced the sounds of orchestras and projectors.

At Gill's Opera House in 1946, when Jinja was turning into the industrial powerhouse of Uganda and the hall still shimmered with promise, the Mengo African Orchestra performed some of their best-known hits, including Kaleri, a song that had become synonymous with their unique fusion of Western ballroom music and Ugandan folk rhythms. The combination of their music and the Opera House's grandeur aptly captured the spirit of a town brimming with energy and ambition, and on its way to becoming Uganda's industrial powerhouse. John Bosa had a magnetic charm, and by this time, he had fallen in love with a beautiful young woman named Christine Nassuna. In her honor, he composed Kaleri, which translates to Sweetheart. Though the song was never recorded, it became a favorite in the Mengo African Orchestra's repertoire. Bosa and Nassuna later married.

At Jinja's Opera House, Mudido and Sevume Salongo were a sensation as they played Hawaiian guitars during a short comedy sketch titled Omuserikari Aseka (The Laughing Soldier). Comedy sketches of this nature were commonly performed by the Rhino Boys during World War II. On this occasion, the band was accompanied by a different set of traditional folk musicians and dancers. Ms. Elizabeth Namale dazzled the audience with her graceful Baakisimba dance to the rhythm of the drums, while a performer named Mary danced to songs accompanied by drums and the endigindi.

The Mengo African Orchestra also performed two of their signature orchestral pieces: Walifu (The Alphabet) and Ssekiriba Kya Ttaka (A Skin of Clay). The latter is based on the Luganda proverb *Ssekiriba Kya Ttaka Mpaawo Attalikyambala*, which translates to " The soil is the garment that spares no one (i.e., everyone must face death)." While Walifu is a pedagogical song teaching the letters of the alphabet, similar to Ya Ye Yi Yo Yu, recorded on the Columbia label when John Bosa was part of Ivan & Co. in the 1930s, Ssekiriba Kya Ttaka is a solemn, sepulchral composition. Sung in Bosa's rich baritone, the song is accompanied by harmonium, violins, and guitars, and reflects on death and the inevitable journey to the afterlife:

<blockquote>
I don't know where Sheol is,
There, where all my ancestors went,
And I too will go there,
The skin of clay—who will not dress in it?
We'll all die and go there,
Leaving this earth behind.
All those who've gone are fortunate,
Joy, true joy,
Truly freed from the suffering of this world.
</blockquote>

John Bosa and the Mengo African Orchestra would go on to record Ssekiriba Kya Ttaka and Walifu on the HMV label. The band, composed mostly of part-time musicians, remained hugely popular for nearly a decade. However, the political winds in Uganda were beginning to shift, setting the stage for profound upheavals that would test even the most beloved cultural institutions.

On November 30, 1953, Sir Andrew Cohen, the British Governor of the Uganda Protectorate, placed Kabaka Mutesa II under arrest and exiled him to London, where he remained until October 17, 1955. The Kabaka's arrest followed a period of escalating tensions between the Buganda Kingdom and the British colonial administration. The British sought to create a closer federation among their East African territories (Uganda, Kenya, and Tanganyika), and Governor Cohen aimed to integrate Buganda more closely with the other regions of the Uganda Protectorate. However, the Buganda Agreement of 1900 had granted the Kabaka significant autonomy over internal affairs, and Mutesa II, along with his chiefs, feared that Cohen's plans for greater integration and federation would undermine the Kabaka's authority and diminish the prestige of his position.

Kabaka Mutesa II's staunch opposition to Cohen's vision culminated in his arrest and exile. Although the Kabaka had not been universally popular before, his exile became a cause célèbre among the people of Buganda. For the people of Buganda, the Kabaka's exile was not merely a political affront; it was an existential crisis. Mutesa II was more than a political leader; he was a cultural symbol, a living embodiment of Buganda's history, traditions, and pride. His removal sparked widespread riots, boycotts, and an intense cultural backlash against anything perceived as foreign or colonial. In the cultural sphere, the effects were immediate and devastating. Nightclubs, once vibrant with the strains of Western ballroom dances, fell silent. The public turned away from rumbas, foxtrots, and tangos, rejecting them as symbols of colonial influence. Many musicians suddenly found themselves without audiences. Venues that had once sold out every weekend now stood empty, their dance floors abandoned and their stages dark, as public gatherings gave way to fervent demands for the Kabaka's return.

The Mengo African Orchestra, the most prominent home-grown post-war band, was affected by the boycott, as were other neotraditional bands of the time. These included the Rhythm Dance Band, Nakawa Band (also known as Nakawa Modern Band), Ballroom Dance, Sanyu Sesame Band, and the Police Band. These groups played in various bars in and around

Kampala, including popular spots such as the Oriental Samba Club in Natete, Sun Park Club on Bombo Road, Palms Restaurant, and Nkumba Happy Bar on the Kampala-Entebbe Road.

With the boycott in full effect, the Mengo African Orchestra ceased their regular Saturday and Sunday performances at the Mengo Social Club, putting an end to their tours. While the band continued rehearsing at John Bosa's home in Busega for a short time, this too eventually stopped. Compounding the band's troubles at the time, Bosa became embroiled in a lengthy and draining legal dispute with his employer, the Uganda Bookshop Printing Press. Court hearings consumed his time and sapped his energy. Without his leadership and with no viable path forward, the orchestra gradually fell apart. By 1954, the Mengo African Orchestra, the group that had once symbolized Kampala's postwar optimism and cosmopolitan aspirations, had quietly disbanded. It was a poignant end to a remarkable era.

Although the band dissolved, individual musicians continued performing and recording on an occasional basis. Kalinimi Mpagi became a regular figure on Uganda Television in the 1970s, where he was often featured playing the keyboard. Yeko Mukasa, another band member, was instrumental in the formation of The Ebonies, one of Uganda's most successful bands in the late 1970s, led by Jimmy Katumba. Mukasa also headed Mukasa's Singing Group, which performed and recorded Christian music. In 1980, under the meticulous arrangement and production of legendary producer and sound engineer Edmund Batte, Yeko Mukasa reworked two Ugandan classics from the 1950s: Kolanga Ofune Okwesiima (Work and Earn Satisfaction) and Ndikuwa Ngoteredde (Yours When You're Settled). The re-recording featured renowned musicians such as Elly Wamala, Charles Ginaro, and Edel Ekodele on rhythm, lead, and bass guitar respectively, with M. Musisi on drums and Kawaga on claves.

It would be thirty-eight years later, on April 4, 1992, that John Bosa returned to the stage at Lugogo Indoor Stadium in Kampala. The concert brought together musicians who had been active from the 1940s through the early 1960s, including Aaron Kiguli, Israel Magembe, Yeko Mukasa,

Nelson Gonzabato, Edmund Batte, and Martin Munyenga. Though a household name in the 1940s and 1950s, Bosa and his Mengo African Orchestra had become relatively unknown in post-independence Uganda. By 1992, the country's music landscape had changed dramatically, with Ugandans born after independence likely never having heard of the orchestra. The world was now more globalized, and Western pop songs such as Londonbeat's I've Been Thinking About You, Luther Vandross' Power of Love, and UB40's The Way You Do the Things You Do dominated street sidewalks and markets. The only real competition to Western music came from Congolese soukous, which had taken Uganda by storm. Hits like Pepe Kalle's Milla and Gerant, Kanda Bongo Man's Monie and Isemba, and Arlus Mabele's Embargo were ubiquitous.

Few Ugandan acts managed to compete significantly with these foreign influences. Moses Matovu's Afrigo Band stood as the rare exception, managing to keep Ugandan music relevant amidst the invasion of outside sounds. Many veteran musicians had either faded into obscurity or found themselves limited to small private performances. Some had moved on to other professions entirely. For John Bosa, the 1992 concert was not just a return to the stage but a rediscovery of a lost era of Ugandan music. On that memorable day at Lugogo Indoor Stadium, the veteran musicians of decades past proved that old could be golden. John Bosa, teaming up with Israel Magembe, took to the stage with a sense of ease and confidence, despite the passage of time. Relishing his brief return to the limelight, Bosa delivered a stirring performance, belting out a cover of the Rhino Boys' classic Ai Empologoma (Aye, the Lion) and other beloved songs from a bygone era, rekindling memories of Uganda's musical past. The audience, a mix of elderly fans who remembered Bosa's heyday and younger music lovers experiencing this heritage for the first time, responded with enthusiastic applause.

The concert served as both a tribute to Uganda's forgotten musical pioneers and a reminder of the rich traditions that had shaped the country's artistic identity. While contemporary audiences had grown accustomed to new genres and influences, the event underscored the timelessness of good music and the deep emotional connections it could forge. For one night, at least, John Bosa and his peers were once again at the heart of Uganda's musical consciousness, their melodies bridging generations and reaffirming their place in the nation's history.

When the Rhino Boys disembarked from the ship that brought them back to East Africa after their long journey from Burma, they still had their musical instruments with them, courtesy of Peter Colmore, who allowed them to keep the equipment. While some band members were eager to return to their families, a core group, mostly from Uganda and Kenya, decided to stick together. Their aim was to bring the music that had entertained tens of thousands of soldiers at the frontlines to civilian audiences. Captain Jeff Seabrook, who had served in the King's African Rifles (KAR) during the war, returned to his military base in Kenya, but his connection to the Rhino Boys was not over.

During the war, nightlife in Mombasa, a city known for its lively taarab and *beni ngoma* music, had fallen into a slump. But with the end of the war and the return of thousands of KAR troops disembarking from ships at Mombasa port, the city's social life experienced a resurgence. The bustling streets of Mombasa, filled with lively bars and hotels, provided the Rhino Boys, now demobilized, an opportunity to restart their civilian lives as professional musicians. By early 1946, the Rhino Boys had reformed, with Seabrook returning to arrange and conduct the band's music. Thanks to Seabrook's involvement and their largely Western-style orchestral repertoire, the band found lucrative gigs performing in predominantly white clubs in Kenya.

The Rhino Boys performed songs in a variety of languages, including Luganda, Swahili, Chinyanja (now known as Chewa), English, Italian, French, and German. Among the band's members were several talented Ugandans. The bandleader, George Senoga-Zake, was a brainy, five-foot-four young man with a gift for both singing and playing the trumpet. Nelson Gonzabato, a shy, soft-spoken man, played both the violin and saxophone. Valentine Muwulya, with sparkling eyes and a distinctive gap between his upper teeth, was known for his cheerful disposition and slender frame. He was the band's lead singer and also a skilled violinist.

Senoga-Zake and Gonzabato had been recruited into the KAR while still students at King's College, Budo. At the time of his recruitment, Senoga-Zake was in his final year of secondary school. Valentine Muwulya had also studied at Budo, where British teachers introduced students to various Western instruments, including the violin. Meanwhile, Charles Ssenkatuka, the band's double bass virtuoso and accomplished saxophonist, came from a different educational background. He had attended Namily-ango College, a Catholic boarding school in Uganda known for its active brass band. Ssenkatuka left school in 1942 and traveled to Nairobi, where he enlisted in the KAR in 1944. Among the band members was the charismatic Honey Wamala, who played the piano. Wamala would later have a brush with stardom when he played the role of Mr. Oyondi in the 1967 British adventure film Africa—Texas Style, directed by Andrew Marton.

Another standout member of the Rhino Boys was Joseph Chuza Kabasele, an exceptionally talented drummer with a compelling personal history. Chuza's family had originally come from the Belgian Congo, now the Democratic Republic of the Congo. The family was part of a group of Congolese Christians who had followed the Ugandan Anglican missionary Apolo Kivebulaya to Uganda. Chuza was around fourteen years old when his family arrived in Uganda, eventually settling in Fort Portal, in western Uganda. Chuza attended Kisubi Technical School, where he trained as a carpenter. It was also at Kisubi Technical that Chuza crossed paths with Abbey Mukungu, another future musical luminary. He was recruited into the KAR from Kisubi Technical, where he played in the school's band. Incidentally, Chuza and Charles Ssenkatuka were not only musical collaborators but also family, as they both married cousins.

The Rhino Boys also boasted several Kenyan musicians, including the guitarists Fundi Konde and Daniel Katuga, the trumpeter Ngala Karani, and the double bass player Baya Toya. In 1948, Israel Magembe, a member of a prominent Ugandan aristocratic family, was recruited as a singer and rhythm guitarist. Notably, Magembe was among the first musicians brought into the band who had not served in World War II. His inclusion marked a shift, as the band began to welcome younger talent into its ranks, keeping their music alive and relevant for post-war audiences.

In the immediate aftermath of the war, the Rhino Boys recorded a series of exhilarating songs on the His Master's Voice (HMV) label. One of their first recordings was Rumba Zetu—Our Rumba. This beautiful instrumental bel canto piece spans both sides of the disc, highlighting the band's ability to move fluently across styles and their deep connection to Western orchestral traditions. Another standout song was Abazira Eno Wala Enyo (Hail the Brave, Faraway Out Here). This riveting foxtrot orchestral piece, delivered with Valentine Muwulya's soaring tenor, offers a sobering reflection on the hazards and waste of World War II while simultaneously celebrating the soldiers' victory:

> Fighting for peace, brethren,
> Like our forefathers,
> They did all they could,
> In their own wars,
> We too have won.

The flip side featured Bwenali Nga Nkumba (When I Used To March), a rollicking waltz. In this melancholic but profound song, Valentine's voice conveyed authenticity and unparalleled virtuosity as he continued the theme of war and homecoming:

> When I was a child,
> I used to sing much,
> My song lulled me to sleep,
> I sing my song in war,
> A war in distant lands,
> I know I will sing in my land,
> To celebrate and rejoice.

Beyond war and victory, the Rhino Boys also delved into themes of love and heartache. With Seabrook conducting, Valentine Muwulya performed a number of passionate love songs in Swahili, recorded on the HMV label. Nakupenda (I Love You) was a lively foxtrot dance song, while Lipi Uli Pendalo (Who Is Your Favorite?) was a tender waltz. In Lipi Uli Pendalo, Valentine's voice, filled with deep emotion, sings of being awestruck by the beauty of his lover's eyes, which gaze at him like moonlight. The same entrancing eyes also engulf his soul with insecurity, and he implores his lover not to despair and leave him.

The band's repertoire wasn't always serious. Omukazi Omubi (An Ugly Woman) was a playful swing song with elements of American folk music, recorded on the Philips label. In this tongue-in-cheek number, George Senoga-Zake humorously advised his listeners to marry the ugliest woman they could find, singing, "If you want to relax in peace, never marry a beautiful woman." He jested that an unattractive wife would "serve your food well" and "pamper you in bed," offering a life of contentment without the worries that come with marrying a beautiful woman.

The Rhino Boys disbanded in 1948 in Kenya, with most of the members reforming under a new name, Kiko Kids. The new lineup included Ugandan musician Honey Wamala. Some former members of the Rhino Boys performed under different names, including the Peter Colmore Band and the Ally Sykes Band, dazzling audiences, mainly white settlers, throughout Kenya. At the time, Kenya's white population was sizable, and strict segregation policies barred Blacks and Indians from many spaces, including exclusive white-only clubs like the Muthaiga Club. This club was frequented by aristocratic white settlers, playboys, and seductresses, making it a hotspot for the wealthy elite.

In 1949, the Peter Colmore Band made history by becoming the first Black African group to perform at the Muthaiga Club, shattering the color bar in a monumental moment. Ugandans Charles Ssenkatuka and Nelson Gonzabato were part of this groundbreaking performance. The white settlers embraced the band's Western-style music with enthusiasm, as it resonated with their own tastes. Under the Ally Sykes Band, the group recorded several tango and foxtrot-themed songs on the East African Sound Studios' Jambo label, which was owned by two British entrepreneurs, Guy Johnson and Eric Blackhart. East African Sound Studios Ltd. was the first local Kenyan recording company to challenge the dominance of multinational record labels in East Africa. Among their hits were Nakupenda Rucky (I Love You, Rucky) and Tabu (Woe), both of which gained wide popularity. Their success convinced Peter Colmore, who was responsible for recording with East African Sound Studios at their home studio in Nairobi, to invest in his own label. This led to the establishment of His Master's Voice Blue Label. Through this label, Colmore produced over 300 songs by musicians from Kenya, Uganda, Malawi, Zambia, Zanzibar, Tanzania, and the Congo. Notably, in 1959, Colmore famously brought the legendary Congolese musician, Jean Bosco Mwenda, to Nairobi to record.

In 1951, several former members of the Rhino Boys left Kenya and relocated to a rumba-crazy Kampala, where the Mengo African Orchestra remained the only Western-style big band. While numerous smaller groups of musicians performed with guitars and banjos, these artists constituted what was locally known as a full band. In Uganda's music scene, the term "full band" came to denote a musical group featuring multiple instrumentalists, typically including a lead guitar, rhythm guitar, double bass guitar, drums, and a trumpet or saxophone. This ensemble setup provided a fuller, richer sound, with each instrument contributing to a layered and dynamic musical experience that became characteristic of popular bands of the time.

Under the leadership of George Senoga-Zake, the Rhino Boys rebranded themselves as Kawonawo Rhino Boys, or more commonly, K-Rhino Boys. The name carried weight and pride. Kawonawo, meaning "war veterans" in Luganda, proudly signaled their origins while hinting at their overseas experiences. They were not merely musicians; they were survivors of a global conflict, carriers of a broader world culture, and ready to dominate Kampala's nightlife. The lineup featured many familiar talents: Charles Ssenkatuka, Nelson Gonzabato, Joseph Chuza, Valentine

Muwulya, and Israel Magembe. However, their fellow Ugandan musician Honey Wamala stayed in Kenya with the Kiko Kids. Kenyan veterans also joined their ranks, including Fundi Konde, Daniel Katuga, Ben Nicholas Apudo, Manuel Ali, and John Karani. Esther Nicholas, wife of Ben Nicholas Apudo, became the group's only female member.

With their orchestral, Western-style arrangements, the K-Rhino Boys won over Kampala's elite. George Senoga-Zake would later recall how the group "held people spellbound with our thrilling music." They began performing at the Mengo Social Center, where they occasionally shared the stage with the Mengo African Orchestra. Their reputation grew steadily, but a decisive turning point arrived in 1952 when they caught the attention of a shrewd businessman with a visionary understanding of Uganda's changing cultural landscape.

Sadru Kamulu, popularly known as Kamulu, was a successful Ugandan businessman and a member of the Khoja Ismaili community in Mengo. Kamulu would become one of the key figures shaping Uganda's nightlife and club scene for nearly two decades. He provided a platform for bands like the K-Rhino Boys to flourish in Kampala's growing entertainment landscape. Born in the late 1920s or early 1930s, Kamulu grew up in Mengo township in a Khoja Ismaili family well integrated into local life, a common experience among Ugandan-Indians in suburban areas. The family was fluent in Luganda and deeply familiar with local customs. After finishing high school in the mid-1940s, Kamulu settled in Mengo, where he and his brother opened a general store on Albert Cook Road. Their shop was one of about a dozen Indian-run stores in the area, offering groceries and household items.

But Kamulu's ambitions stretched beyond the role of a simple neighborhood dukkawallah. At the time, Mengo had about twelve dukas, most of them operated by Khoja Ismailis. Behind the shopfront of his own duka was a spacious hall, which he transformed into a bar and nightclub called Hollywood Social Club, more commonly known as ewa Kamulu—Kamulu's place. The club was unlike any other owned by whites or Indians in Uganda at the time. It had no color bar and welcomed Black patrons openly. Kamulu's opposition to racial segregation was widely known, and he embraced a multicultural outlook long before it became a popular ideal. His affinity for Black Ugandan culture ran deep, reflected not just in his business ventures but also in his personal relationships.

Kamulu was a close friend of the Kabaka, Sir Edward Mutesa, businessman Lwanga Miti, and frequently spent time with Polycarp Kakooza, who, along with John Bosa, composed the Buganda anthem Ekitiibwa Kya Buganda. A lesser-known detail of Kamulu's life is that he was a cousin of Hassan Sunderani, a transformative figure in the history of Ugandan sport. Sunderani played a significant role in launching the athletic career of Uganda's 1972 Olympic gold medalist, John Akii-Bua, a world-class hurdler. He was also a familiar face on national television, hosting the weekly Uganda Television program Sports Review, which made him one of the most recognized sports broadcasters of the 1960s. Like his cousin, Kamulu was a passionate sports enthusiast. He contributed significantly to the development of sports infrastructure, notably as a major donor, alongside the Madhvani family of Jinja, to the construction of Bugembe Stadium, a venue that would go on to host major sporting events, including national soccer matches and athletics competitions.

Kamulu's Hollywood Social Club soon became one of Kampala's most popular nightspots. People from all backgrounds, Black Africans, Asians, and Europeans, gathered to drink, dance, and enjoy live music. The atmosphere was vibrant, sometimes rowdy, with occasional scuffles often sparked by jealousy or flirtation. As the nightclub's reputation grew, it stood as a microcosm of the changing times, a space where post-war Kampala's social boundaries began to blur, and a new musical culture found room to grow.

When Kamulu encountered the K-Rhino Boys, he recognized immediately that they embodied the musical sophistication his club needed. Their blend of rumba, tango, and foxtrot perfectly captured the fusion that Kamulu envisioned for his clientele. He wasted no time. In 1952, Kamulu signed the K-Rhino Boys as the second resident band at the Hollywood Social Club, complementing his existing house band, the Hollywood Jazz

Band. Under the leadership of frontman George Senoga-Zake, and with their irresistible music, the band became a favorite among Kampala's elite. At the time, the city's obsession was with the swing, popularly known as "spot dance."

The K-Rhino Boys initially performed on Saturday evenings, but due to their popularity and the growing enthusiasm for ballroom dancing, they soon expanded to include Sunday performances. The rest of their week was spent rehearsing or touring other venues. The entry fee to Kamulu's was set at 3 shillings for men and 2 shillings for women, with audiences flocking to witness the band's stellar performances. Their repertoire included hits like Pena Langu, a tango full of raw passion and sensuality with an undercurrent of nostalgia and sadness. Other crowd-pleasers included Soya Bini (Soybean), a foxtrot celebrating the virtues of growing soybeans, and Mpulira Oluimba (I Hear a Song), an exciting rumba that had the band shimmying across the floor, hips swaying to the rhythm. Couples moved together in the heat of the moment, male hands clasping women's waists, embodying a modern expression of sexuality and sensuality. For many young Ugandans, Hollywood Social Club was an education in style, music, romance, and urbanity. Men learned to court with a respectful bow and a quickstep. Women practiced the art of elegant flirtation in tight-fitting shiny dresses. Together, they invented a new language of aspiration, one shaped by the sounds of a full orchestra and the dreams of a freer, more modern life. Kamulu, observing it all from a seat in the back of the dance-hall, knew he had achieved something rare: a space where people could dream aloud, where new forms of community and identity could take root through the simple, stubborn, joyful act of dancing.

The surge of excitement that Hollywood Social Club and the K-Rhino Boys brought to Kampala's nightlife was impossible to ignore. Every Saturday and Sunday, crowds of stylish men and elegantly dressed women packed the dance floor. But not everyone in Buganda viewed this flourishing nightlife with approval. The same postwar era that birthed new musical forms also revived the guardians of traditional moral order, especially among Buganda's older chiefs. To them, the sight of young women in fitted dresses and men in sharply cut suits, dancing closely to foreign music, symbolized a dangerous and scandalous erosion of cultural values.

This tension between modern and traditional values found its way into music, as seen in Eva Nanyonga's Gyoyagala Gyobolaga (Go Wherever You Want To). Nanyonga, an influential 1950s female guitarist, singer, and songwriter, lamented a husband who abandoned his marital home for the thrill of dancing at Kamulu's. Her soft, tender voice, accompanied by gentle guitar strumming and maracas, conveyed the betrayal she squarely blamed on Kamulu's:

If my husband were to return,
I wouldn't pay attention,
At Kamulu's, he's dancing the samba,
At Kamulu's, he's dancing the rumba,
And I rejoice in my tango,
Darling, don't walk away,
My dear, don't leave.
My man, I don't care,
Goodbye to you now,
Work wherever you please,
Go wherever you like.
My man was even laid off,
Find work wherever your journey takes you,
My man, you're late to the rumba,
At Kamulu's, you chugged your drink,
Where you spend your nights,
They should pay your wages and cook for you,
You, my man, can leave,
Off to Kamulu's where you pass the nights,
Work wherever you please,
Go wherever you like.
You no longer wish to work,
You've become a nuisance,

> My man, you've brought me shame,
> When I play my guitar, you run away,
> When I sing my songs, you turn away,
> Work wherever you please,
> Go wherever you like.

The tension between the modern and traditional simmered, then boiled over. In early 1953, Buganda's prime minister, Paul Kavuma, pressured by conservative factions within Buganda's parliament, the Lukiko, announced plans to ban Western-style dancing.

The proposed ban caused an immediate uproar among Kampala's urbanites. For many, dance was not merely recreation; it was a declaration of modern identity, a joyful defiance of old restrictions. The threatened prohibition was seen not just as an attack on fun, but on the right to imagine new social futures. Among the loudest and most articulate voices opposing the ban was Joseph "Jolly Joe" Kiwanuka. He had long promoted Western-style dance as a vehicle for self-improvement and cosmopolitanism. Through his various community initiatives, he had founded ballroom dance clubs across Kampala, bringing lessons in foxtrot, waltz, quickstep, and samba to a new generation of Ugandans eager to step confidently onto the world stage.

Jolly Joe's anger was immediate and unfiltered. In a blistering editorial in the *Uganda Post*, he lambasted the proposed ban, calling it "an absurd and backward decree" and accusing Kavuma of being a "clueless ignoramus." He reminded readers that the colonial government itself, through its Department of Public Relations and Social Welfare, had promoted Western cultural education, sponsoring community centers like Buyala Social Club, Rubaga Women's Club, and Sekenzi Boys Club, all of which offered dance classes as part of modern civic engagement. These clubs participated in annual competitions like the African Club Festival.

Arrested and briefly detained for his outspokenness, Jolly Joe refused to back down. The matter was brought before the court. The legal battle over the dance ban climaxed in mid-1953 when courts declared the ban on western dancing was illegal. The judges acknowledged that while social change inevitably unsettled some, the right to gather, dance, and express oneself within reasonable limits could not be prohibited under colonial law. Young men and women saw in Jolly Joe a defender of their newfound freedoms, a voice willing to stand against the heavy hand of tradition when it threatened to stifle personal and cultural expression.

Jolly Joe's victory over Kavuma's ban was immortalized in Fred Masagazi's 1960s song Kiwanuka ne Dansi, which praised Kiwanuka's fight against the proposed ban. Masagazi's lyrics reflect the popular sentiment: "What had entered the prime minister's head to enact such an unfair ban?"

After the ban on western dancing was reversed, the K-Rhino Boys and other musicians resumed entertaining fans across Uganda's major towns with renewed enthusiasm. On June 3, 1953, the day after Queen Elizabeth II's coronation, the K-Rhino Boys performed at the Green Gardens Club in Buikwe township as part of nationwide celebrations. Revelers were asked to wear their best attire, and prizes were awarded to the best-dressed and best-dancing couples. The music began at 2:30 pm, and the club's hall filled with enthusiasts of western-style dance. The K-Rhino Boys were in high demand, receiving invitations to perform at various venues and events. Along with the Mengo African Orchestra, they had sparked a dance craze in Kampala and other urban centers.

As the K-Rhino Boys' fame soared, cracks began to appear in their relationship with Kamulu. What had started as a fruitful collaboration increasingly turned into a struggle over control and creative freedom. Kamulu, proud of the role he had played in boosting their success, viewed the band as an extension of his establishment. In his mind, the K-Rhino Boys were not merely performers at the Hollywood Social Club; they were part of his brand, essential to its prestige and profitability. Reflecting this vision, the band was even rebranded as the Kamulu Rhino Boys.

Kamulu had drawn up contracts specifying that the band could not perform elsewhere without his explicit permission. These restrictions, however, chafed at the musicians, who saw their growing popularity as a chance to expand their influence across Uganda. Invitations to perform at weddings, private events, and other venues poured in. Turning them down, in the musicians' view, meant stifling their careers and missing out on much-needed income. Tensions escalated when the K-Rhino Boys began accepting offers to perform outside Hollywood Social Club without seeking Kamulu's approval. Feeling betrayed and determined to assert his authority, Kamulu responded forcefully. He published a stern legal notice in the pages of *Uganda Empya*, warning that any person or venue hiring the K-Rhino Boys without his consent would face legal action.

Led by George Senoga-Zake, the K-Rhino Boys decided to take a bold step. They severed their ties with Kamulu and moved their base of operations to Kawoya's Blue Gardens. This defection sparked one of the most intense rivalries in Uganda's music scene. Kamulu harbored a lasting grudge against Blue Garden, and the rivalry only intensified after Blue Garden was later purchased by Jolly Joe Kiwanuka, renaming it White Nile Club. Kamulu and Jolly Joe would stop at nothing to undercut each other's clubs, frequently attempting, often successfully, to lure top musicians from the rival establishment. Bribes, poaching, and subtle sabotage were fair game as each tried to undermine the other's success. Although the rivalry between Kamulu and Jolly Joe was fierce, it was curiously respectful. They shared an unspoken understanding. Both were builders of Uganda's nightlife. They were cultural patrons who had helped create spaces where music, dance, and modern African identity could flourish. Even as they competed for bands and patrons, Kamulu and Jolly Joe maintained cordial personal relations. They dined at the same restaurants, attended the same civic functions, and occasionally even collaborated on charity events. Their rivalry was professional, not personal. It was a spirited competition that, in the end, enriched Kampala's cultural life immeasurably.

The K-Rhino Boys might have stayed longer at Blue Gardens if not for the political unrest, including a boycott of western businesses and cultural expressions that followed the Kabaka's exile in late 1953. Like the Mengo African Orchestra, the K-Rhino Boys enjoyed the Kabaka's patronage, having composed and recorded Ai Empologoma (Aye, The Lion), a slow foxtrot that praised the Kabaka and wished him a long life.

Valentine Muwulya's smooth vocals made the song a favorite, and it was later covered by Fundi Konde in an instrumental version. The K-Rhino Boys relocated to Nairobi around December 1953, as the boycott severely affected their performances in Uganda.

In addition to their own hits, the K-Rhino Boys collaborated with several Ugandan female musicians, producing well-regarded songs. Fundi Konde worked with Eva Nanyonga to record Ai Tabisa Wandeeka Nkaba (Ah Tabisa, You Left Me Crying) and Ekisera Kituse (Time Has Come) on the HMV label. Meanwhile, guitarist Joseph Daniel Katuga met the stunning Jane Kyahurwa during their time in Kampala and wrote Eliso Lya Dalli (My Darling's Eyes) in admiration of her beauty. The flip side of the record featured Kyahurwa's haunting vocals on Nazalibwa Kunsi (I Was Born Into the World), accompanied by Katuga and E. Joseph (Joseph Ndalo) on guitar. The song tells the story of a young woman abandoned by her family:

> I was born into this world and lived as a child,
> But when the world betrayed me, I was like a servant,
> Suffering came my way, with no one to call,
> All who once called me Jane disappeared.
> Now, I make my own friends—
> What good are relatives?
> When trouble strikes, they'll abandon you.
> Dad left me, and mom did too,
> Don't know where they went,
> Just left me as I am.
> I had younger siblings, but I lost them too,
> Left me searching for Dad.

Kyahurwa also recorded Ogenda Wa (Where Are You Going?), another poignant song with Katuga and Joseph on guitars. These songs, recorded at Nsambya by Hugh Tracey and released on the South African Gallotone label, highlighted the depth of emotion and storytelling that characterized much of Ugandan music at the time.

The call to boycott Western businesses, including western-style dancing, coupled with the dissolution of the Mengo African Orchestra and the relocation of the K-Rhino Boys, marked the end of Uganda's big orchestral bands and the elegant ballroom dancing era. Both ensembles had elevated the idea of the "full band" to new artistic heights, leaving behind a legacy of memorable music. The years between the Kabaka's return and Uganda's independence in 1962 were marked by political unrest and cultural realignment that deeply affected Kampala's nightlife. Tensions simmered toward foreign-owned businesses, particularly those run by people of South Asian ancestry and Europeans. Among the most visible sources of resentment was the South Asian monopoly over cotton ginning, a highly profitable sector that symbolized the broader economic exclusion of Africans. An atmosphere of revolution hung over the major urban centers, fueled by growing frustration with racial discrimination, economic inequalities, and the enduring grip of colonial rule. African leaders began to push forcefully for greater African participation in commerce and demanded meaningful political reforms from the colonial administration.

In this shifting landscape, even astute cultural entrepreneurs like Kamulu found themselves vulnerable. Aware of the rising nationalist sentiment, and sensing that his public image as a Ugandan of Indian ancestry might attract unwanted scrutiny, Kamulu decided to quietly step back. In 1958, he withdrew from the frontline of Kampala's nightlife. Hollywood Social Club, the pioneering venue he had built with such passion and vision, was sold, or at least formally transferred, to Lwanga Miti, a Ugandan entrepreneur and longtime associate. Miti also owned the Skyline Bar in Natete, which was later renamed the New Era Bar after it was acquired by the Kaala family. Miti hailed from a respected lineage, being the son of James Kibuka Miti Kabazzi, a prominent Buganda chief and clan leader. Under Miti's stewardship, the club was rebranded as Top Life, later affectionately shortened to "Top" by Kampala's socialites. It was Top Life that brought the Kenya Twist into vogue in Uganda.

However, the full story of Miti's ownership of Top Life was likely more nuanced and complex than it appeared. It was widely believed that

Miti, though a competent businessman in his own right, acted in part as a front for Kamulu, shielding him from the growing political and cultural backlash against figures perceived as too closely tied to western culture. Behind the scenes, Kamulu remained involved in club operations, quietly guiding the venue's transformation while allowing others to take the public spotlight. This quiet handover allowed Kamulu to preserve his business interests without becoming a target during a time when nationalist fervor could easily turn against even those who had once been champions of inclusion. It was a delicate balancing act, and Kamulu played it with characteristic foresight.

By 1964, as the political atmosphere stabilized somewhat following Uganda's independence in 1962, Kamulu felt the time was right to reemerge. He formally repossessed the club and gave it a new name: New Life Nightclub. The name preserved a subtle link to its previous identity under Miti, while also signaling a fresh chapter following the cultural boycott that had prompted Kamulu's earlier retreat. As he resumed a more visible presence, he was joined by his son, who also went by the same name. The junior Kamulu was a charismatic, outgoing figure with an approachable demeanor. Driving a sleek Mercedes Benz through Kampala's streets, he projected an image of youthful confidence and modern entrepreneurial ambition. His vitiligo, a skin condition that visibly marked his complexion, never diminished his warmth or social ease. Like many in the Ismaili community of Mengo, he spoke fluent Luganda and, following in his father's footsteps, held a deep appreciation for Ugandan culture and a firm disdain for racism. This cultural affinity shaped his personal life as well. The younger Kamulu was married to a Black Ugandan woman from Jinja. During her time with the junior Kamulu, she played an instrumental role in the family's vast business holdings, managing the New Life Nightclub in Bugembe, Jinja. Under her leadership, the club thrived, becoming a lively nightlife hub that attracted patrons from across eastern Uganda and even neighboring Kenya. In addition to his work in entertainment, the younger Kamulu also managed the family's jaggery factory near Bujagali Falls, then the largest in Jinja.

Proud Ugandans of Khoja Ismaili heritage, the Kamulus were more than just nightclub proprietors. They were astute businessmen with a deep affection for their country and a strong commitment to community service. They imagined a Uganda where race posed no obstacle to friendship, collaboration, or joy. Through their nightclubs, they fostered spaces where music and dance transcended boundaries of class, ethnicity, and creed. In doing so, they helped shape a more inclusive cultural life in Kampala and contributed meaningfully to the broader national fabric.

CHAPTER 4

Eva Nanyonga, Kampala City Six and the Twilight of a Musical Era

The era of the big orchestral bands in Uganda effectively ended in 1954, with the dissolution of the Mengo African Orchestra. The distinct style and impact of orchestral bands led by figures like John Bosa and George Senoga-Zake were not replicated, even after Kabaka Mutesa II's return from exile in London on October 17, 1955. Although these pioneering bands no longer performed, they had set a template that subsequent Ugandan musicians would build upon.

The Kabaka's exile to Britain was met with two years of unrelenting hostility from his subjects, who actively resisted and obstructed nearly every initiative of the British colonial administration and its Governor, Sir Andrew Cohen. Faced with growing unrest and political pressure, Cohen ultimately conceded, and the Kabaka was allowed to return to Uganda in 1955. His return came with new conditions: he would rule as a constitutional monarch, thus relinquishing the absolute authority that his predecessors had wielded. Known in his early years for leading an opulent lifestyle, Mutesa had appeared detached from the daily struggles of his people, an image that distanced him from many of his subjects. However, his forced exile by the British colonial administration had an unintended consequence. Rather than diminishing his influence, the king's exile awakened a powerful sense of loyalty and pride among the Baganda. On his triumphant return, Mutesa was no longer seen merely as a royal figure but as a symbol of resistance and cultural pride. His defiance of British powers endeared him to his people, who saw in him a unifying leader who had risked everything for Buganda's dignity and autonomy.

Songs honoring the Kabaka flourished, and even the Trinidadian calypso king Aldwyn Roberts, known as Lord Kitchener, recorded "King Freddie (HRH The Kabaka)" on the Melodisc label in 1956. Such was the fame within the British Empire of an African king who had defied the British colonial masters, returning from exile clothed in honor and dignity. In Kenya, four members of the K-Rhino Boys paid tribute to the Kabaka with two songs, Mulembe Omutesa (Peace to the Councilor) and Tusabire Kabaka (We Pray for the Kabaka), which were recorded under the name The Four Brothers. The group included Valentine Muwulya and Nelson Gonzabato on violins, Daniel Katuga on guitar, and Charles Ssenkatuka on double bass. The K-Rhino Boys continued performing in Nairobi until 1957 when the group formally disbanded.

Bandleader George Senoga-Zake left popular music altogether following a chance encounter with American researcher Philip Foster in Mombasa. Foster encouraged him to pursue formal music studies. This support led Senoga-Zake to the Kenya Conservatoire of Music and eventually to Trinity College of Music in London. He returned to Kenya to help establish the music department at Kenyatta University, where he later served as a professor, away from the nightclub spotlight. In 1963, Senoga-Zake co-wrote Kenya's national anthem, creating a lasting legacy.

Meanwhile, other K-Rhino Boys members continued their musical journeys. Fundi Konde and Daniel Katuga formed the Nairobi City Five, while Valentine Muwulya recorded under the Columbia label, producing notable songs like Sabagenda Muninde (Wanderer, Wait for Me) and Sanyu Lyobuvubuka (The Joy of Youth). A splinter group from the K-Rhino Boys formed City Five, led by Joseph Chuza Kabaselle, with members including Charles Ssenkatuka, Ben Nicholas Apudo, Manuel Ali, and

John Karani. In 1957, the group left Nairobi for Leopoldville (now Kinshasa) in the Democratic Republic of Congo. On their way to the Congo, City Five spent around nine months in Kampala, performing at various venues, including the Mengo Social Club and the Blue Garden. Around this time, Israel Magembe rejoined his former bandmates and eventually accompanied them on a trip to Kinshasa.

Once in Kinshasa, the group was rebranded as The City Five Le Noir band, which comprised two distinct bands with a total of about sixteen members: The City Five and Le Noir. The City Five focused on Western music, performing mostly English, French and Spanish covers, with Charles Ssenkatuka as one of the lead singers. Their signature song, "Rythmo City-Five," was sung in Spanish and later recorded in the 1960s on the Nairobi ASL label, featuring Ssenkatuka and the celebrated Congolese guitarist and vocalist Eugene Ngoy, also known as Theo Gogene. Gogene was an accomplished musician who had previously performed with well-known Congolese bands, including African Jazz and Rock-A-Mambo.

Le Noir, on the other hand, specialized in rumba la Congolaise, with Leon Amba Zozo as the main vocalist, singing in Lingala. For several years, the band operated out of Kinshasa's popular Afro Mogambo nightclub. Their reach extended beyond the Congo, including a performance tour in Belgium in 1963. In May 1970, Chuza returned to Kampala with his City Five Le Noir band, where Zozo was a crowd favorite during their performances at Kampala's New Life nightclub.

In Uganda, a dramatic cultural shift unfolded as the grand orchestras faded into memory, leaving a void filled by vibrant, smaller acts. Solo performers and intimate groups emerged, armed with guitars, mandolins, and accordions, instruments that underscored a new era of simplicity and authenticity. These musicians stripped away the complexity of their orchestral predecessors, favoring an unvarnished sound that resonated with ordinary Ugandans. This transition marked a democratization of music, one where heartfelt lyrics and accessible melodies spoke directly to the local experience, a departure from the operatic singing style championed by celebrated figures like Valentine Muwulya, George Senoga-Zake, Nelson

Gonzabato, and Charles Ssenkatuka. Without easy access to recording studios, this cohort of new musicians turned to live performance as their primary way of reaching audiences. Their instruments became tools of expression and engagement, allowing them to share their stories, emotions, and social commentary directly with listeners. Their impromptu performances became part of the rhythm of daily life, echoing through community gatherings, marketplaces, and local festivities. Adding a unique twist to this evolution were the resourceful Indian shopkeepers in rural townships. With a keen sense for business and community spirit, they hired local musicians to play outside their stores. This clever strategy not only attracted customers but also helped spread the contagious energy of guitar-based music throughout the country, bringing it into the fabric of everyday life.

One of the popular Ugandan groups of the 1950s was the Buye Kigowa Galimasani (BKG) music club, popularly known as the BKG band, which was under the dynamic leadership of Joseph Bukenya. A multifaceted talent, part musician, part auto mechanic, and part entrepreneur, Bukenya not only fronted the band but also owned several popular bars in Kampala's Kiswa and Ntinda suburbs. BKG was well-loved in rural townships.

A defining moment for Bukenya's band came in March 1953, when BKG scheduled a performance in Kituntu township, Mawokota, about 70 miles southwest of Kampala. For months, BKG had been the talk of the township and the surrounding areas, with fans eagerly anticipating the opportunity to dance and lose themselves in the band's music. The atmosphere was one of excitement and celebration. But as BKG prepared to take the stage, the festive occasion took an unexpected and dramatic turn. A conservative *gombolola* (sub-county) chief, deeply entrenched in the old ways and a staunch advocate for preserving Buganda's heritage, arrived with the intent to stop the show. He denounced the Western-style dancing and emerging syncretic music as corrupting forces, claiming it was an affront to traditional morals and culture. Despite ongoing legal challenges to the Buganda Prime Minister's ban on Western dancing, as exemplified by the lawsuit filed by Jolly Joe Kiwanuka, the chief pressed on, determined to assert his authority. The crowd, fueled by months of anticipation and a growing sense of injustice, erupted in anger. What had begun as a joyful cultural gathering quickly descended into chaos, with the chief's intervention sparking a full-blown revolt. Realizing the dangerous path he had taken, the gombolola chief fled the scene, leaving the crowd in a state of defiance.

As the chief disappeared into the night, Bukenya and his band took the stage. The defiant performance was a resounding act of rebellion against stifling tradition. Bukenya and his BKG carried this spirit of defiance, and this connection to rural audiences, well into the early 1970s. BKG was also a crucible for emerging musical talent. Young musicians, drawn to Bukenya's energy and unyielding spirit, found space within the band's dynamic ranks. Future stars such as Frank Mbalire, Billy Mutebi, and Peter "Gastone Soso" Kabale all honed their craft under Bukenya's wing. These artists would go on to define and shape the golden age of Uganda's music in the 1970s, but it is within BKG's vibrant ecosystem that their journeys truly began.

Among the many Ugandan artists of the 1950s skilled in playing Western instruments, a fortunate few, primarily based in Kampala and nearby areas, had the opportunity to record their music on disc, preserving their creativity for posterity. Many of these recordings were facilitated by Hugh Tracey, a British ethnomusicologist who had previously worked for the South African Broadcasting Corporation and Gallo Ltd. of Johannesburg. In 1947, Tracey founded the African Music Society and later established the International Library of African Music (ILAM) in Roodepoort, a suburb of Johannesburg.

In the July 1970 issue of *The Quarterly Journal of the Library of Congress*, Jabbour and Hickerson described Tracey as "perhaps the most indefatigable collector of and commentator on sub-Saharan African music" of the mid-twentieth century. Tracey visited Uganda in 1950 and 1952, recording numerous musicians and groups at a variety of venues, including football fields, royal palaces, and Christian cathedrals. Some of his recordings captured public entertainers employed by local municipalities to perform in public beer halls, where they displayed their expertise with traditional instruments such as lutes, lyres, and drums. At the Kabaka's palace in Mengo, Tracey recorded the Kabaka's ensemble performing traditional songs. This was the same group that had recorded for the Odeon label in 1930.

One of Tracey's most notable recordings from Uganda was that of the legendary harpist to the Kabaka, Temusewo Mukasa, performing the spectacular piece Okwagala Omulungi Kwesengereza (To Love a Beauty Is to Beseech). Released on the Gallotone label, this recording garnered international attention among enthusiasts of African music. Okwagala Omulungi Kwesengereza was one of three songs to win the inaugural Osborne Award in 1952, making Temusewo Mukasa the first Ugandan musician to receive an internationally recognized music award. The other award recipients were Congolese musician Jean Bosco Mwenda for his guitar piece Masanga (Beer) and Zambian musician Josias Yemba Mate for his mbira composition Sitimela (The Train). The Osborne Award, launched in 1952 by the Dr. Tom Osborn Memorial Trust, aimed to recognize the finest recordings of African music each year. The award was greeted with great expectations, with many hoping it would hold a prestigious place in the burgeoning world of African music. W. A. Chislett, an avid record reviewer and critic who wrote extensively on music after World War II for the *Oxford Mail*, captured this sentiment. In his article "The Fascination of the Talking Drums," published in the January 1954 issue of the *Journal of African Music*, Chislett noted that there were "high hopes that the 'Osborn' would become as coveted in the new world of African music as an 'Oscar' is in the world of films."

The 1953 Osborn Award recognized eleven African songs, including Kyuma (Machine), a symphonic poem for fifteen drums performed by the royal drummers of the Kabaka of Buganda. Following in the footsteps of Columbia Gramophone Company engineers before him, Hugh Tracey also recorded the choir of St. Paul's Cathedral Namirembe, now under the direction of its skilled organist and conductor, Eriya Kayizzi. Struck by the choir's beauty and exceptional performance quality, Tracey considered it one of the finest examples of African choral music he encountered during his recording tours. In his article "Recording Tour, May to November 1950 East Africa," published in the *African Music Society Journal* in June 1951, he noted, "With the one exception of the 'Singers of the Copper Cross' in Elisabethville (present-day Lubumbashi in the Democratic Republic of the Congo), we have heard no religious music so well performed by Africans as that which we recorded that late September afternoon at Namirembe Cathedral."

Alongside his extensive recordings of traditional music from across Uganda, Hugh Tracey, who famously opposed the spread of European musical styles in Africa, also captured performances by Ugandan musicians playing guitars, banjos, and mandolins. One of these musicians was Matia Kaberuka from western Uganda, who performed with a group called the Western Province Demonstration Team. Kaberuka recorded several songs in the Runyakitara language with Tracey, many of which carried a patriotic tone, encouraging unity and progress among his region's people. Notable songs accompanied by banjo and mandolin include Banyankole Itwe Tukore Tuta (What Shall We Do, We the Banyakole People?), Ewaro Yaitu Eya Bunyoro (Our Land of Bunyoro), and Abahima Twerinde (The Hima People, Let's Protect Ourselves). In Tuterane Itwena Aba Bugwaizoba (All Unite Today), Kaberuka, unlike in his other songs, weaves in a dreamy Hawaiian guitar melody that lends the song a graceful lilt.

Another lively contributor was guitarist Dasane Ibanda, who sang in his native Lusoga language. Hailing from Nsube, a township north of Jinja, Ibanda recorded two songs with Tracey in 1952: Mwoyo Gwomukwano (A Heart Of Love) and Kaduma (a male name). Kaduma is a roman à clef, a thinly veiled autobiographical tale that recounts the heartbreak of a young Ibanda who arrives at his lover Milionsi's home, only to find she has eloped with an illiterate villager named Mpata. Despite his pleas for her to leave Mpata for the educated, banjo-playing Ibanda, Milionsi remains firm in her choice. Crestfallen, he mounts his bicycle for the long ride back to Nsube, lamenting what he sees as the misguided decisions of young women.

One of the most influential musicians of the time and a standout figure in mid-1950s Ugandan music was Ms. Eva "Varnish" Nanyonga, a self-taught guitarist. In a country where guitar players were often scorned at and associated with a boisterous lifestyle of drinking, partying, and lewdness, the rise of a female guitarist was nothing short of revolutionary. In a male-dominated world, her genial and polite nature, combined with her undeniable talent, made her a remarkable pioneer. Nanyonga, along with her friend Mrs. Dezi "Bitumbwe" Mwire, the stunning wife of Kampala musician John Mwire, were the first Black Ugandan female guitarists to perform publicly, generating much hubbub.

Born to a father from Buganda and a mother from Bunyoro in western Uganda, Nanyonga's early years were steeped in cultural diversity. Raised in Hoima by her maternal grandfather, Mr. Kaboga, she developed a resilient character and an independent spirit. By the time she was about twenty, coinciding with the departure of the K-Rhino Boys for Nairobi, her prodigious talent on the guitar was already beginning to command attention. Nanyonga possessed a striking beauty. She was tall and slender with warm and expressive eyes. It has often been said that her radiant smile lit up even the simplest moments. She carried herself with a natural confidence and a sense of purpose. This charisma proved irresistible and became the backdrop for a profound, cross-cultural romance with a European man, a relationship that blossomed over more than two decades.

Nanyonga famously embraced her distinctive physique in a culture that prized curvier figures. Unapologetically, she sang about her *museberende*, or flat backside. In her self-deprecating song Omto Mtono (Young and Slender), she sings about her young lover, Mahmood, and a night on the dance floor where "girls with well-endowed backsides have fun" while she "shakes her museberende," wondering what Mahmood sees when he glances in her direction. Nanyonga's early music, performed with commanding presence and composure, was often semi-autobiographical. Through her charmingly simple songs, we gain insight into the syncretic music scene that emerged in the wake of the Mengo African Orchestra.

Nanyonga made a striking impression performing in small venues across Kampala's native neighborhoods, such as Kibuye, Bwaise, Kawempe, and Kibuli. However, she was also a friend of the Kabaka, King Freddie, who invited her to perform at his palace on numerous occasions. The Kabaka showered her with lavish gifts, a generosity Nanyonga briefly alludes to in her song Chana Kitoo (Young Beauty). In the song, she describes herself as a fun-loving girl seeking excitement at Nyakasura High School near Fort Portal, only to be cold-shouldered by a jealous young lover. This lover's jealousy is sparked by a ring on her finger and a fancy glass goblet, gifts that Nanyonga coyly hints may have come from either someone at Nyakasura or the Kabaka himself. It was also the Kabaka who gifted her first electric guitar in the late 1950s, an instrument she played with great enthusiasm.

In her songs Omto Mtono and Nanyoga Rumba, recorded for Columbia Records, Nanyonga paints a vivid picture of Kampala's 1950s dance scene. One can imagine an evening at musician John Mwire's walled backyard, where Nanyonga entertained rumba-loving fans. Mwire's home, near the famous "Kibuye kubiri" (Kibuye at two miles) bus stop on the old Kampala-Entebbe Road, was a haven for rumba enthusiasts. There, music stars like Nanyonga, John Mwire, and several lesser-known artists without the prominence of the Mengo African Orchestra or K-Rhino Boys pedigree could perform for adoring audiences.

John Mwire, a talented guitarist from the Busoga region, had recorded with the Jambo record label, producing songs such as Mukwano Gwange Dezi (My Darling Dezi) and Omuto Omulungi (Young and Pretty), both tributes to his beautiful wife, Dezi "Bitumbwe." Although a proficient banjo and guitar player, Dezi never recorded her own songs. It is Mwire who helped Nanyonga, and his wife Dezi, hone their guitar skills. His backyard became a vibrant space where revelers danced to locally adapted rumba, tango, and samba songs.

Nanyonga's performing ensemble, known as "Nanyonga & Party," included a close-knit group of musicians from diverse backgrounds. Among them were John-Paul, a Kenyan police officer assigned to Kibuye station;

Makumbi, a Kenyan working with the East African Trade and Customs department; Dr. Raymond Kafamba, then a medical student at Makerere University and a member of a prominent Haya family from Tanzania; and Livingstone Ngadha Mdigos, a Kenyan meteorologist with the East African Meteorological Department at Entebbe. Another core member of this group was the renowned Ben S. S. Edebe, a Kenyan Luhya from Ivonda village in western Kenya. Edebe, Uganda's leading tailor at the time, had studied tailoring at the London Taylor & Cutter Academy and previously worked for Deacons Ltd in Nairobi before establishing a successful business in Kampala's Katwe suburb, a hub for skilled African artisans. He was likely the first Black African to manage a hugely successful and thriving enterprise in Katwe. Edebe was briefly married to Edisa Nabweteme, a daughter of Kabaka Daudi Chwa and sister to Kabaka Mutesa II, with whom he had a daughter, Winnie Naava Edebe. In addition to his tailoring expertise, serving high-profile clients like Kabaka Mutesa II and Lady Cohen, wife of the British governor to Uganda, Edebe was also a gifted vocalist.

It is easy to imagine a "full band" scene at Mwire's home. On warm, starlit evenings, revelers packed into the backyard, drawn by the rhythms of locally adapted rumba, tango, and samba. The atmosphere buzzed with camaraderie, as clerks from the protectorate government, representing the small African elite, mingled with members of the urban working class who eked out a living in native neighborhoods like Katwe, Kisenyi, and Nsambya. For one night, they could set aside their daily struggles, united by music and a shared love of dancing. Excitement filled the air as revelers lost themselves on the makeshift dance floor in the backyard, their laughter and voices rising above the steady heartbeat of drums and guitars. Kerosene lanterns strung around the yard cast a warm glow over cheerful faces as dancers swayed and spun, kicking up dust beneath their feet.

At the heart of it all was Nanyonga, the undisputed queen of the music scene, taking center stage. Her luminous voice and magnetic charm drew in the crowd as she sang, accompanied by Mdigos on the banjo, with Kafamba and Edebe adding rich harmony as backup vocalists. The regular patrons and standout dancers earned special recognition, as Nanyonga gave shout-outs in her catchy tunes, with some even immortalized in her lyrics. As the night wore on, the music grew bolder, the dancers more animated, and the laughter louder. In this backyard haven, the revelers escaped the challenges of urban life, immersing themselves in a night of joy, music, and unity under the wide African sky. Mwire's backyard had become more than a gathering place. It was the hottest ticket in town, a cherished refuge where the city's heartbeat thrived.

In Nanyoga Rumba, she introduces herself as "Ms. Varnish," a woman with a smooth voice, daughter of a mother from Bunyoro and a member of the Buganda clan Nyonyi Nyange, the Egret clan. She invites the star dancers of the night, who included Mr. and Mrs. Abdallah, Mr. Saleh, and Mr. Mahmood, to exhibit their rumba skills on the floor. In Omto Mtono, she sings of her lover, Mahmood: "The one I constantly think about, the one I chose from among many, the one I love most." In Mganzi Wange (My Beloved), Nanyonga takes on the perspective of her good friend and mentor, John Mwire, dedicating a love song to his wife, Dezi Mwire, describing her as graceful and beautiful. Nanyonga sings of Mwire's pride in his wife, whom he jealously guarded with nine bodyguards, requiring admirers to submit written requests to meet her.

Nanyonga enjoyed widespread success throughout the 1950s, becoming a fixture in Kampala's entertainment circles and recording many songs on various labels. She collaborated with Fundi Konde on two songs recorded with HMV: Ai Tabisa Wandeka Nkaba (Ah, Tabisa, You Left Me Crying) and Ekisera Kituse (Time Has Come). Also on HMV were her popular songs Gyoyagala Gyobolaga (Go Wherever You Want To) and Okulya Ebyange (You Ate What Was Mine), a fast-paced tune with lively guitar lines. Sung in both Luganda and Runyoro, the song is playful and suggestive, telling of a dapper man who charms her into giving up something precious, only to flee to Mombasa, Tanganyika, or Fort Portal. In her lament, Nanyonga scolds, "Shame on you for eating my goods and fleeing. Goodbye, buddy. You indeed ate my goods."

Nanyonga also recorded extensively with the Kenya Jambo label, producing songs such as Maria Tamanyi Mukwano (Maria Knows No

Love), Kondare Kondare, Bulikaseka (All That Laughs), Omwagalwa (Beloved), Eriso (The Eye), Ndikuwa (I'll Give You), Gurii and Katusha (a boy's name). The song title Katusha was a misspelling, and it should have appeared as Katisa. The song was a dedication to her friend and fellow member of Nanyonga and Party, Mr. Mdigos. Mdigos, a light-skinned man, had married into the extended Ham Mukasa family. Because of his fair complexion, Ham Mukasa nicknamed him Katisa, a word that traditionally refers to someone who inspires fear. However, in this context it was used playfully to mean "the fair-skinned specter." The Gurii title was a misspelling too; it was meant to be Enguli, referring to a potent home-brewed gin. In Enguli, Nanyonga praises the drink at length, asserting, "If you are unaware of enguli, you've been long dead," and "If you do not like enguli, don't even think of entering into a relationship with me."

The subject of enguli, also known as waragi or Kasese or Lira-Lira, was explored by various musicians. Zakaria Kasasa, a traditional folk musician accompanied by lyre, lutes, and drums with his group Abadongo Abaganda, recorded an Enguli song on the Gallotone label. Edward Seruwagi, accompanied by guitar and mandolin, also recorded Enguli on the Gallotone label in 1952, another of the sessions captured by Hugh Tracey. Unlike Nanyonga, whose treatment of the subject was more celebratory, Seruwagi warned of the societal harms of enguli, urging Ugandans to steer clear of the locally brewed gin. Similarly, Zakaria and Party recorded Enguli Eswaza (Enguli Humiliates) on the local Ugandan G.L.K label, decrying the destruction caused by excessive drinking.

Nanyonga's influence was profound. She was a defining figure of the post-big band era, proving that a solo musician with an acoustic guitar, a *kadongo kamu* player, could command the attention of a large audience, including royalty. Kadongo kamu, which translates to "one guitar," is a genre in which musicians accompany their storytelling lyrics with a single acoustic guitar. It represents the closest expression of a truly national music style in Uganda. Nanyonga, often playing her electric guitar, was one of the main acts during Kampala's official celebrations of Uganda's independence from Britain in October 1962.

Many later Ugandan musicians cited her as a significant inspiration. Hadija Namale, a popular musician from the late 1960s to the mid-1970s, recalled that as a young girl of five, she had memorized many of Nanyonga's songs heard on the family gramophone. During a 2020 interview, she broke into song, singing Nanyonga's Sala Bulago (Cut the Throat), a song widely regarded as a tongue-in-cheek risqué commentary. It depicts a chance meeting between a man and a beautiful woman on a deserted path at dusk. He is clearly smitten and confesses his admiration. Her response is an invitation to "cut her throat," a metaphorical suggestion to cast aside hesitation and embrace the wild passion of the moment:

Ah, cut the throat
Maiden, you are so beautiful,
Maiden, fertile with children,
Ah, cut the throat,
She was lashed with twelve strokes of the cane
For fun-seeking late evening,
Ah, cut the throat,
Men about here never rest at night,
Men about here never sleep.
Just cut the throat so I can go home.
Let me tell you what sends you out late in the evening,
Matters of pleasure can be painful,
Just cut the throat so I can go home.
One hundred waterspouts opened,
And she was smeared in oil

Released on the Kenya Jambo label in the mid-1950s, Sala Bulago became a hit despite its suggestive lyrics. Though it received limited radio play due to its double entendre, it was a favorite in bars, blaring from jukeboxes. Parents often forbade their children from singing it, and violators faced punishment.

Nanyonga was an important and influential musician who inspired many fledgling and aspiring musicians. Her immense talent and dedication to the guitar not only challenged societal expectations but also left an indelible mark on Ugandan music, serving as a powerful inspiration for generations of musicians. For example, musician Elly Wamala cited Nanyonga and Polycarp Kakooza as major influences. Wamala had a particular fondness for Nanyonga's song Ndikuwa Maama Wange (I'll Give You My Mother), a cherished classic.

Nanyonga's popularity waned following the 1959–60 boycott of businesses run by non-Africans. Nanyonga was a true entertainer, with music as her lifeblood. In the 1970s, she and her longtime European boyfriend operated a bar off Kampala's Nakivubo Place Road (now Ssebaana Kizito Road). Most evenings, when she was at the bar, Nanyonga would take out her guitar and perform for the guests. The revelers, nostalgic for the music of the 1950s and 1960s, could not get enough of the Queen of the "full band" era. She played her own hits from the 1950s and occasionally covered popular songs by other artists, notably Elly Wamala's Nabutono. Sometimes, she would invite fellow musicians to join her on stage.

One of her frequent guests was Hadija Namale, who, after her acclaimed time with the Rwenzori Band in the mid-1970s, was often invited by her idol, Nanyonga, to perform at the bar. The two women bonded over their shared love of music and became close friends. Nanyonga was especially fond of Namale's Gwe Musanyusa (You Are Joyfulness), a mellow and heartfelt song with clean guitar lines that Namale recorded in 1974 on A. P. Chandarana's Upendo label. Together, they would sing Gwe Musanyusa, a soothing melody that gently rocked the soul:

I too think much about you,
You're the one who stands above all,
When I think of you, peace fills my heart,
I've given you names, a growing list,
You are the genius,
You are the muse,
You are Happiness.

The disruptive and sometimes violent boycott of 1959–60 was organized by the Uganda National Movement (UNM), a neo-traditional party led by the charismatic 29-year-old building contractor, Augustine Kamya. Representing the interests of a traditional Buganda, the UNM feared that British plans for an independent and unified Uganda that protected minority rights would diminish Buganda's historical prominence. Kamya and the UNM launched the boycott to disrupt ongoing talks about Uganda's self-rule and independence, disguising it as opposition to racial discrimination, economic inequalities, and colonial domination. As Yoga Adhola, a Ugandan politician, would later astutely observe in a September 2020 *Monitor* newspaper article, "UNM leadership ingeniously chose the dominance by non-Africans of trade and business as the issue to rally around. Because of the widespread dislike of Asian traders throughout Uganda, a trade boycott was bound to enlist popular support; indeed, the boycott they called for was an immediate and total success in Buganda."

The UNM held large rallies across central Uganda, urging crowds to persevere in the boycott and avoid patronizing non-African businesses. These rallies often concluded with crowds facing Mengo, the Kabaka's palace, and passionately singing Ekitibwa Kya Buganda (The Pride of Buganda), the Buganda Kingdom anthem composed by John Bosa and Polycarp Kakooza. Central Uganda's Black population largely refused to buy goods or services from non-African businesses and shunned foreign consumer goods, including bottled beer and Brooke Bond tea, once staples in most Ugandan households. Black employees of Asian or European families or businesses were encouraged to quit. The boycott was vigorously enforced by UNM retainers who operated like guerilla fighters, avoiding British colonial administrators. On one occasion, the colonial police used brutal force against protesters, resulting in fatalities. Those seen or suspected of doing business with Asians or Europeans faced threats, beatings, and in some cases, even death at the hands of UNM enforcers. In July 1959, UNM agitators left leaflets at Lwanga Miti's Top Life nightclub in Mengo, urging patrons to join the boycott. Because bottled beer was a main attraction at Top Life, even patrons who did not support the boycott stayed away, fearing reprisals from the boycott's enforcers. Staff, including the nightclub's popular barmaids, also stopped coming to work. The boycott had a dampening effect on Kampala's nightlife, and the clubs suffered considerable economic loss. Miti struggled to keep the business afloat as the economic impact of the boycott deepened. Not long after the boycott ended, a Kampala choral ensemble known as the African Music Society released Twalinya Mukyoto (We Trampled the Fireplace) on the CMS label. The song praised the UNM in glowing terms, portraying the boycott as a necessary and justified act of resistance. In a striking and derogatory metaphor, it referred to foreign traders as a "jigger" that needed to be removed from the African body. The tone was unapologetic, reflecting the heightened emotions and polarizing rhetoric of the time. This ensemble should not be confused with the similarly named organization founded by Hugh Tracey to research and document African music.

The boycott also impacted the Opel Gramophone Record and Battery Factory, Uganda's first recording studio. Founded in 1956 by Georg von Opel, the German multimillionaire and grandson of the founder of Opel Automobile Works, the factory included a record pressing plant and was based in Kampala's industrial area. Opel had initially come to Uganda in 1955 as part of an expedition to collect African animals for a private zoo he was establishing in Kronberg, Germany. Like many Western visitors, he fell under the spell of Uganda's natural beauty and culture. When Winston Churchill visited Uganda in 1907, he famously declared it "the Pearl of Africa," marveling at the country's magnificent landscapes, vibrant wildlife, and diversity. This sentiment resonated with von Opel. Inspired by his experience, von Opel decided not only to collect animals but also to help preserve the region's musical heritage by founding the Opel Gramophone Record and Battery Factory.

The factory produced shellac records under its Tom Tom label and became one of Kampala's major employers. At its peak, it provided jobs for around 200 workers and manufactured an average of 50,000 78 RPM shellac records per month. This output included recordings for other local labels, such as the Mzuri label owned by Assanand & Sons. Opel

Gramophone recorded artists from across East Africa, focusing primarily on traditional folk musicians. Among the company's employees was a young receptionist, Elisham "Elly" Wamala, a talented guitarist and singer who also played in the Opel Gramophone studio band. During his time at Opel, Wamala collaborated with singer Simon Kaate Nsubuga to record one of his early singles, Nabutono.

Although Opel was the most significant recording studio in Uganda at the time, it was not the only one. In eastern Uganda, a Ugandan Indian based in Iganga ran a smaller operation under the SUKARI label, which focused on preserving and publishing traditional folk music of the Basoga and other communities in the region. While modest in scale, such efforts reflected a growing interest in documenting local musical traditions beyond Kampala. However, Opel's prominence also made it a target. The UNM boycott soon turned its attention to Opel Gramophone, urging workers to abandon their posts. Faced with mounting pressure, von Opel ultimately decided to close the company in 1960, marking the end of Uganda's first major music recording operation. This closure was devastating for local musicians, both established and aspiring, who now lacked reliable recording facilities in Uganda. Many were forced to travel to Nairobi, Kenya, to record their music, a costly and arduous journey.

When the boycott ended in 1960, a new wave of Ugandan musicians emerged, overshadowing earlier stars like Eva Nanyonga. These young musicians looked to Kenya and Congo for inspiration, embracing the "twist" style popularized in Kenya or drawing from Congo's la rumba Congolaise, which had become a staple on Radio Uganda, the country's first broadcaster since 1954. A prominent figure on Radio Uganda was Ms. Nanfuka Kigozi, the first Ugandan woman to host a radio show. Stunningly charming and charismatic, Nanfuka became a beloved voice on the airwaves. Her one-hour program, *Enyimba Enga'nzi* (Popular Music), was widely listened to across Uganda and exposed audiences to local talent and a variety of music from other parts of Africa, Europe, and the Americas. It became a cherished platform for musical discovery. Tragically, at the height of her popularity, Ms. Nanfuka was involved in a fatal car accident in Kampala's Bakuli suburb.

Program Ya'balimi (Farmers' Program) on Radio Uganda was another popular show that introduced a wide array of domestic, regional, and international music to Ugandan audiences. The program began with its lively signature song, Kolanga Ofune Okwesima (Work Gets You Rewarded) by the K-Rhino Boys. This song, first revived by Yeko Mukasa and later reimagined by veteran musician Frank Mbalire with Ziwuuna Band in 2020, celebrates the dignity of hard work. Its lyrics champion labor as the path to food, drink, money, and fine clothing, urging listeners to rise, toil, and triumph over poverty. The 1960s also saw the rise of Tom Ndugga, whose *Saturday Club* program became a sensation, particularly among teenagers and young adults. Ndugga's show was eagerly awaited each week, as it was the ultimate source for the latest British and American pop songs. In addition to his role as a DJ, Ndugga was a prominent news anchor and covered Uganda's independence ceremony for the national broadcaster. His influence on youth culture at the time was profound, bridging the sounds of international pop with the tastes of a young Ugandan audience eager for global music trends.

Radio Uganda, more than any other platform, transformed the musical landscape of ordinary Ugandans. Through its broadcasts, the radio fostered a thriving musical culture with listeners introduced not only to local and traditional music but also to the energetic Afro-Cuban rhythms and instrumentation of Congolese rumba, which swiftly riveted the nation. Congolese musicians like Antoine "Wendo" Kolosoy and Joseph Kabasele "Le Grand Kalle" became household names, their songs reverberating across Ugandan towns and villages. Frank Mbalire, a renowned Ugandan guitarist, recalls the tremendous popularity of Wendo's Marie Louise in the 1950s, a period when he himself was just a young boy in elementary school. This song, with its irresistible rhythms, marked one of Mbalire's earliest encounters with music and left a lasting impression on his budding musical career.

As Nanyonga's popularity declined, Israel Wamala Magembe and his Kampala City Six band rose to prominence, becoming Uganda's leading popular music group. Magembe was a tall, charming figure and a talented, charismatic singer and songwriter. Born in 1928 into an aristocratic Buganda family, he was the son of Samwiri (Samuel) Wamala, a former Prime Minister of the Buganda Kingdom. Magembe attended Bishop Tucker in Mukono and later King's College, Budo, where he graduated in 1944. It was at Budo that his passion for music truly blossomed. Guided by his teacher, Mr. Bamutire, he began learning guitar. After Bamutire left to work for the Kingdom of Busoga, Magembe continued his studies with Mr. Apollo Kironde, a teacher from a musical family. Kironde, whose father Asanasiyo Kironde was one of Uganda's early recording artists, had learned various Western instruments at University College of South Africa, Fort Hare, and had even recorded Negro spirituals under the name "Kironde & Party" with his students at Budo. Under Kironde's mentorship, Magembe's musical talents matured.

Magembe also drew inspiration from American country musician Jimmie Rodgers. During social evenings at Budo, he entertained students and faculty alike with his renditions of Rodgers' songs. In 1944, Magembe's adventurous spirit led him to Kenya, where he eventually settled in Mombasa. Accounts of how he joined the Rhino Boys band in Mombasa in 1948 vary. In one version, he claimed he had gone to Mombasa for a civil service job with the municipality, moonlighting with the Rhino Boys at the Mombasa European Club. In another account, he said he was personally recruited by the wealthy owner of the band after he had seen him perform in Kampala. Regardless, Magembe soon joined his compatriots Senoga-Zake, Charles Ssenkatuka, Muwulya, and Nelson Gonzabato in the Rhino Boys in Mombasa, playing with them for a few months before the group disbanded that year and splintered into various groups, including the K-Rhino Boys.

The K-Rhino Boys relocated to Uganda in 1951, becoming the resident band at Kamulu's Hollywood Social Club. Magembe switched from rhythm to lead guitar. He stayed with the band until their departure back to Kenya in December 1953. This time, Magembe chose to remain in Uganda, forming his own band, Black and White. The band struggled to gain an audience in Kampala, so Magembe relocated to Fort Portal, a town with a significant white population, largely tea planters. Black and White played covers of popular Western and Caribbean songs, with a focus on calypso music inspired by Lord Kitchener's playful and humorous songs, including King Freddie (HRH The Kabaka) and January Girls. Inspired by his love for calypso, Magembe renamed his band The Calypso Band.

In 1957, however, Magembe's Fort Portal venture came to an end when the K-Rhino Boys returned to Kampala. Unable to resist rejoining his bandmates, especially his close friend Charles Ssenkatuka, Magembe became part of the group. The K-Rhino Boys, now calling themselves the City Five Band and led by Joseph Chuza Kabaselle, soon left for Kinshasa in the Democratic Republic of Congo, and this time Magembe went with them. In Kinshasa, City Five established a residency at the Afro Negro nightclub (renamed Afro Mogambo) on Avenue De Gaulle, which would later become Avenue du Commerce. One of the city's most sought-after venues for live music and dancing, Afro Negro was renowned for its pulsating rhythms and cosmopolitan ambiance, it attracted a diverse clientele, including locals, expatriates, and United Nations personnel stationed in the city. According to some accounts, Charles Ssenkatuka eventually purchased the club when it had changed names to Afro Mogambo, becoming the first East African to own such an establishment in Kinshasa. Under City Five's spell, the venue gained further fame for its dynamic performances of Western-influenced styles, including jazz, and became known for drawing Kinshasa's most fashionable women and Western tourists in search of the city's vibrant nightlife.

Several future Congolese music stars spent time with City Five. Virtuoso guitarist Dicky Nicolas Baroza, younger brother of L'African Jazz guitarist Tino Baroza and cousin to guitar legends Nico "Dr. Nico" Kasanda and Charles Mwamba, played with City Five at Afro Mogambo. Leon "Bholen" Bombolo, who would later join Franco Luambo Makiadi's OK Jazz and Le Negro Success, also performed with City Five in its early days.

Magembe's time in Kinshasa, however, was short-lived. Struggling with homesickness and frequent bouts of illness, he returned to Kampala in 1959. Meanwhile, Ssenkatuka remained in Kinshasa with City Five, recording several hit songs of the era. Magembe's experience in Congo had left him with a deep appreciation for the rhythms of la rumba Congolaise, and he was eager to introduce this style to Uganda's music scene, confident that the Congolese sound would resonate with Ugandans across social classes.

To help him in this enterprise was a Congolese saxophonist, Michel, who he had befriended. He convinced him to make the trip to Kampala with him, and together they would tap into the deep pool of promising young musicians to form a group that was unlike any the country had ever seen. Michel traveled to Kampala, eager to embark on a new musical adventure together with his friend.

With the end of the UNM boycott of Western businesses in 1960, Magembe purchased musical instruments from Assanand & Sons on Kampala Road, Uganda's leading music store. He began recruiting and mentoring a new generation of young musicians, forming a band he called Kampala City Six. The group served as an incubator for emerging talent and played a vital role in launching the careers of many Ugandan musicians during the 1960s.

The initial line-up of the band blended the two seasoned musicians, Magembe and Michel, with young, eager talent. Magembe himself played lead guitar and provided the direction and the sound that defined Kampala City Six. Joining him was Michel on the saxophone, and Simon Kaate Nsubuga played the rhythm guitar and also sang. Ecklas Masembe Kawalya, a shy young man that Magembe had met at the Opel Studio just before it closed, was the band's double bass player. He also doubled as the lead vocalist. Kalule was on drums. Other musicians that joined Kampala City Six in 1960 and 1961 included Steven Sempasa, E. Lukwata, Fred Kanyike, Andrew Kyambadde, Bonny Steven Kyambadde (B. K. Steven), Willy Mujwala, and Fred Masagazi. Elliot Adwong, a Kenyan saxophonist, was another prominent alumnus who joined Kampala City

Six briefly in the mid-1960s. Sarah Namagembe, Margaret Nakibuuka, and Mary Nattima made their live debuts with Kampala City Six as guest backup artists. Although they initially performed in supporting roles, each eventually emerged as a distinguished musician in her own right.

While David Jingo is sometimes mistakenly associated with Kampala City Six, he actually performed with the Kampala City Boys, a separate group founded by Israel Magembe and featuring younger musicians. Recognizing the strength of a unified voice, Magembe believed that banding together could improve the musicians' earnings. In an effort to empower musicians and wrest control of their music from record companies, he founded the Uganda Musicians Union in 1960. His goal was to secure royalties from record sales that would benefit all artists. However, the union was short-lived, as he was unable to garner sufficient support from his fellow musicians.

Israel Magembe did not simply mold musicians; he helped shape the very future of Uganda's syncretic music scene. Kampala City Six's distinctive sound was deeply influenced by the works of Congolese pioneers like Wendo Kolosoy and Joseph Kabasale "Le Grand Kallé." Drawing inspiration from Kallé's groundbreaking band, L'African Jazz, the group adopted African jazz's rhythmic structures and melodic sensibilities and infused them with Ugandan identity.

Magembe held deep admiration for Kallé's innovative fusion of traditional African rhythms with Cuban rumba, and this admiration found direct expression in Kampala City Six's compositions. One notable example is their hit song Buganda Dembe ("Buganda Is Peace"), a clear homage to Grand Kallé's Tembe Nye ("No Doubt"). The melodic framework of the two songs is nearly identical. In Buganda Dembe, the lyrics were reworked in Luganda, and the title reflects a clever linguistic adaptation: *ntembe* becomes *dembe*, the Luganda word for peace, showing the fluid relationship between Lingala and Luganda. This practice of adapting Congolese melodies into locally resonant forms became a hallmark of Magembe's style. It reflected his broader vision to blend African musical traditions with global influences and to forge a uniquely Ugandan sound grounded in shared continental rhythms.

Kampala City Six initially rehearsed at Planet, a bar located in Bwaise on the outskirts of Kampala. The bar was owned by businessman Ignatius Sebalamu, whose establishment became a cornerstone of the local music scene. Locals affectionately referred to the venue by several names, with the most iconic being Sebalamu's and, perhaps most intriguingly, *Kyeggunda*. The latter was not just a nickname; it was a term deeply embedded in the cultural fabric of Kampala's nightlife. Kyeggunda was used to describe any venue where live music pulsed through the night, a place where the city's heart seemed to beat louder with each passing hour. The word itself perfectly encapsulated the experience: the deep, resonant "boom-boom" of the loudspeakers that vibrated through the walls of the club, the energy spilling out into the streets, pulling people in from every direction. Kyeggunda was more than a name; it was a feeling, the very essence of the vibrant nightlife that defined Kampala. It evoked the idea of a powerful, almost living heartbeat, a rhythm that reverberated through the warm air and brought the city's nights to life.

Because of Kampala City Six's regular gig at Planet, the bar earned a reputation as a musical landmark, helping shape the nightlife scene on the outskirts of the city. Over time, Planet became synonymous with the music of Kampala, where every night was alive with energy, rhythm, and a sense of community. It was not just a bar; it was a place where memories were made, where music lovers gathered, and where the pulse of Kampala could be felt most strongly.

In 1961, after years of ownership, Sebalamu sold Planet Nightclub to Miti Lwanga. Miti renamed the venue Top Life. Around the same time, he returned Hollywood Nightclub in Mengo to its original owner, the Ismaili businessman Kamulu. Though Kamulu was said to have sold the club to Miti years earlier, it is now believed that Miti may have simply acted as a front, maintaining operations while Kamulu lay low, waiting for the choppy political waters to settle. In September 1964, after several months of renovation during which the club remained closed, Top

Life reopened with much fanfare. The event was graced by Sir Edward Mutesa, the Kabaka (King) of Buganda, who officially inaugurated the newly refurbished venue. The reopening ceremony drew a distinguished crowd, including top government officials and prominent business leaders, many from the Ugandan-Asian community. In collaboration with Hassan Sunderani, who would go on to lead Uganda's Olympic team to the 1964 Games in Tokyo, Miti used the event as an opportunity to give back. All proceeds from the day were donated to support the national Olympic team. It is worth noting that Sunderani and Kamulu, who were cousins, shared a commitment to fostering both cultural life and national pride in Uganda. Later, in 1971, the club saw yet another transformation when it was purchased by Ramadan Mustafa, a businessman from the Nubian community in Bombo. Mustafa renamed the venue Lumumba Nightclub, in honor of the late Congolese leader Patrice Lumumba. Despite this, the nightclub became more closely associated with its manager, James Sseba Mukasa, who was often mistaken for the owner.

Following the sale of Planet, Kampala City Six relocated to Jolly Joe Kiwanuka's White Nile Club in Kibuye, also simply referred to as "White". Kampala City Six was formed at a time of rapid political change in Uganda. The British were preparing the country for self-rule and eventual independence, and political fervor was high. Various political groups were mobilizing, ranging from regional monarchists loyal to the Kabaka, who were wary of British intentions, to staunch nationalists who championed a united Uganda, a nation that would bring together diverse tribes to shape their shared future.

As a scion of an aristocratic Buganda family closely linked to the monarchy, Magembe reflected his political beliefs in some of his music. In Abataka Abasajja (The Clan Headmen), with vocals by Ecklas Kawalya, he captured the prevailing political sentiment from the perspective of a Buganda loyalist. At that time, Buganda's clan leaders, known as the *Abataka*, were leading efforts to resist British plans for Ugandan independence, fearing that a united Uganda would diminish the Kabaka's role and strip

Buganda of its privileges under the 1900 Buganda Agreement. In a beautifully rendered voice accompanied by an upbeat saxophone and rhythmic guitar, Kawalya sings about the clan leaders' loyalty and resistance:

<blockquote>
The clan headmen,
Rejected political parties,
For the King and Buganda Parliament,
All rally behind the Buganda Parliament,
Time is nigh,
For Buganda's self-rule.
</blockquote>

<blockquote>
The King flew away,
The prime minister left too,
So did the county chiefs and legislators,
They saw it was past time,
For Buganda's self-rule.
</blockquote>

Abataka Abasajja became a major hit on the eve of Uganda's independence in 1962, marking the start of Kawalya's rise to fame. As lead vocalist, Kawalya gained wider recognition than Magembe, who was content to take a step back, encouraging his protégé to record some of the most iconic songs of the early 1960s. Other early 1960s hits sung by Kawalya and mostly composed by Magembe included Ayida Mama, Millie Gwe Sherry (My Darling Millie), Mweraba (Bye-Bye), and the very successful Ninda Kabandole (Waiting for the Double-Decker Bus), where he sings about a burning desire to get on the double-decker bus to go to Ndebba, to visit his beloved, Lucy, for he has a heartache. Steven Sempasa composed Ninda Kabandole.

Years later, in the late 1960s, Magembe revisited Millie Gwe Sherry, calling it Sherry Wange, and re-recorded it alongside Omukwano Gwaffe Guffe (Let Our Love Die) for the Serena label in 1970. On this version, Kawalya was replaced by Tony Ssenkebejje and Geoffrey Nsereko as the lead singers. While their contributions went uncredited (the song is credited to Israel Magembe), Ssenkebejje and Nsereko brought their own unique styles to the songs, resulting in beloved reinterpretations that breathed new life into Magembe's vibrant originals.

Kampala City Six recorded on various labels, including South Africa's New Sound (owned by Gallo Record Company), which released Okwagala Kwenina (The Love I Have) and Banabatu Nkole Ntya (Friends, What Should I Do?). On the CMS label, they recorded Jukira Byewalayira (Remember Your Promise), Abaganda Bafirwa (The Loss of the Baganda People), Wesirya (If I Don't Eat) and Omukwano Guffe (Let Love Die).

In one memorable instance, the Kabaka, Sir Edward Mutesa, invited Kampala City Six to perform at his Ndaiga Hunting Lodge. The musicians' families and friends advised them not to bring their girlfriends or wives to the lodge. The Kabaka was renowned for his amorous pursuits. He saw himself as entitled to any woman in his kingdom, married or not, and his position allowed him to act on these desires with impunity. This behavior, while shocking to outsiders, was largely accepted within the cultural norms of the time. Andrew Kyambadde, a band member who joined the trip, noted that many musicians did not mind sharing their girlfriends with the king. It was considered an honor, as the Kabaka was seen as the symbolic husband of all his subjects.

The visit to Ndaiga was unforgettable, filled with evenings of music, dancing, and schmoozing with the Kabaka, against a backdrop of much indulgence. Excessive drinking, smoking, and unabashed debauchery defined the trip, which Kawalya later immortalized in his song Tugende Endayiga Omutanda Akola (Let's Go to Ndaiga, the Sovereign Is at Work). However, it was rumored that Kawalya, a devout Christian in his early twenties, was privately uncomfortable with the excesses of the Ndaiga visit. His song Sifaayo (Don't Care), a duet with the talented Yunia Nalwanga, was seen by some as a subtle critique of the Kabaka's libertine lifestyle. In the song, Kawalya pleads with his lover not to leave him for a wealthier rival, a suave, Mercedes-driving man, while Yunia, singing as his lover, passionately declares her devotion to this rival, even professing she would lay down her life for him. Kawalya counters, insisting that he is the better man. Though Sifaayo was a beautifully crafted song, it stirred controversy among Buganda traditionalists, who saw it as irreverent toward the Kabaka. Some even called for a boycott, but the song's charm won over the public, and it became a popular duet known for its soothing, reassuring tone.

Kampala City Six was undeniably Uganda's premier Black musical act and very much in demand in the early 1960s. The band also gained a taste of international acclaim when jazz legend Louis Armstrong visited Uganda in October 1960 with his All Stars band. On the evening of his arrival from the Congo, where he just completed another leg of his African tour, Entebbe Airport shimmered under the glow of floodlights, the humid air scented faintly with lake breeze and aviation fuel. Crowds pressed forward, eager to glimpse the jazz legend as his aircraft taxied to a halt. Waiting near the terminal, Kampala City Six tuned their instruments, their crisp suits catching the light. Known for slipping Armstrong's classics into their own sets, they were the perfect musical ambassadors. Alongside them stood the resident band from Kampala's Bagatelle Nightclub, its lead singer, Lariki, a striking figure from the Tanganyika coast whose voice carried the salt and sun of her homeland. Most members of the band were Kenyans. The Bagatelle bar was a popular haunt for colonial administrators as well as Kampala's Asian and Black elite. Among the latter were figures such as Daudi Ochieng and Michael Kaggwa. It gained a reputation for its resident band, which performed European and American covers. The Bagatelle, like La Quinta, was owned by Norman Godinho. It was located on William Street, a short distance across from the Equatoria Hotel, in the three-story Bank of Uganda building. Today, that building houses the Central Bank of Uganda Staff Clinic and various bank departments. When the Bank of Uganda was established in 1966, this building served as its initial premises for a few months before operations moved to Liverpool House on Parliamentary Avenue. In 1970, the bank relocated to its current head office on Kampala Road.

When Armstrong stepped into view, the two local bands launched into a spirited welcome. Brass and saxophones cut through the evening air, the rhythm section locked into a swinging groove, and Lariki's vocals curled effortlessly around the melodies. When they finished, Armstrong clapped and exclaimed, "They really swung that Mark The Knife!" The crowd erupted, their applause mingling with the music in a moment that bridged continents. In the days that followed, Nakivubo Stadium became the stage for two extraordinary concerts. Kampala's residents arrived in droves, some in elegant evening dress, others in their Sunday best, the crowd a patchwork of color and anticipation. As Armstrong's first notes soared into the warm night, a roar rose from the stands. People swayed, clapped, and shouted in delight, swept into a celebration that blurred the lines between performer and audience. For Kampala City Six, and for all who were there, those nights became a living memory of the moment when the heart of East Africa danced to the beat of New Orleans jazz.

At the official opening of Kamulu's New Life Nightclub in Mengo in March 1964, Kampala City Six performed for an enthusiastic audience, and it was here that many first encountered the young and extraordinarily talented Sarah Namagembe, who had made her live debut earlier at Planet singing alongside Magembe. With a voice that was both expressive and soulful, Namagembe graced the stage alongside Magembe, and the chemistry between the two was palpable.

Magembe, in addition to his musical pursuits, was committed to community causes. In July 1964, as chair of the Uganda Musicians Union, he organized a charity fundraiser for the destitute and disabled at the New African Club in Nakulabye. The venue had opened its doors in 1963 under the ownership of Aloysius Darlington "A.D." Lubowa, a minister in the Kabaka's government, who brought in four musicians from Southern Rhodesia, now Zimbabwe: Shelton Mazowe, Richard Majola, Henry Mumbu, and Ernest Zulu, to manage and perform at the club. The four had settled in Uganda in the late 1950s and were known for their talent and stage presence. The building that housed the club belonged to Mr. Katatanzi, from whom it had been leased. Despite the promising start, the club soon ran into financial trouble under the management of the musicians.

To keep the venue afloat, a group of well-connected Ugandans stepped in with both funding and moral support. They were Sam Odaka, minister of foreign affairs; Erifaz Kalangi Ntende (aka Phan Ntende), chairman of the Lint Marketing Board; Roger Mukasa, chairman of the Coffee Marketing Board; and Sam Mukasa, then manager of Shell in Uganda. This fun-loving circle of friends were more than just financiers. They were the club's earliest and most loyal patrons, known for their easy camaraderie and shared enthusiasm for Kampala's nightlife. Their presence helped shape the atmosphere of the venue, giving it a convivial, welcoming spirit. With their support, the club was saved from closure. Later that year, it was renamed Susana Night Club, a name that would soon come to define one of Kampala's most glamorous and vibrant gathering spots.

It was in this setting that Magembe's gala evening unfolded, with the invited musicians dressed in tuxedos and the city's elite in attendance. The guest of honor was Miria Obote, the stylish wife of Prime Minister Milton Obote, whose presence lent an additional air of prestige. Dressed in a shimmering silk gown, she embodied grace as she joined Magembe on the dance floor. He, resplendent in a crisp white tuxedo and bowtie, moved with practiced elegance. Their poised ballroom steps, performed before a cheering crowd of dignitaries and socialites, made the evening unforgettable, not only as a fundraiser but also as a milestone moment in the early history of Susana.

It was also on that glittering night that Kampala's residents first encountered a musical force who had already captured hearts across the country: Aloziyo Nnyago. Although his fame had risen on the strength of his hit song Ekitobero ("One-Pot Dish"), it was at this event that he proved his star power could match that of the capital's most respected performers. Many of these performers often viewed musicians from outside the city as unsophisticated cousins. Nnyago stood tall, dark, and supremely self-assured. In a sharp black tuxedo and crisp white shirt, with golden cufflinks catching the light, he looked every bit the part of a national icon. His voice, rich and resonant, filled the room effortlessly when he took the stage to perform Ekitobero. The crowd erupted as his lyrics rang out, and by the chorus, the entire hall was singing along in unison. Beyond Ekitobero, Nnyago had a string of well-received recordings on the CMS label, including Getulida (a female name), Ekivulu ("Festival"), U.P.C. Obote, and Kyabazinga. The latter paid tribute to the cultural head of the Busoga region, an institution created by British colonial administrators in 1939 to unify the fragmented chiefdoms under a single ruler during the Uganda Protectorate. At the time, the Kyabazinga was William Wilberforce Nadiope Kadhumbula, a prominent royal figure and respected leader who later served as Uganda's first Vice President.

Despite his immense talent and popularity, Nnyago was a volatile and flamboyant figure, known for his fiery temper and, at times, violent outbursts. Behind the polished exterior was a man often drawn to trouble. In the years following his musical peak, Nnyago became entangled in Busoga's criminal underworld, joining gangs involved in violent robberies. Accounts of his final days vary, but the most widely reported version suggests that in the 1980s, during a robbery in Nankoma township in Bukooli, his violent lifestyle finally caught up with him. Government soldiers, called in to rescue the victims, engaged in a firefight with the gang. Nnyago was killed in the confrontation.

In 1964, Ecklas Kawalya and Fred Kanyike left Kampala City Six to form their own band, The Stars. This move followed a trend set by Andrew Kyambadde, Simon Kaate Nsubuga, and Fred Masagazi, who had earlier departed from Kampala City Six to pursue more lucrative opportunities in other musical ventures. The departure of Kawalya and Kanyike dealt a crushing blow to Kampala City Six, stripping the group of two of its top talents and further destabilizing the already fragile band. The timing of Kanyike's and Kawalya's exit could not have been worse. Kampala City Six faced mounting pressure from the rising dominance of Kampala's Congolese bands, which were better organized and boasted a deeper, more versatile talent pool. At the same time, the musical tastes of club-goers were rapidly shifting, influenced by the vibrant, dynamic rhythms of Congolese icons such as Franco Luambo Makiadi, Tabu Ley Rochereau, and Dr. Nico Kassanda. Their songs featured ricocheting guitar lines and complex arrangements that delighted Ugandan audiences. This new, infectious energy stood in stark contrast to the sound Kampala City

Six had long cultivated, a Cuban-inspired fusion rooted in the 1950s African Jazz style of Grand Kallé. As the Congolese wave swept through Kampala's dance halls, Kampala City Six struggled to keep pace.

By 1968, the band found itself increasingly marginalized from the nightlife scene that had once sustained its popularity. In June of that year, however, they mounted one final high-profile appearance at a charity concert held at Florida Nightclub in Kibuye, an area popularly known as "Kubiri" (Two Miles), bustling with bars and located on the outskirts of the city's main business district. The venue itself had a rich and layered history. It originally opened in the late 1950s as the Kit Kat Bar, under the ownership of Patel, an Indian-Ugandan businessman. In 1964, Patel sold the establishment to Erifaz Kalangi Ntende, chairman of the Lint Marketing Board, and Joseph Mary Mubiru, who would later become the first Governor of the Bank of Uganda. After acquiring the venue, they renamed it Satellite Nightclub, marking a new chapter in its history.

Four years later, in 1968, ownership passed to Mrs. Florence Alice Lubega, sister of Israel Magembe. Lubega had already made history as the first Ugandan woman appointed to the Legislative Council and, at independence in 1962, as the country's first female Member of Parliament. In 1967, she was appointed Deputy Minister for Community Development and Labor, becoming the first Ugandan woman to hold any ministerial-level position. She continued in this role even after Idi Amin overthrew Milton Obote's government in 1971.

By acquiring the nightclub, Lubega broke another important barrier. She became the first Ugandan woman to own and manage a major nightclub in Kampala. This was a remarkable achievement at a time when few women were seen in leadership roles in the private sector, let alone in the nightlife and entertainment industry. Her decision to step into this male-dominated space challenged conventional expectations of what women in politics or public life could do. It reflected a strong spirit of independence and a clear desire to shape cultural spaces on her own terms. She renamed the venue Florida, a nod to her own first name, and brought to it both elegance and a well-honed political instinct. Determined to establish Florida as Kampala's premier nightclub, Florence Lubega engaged in careful and strategic negotiations until she succeeded in attracting Vox Nationale, the celebrated Congolese rumba band that had brought fame to Kamulu's New Life nightclub. The move sent shockwaves through Kampala's music community. Kamulu, long known for his fierce competitiveness and relentless pursuit of top musical talent, had been outmaneuvered by Lubega's quiet persistence and shrewd leadership.

With Vox Nationale installed as the resident band and supported by a second ensemble, the Florida Fiesta Band, the venue swiftly rose in stature. Florida became one of Kampala's most respected nightclubs, known for its polished performances, elegant atmosphere, and diverse clientele. Florence Lubega drew some of the country's finest performers to the stage, including Sarah Namagembe, Fred Masagazi, and Fred Kanyike. Louise Bagenda also became a frequent guest artist, adding further prestige to the club's musical lineup.

Lubega managed Florida until 1971. That year, as President Amin began to show an unwelcome personal interest in her affairs, she made the decision to sell the nightclub and leave the country. She went into exile in the United Kingdom. The venue changed ownership once more and was renamed the Arizona Nightclub. Although her time as a nightclub proprietor came to a close, the impact of Florence Lubega's accomplishments endured. Florida was not merely a nightclub under her stewardship. It became a powerful symbol of how a woman with vision, courage, and determination could redefine her role in public life and leave a lasting imprint on Uganda's cultural and social history.

Israel Magembe attempted a comeback in 1970, but by this time, the original lineup of Kampala City Six had disbanded and all the founding members had moved on. To breathe new life into his music, Magembe enlisted the help of the Top Ten Band of Joseph Ndugga and the vocal delivery of Tony Ssenkebejje and Geoffrey Nsereko. However, due to legal and contractual constraints, the band could not record under its usual name. To navigate this thorny issue, they adopted the name United Artists Band for the recording session. The songs that were finally released included some of Magembe's earlier hits, including Millie Gwe Sherry and Omukwano Gwaffe Guffe. Magembe also recorded and released new songs, such as Olunaku Lwenkya (The Day of Tomorrow) and Jane Jukira (Remember Jane). Despite this effort, the songs failed to capture the magic of his earlier successes, and Magembe's attempt to reclaim his former glory remained largely unfulfilled. The once-promising star of Kampala City Six had dimmed, overshadowed by the changing tides of the music industry and the rise of new, more influential musical forces.

In November 1969, Sir Edward Mutesa died in poverty in a modest London apartment. After the overthrow of Milton Obote in January 1971, the new military government under Gen. Idi Amin arranged for Mutesa's body to be returned to Uganda as an "act of national reconciliation." An estimated 200,000 Ugandans filed past the body as it lay in state for three days at Namirembe Anglican Cathedral. Magembe, a close friend of the late Kabaka, collaborated with Fred Kabuye and Paul Kasozi to release Amada Genjole (The Return of the Body), a mournful song expressing their love for the king and sorrow at his death in exile. The song sharply criticized Obote for exiling the Kabaka and deposing him from his throne. Unlike Magembe's earlier rumba-style songs, Amada Genjole was composed in the kadongo kamu style. However, it received little airplay and remained relatively unknown.

By the mid-1970s, Magembe was seen to be over the hill with nothing new to offer. He had, in fact, stepped away from the leadership of Kampala City Six, passing the baton to Elly Bukenya, who assumed control of what remained of the group. Under Bukenya's leadership, the band continued to perform sporadically, mainly in and around Kampala. However, despite Bukenya's best efforts, he struggled to restore the band to the heights of its 1960s glory. The group's prominence had diminished, and the vibrant energy they once commanded was elusive and out of reach. Nonetheless, Kampala City Six had undeniably played a significant role in the development of the music scene in Uganda. Their influence was lasting, and their contribution to Uganda's music culture remained significant, even if their later years were marked by challenges in recapturing past success.

CHAPTER 5

Charles Sonko and the Kenyan Influence on Uganda's Music

Uganda's vibrant popular music scene of the late 1950s to mid-1960s emerged with remarkable energy, drawing significant influence from Kenyan musical innovation. At the heart of this evolution was the Kenyan Twist, a dynamic style that emerged from the famed Equator Sound Studios on Victoria Street in Nairobi. Kenyan Twist seamlessly blended the rebellious edge of rock 'n' roll, the intricate rhythms of Congolese rumba, the pulsating beats of South African kwela, and the soulful melodies of traditional Kenyan instruments, creating a sound that Ugandan audiences could easily relate to. Although Ugandans might not have seen Chubby Checker, the face and voice behind the Twist phenomenon, perform, they embraced the dance with enthusiasm and made it their own.

Kenyan musicians were much beloved in Uganda, with celebrated artists such as Fundi Konde, Daniel Katuga, Ben Nicholas, Esther Nicholas, and George Mukabi capturing the public's imagination. One standout hit was the ballad Kipenzi Waniua Ua (Sweetheart Killing Me Softly), composed by Joseph Ndalo. Featuring Ben Nicholas on clarinet and vocals, Esther Nicholas on vocals, and Fundi Konde's expressive guitar work, the song became a major sensation. Another memorable contribution to this era was George Mukabi's Mtoto Si Nguo (A Child Is Not a Piece of Cloth). Mukabi, renowned for his intricate finger-picking technique and sharp social commentary, even incorporated a Fanta bottle as a percussion instrument. His lyrics powerfully conveyed the message that a child, unlike a dress that can be lent or returned, must be treated with deeper care and responsibility, a theme that struck a particularly strong chord in Uganda.

The advent of the Kenya Twist further enriched Uganda's musical offerings, introducing an even broader array of talented Kenyan performers. This new wave featured figures such as Daudi Kabaka, affectionately known as the "King of Twist." Kabaka was born in Kyambogo, Uganda, and later returned to Kenya in the late 1950s. He was named after Kabaka Daudi Chwa, as he was born in the same year the Kabaka passed away. Alongside him were celebrated artists like Fadhili William of Malaika fame, David Amunga, John Ondolo, John Mwale, John Nzenze (also known as John Amutabi), Edward Nandwa, and many others. Notably, David Amunga's America to Africa, performed in English, evoked a nostalgic longing for the continent and demonstrated how Kenyan musical innovation could capture the airwaves in Uganda.

Several factors explain Uganda's gravitation towards Kenyan music and the subsequent adoption of emerging Kenyan popular styles. This was not mere imitation but rather a natural convergence of cultural, economic, and historical forces that had long bound the two regions. Long before colonial borders were imposed, the areas now divided between Uganda and Kenya formed a culturally continuous landscape. Communities such as the Samia, Gisu, and Teso originally lived in a unified and contiguous region that was later divided by colonial boundaries. These groups maintained close familial, linguistic, and social ties across what would become an artificial boundary drawn by British administrators. Especially in the pre-independence era, the porous nature of this border enabled the free movement of people, ideas, and, crucially, musical influences that flowed naturally across the region.

Moreover, during the 1950s and 1960s, Uganda emerged as an attractive destination for many Kenyans seeking new opportunities. The promise of work on coffee, sugar, and tea plantations, combined with the rise of modern industries in towns like Tororo, Mbale, Jinja, and Kampala, drew large numbers of Kenyans, especially from the western province. This migration was further encouraged by economic policies implemented by the British colonial administrations, which actively promoted closer ties between the two territories. A Customs Union was established as early as 1917, and by the 1930s integrated services such as the East African Meteorological Service (1929) and the postal and telegram system (1933) were in place. The formation of the East African Common Services at the end of 1961 further strengthened these ties, prompting Kenyans to move to Uganda for positions with the East African Railways and Harbors. In Kampala, many Kenyans settled in neighborhoods such as Naguru Housing Estate, Kiswa, Nakawa, Kibuli, Nsambya, Wabigalo and Makerere. This influx not only enriched Uganda's workforce but also spurred a dynamic cultural exchange, as shared urban experiences of both hardship and hope found expression in music.

The music brought by these Kenyan migrants found a natural connection with Ugandan audiences. Its exciting melodies and vibrant rhythms shared the tonal warmth and percussive character of traditional Ugandan instruments like the endongo lyre, the ndigidi fiddle, the endere flute, and various drums. The use of Swahili in lyrics, a language widely understood in both countries, made the songs accessible to the burgeoning urban middle class. For instance, John Nzenze's Angelike Twist was more than a catchy tune; it evoked a deep sense of longing and nostalgia, allowing urban listeners to imagine the beauty and calm of the rural life they had left behind. His Simu Kutoka Ulaya (A Phone Call from Europe), a romantic plea wrapped in playful sensuality, placed the beloved Amina in a faraway place, symbolically in Europe, but more profoundly representing the emotional distance between two worlds. While Europe suggested glamour and remoteness, the song spoke to a more familiar divide: the gulf between those who had moved to town and those left behind in the village. In asking Amina for just one kiss to bring him joy, Nzenze captured the ache of separation, the strain of love stretched across physical and emotional borders. Beneath its light-hearted tone lay a quiet sadness, an expression of the loneliness, longing, and fractured intimacy that often accompanied migration to the city.

Daudi Kabaka captured the zeitgeist of urban life with Bachelor Boy, a song that explored the allure of hedonism while rejecting the traditional expectations of marriage. Similarly, Isaya Mwinamo's Julieta Uko Wapi (Where Are You, Julieta?) tapped into the universal theme of longing for a loved one. Beyond romance, Kenyan musicians also addressed the everyday struggles of urban living. These narratives of hardship and aspiration, reflected in songs that became anthems of the time, resonated deeply in Uganda and even influenced the adoption of the twist dance. The songs, which vividly portrayed the challenges faced by new city dwellers, became deeply woven into the rhythms of daily life in the townships.

In the 1960s and 1970s, Ugandan musicians such as Stanley Kamparo and Freddie Kanyike explored similar themes, crafting sharp, relatable narratives about the triumphs and trials of urban existence. Their lyrics conveyed urgency, wit, and realism, as heard in Kanyike's Sitenda Kiri Kampala (Can't Chronicle Enough What Is In Kampala) and Kamparo's Kampala City. These songs spoke directly to the growing wave of rural migrants who had descended upon Kampala and other Ugandan towns in search of opportunity and a better life. What many encountered instead was a jarring reality: everything came at a cost, even water, starkly contrasting with the expectations and communal rhythms of the villages they had left behind. The city, however, did not sever ties with the countryside. Migrants maintained homes and land in their villages, sent remittances, and returned regularly, creating a rural-urban continuum that shaped not only their daily lives but also the music itself, giving it a dual texture that was modern in outlook yet still deeply rooted in rural identity.

The popularity of Kenyan musicians in Uganda can also be traced to their successful tours and collaborations with Ugandan musicians. The exchange between Kenyan and Ugandan music was not confined to radio waves and record sales. Live performances played a crucial role, with numerous Kenyan musicians undertaking successful tours of Uganda and leaving a lasting impression on the local scene. Fundi Konde, Ben Nicholas, Esther Nicholas, and Daniel Katuga, luminaries of Kenyan music, spent significant time in Uganda, notably collaborating with the K-Rhino Boys at Kamulu's in Mengo. Their presence sparked a creative synergy, which led to collaborations with Ugandan talents such as Eva Nanyonga and Jane Kyahurwa in the early 1950s. Among the more distinctive figures was the talented Kenyan Luhya musician Sichangi Wambilianga, who gained popularity in Uganda with songs sung in fluent Luganda. Released on the Kenyan CMS label, his hits included Suzza (a female name) and Kutereka Sente (Saving Money). In Kutereka Sente, Sichangi playfully praises the modern woman's remarkable ability to save money, often more than men. With tongue-in-cheek humor, he asks, "Where do the women get their money from?" and answers that it is actually the men who give it to them. The song, lighthearted and witty, was a smashing favorite among Ugandan listeners.

The mid-1950s also saw Fadhili William and his Chem Chem Kids Band thrilling Kampala audiences with their energetic performances. Their concerts drew massive crowds, underscoring the popularity of Kenyan music in Uganda. However, it was the arrival of Sheila Monroe in 1961 that truly ignited a frenzy.

Sheila Monroe, an alluring and charismatic Kenyan singer and a member of the iconic Jambo Boys (later renamed Equator Boys Band), was already a star in her own right. She had also established herself as a solo performer at Nairobi's New Swiss Grill Club and Hotel on Salisbury Road, where she excelled at interpreting popular English songs. Her arrival in Kampala was highly anticipated, especially with the opening of La Quinta, a new nightclub owned by Norman Godinho.

Norman Godinho, a Goan business magnate who had made Uganda his home since 1906, transformed the former Tabaris, a social gathering place for the Goan community, into La Quinta, a sophisticated nightclub located on the upper floor of the Norman Cinema building on Bombo Road. Godinho envisioned La Quinta as a premier entertainment venue, catering to the British colonial administrators, businessmen, and a select few Asians and Black Ugandans. The club's resident band was tasked with playing western music, reflecting the tastes of its intended clientele. The grand opening of La Quinta in April 1961 was to feature Sheila Monroe as the star attraction. Godinho promised a lavish night of entertainment, and Sheila arrived at Entebbe Airport in the early afternoon, proceeding to the Speke Hotel (also owned by Godinho) to prepare for her performance. The resident band at La Quinta consisted mostly of Makerere University students, many of whom also played in the Makerere Jazz Band led by Peter Nazareth. Though bright and eager, they lacked the polish and adaptability of seasoned professionals. As the band launched into the opening number, Sheila Monroe, elegant and exacting, froze in place. She raised a hand, cutting the music short, and demanded a restart. But when the second attempt fell just as flat, she turned to the audience and, with a dramatic flourish, announced, "I cannot sing with this combination. There's no piano, and the boys are not used to changing key. Without a change in key, when needed, no chanteuse can sing." With that, she walked off the stage, leaving behind stunned silence and murmurs rippling through the crowd.

Instead, Sheila embarked on a spontaneous tour of Kampala's indigenous nightclubs, places frequented by Black Ugandans. Dressed in a striking rose-pink gown, she was instantly recognized and warmly welcomed. The bands invited her to perform, and she obliged, singing a few songs at each venue to the delight of the enthusiastic crowds. While it is plausible that Sheila's departure from La Quinta was motivated by her perception of its discriminatory practices, it is important to note that the nightclub later evolved into an inclusive venue, featuring local Ugandan musicians. Indeed, Norman Godinho played a significant role in promoting racial harmony in a society deeply divided by segregation. His actions, while perhaps initially guided by business interests, contributed to a gradual shift towards inclusivity.

The dominance of Kenyan music in Uganda was fueled not only by cultural and economic ties but also by the ease with which Kenyan musicians accessed modern recording facilities. Whereas Uganda had only one commercial recording studio—Opel Gramophone Records, owned by Georg von Opel, which was forced to close in 1960 due to the Uganda National Movement boycott of foreign-owned businesses—commercial recording in Kenya thrived. Kenya boasted several well-run studios and prestigious record labels, meaning that Ugandan musicians often traveled east of the border to record their songs, and they were spoiled for choice.

In the early 1950s, the South African Gallo Record Company established an office and state-of-the-art recording studios in Nairobi. By 1961, Gallo's recording business had been sold to the United Kingdom's Green Brothers, who then set up a wholly owned Kenyan subsidiary, Associated Sound (East Africa) Limited. Their famous ASL label focused on Congolese musicians who were rising in popularity across East Africa. Additionally, Assanand & Son released songs on the Mzuri label, further enriching Kenya's musical offerings.

Among the recording studios, three Kenyan companies stood out for releasing the bulk of Ugandan music on vinyl from the late 1950s to the mid-1960s. These were Capitol Music Store (CMS), owned by Meghji Karm Shah; Africa Gramophone Service (later known as Africa Gramophone Store, or AGS), founded by Maganlal Jethalal Shah; and Charles Worrod's Equator Sound Studio Ltd, which was originally known as East African Records when he acquired it. East African Records had previously operated the Jambo label, with the Jambo Boys Band as its house ensemble. Each of these studios maintained their own stable of session musicians, predominantly Kenyan, but they also featured artists from across the region, including Zambians Peter "Tsotsi" Juma and Nashil Pichen Kazembe, as well as the versatile Ugandan musician Charles Sonko.

Charles Sonko's contributions to this vibrant musical era illustrate the kind of cross-border exchange that enriched East African popular music. Charles was born in 1932 in Kidukulu, a small village along the banks of River Lugogo in Bulemezi, central Uganda, to Mr. Blasio Kasiko (a Muganda) and his Mutoro wife, Kasalina. He was the younger half-brother of Frida Basuta, widely known as Frida Sonko, one of the most iconic Ugandan female musicians of the post-independence era and among the most recognizable voices of her generation. Frida and Charles shared the same mother, but not the same father. Frida's biological father was never identified, although she grew up regarding Kasiko as her own. Sonko began his schooling in Kidukulu but dropped out around the age of twelve. In 1944, he and his older sister Frida, who was two years his senior, left for Nairobi to join their parents, who had moved there in search of work as casual laborers.

From a young age, Charles Sonko showed a deep interest in music, particularly the guitar. He was inspired by Ugandan groups such as the Rhino Boys and the Mengo African Orchestra. He also drew significant influence from pioneering Kenyan musicians including Fundi Konde and Daniel Katuga. In Nairobi, Sonko did not return to school but instead took a job as a shamba boy, tending the lush green gardens of a colonial-style home owned by an Italian family in Nakuru. It was in this household that he first encountered the Hawaiian guitar. The master of the home played the instrument and taught Sonko how to use it. Sonko proved a quick and gifted learner, eventually playing the guitar with even greater finesse than his teacher. His mastery was so unexpected that the Italian man was astonished at how naturally Sonko had taken to the instrument. He developed a signature style that combined a distinctive walking bass line with the fluid and expressive tones of the Hawaiian guitar.

Confident in his abilities, Sonko left Nakuru for Kisumu, where he secured a regular performance slot with the resident band at Kamal's Hotel. Known for his muscular build, engaging stage presence, and free-spirited nature, Sonko quickly became a popular figure in Kisumu's lively social scene. He fully embraced the nightlife, which included drinking, smoking, and romantic escapades, all while enchanting audiences with his remarkably mature and soulful voice. While in Kisumu, Sonko fell deeply in love with a local Jaluo woman named Auma. Their passionate romance inspired the Swahili song Mahaba ya Dunia (World of Love), recorded in the early 1960s on the CMS label. In this evocative track, with Sonko on bass and Abudu Kazoba on rhythm guitar, he reflects on Auma's genuine affection and the sleepless nights he spent yearning for her. The song paints a tender and revealing portrait of Jaluo love. Despite their bond, Auma's love was not enough to keep him in Kisumu. Bored with the routine at Kamal's Hotel and driven by a desire to record his own music, Sonko began seeking new opportunities.

At the time, Kisumu had no modern recording studio, so in the early 1950s he returned to Nairobi. There, he immersed himself in the thriving musical scene along the city's famed River Road, where artists from across East Africa converged to create, perform, and record. This marked a new chapter in Sonko's musical journey, one that would see him emerge as one of the most distinctive and influential Ugandan musicians of his generation.

River Road pulsed with a raw, energetic rhythm, a stark contrast to the more sedate avenues of colonial Nairobi. It was a place where the city's heartbeat was palpable, a mix of commerce, ambition, and the daily struggle for survival. This bustling thoroughfare was dotted with Indian-run shops and many African street vendors hawking their wares. But most importantly, River Road was home to music recording studios that attracted artists from across the region. By day, its streets teemed with vendors and local chatter; by night, neon lights and the pulse of live music transformed it into a haven for musicians seeking inspiration and collaboration. Here, Sonko forged bonds with fellow artists such as Tom Miti, Fadhili William, Abudu Kazoba, Nashil Pichen, and Peter Tsotsi, sharing ideas and dreams amid the electrifying musical energy of the city.

Before long, Sonko was backing many of these musicians during studio sessions, earning modest shillings for his contributions. The energy of River Road, combined with the vibrancy of Majengo and Eastleigh, became a wellspring of inspiration for his growing artistry. Sonko lived on the border of Majengo and Eastleigh, a Nairobi neighborhood that embodied the city's shifting identity. Its narrow, winding, and often unpaved streets buzzed with life, teeming with diverse communities that included local Kenyan tribes, other Africans, Indians, and Yemenis. Modest shops and makeshift market stalls overflowed with goods ranging from fragrant spices and vivid textiles to fresh produce and handmade trinkets. For a young musician, it was a world alive with rhythm, color, and endless possibility.

Charles Sonko's journey took a significant turn when he secured a position with East African Records Ltd. Working as a studio assistant and bass guitarist, he became part of the itinerant group of session musicians known as the Jambo Boys Band. These freelance players were called upon whenever the studio needed their expertise. They were not salaried employees, but their talent was indispensable. A fortuitous encounter with Daniel Katuga would dramatically alter Sonko's fortunes. Katuga, who had spent time in Uganda and fallen in love with the Ugandan musician Jane Kyahurwa, was a former member of the Rhino Boys and K-Rhino Boys. He was an ardent admirer of Uganda's cultural heritage and even learned Luganda to deepen his connection. Impressed by Sonko's bass guitar prowess and stirring vocals, Katuga recognized a kindred spirit. Sonko had already recorded some of his early songs on the South African Gallotone label in the early 1950s, including Tabu Juyake (Problems Because of Him/Her) and Bwana Byo Malaya (The Pimp). With contacts at CMS, Katuga introduced Sonko to studio managers, opening doors that had previously been closed.

Around this time in the late 1950s, Sonko and his close associates, Nashil Pichen, Peter Tsotsi, and Fadhili William, formed the short-lived Congo River Band. This pioneering ensemble is reputed to have been the first Kenyan band to routinely incorporate Congolese-style rhumba songs into their repertoire. Their innovative blend of styles marked a significant milestone in the evolution of Kenyan popular music. The band achieved notable success on the CMS label with a string of Swahili hits, including Zainabu Ukowapi (Zainabu, Where Are You?), Hata Kaburini (Till Death), and Kazi Na Fanya (I Work at a Job). Their repertoire also featured evocative tracks such as Wezi wa Mifuko (Pickpockets) and Wakora wa Eastleigh (The Crooks of Eastleigh), which powerfully narrated the hardships faced by many Black Africans in Nairobi's rundown neighborhoods.

During the Congo River Band period, Charles Sonko also recorded under the name K.B. Charles on the CMS label. The initials "K.B." stood for Kasiko Balaba, with Kasiko being his father's name, and Balaba a cherished uncle who had no children of his own but treated Sonko like the son he never had. In adopting these initials, Sonko paid homage to the two men who shaped his early life, grounding his musical identity in family loyalty and love. His catalog from this period includes several memorable songs marked by the gentle sway of Hawaiian guitar melodies, such as Abakyala Nokusaba (The Entreaties of Women) and Abaganda Edda (The Baganda [People] of the Past). Sonko continued to contribute prolifically to the CMS roster, later recording Komawo Jaliya (Come Back Jaliya) and the resonant duet Teridagala Mukwagala (There Is No Medicine in Love) with influential Ugandan musician Margaret Nakibuuka. In this lively twist beat, punctuated by bouncy, syncopated chords, Sonko and Nakibuuka sang about the irresistible law of attraction that binds lovers together. Their message was clear: those who disapprove should keep their judgment to themselves, for "love is love, everywhere," and no one should be chained or beaten simply for choosing their own partner.

Continuing the celebration of personal choice in love, Sonko extended this theme with a soulful duet in the Congolese rhumba style titled Mulekere Amwagala (Leave It to the Lover). In this heartfelt collaboration with his sister Frida, the song emphasized that a couple's decision to love each other is a private matter deserving respect, free from the judgment of others. The gentle interplay of harmonized vocals, intricate guitar work, and smooth percussion created a warm, inviting atmosphere that encouraged listeners to honor the sanctity of personal relationships and let love flourish on its own terms:

> Why does a red chili pepper you have never tasted still burn you?
> None of them share your bed
> How could you even recognize their scent?
> This is not your concern; release your jealousy.
> Why they love each other
> Is theirs alone to understand.
> When you love someone else,
> You do not dwell on their flaws.
> Even if you speak endless words,

It changes nothing:
When two souls are in love,
Your jealousy becomes irrelevant.

Through his collaborations, recordings, and growing reputation, Charles Sonko positioned himself as a bridge between Ugandan and Kenyan popular music, setting the stage for even greater influence in the years to come. When Charles Worrod acquired East African Records in 1960 and rebranded the studio as Equator Sound Studios Ltd. the following year, a new chapter began in the region's musical evolution. Charles Sonko remained an integral member of the studio band, known as the Equator Boys or, alternatively, the Equator Sounds Band. The original lineup included prominent talents such as Fadhili William, Daudi Kabaka, Peter "Tsotsi" Juma, Benson Simbeye, and Nashil Pichen Kazembe. Later, the group expanded with the addition of Gabriel Omolo, who would later achieve fame with his 1970s hit Lunch Time, and Frida Basuta, Charles' sister, who provided backup vocals on numerous tracks. Frida later adopted her brother's surname and became more widely known as Frida Sonko. However, her earliest recordings were released under her birth name, Frida Basuta. Among these were 1961 duets with Moses Katazza on the CMS label, including Mukwano Gwange Twist (My Friend Twist), Uganda Cha Cha Cha, and Mukyala Twist (Lady Twist). She would go on to enjoy a successful solo career, building on the momentum of those early performances.

Charles Sonko emerged as a prolific composer, releasing a remarkable array of songs on the studio's Equator label. Among his most influential contributions was the seminal track Harambee (Let's Pull Together), a collaboration with Daudi Kabaka and Fadhili William released in 1964. This landmark song was set to a medley combining the stirring American marching tune John Brown's Body with the British patriotic anthem Rule Britannia. By fusing these familiar melodies in an innovative way, Harambee struck a chord with listeners from diverse backgrounds. With lyrics penned by Daudi Kabaka and arranged in the distinctive Kenya twist rhythm, a style in which all three artists excelled, the song was embraced with enthusiasm across the nation. Its innovative blend of musical traditions and impassioned call for unity elevated Harambee to the status of a second national anthem in Kenya. The instrumental rendition by the Kenya Army Band, later adopted as the Voice of Kenya radio news theme tune, ensured that its stirring message remained iconic well into the 1990s.

The song resonated powerfully during a pivotal moment in Kenyan history. In December 1963 at Uhuru Stadium in Nairobi, the British Union Jack was lowered and replaced by the new flag featuring black, red, and green, a symbol of the dawn of independence and the end of British colonial rule in East Africa. As the colonial power withdrew, Kenya was determined to nurture the spirit of unity forged during its arduous struggle for freedom. The following year, Harambee captured this fervent sentiment perfectly, urging the nation to pull together for progress and the common good.

At Equator Sound Studios, Charles Sonko balanced roles as both a session musician and a studio assistant. As part of the Equator Boys, he and his fellow musicians received a retainer fee for recording projects while retaining the freedom to work with other labels. Their creative fluency and instrumental skill carried over to live performances as well. Their debut public performance took place in Nairobi at the grand opening ceremony of Noormohamed Hirji's Hallian's Nightclub on Victoria Street, now known as Tom Mboya Street.

Throughout his prolific musical career spanning over four decades, Charles Sonko worked on numerous solo and collaborative projects, amassing a rich recorded repertory that featured major hits across multiple Kenyan record labels. His artistic vision was both bold and eclectic, experimenting with a wide range of musical genres in a way that few Ugandan musicians had ever attempted. This adventurous spirit, coupled with his considerable success, enshrines Charles Sonko in the annals of Ugandan music as one of its most fascinating and remarkable artists.

In 1979, while in Nairobi, Jamie Candelaria-Greene, an American professor of special education volunteering with the Peace Corps, had the opportunity to meet Sonko. An amateur musician herself, Jamie collab-orated with him on at least four songs. Among these were the two-part Refugee Song, released on the Kenya CBS label, and a reworking of the early 1960s classic I Must Confess, originally recorded by Charles and his sister Frida Sonko on the Equator label. Although the version with Jamie was never officially released, Jamie recalled her experience with great admiration. She described Charles Sonko as an easy-going, multidimen-sional musician with gracious mannerisms, comparing him to influential figures like George Martin and Quincy Jones. According to Jamie, had Sonko resided in the industrialized West, his innovative artistry might have earned him worldwide acclaim as one of the most influential musicians of the latter half of the twentieth century.

Charles Sonko's musical journey continued to evolve under the aegis of Charles Worrod's Equator Sound Studio, which was instrumental in creating and popularizing the Kenya twist rhythm throughout East Africa in the early 1960s. In embracing this exuberant style, Sonko did more than master the Kenya twist, using it as a springboard to deepen and diversify his musical expression. Among his forays into the genre, Kampala Twist and Heart Beat Twist stand out not merely as catchy dance tunes, but as artful compositions that reveal his rhythmic ingenuity. Recorded on the Equator label with the dynamic backing of the Banana Boys, a group of friends assembled specifically for the session, both tracks were later licensed to Associated Sound (East Africa) Limited and released under the ASL label. Kampala Twist explodes with an energetic, driving lead guitar, a doo-wop rhythm, and a feisty bassline, all complementing Sonko's urgent, impassioned croon. In this track, he sings to Namuddu, a beauty from his past, imploring her to wait a little longer as he prepares to ask for her hand in marriage. His emotional lyrics, "Namuddu, you sure cause me to suffer / Namuddu, mama / Heard you haven't married / Namuddu, I too haven't / Namuddu, keep our promise," capture the poignant yearning and anticipation of young love.

In contrast, Heart Beat Twist adopts a slightly more measured pace, unfolding as a delightful love ballad infused with echoes of American country music. This track not only highlights Sonko's versatility but also his ability to weave together diverse musical influences into a cohesive and emotionally resonant narrative. Charles Sonko sings in a deliberate, measured tone:

My heart loves you,
My blood gives its blessing,
My eyes behold you,
My body urges me
To love you,
To hold you within my soul,
Just the two of us in our home,
Celebrating each day.

Charles Sonko also embraced the Hawaiian guitar, drawing inspiration from the K-Rhino Boys and the 1950s Congolese musician Zacharie "Jhimmy" Elenga, who is credited with introducing the slack-key guitar style to Congolese music. This innovative technique was later adopted by his protégé and fellow Congolese musician, Dr. Nico Kasanda wa Mikalay. Sonko's own sliding guitar style is evident in his early recordings on the AGS label during the latter half of the 1950s. Notable examples include Nini Bibi We (What's the Matter, Lady?) and Maria Sweet Rudi (Come Back, Sweet Maria). The latter, set to the tune of Harry Belafonte's Jamaica Farewell, was performed in collaboration with the Kenyan guitarist and singer Tom Miti, and both tracks exude a distinct calypso feel. Another early AGS recording illustrated Sonko's versatility through the dual piece Anna Maria and Ogabira Nongo (Gift the Lyre). In this work, Anna Maria, sung in the Lutoro language of his mother, carries a relaxed, jazzy flair, while Ogabira Nongo draws on influences from Hawaiian and Latin music traditions.

Further expanding his creative horizons, in 1960 Sonko teamed up with his compatriot and friend, Saimon "Sai" Kaate Nsubuga, who provided backup vocals and played lead guitar, to release two Congolese rhumba-style songs on the AGS African Voice label: Oyo Akimanye (That One Ought to Know) and Eroni Yabula (Eroni Is Missing). The latter drew directly from Sonko's personal life. It tells the poignant story of his wife, Eroni Nalunga, a deeply poised and radiant woman, whose memory remained etched in Sonko's heart long after their parting. Though he had many women in his life, Eroni was his one true love. Their marriage ended in separation, a heartbreak from which he never fully recovered. A heartbroken Sonko sang:

I cry for the one I have lost,
Eroni, oh Eroni,
I cry for the one who has left,
Eroni, oh Eroni,
I cry for my dearest Eroni.
I saw another face,
But none can match your light,
I found someone new,
But they never shine as bright,
Even a youthful love I embraced,
Leaves a hunger in my heart.

Eroni is also the subject of another of Sonko's memorable songs, Ani Atanfako (Who Is Ignoring Me). In this poignant composition, he laments the loss of Eroni, who abandoned him in Nairobi to return to Kampala, while simultaneously expressing gratitude for the children she bore him. The song captures a bittersweet mix of sorrow and thankfulness.

In Oyo Akimanye (That One Should Know), Sonko made his debut in the challenging realm of political commentary and subtle flattery. At a time when Uganda was preparing for independence from Britain, the nation was divided between two contrasting political factions. On one side were the neo-traditionalists and tribalists, staunch defenders of tribal solidarity under the Kabaka of Buganda, who championed his unchallenged political leadership and sought special status for his kingdom and subjects in an independent Uganda. On the other side was a multi-tribal coalition that embraced the broader promise of national independence. The former group eventually coalesced into a loyalist movement known as Kabaka Yekka (Only the King). Oyo Akimanye served as a propagandistic anthem for the Kabaka Yekka movement, stirring up local Buganda patriotism and warning against any challenge to the Kabaka's political authority. The song appears to have been aimed at prominent Baganda nationalists such as Benedicto Kiwanuka, Jolly Joe Kiwanuka, E.M.K. Mulira, Ignatius Musazi, and others who were perceived as traitors for placing loyalty to an independent Uganda above unwavering fealty to the Kabaka. The title Oyo Akimanye is a stern reminder that loyalty to Buganda and the Kabaka must never be compromised.

Beyond his contributions as a composer and vocalist, Charles Sonko was also a virtuoso on the guitar. He served as the bass guitarist on almost every Equator label recording from the label's inception until the mid-1960s, and he was the creative force behind the lilting, sliding guitar sounds that became a signature of Equator Sound Studio's productions.

In Teri Amusinga (There's No Better One), one of the many songs in which he backs his sister Frida Sonko, Charles Sonko lends his signature touch to the Hawaiian guitar, creating a shifting silhouette of an otherworldly sound. Teri Amusinga is a testament to the enduring power of love and the emotional rollercoaster it inspires. In this standout track, Charles weaves a wonderfully woozy twang, a mesmerizing blend of calming serenity and assertive passion, which perfectly complements Frida's heartfelt vocals. Frida, with her charmingly vulnerable delivery, lays bare the depths of her affection for a lover, confessing to a profound longing that borders on pain when they are apart:

> This love I have for you,
> It's a love I've never known before.
> Just listen!

When you're gone, the Mercedes gather,
Whispering and gossiping.
But I am not deceived.

When you're gone, the Volkswagens gather,
Buzzing and swirling around.
But I pay them no mind.

Then I see your car arrive,
And joy overwhelms me.
My hair stands on end, my blood races.

You begin to shine,
You sparkle from within.
And this feeling inside,
Should I weep, or should I rejoice?
I feel like I am floating, not of this world.

With the Equator Sound band, Charles Sonko enjoyed a series of mega-hits that were warmly received in Uganda. One standout track was Leero Wanyita (You Kill Me), an energetic song set to Latin mambo rhythms. Sung in the Lutoro language of western Uganda and released in 1964, this track, along with several others featuring his sister Frida, remains among the most remarkable and refreshing recordings of the 1960s. Charles, a prolific songwriter, was responsible for many of Frida's iconic hits. His compositions include Oh! Please Baby Love Me, I Must Confess, Omutwe Gwa Amaka (Head of Household), and Alojja Omukwano (Testifying About Love). The latter, better known as Wambuza (You Asked Me), emerged as a defining anthem of 1960s Uganda, celebrated for its evocative lyrics and mellow melody.

In Nairobi, Sonko's life appeared to be thriving. Although he possessed a fierce edge, he had a heart of gold. He was well-groomed, polite, and welcoming, often opening his doors to Ugandan musicians who traveled to Nairobi to record. He developed a close friendship with Moses Katazza, who spent many months at his Nairobi home, which he shared with his sister Frida. Sonko earned respect as a key member of the Equator Boys Band and, under the guidance of Charles Worrod, was promoted to assistant studio manager. This role, which came with the benefits of a salaried position, alleviated some of his chronic worries about money, a constant concern throughout his career. Worrod even allowed Sonko and his bandmates to use studio instruments for performances outside the studio, which further enhanced their musical output and improved their earnings.

Alongside his colleagues Nashil Pichen and Peter Tsotsi, Sonko co-founded the Golden Band Singers. This group performed in Nairobi clubs, and their cabaret shows featuring energetic Zulu dances were a great success. However, internal disagreements eventually led to the disbandment of the Golden Band Singers. Following this setback, Sonko left the Equator Boys Band and secured a position as a studio assistant at High Fidelity. There, he found a mentor in Mr. Hakam, a Kenyan of Indian origin who served as the studio controller. Hakam took Sonko under his wing, teaching him the intricacies of studio and recording work. It was at High Fidelity that Charles, together with his sister Frida, recorded the beautifully rendered rhumba duet Nga Walaganyiza (When You Have A Date Night) on the Philips label in 1967.

For years, Charles Sonko had yearned to return to Uganda, and in 1967, the pull of home proved irresistible. Ugandan music lovers greeted his return to Kampala with great enthusiasm. Initially, he worked with Kiyingi Studios, then a leading producer of catchy commercial jingles for Radio Uganda. Soon after, his friend and fellow musician Shelton Mazowe, affiliated with the management of Susana Nightclub in Nakulabye, offered him the position of club manager. In an April 1968 interview with *Taifa Empya*, a Ugandan newspaper, Sonko explained that his decision to return was driven by a desire to uplift the standard of Ugandan music. He also shared plans to build a recording studio in Kampala, a venture aimed at sparing local musicians from the costly journey to Nairobi for recording sessions. Even while managing Susana Nightclub, Sonko continued to appear on stage. Together with his sister Frida, who had also returned from Nairobi, they performed as part of the Susana Band, belting out their old hits that were favorites across the country.

By the late 1960s, Sonko grew increasingly disillusioned with his managerial role at Susana. Despite holding the title, he felt powerless to effect the changes needed to instill professionalism among the bar servers, whose recurrent absences and lack of courtesy frustrated him. Although he occasionally fired staff members, upper management routinely reinstated them without consultation, leaving him feeling undermined. Frustrated by these challenges, Sonko eventually resigned and formed the Sonko Dancers Group. The new group soon became a familiar presence on Ugandan television and Radio Uganda. Among the group's standout performers was Madina Najjemba, a graceful and captivating dancer. Madina came from a family with a rich tradition of performance, descended from generations of dancers who had entertained the kings of Buganda. In 1972, she married President Idi Amin, becoming his fourth wife.

Around this period, Sonko also recorded and released several compelling traditional songs such as Omukazi Wange (My Lady). In these tracks, he innovatively incorporated Western instruments into traditional melodies, creating a fusion style locally known as Kagutema. However, the creation of Kagutema in the early 1960s is credited to pioneers like Fred Masagazi and Ecklas Kawalya. Notably, Sonko and Frida had already made waves in this genre with the blistering 1968 hit Nawuliranga (I Will Always Obey), recorded on the Philips label and backed by a studio-created band named Orchestre Melo Success, which Sonko had founded. This studio band went on to provide instrumentation for other artists as well. They backed Margaret Nakibuuka and Betty Nankya on their songs Debula and Namusazi, and also supported Nelson Sabavuma on Ggolo Eri Emu (There's One Goal) and Steven Sempasa on Obuwulu Bunemye (Can't Bear Being Alone).

In Uganda during the 1960s and 1970s, it was common practice for musicians to assemble ad hoc studio groups for specific recordings. These were not standing bands in the traditional sense but rather flexible collectives of available instrumentalists and vocalists who would rehearse a song, often for just a few days, record it, and then disband. The same musicians might regroup under a different name for another project, depending on who initiated the recording. To lend these ephemeral groups an air of prestige or mystique, and often to suggest a Congolese pedigree, musicians would give them fancy-sounding names such as Orchestre Melo Success, Orchestre Bella Success, Orchestre Mambo Jazz, or Orchestre Success d'Afrique. The use of the term "Orchestre" was especially popular, having been borrowed from the naming conventions of Congolese bands whose influence loomed large over the region's musical imagination.

In many cases, the musicians behind these Ugandan recordings were members of Joseph Ndugga's Top Ten Band, who were contractually bound to Serenade Studios as session musicians and thus prohibited from recording elsewhere. To sidestep this limitation, they adopted alternate band names and moonlighted on the side. This improvisational and pragmatic approach to band formation reflected both the economic constraints of the local music industry and the collaborative spirit that defined the 1960s and early 1970s popular music scene in Uganda.

The Sonko Dancers Group enjoyed significant success in the early 1970s, securing a regular performance contract at the prestigious Kampala International Hotel, formerly known as Apollo Hotel during the 1960s. In 1971, Charles Sonko reached a turning point in his musical career. Motivated by a desire to serve his country, he made the momentous decision to join the Uganda Army. This choice must be understood within the wider political context and emotional climate of the time.

In January 1971, Uganda's military overthrew the increasingly repressive regime of Dr. Milton Obote. Obote, who had served as Prime Minister at independence in 1962, had removed the ceremonial President, Kabaka Mutesa II (King Freddie), in a violent 1966 coup. He then declared himself President and abolished the country's traditional kingdoms, including Buganda, a move that deeply alienated monarchists and plunged the region into a period of figurative mourning. When Maj. Gen. Idi Amin seized power, promising to restore law and order, organize free and fair elections, and return Uganda to civilian rule, the country erupted in celebration. Many, including Sonko, believed in the sincerity of Amin's promises. Having previously sung praises to the Kabaka, Sonko was swept up in the wave of hope that followed the coup. The military, eager to harness the power of music for morale and public image, actively courted artists like him.

Recognizing his popularity and artistic influence, the army made generous accommodations. Sonko was allowed to continue leading his traditional dance troupe while serving in uniform. In 1972, the military provided him with Western musical instruments, enabling him to form and manage a pop band based at the Mbuya army barracks called Charles Sonko & Party. He even recruited his sister Frida into the group. Grateful for the support and privileges extended by the new regime, Sonko publicly converted to Islam in a widely reported ceremony, adopting the name Rashid Charles Sonko. Like many such conversions at the time, the move helped consolidate his position within a government increasingly dominated by Muslim military and political elites. Alongside his band, Sonko continued to direct the Sonko Dancers Group, which soon caught the attention of Maj. Gen. Francis Nyangweso, Uganda's Minister of Culture and Community Development. Impressed by their skill and professionalism, Nyangweso brought the troupe under the ministry's patronage and ensured their participation in national festivals. Their prominence grew further after Madina Najjemba married President Idi Amin in 1972. Though she stopped performing after her marriage, now known as Madina Amin, she used her new position to advocate for the group and ensure they were well supported. From that point on, the Sonko Dancers Group operated as a semi-official national troupe, representing Uganda at cultural events and state functions.

With state backing, the troupe emerged as Uganda's cultural ambassadors, offering audiences at home and abroad a compelling window into the nation's heritage. In 1973, they received a major honor when they were invited to perform at State House in Nairobi before Mzee Jomo Kenyatta, Kenya's President. International tours followed, taking the group to Zaire (now the Democratic Republic of the Congo), Algeria, and even Moscow, all part of Amin's broader strategy of using cultural diplomacy to enhance Uganda's global image.

Later, Maj. Gen. Nyangweso integrated the Sonko Dancers Group into the national folklore ensemble known as Heartbeat of Africa. The group celebrated Uganda's rich cultural diversity and featured dancers from across the country, capable of performing a wide range of traditional dances, from the lively Baakisimba of Buganda to the graceful Larakaraka, a courtship dance of the Acholi people in the north. Under the banner of Heartbeat of Africa, Sonko and several members of the Sonko Dancers Group represented Uganda at the 1977 Festival of Arts and Culture (FESTAC '77) in Lagos, Nigeria. FESTAC '77 was a vibrant, month-long celebration that brought together thousands of people of African descent, aiming to revive and promote Black culture, values, and political solidarity. The Ugandan delegation, featuring a spirited performance by Heartbeat of Africa, garnered widespread acclaim. Among the highlights was Byron Kawadwa's play *Oluyimba Lwa Wankoko* (Song of the Rooster), a satirical critique of autocratic rule first staged in Uganda in 1969. Its performance in Lagos was met with enthusiasm, as many in the audience saw it as a timely call for justice and the restoration of the rule of law. With over 20 democratically elected governments across Africa having been overthrown by the military by the mid-1970s, the play's message found a receptive audience in a continent grappling with repression and disillusionment.

However, amid the celebrations, darker currents began to emerge. The FESTAC '77 experience was marred by tragedy and political turmoil. A week before the festival's official start, Prof. Pio Zirimu, a prominent Ugandan linguist and academic chosen to chair FESTAC's Colloquium, was found dead in his rental apartment in Lagos under mysterious circumstances. Many have suspected that his death had links to Idi Amin, and what lends credence to this suspicion was the fact that Ugandan newspapers at the time never mentioned Prof. Zirimu's death.

When Sonko and others returned from FESTAC, the political climate in Uganda had deteriorated sharply. The economy was in freefall, basic commodities had become scarce, and fear gripped the nation as people were routinely abducted and disappeared without a trace. Tensions rose further following the deaths of Most Rev. Janan Luwum, the Anglican Archbishop of Uganda, and cabinet ministers Erinayo Oryema and Charles Oboth Ofumbi. Though officially reported as victims of a car accident shortly after their arrest for allegedly plotting against Idi Amin's regime, few believed the story. Most were convinced that the killings had been ordered by Amin himself, and the shadow of state-sanctioned violence grew darker.

Tragedy continued to stalk the Uganda delegation that had attended FESTAC '77. Just a day after Archbishop Luwum's death, Byron Kawaddwa, who had returned early from Lagos with members of Heartbeat of Africa, was abducted by agents of the State Research Bureau (SRB) from the National Theatre in Kampala. He was forced into the trunk of a car and murdered the same day, his mutilated body later discovered in Namanve Forest along the Kampala-Jinja Road. In August 1977, Edward Galabuzi Mukasa, son of the respected Chief Ham Mukasa and the leader of the Heartbeat of Africa troupe, was also arrested by SRB operatives. His body was never found, though it is widely believed he died under torture.

These deaths struck Charles Sonko deeply. He had been close to both Kawaddwa and Galabuzi Mukasa, and had also known Professor Pio Zirimu. The succession of killings left him increasingly shaken. Although Sonko had made a public show of converting to Islam and was given the Muslim name Rashid, those closest to him continued to call him Charles. His ties to the Anglican Church had never been fully severed. Some even suggested that his conversion was symbolic rather than spiritual, and that he remained active in the church community. As Christians became increasingly targeted, the killing of Archbishop Luwum seemed to confirm his growing fears that Christianity itself was under siege. Despite holding the military rank of Warrant Officer II and enjoying privileges under Amin's patronage, Sonko could no longer, in good conscience, reconcile himself to the brutality of the regime. He came to believe that he, along with others who had participated in FESTAC, were now targets. Disillusioned and fearing for his life, he made the painful decision to flee Uganda in 1977 and seek political asylum in Kenya.

Back in Kenya, Charles Sonko sought to reconnect with his old musical comrades, only to find that many had taken a break from creating music. Determined to forge a new path and lead his own group, he soon discovered that money was hard to come by. Funding was elusive, as few were willing to invest in his vision amid a thriving musical scene. Nairobi was already awash with successful bands such as Simba Wanyika, Maroon Commandos, Shika Shika, Super Mazembe, Bana Ngenge, and Orchestre Les Mangelepa. Each of these groups captured the public's attention with their distinctive sounds. Even reaching out to old friends from his Equator Boys days proved challenging, as many had either retired from performing or were unwilling to return to the grueling schedule of live gigs.

Undeterred by these setbacks, Sonko took matters into his own hands by booking studio time at Doromy Studios in Nairobi. There, he assembled a new group of musicians, naming them L'Orchestre Kyaddondo International, a nod both to his roots in Uganda (Greater Kampala is part of the old Buganda Kyadondo County) and to his aspirations for a fresh musical chapter. The ensemble featured talents such as John "Negro" Kiwanuka, Elliot Adwong, and Okuni Festus, among others. Together, Sonko and L'Orchestre Kyaddondo recorded Gkinumanze (It Hurts Me), a track that features a pulsating Afrobeat sound marked by a surging bass riff and accented with rhythmic guitar lines. The solo guitarist delivered knockout, pealing lines that were utterly hypnotic, giving the song its distinctive edge.

Recorded on the Doromy label, Gkinumanze was heavily influenced by the innovative sounds of Fela Kuti. Sonko's exposure to Afrobeat's transformative power had deep roots in his experiences at FESTAC '77. There, alongside other Ugandan artists, he had the rare opportunity to visit Fela's Kalakuta Republic, a two-story building nestled in the sprawling Lagos slum of Surulere, where the irascible but brilliant mega-star performed some of his greatest hits. The impact of Fela's Afrobeat style is unmistakably woven into the fabric of Gkinumanze. Lyrically, the song is a heart-rending narrative of love and rejection. Sonko sings about the agony of giving his all, dressing smartly, wining and dining his lover, and attending to her every need, only to be met with the sting of rejection. Despite his best efforts to make the relationship strong and durable, the pain of dejection leaves him struggling with the hurt of unreturned love. This expression of vulnerability and resilience captures not only his personal heartbreak from Eroni Nalunga but also the universal longing for reciprocated affection.

Unable to form a band and secure a regular gig at Nairobi's trendy nightclubs, Charles Sonko was forced to take on odd jobs, including working as a cab driver to make ends meet. The harsh reality of life as a refugee in Kenya weighed heavily on him, but his creative spirit remained undiminished. In 1980, drawing from the depth of his experiences and the pain of displacement, Sonko composed and recorded a moving track titled Refugee Song on the CBS (K) label. He was accompanied by Orchestre Les Afrikanos, a collective of close friends who had rehearsed and collaborated with him. Refugee Song features a sweet, upbeat reggae sound interwoven with spiritual and contemplative lyrics. The song powerfully conveys the plight of refugees, reminding listeners that anyone, under certain circumstances, might be forced to flee their home. Sonko's words carried a personal resonance; he had witnessed firsthand the brutal consequences inflicted by a repressive regime.

In the 1980s, seeking to reconnect with his roots, Sonko eventually returned to Uganda. There, he joined Moses Matovu's Afrigo as a traditional dancer, a poignant attempt to recapture the brilliance of his musical past. However, the homecoming was bittersweet. Despite his undeniable talent and the echoes of his former glory, he struggled to regain the prominence he once enjoyed. The shifting tides of the music scene, coupled with the lingering scars of his exile, proved insurmountable. Over time, his star faded, and he ultimately died in obscurity and poverty, a tragic end for a man who had poured his soul into his art.

Charles Sonko's legacy transcends the circumstances of his passing. His innovative fusion of traditional Ugandan sounds with contemporary influences, his ability to weave deeply personal narratives into beautiful melodies, created an admirable body of work. He was a musical innovator, a storyteller, and a voice for the displaced, masterfully employing a smorgasbord of musical genres. Sonko's music lives on, a haunting and beautiful reminder that even in the face of adversity, the human spirit, expressed through art, can endure, and continue to speak to new generations.

CHAPTER 6

The Scout of River Road: How Freddie Kanyike Shaped a Musical Generation

As Charles Sonko was establishing himself as a leading musician on the Kenyan scene, a new generation of Ugandan artists was eager to join the Kenyan Twist revolution, a musical style that swept through Kampala's vibrant nightclubs. Although these emerging artists delivered energetic live performances, they longed for the opportunity to record and broadcast their songs on Radio Uganda. Unfortunately, Kampala did not have a dedicated recording studio at the time. This forced many musicians to travel to Nairobi's famed River Road studios in search of quality recording facilities. The situation was compounded in 1960 when the Opel Gramophone Record and Battery Factory closed following a boycott of foreign businesses, further stifling local recording efforts.

In 1961, childhood friends Freddie Kanyike and Andy Kyambadde from the Busega and Natete neighborhoods took decisive steps toward realizing their recording dreams. Both members of Israel Magembe's Kampala City Six, they had already tasted success with the release of their debut single, Lupiya Zange (My Rupees), on the Tom Tom label. Recruited by Magembe in 1960, they were not only determined to record their music but were also deeply influenced by the broader regional musical community, admiring the Twist beats coming in from Kenyan artists. They had also forged important connections with established musical figures who happened to live in their neighborhood, such as John Bosa, the charismatic leader of the Mengo African Orchestra, as well as his son Moses Katazza and Nelson Sabavuma.

Freddie Kanyike's musical journey began at an early age. Born in Busega in 1938, he attended Natete Primary School, Bishop Tucker in Mukono, Gombe Junior Secondary, and later Mengo Senior Secondary School. Inspired by legendary musician Elly Wamala, Freddie aspired to forge a professional career in music. Alongside Andy Kyambadde, he spent countless evenings at Top Life in Mengo, where he absorbed the artistry of live rehearsals by the club's musicians. Members of the Top Life Band, including Livingstone Damulira and Wapamba, recognized the duo's potential and encouraged them to write and compose their own songs. Damulira, who would go on to lead the influential Five Stars Jazz Band, was central in shaping their early development.

Kanyike and Andrew Kyambadde charmed audiences at Planet Nightclub in Bwaise, the home base for Kampala City Six. Despite consistently winning over the crowd with their engaging live shows, they aspired to achieve more than nightly performances. Undeterred by the Opel Gramophone Record and Battery Factory closure, they remained determined to document their music and set their sights on Nairobi, a regional hub for recording facilities. However, their mentor, Israel Magembe, appeared hesitant to arrange a recording trip. Not willing to let that hesitation stall their progress, Kanyike and Andy Kyambadde took the initiative. In the first half of 1961, they embarked on a journey to Nairobi's famed River Road to record their own material.

This venture marked a new phase in their careers. It was Andy Kyambadde's first trip outside Uganda, expanding his horizons and exposing him to new musical influences. Kanyike was already familiar with Nairobi, having spent many school holidays there while his father worked for the East African Railways and Harbors Corporation. His deep knowledge of the city, combined with his extroverted and confident demeanor, proved invaluable. It helped smooth out logistical challenges and enabled them to forge connections within Nairobi's burgeoning music scene.

The allure of Nairobi was undeniable. The young men were inspired by the tales of Charles Sonko's success, viewing the city as a musical mecca. Beyond Sonko, other Ugandan artists thrived there, reinforcing this perception. Hanny Wamala, formerly of the Rhino Boys, had carved a successful career with the Kiko Boys, releasing popular tracks like Ensi Yafe (Our Country) and Ebyenaku Zino (Modern Times) on the Jambo label in the late 1950s. Adding to the city's magnetic pull was the presence of Elly Wamala, a significant influence on Kanyike and Kyambadde. Elly Wamala, who had played a crucial role in facilitating their recording of Lupiya Zange while working at the Opel Gramophone Record and Battery Factory in Kampala, had since relocated to Nairobi. Stories circulated about his fulfilling life, performing with Msafiri Mori Mori's Sportsman Cha Cha Band and touring across East Africa. Before moving to Nairobi, Elly Wamala had lived in Bulenga. This was close to Busega-Natete area where Kyambadde and Kanyike were from. Within the Sportsman Cha Cha Band, another Ugandan, Joseph Ndugga, held the vital role of drummer. Like Israel Magembe, Ndugga hailed from Ndeeba, another Kampala neighborhood bordering Natete. This presence of fellow countrymen in Nairobi provided a sense of community and support, easing the anxiety that Kanyike and Kyambadde may have felt.

Fueled by youthful ambition and a shared dream, Freddie Kanyike and Andrew Kyambadde boarded a bus to Nairobi, determined to record their music. The journey was more than a physical relocation; it marked a bold step toward professional recognition and a place within the broader East African music scene. They weren't just chasing a recording. They were seeking validation, airplay, and the possibility of building sustainable musical careers. However, once in Nairobi, they encountered the vibrant yet fiercely competitive world of River Road. The studios, often cramped and bustling with activity, pulsed with ambition and creativity. Artists from across the region converged there, each hoping to be heard. Despite lacking a prior appointment, the pair threw themselves into this dynamic environment, hoping to carve out their place in the ever-evolving musical landscape.

They eventually made their way to AGS Studios, located at Plot 138 on River Road. According to Andrew Kyambadde, they confidently introduced themselves to the Kenyan-Indian studio manager as well-known Ugandan musicians. This was not an empty claim. They had built a loyal following at Planet Bar in Bwaise, and their song Lupiya Zange had achieved notable local success. Mr. Maganlal Jethalal Shah, the manager of AGS, had limited awareness of Uganda's broader musical talent, knowing mainly Charles Sonko. Sonko was generally regarded as a Nairobi-based performer, more connected to Kenya's music scene than to Uganda's growing artistic movement. That perception shifted significantly during the a cappella audition by Fred Kanyike and Andrew Kyambadde. Their rich harmonies, emotional depth, and vocal precision made an immediate impact. Shah offered them a recording session later that same afternoon.

There was just one problem: the AGS Boys, the studio's regular session musicians, were unavailable. Without hesitation, Kanyike offered to find them. Speaking fluent Swahili and familiar with Nairobi's rhythms, he made his way through the River Road district. Eventually, he found one of the musicians at a nearby bar, visibly intoxicated and hesitant to leave his drink or his friends behind. But Kanyike's persistence paid off. He persuaded the man to come along, and together they gathered enough musicians to assemble a full band. The session that followed was rushed, with minimal time to rehearse, yet the results were unexpectedly strong. The recordings captured the essence of the River Road style, complete with warm harmonies, lively guitar lines, and a rhythmic foundation of bass, maracas, and tambourine. Studio staff were surprised by how well the songs turned out, especially given the circumstances. Most importantly, Shah was impressed, and not just by the music, but by Kanyike's initiative, musical instincts, and ability to make things happen. Realizing there was far more to Uganda's music scene than he had initially assumed, Shah offered Kanyike a new role as AGS's talent scout in Uganda, tasking him with identifying and developing promising artists. This marked the beginning of Kanyike's long and influential association with the AGS label, and the start of a musical career that would stretch well into the 1980s.

Shah also gave Kanyike more time to record his own material. He admired his voice, the ease of his delivery, and his upbeat, engaging personality. Kanyike's cheerful disposition helped set the AGS Boys at ease as well. They saw in him a kindred spirit, someone who shared their humor and bantered with them comfortably in Swahili. During that first recording session, Kanyike began to establish himself as a core artist on the AGS label, producing a string of popular tracks: Kimanda Sherry (Kimanda Darling), Nalunga (a female name), Dali Malina (Darling Malina), Mulungi Regina (Beautiful Regina), Oh! Oh! Covia (Covia was Scovia), and Abaganda Abazira (The Brave Baganda).

At the same time, Andrew Kyambadde recorded a single disc featuring Alice and Uganda Yefuga (Uganda Has Self-Rule). Eager to record more of his compositions, Kyambadde grew frustrated when Shah cited limited studio time. Most of the time had been allocated to Kanyike's recordings. In response, Kyambadde suggested to Kanyike that they explore other studios. Though initially reluctant, mindful of his new arrangement with AGS and uneasy about appearing disloyal, Kanyike eventually gave in to Kyambadde's persistence. They turned to CMS Studios on River Road, which had once been co-owned by Maganlal Shah and Meghji "Kaka" Shah. At CMS, they were welcomed by Kaka without hesitation. Together, Kanyike and Kyambadde recorded several tracks at CMS, including Ekibuga Katwe (Katwe Town), Nalina Jajja (I Had a Grandparent), and Night Mama. In the latter, "Night" refers to a name traditionally given to girls born at night. Kanyike also recorded additional songs at the studio, such as Elena Wange (My Elena) and Olowoza Kwani (Who're You Thinking About?).

Determined to make the most of his first visit to Nairobi, Kyambadde was driven to produce a body of work that matched Kanyike's growing discography. This ambition led him to branch out further, eventually recording at Equator Sound Studios, the recording base of Charles Sonko. There, he produced Menda (a female name) and Uganda Twist

(Wetingonyole Twist). Over time, a clear distinction emerged between the two musicians. Kanyike remained mostly loyal to AGS, believing it offered greater room for artistic and professional growth. Kyambadde, by contrast, found his creative stride at CMS, where he continued to explore and expand his musical voice. Through Kanyike's initiative, AGS began to capture the distinctive sound of Ugandan popular music. His keen ear for talent and ability to nurture emerging artists greatly added to the label's evolving catalogue. Among his earliest achievements was persuading Charles Sonko to record with AGS. The result was a series of well-received tracks, including Komawo (Come Back) and Dali Kichoncho (Darling Kichoncho), both of which enjoyed widespread popularity.

Kanyike's influence grew considerably as he brought a wave of artists into the studio, helping to shape the sound of a new musical era. Among the many musicians he ushered into AGS were performers who would go on to become household names. One of the most distinctive was Samuel Wamala, whose voice became one of the most recognizable and admired in the early 1960s. Often confused with Elly Wamala, Samuel had a kadongo kamu style entirely his own. It was introspective, gentle, and filled with lyrical longing. A carpenter by trade, he rarely performed live, preferring the solitude of studio sessions in Nairobi, where he worked with professional session musicians. He otherwise lived a quiet life and was considered something of a recluse. Wamala made his home in Kampala's neighborhood of Nsambya. Outside the more orderly quarters of the Police barracks, the East African Railways and Harbors Corporation estate, and institutions like St. Francis Hospital and St. Joseph's Girls' Senior Secondary School, Nsambya was a sprawling slum, crowded and makeshift. But it was here, in these dense and dusty surroundings, that Wamala found his comfort and rootedness. His songs, including Namudu (a female name), Agalikadiwa (What Will Grow Old), Topi (a female name), Fena Mu Uganda (All of Us in Uganda), and Merida (a female name), captured the quiet dignity of ordinary lives and became staples on Radio Uganda.

Beyond Samuel Wamala, Kanyike became the quiet architect behind a golden wave of Ugandan sound. At AGS and its offshoot labels such as Super, Twist, and Rock, he brought a steady stream of voices into the studio, each bringing their own flavor, each adding to the growing pulse of the Uganda's popular music. Among them were Ecklas Kawalya, Christopher Ssebadduka, Yunia Nalwanga, Rose Musoke, Mary Nattima, Dominico Sentamu, Simon Kaate Nsubuga, Stanley Kyeranyi, Evalisto Muyinda, and Benon Mayambala. There was Edmund Batte, J. Mukasa, Fred Masagazi, Nelson Sabavuma, Steven Sempasa, Bonnie Steven Kyambadde, Sarah Namagembe, Gerald (also spelled Jared) Mukasa, Simon Berunga, Freddie Mukasa, Billy Mbowa, Eddy Masembe, Tony Ssenkebejje, Rock Luganzi, and Matia Kyakamala. But Kanyike didn't stop with the stars. He scouted the neighborhoods, listening for untapped promise. From the backyards of Kampala came Jackson Mukibi, Vincent Nsubuga, and Wilson Mutumba. They were little known at the time, but Kanyike gave them the opportunity to record under AGS's labels.

Encouraged by Kanyike's warm reception at AGS Studio, Israel Magembe was inspired to travel to Nairobi with Kampala City Six. Unlike the other Ugandan artists that Kanyike introduced to AGS Studios, who typically performed with the AGS Boys, Kampala City Six contributed their own live instrumentation. At the studio they recorded several tracks, including E. Lukwata's Enyambala Yo Mwami (A Gentleman's Style) and Siruma Sifayo (Unhurt, Unbothered); Fred Masagazi's Namazzi (a female name that was erroneously printed on the disc as Nanamazi); Fred Kanyike's Mukyala Jerida (Lady Jerida), a composition by Bonnie Steven Kyambadde; and Kawalya's Ninda Kabandole (Waiting for the Double-decker), a composition by Steven Sempasa with vocals credited to Israel Magembe on the disc. Additionally, the track Ayida Mama, sung by Kawalya in collaboration with Kampala City Six, was also credited to Israel Magembe.

Andrew Kyambadde later returned to AGS Studios with his then-girlfriend and later common-law wife Margaret Nakibuuka. Together, they recorded their first duets, including Erioth-Twist (with "Erioth" being a female name), Muhonya Yabula (Muhonya Got Lost), Malina (a female name), and Zisanze (Alas, Hard Times). Nakibuuka, a slender and energetic woman with a strong personality, emerged as a formidable musical partner. The duo formed a powerhouse act whose duets went on to become huge successes in Uganda.

Kanyike and Andrew Kyambadde's success in Nairobi sparked a broader wave of interest among Ugandan musicians. Inspired by the opportunities available at AGS and CMS, many others followed, traveling to the Kenyan capital to pursue recording sessions. In addition to AGS, which welcomed Ugandan artists, CMS also opened its doors to a wide range of Ugandan acts performing in genres from pop to kadongo kamu. These included Kampala City Six, Simon Kaate Nsubuga (who recorded under various names such as Saimon & Party, Saimon & Kampala Wonderers Jazz Band, and Saimon & Kampala Jazz), Aloziyo Nnyago, Gerald Mukasa, Christopher Ssebadduka, Dominico Sentamu (also spelled Dominiko), Samuel Wamala, Stanley Kyeranji, Nelson Sabavuma, Frederick "Fred" Mwanje, Fred "Freddie" Mukasa, and Wilson Mutumba. The latter released charming songs, enriched by a penny whistle, titled Muchala Mukulu (Senior Wife) and Nkufunile Omulungi (I'll Get You a Beauty). Among the most prolific artists to record with CMS and its sister imprint, Africa Voice, were Simon Kaate Nsubuga, Fred Mwanje, Gerald Mukasa, Nelson Sabavuma, and the duo Andrew Kyambadde and Margaret Nakibuuka.

For Kanyike, that first connection with AGS Studio proved transformative, and propelled him to remarkable musical prominence in Uganda. His outstanding vocal abilities, coupled with consistent access to quality recording facilities, enabled him to produce a substantial catalog of songs that deeply moved music enthusiasts across the country. At AGS, he cultivated strong relationships with the AGS Boys session musicians: Edward Nandwa, Joseph Abbas, John Nzenze, Reuben Shimbiro, John Mwale, John Luongo, and Tom Miti. Their shared musical understanding and collaborative energy transformed each recording session into a display of fresh ideas and dynamic sounds.

Between 1961 and 1964, Kanyike recorded over 30 songs for various AGS labels, including the eponymous AGS, Super, Twist, and Rock. This extraordinary output was unprecedented in Uganda, establishing him as a pioneering recording artist. Each new record was highly anticipated at

Kampala's music stores, attracting fans eager for his latest releases. Popular hits like Dali Malina (Darling Malina) and Kinjagaza Milly (Why I Love Milly) became staples, while deeply felt tracks such as Eramirembe Rhoda (Be At Peace Rhoda) and Guma Omwoyo Irene (Don't Lose Heart Irene) connected with listeners through their emotional lyrics and memorable tunes.

Although Kanyike primarily sang in Luganda, his adaptability was evident in Lonely Boy, an English-language track featuring a gentle, waltz-like arrangement:

If you want to be my baby
If you want to be my girl
Just come to me and treat me nice
Just come to me and see me baby
Oh, I'm a lonely boy
Have no daddy or brothers
Mummy is away
Oh, I dream
I'm a lonely boy come to me
Please my baby save my life
Oh, I'm a lonely boy
Let me hope
Mary come
Come to me
The world is dull
I'm so lonely
Listen to me darling Mary
The world is dull without you
I'm a lonely boy come to me
Please my baby save my life

Beyond his recording sessions in Nairobi, Kanyike remained a central figure in Kampala's live music scene. At Sebalamu's Planet Bar in Bwaise, the members of Kampala City Six included Freddie Kanyike, Ecklas Kawalya, Bonnie Kyambadde, Andrew Kyambadde, Fred Masagazi, Simon Kaate Nsubuga, and Israel Magembe. Night after night, they joined forces to deliver performances that sparked lively interaction among the audience. Their repertoire ranged from gentle waltzes and spirited rhumbas to the ever-popular Kenyan Twist tunes that drew nearly every patron onto the dance floor. The atmosphere was electric: Kaate Nsubuga, suave and sure, would glide into Bana Bawala (Girls), a crisp Cha Cha number with a beautiful horn section; Kanyike followed with the relaxed charm of Elena Wange (My Elena), his voice smooth and unhurried; then came Kawalya, whose rich delivery of Obukyayi (Hatred), a slow, luxuriant swing tune, often drew cheers before the first verse ended. These performances, as lively as they were polished, brought to life the very songs that would later appear on the CMS label. The ensemble's performances fostered an atmosphere of warmth and good fellowship, providing a welcome reprieve after a long day's labor.

Kanyike's focus on love songs matched his natural charm and flair for seduction. His romantic escapades, which became the stuff of Kampala lore, often served as inspiration for his music. When he was smitten, he never hesitated to share his personal joys and heartaches with the public through song. Kanyike's well-known romantic adventures stirred much conversation, and many believed that his ballads carried hints of his own passionate encounters. One notable example is the song Vida, composed under the spell of love in honor of an elegant Kampala beau named Vida, one of Apollo Kironde's half-sisters. Her sister Jida had already received a dedication titled Dear Jida from Steven Sempasa and Kanyike on the AGS label in 1962. Vida is a graceful, dreamy composition filled with heartfelt passion, frustration, and urgency that continues to be a favorite among Kanyike's fans:

> I felt my heart flutter in the absence of Vida,
> So much so that I could hardly swallow my food,
> And even the tea tasted bitter.

Once I was robust, but now I've grown thin,
Burdened by an endless stream of thoughts.
Vida, if you love me,
Come back to me, I am in deep distress.
I traveled to Mengo, your birthplace,
Hoping to find you there, but you were nowhere to be seen.
I even went to Sam's in Jinja, thinking that might be where you stayed.
My heart has lost its steadiness because you are not here.
Love feels overwhelming, my dear
Please, return to me, Vida!
Listen, and I will share with you the story of how you came to be.
They say that the gap in your front teeth draws the gaze of everyone
who sees you,
And your kindness flows as naturally as a gentle stream.
All these qualities together are the very essence of you
The essence that now troubles me so.
Perhaps one day you will return,
And our wedding will be beyond description.
Perhaps I will shed tears of pure joy.
My heart still skips a beat in your absence.
Vida, if you truly care for me, come back,
For I suffer in your absence.

The story of Vida and Kanyike's romance carries all the drama and intrigue of a Nollywood script. When Kanyike composed a song in her honor, Vida was already widely known as one of Jolly Joe Kiwanuka's mistresses. Jolly Joe, the powerful owner of the White Nile nightclub, was married but notorious in Kampala's social circles for his long string of affairs. Vida, however, was different. Her easy smile and the unmistakable sparkle in her eyes made her one of the most admired women in the city.

Kanyike, celebrated for his charm and flair, was no stranger to romance. But with Vida, there was something more. He offered her what Jolly Joe never could, a love grounded in loyalty, stability, and the quiet assurance of something lasting. To prove his devotion, he composed a song in her name. The track played constantly on Radio Uganda, its tender lyrics and measured rhythm laying bare the depth of his affection and the ache of separation. Touched by his sincerity, Vida made a bold choice. She walked away from the wealth of Jolly Joe and began a relationship with Kanyike that would last until his departure into political exile in the United States in the mid-1970s.

By the time their relationship began, Kanyike had already left the Kampala City Six and joined the Stars Band. The group, which included Freddie Kanyike, Ecklas Kawalya, and Bonnie Steven Kyambadde, had been performing regularly at the White Nile nightclub since 1964. News of Vida's defection to Kanyike was met with fury. Jolly Joe did not take the betrayal lightly. In a fit of rage, he drove to Kanyike's house in Lungujja, a quiet suburb of Kampala. Towering, broad-shouldered, and feared for his violent temper, Jolly Joe had long ruled the nightlife with a heavy hand. That day, his rage boiled over. He found Kanyike's green Triumph Herald coupe parked outside and smashed its windows in a shower of glass. Kanyike, sensing danger, fled to the banana grove at the back of the property, hiding among the trees as the man he had crossed roared outside.

The incident soon became the talk of Kampala's entertainment scene. In the aftermath, Kanyike and the Stars Band were no longer welcome at White Nile. Ironically, the two rivals were connected by marriage, a fact that only deepened the personal strain. What began as a romantic entanglement had turned into a bitter, combustible feud that would haunt both men long after the shattered glass was swept away.

Kanyike sang about another one of his loves in the song Eddy, a duet with Rose Musoke. Edisa "Eddy," affectionately nicknamed Kinyonyi (The Bird), was a wide-hipped, curvaceous woman of medium height with an exceptionally pretty face and smooth, espresso-brown skin. She embodied beauty in its purest form. Beyond her striking appearance, Eddy served as the cashier at Kaala's New Era bar, a popular Natete dive bar during the 1950s and 1960s, a role that was crucial at the time. As the keeper of the funds, she was responsible for ensuring the bar's financial stability while maintaining a warm and approachable demeanor.

New Era itself was a hub of activity, exuding a homely but exhilarating atmosphere. It was more than a neighborhood hangout. In one corner, a jukebox played an eclectic mix of tunes, while tables and chairs were scattered in a casual, unarranged fashion. The walls were decorated with posters promoting Sportsman cigarettes and Nile beer, along with cover pages from Drum magazine featuring beautiful African women. Although the bar was not particularly fancy, its functional design and welcoming ambiance made it a favorite among locals. Patrons would collect their drinks at the counter, settle their bills with Eddy, and often engage in light conversation or playful banter before joining a lively crowd that gathered to discuss everything from local politics to the challenges of urban life. Some male patrons flirted with the barmaids.

New Era was also a favorite haunt for musicians from the area, including Kanyike, Andrew Kyambadde, B. K. Steven, Magembe, and Nelson Sabavuma. The bar offered a relaxed, pressure-free environment where these artists could unwind with friends. It was a place where, away from the stage, they could enjoy the conviviality of a familiar local bar and be themselves.

Kanyike's affection for Edisa was deep and genuine. She was known not only for her beauty but also for her generosity, often lending money to the musicians during lean times. Edisa's connection to the world of music extended through her family as well. Her cousin, Yunia Nalwanga, a nurse trained at Mulago School of Nursing and Midwifery, Uganda's premier institution, possessed a remarkably beautiful singing voice. Yunia would often assist Edisa on the busiest nights, especially at the end of the month when newly paid patrons flocked to the bar.

When Edisa introduced Yunia to Kanyike in the early 1960s, the young woman, then about 23, immediately impressed him with her vocal talent. Kanyike not only fell for her voice but also developed romantic feelings for her. Although other prominent musicians like Fred Masagazi, Andrew Kyambadde, and Nelson Sabavuma made attempts to court Yunia, none could match the allure of Kanyike's charm. The secret romantic and musical partnership between Kanyike and Yunia soon led to groundbreaking duets, which were among the first in Uganda's popular music to feature both male and female voices.

Even as he embarked on this clandestine relationship with Yunia, Kanyike's profound love for Edisa remained undeniable. He often recalled how she had come to his aid during times of financial hardship. In the song Eddy, enhanced by the gentle melody of a pennywhistle, Kanyike poured out his heartfelt tribute to Edisa. Although he had a brother named Eddy, the song was solely an ode to Edisa "Kinyonyi" at New Era, a passionate homage to the woman with whom he shared a complex and deeply felt romantic bond:

I long to go to Natete
To behold the much-talked-about Eddy.
Even if I must pay to see her,
I am determined to do so.
I recall when I was in Moshi,
I saw her in pictures.
Truly, Eddy was opulent,
Dressed in ivory and gold.
Her beauty isn't merely from her clothes,
It is natural and undeniable.
Just look at the way she wears that tight dress,
You simply cannot leave Eddy behind.
And most importantly,
She carries a radiant smile.
Even if I must pay to see her,
I remain determined.
I long to go to Natete
To behold the much-talked-about Eddy.

In Nalwanga, a duet enhanced by the charming sound of a pennywhistle much like Eddy and recorded on AGS's Rock label, Yunia Nalwanga and

Kanyike explore the bittersweet complications of their secret love affair. Despite their deep affection for one another, they found no clear path to marriage. The lyrics capture this hesitation:

> What you say about marrying you is good, and I agree
> But one thing, my dear, that frightens me
> Marrying you and then leaving me.

In this poignant moment, a visibly tormented Kanyike pleads with Yunia to promise that she will never leave him, regardless of whether they face poverty or prosperity. However, the delicate balance of their relationship was shattered when Edisa heard the song Nalwanga and discovered that her trusted cousin had been romantically entangled with Kanyike. Incensed, Edisa vowed to take drastic measures against Kanyike, and her harsh words marked an irreversible rupture between her, Kanyike and Yunia.

This episode also signaled the beginning of the end for Yunia's brief but brilliant recording career. Although she was musically active for only about four years, Yunia was one of the most recognizable female voices of her time. In her short music career, she performed alongside leading male artists such as Freddie Kanyike, Bonnie Kyambadde, and Ecklas Kawalya, leaving a deep legacy on Uganda's popular music scene before her final recordings in 1965. Yunia was by far the most preeminent female artist of the early to mid-1960s.

Meanwhile, Kanyike continued to forge his musical legacy with a series of hit songs. In 1965, he charmed audiences with Abana Munyiikire Okusoma (Work Hard in School, Children). The following year, he released further hits like Sijja Kwagala Bangi (Not Gonna Love Many) and Sandinyize Nnyo (Shouldn't Have Been So Angry). Another standout track from 1966 was Nonya Lukia (Searching for Lukia), a wistful and melodious tune.

Kanyike played a key role in launching the musical careers of many Ugandan artists, serving as the influential gatekeeper at AGS Studios. While the venture brought financial rewards, these were not his primary motivation. His deeper drive came from a passion to elevate Ugandan music and musicians, helping them record their songs as reflections of the nation's lived experiences. He saw these recordings as a cultural legacy to be preserved and shared with future generations. Accounts of his methods, however, remain mixed. Some praised his sharp instinct for identifying fresh talent and introducing new voices to wider audiences. Others questioned his integrity, alleging that personal rivalry often clouded his decisions. Nearly every Ugandan musician who recorded on the AGS label was required to audition before Kanyike. According to some accounts, he occasionally rejected songs during auditions, only to later record similar versions with different artists. Critics viewed this not as a matter of competition but as an act of jealousy, rooted in the belief that no one else should outshine him. Kanyike reportedly considered himself the finest musician in the country and regarded others as merely secondary.

One notable example of the allegations surrounding Kanyike's methods involves Willy Mujwala, the half-brother of Elly Wamala. Mujwala occasionally performed with the Kampala City Six and had recorded two songs with the band in 1960: Njawulirawo (Help Me Decide) and Muliranwa (Neighbor). In 1962, he auditioned again with a new set of songs that Kanyike approved for recording. A bus trip to Nairobi was arranged, with Kanyike promising to hand Mujwala the ticket on the appointed day at the Kampala bus station. He also assured him that all expenses in Nairobi would be covered. When the day arrived, Mujwala went to the bus park only to find that the Akamba bus to Nairobi had left hours earlier. Confused and distressed, and unable to afford a ticket on his own, he turned to Edisa, the cashier at New Era in Natete, who generously gave him the fare. Mujwala eventually made it to the AGS studios and auditioned again, though by then Kanyike had already returned to Uganda. To his shock, Mujwala learned that the very songs he had planned to record had already been recorded by other Ugandan musicians.

Mujwala came to believe that Kanyike had deliberately misled him about the time and date of departure. He chose not to name the songs he claimed were taken from him, though he alleged that some had gone on to become major hits. While Mujwala would later find success on the Equator label with tracks such as Silvia Walagawa (Where Did You Go

Silvia?) and Nasali Omulungi (Beautiful Nasali), the episode remained, in his mind, a bitter reminder of the more troubling side of Kanyike's influence. In November 1970, several years after the Nairobi incident, Mujwala attempted to improve the lot of local musicians by forming the Uganda Picking Guitarists Union, an association that sought to fight for copyright protection and prevent exploitation. Mujwala served as president, Paul Damulira as secretary, and Vincent Nsubuga as treasurer. The initiative, however, was short-lived. As with other efforts to unite Ugandan musicians under a common umbrella, it faltered because many performers did not appreciate the value of copyright and were suspicious of those behind such organizations, fearing they might be motivated by self-interest.

Regardless of these controversies, Kanyike's impact on Ugandan music is undeniable. His influence opened doors for numerous artists, including fellow Kampala City Six members Fred Masagazi, Bonnie Steven Kyambadde, and Ecklas Kawalya. While Fred Masagazi eventually moved on from AGS to record with Charles Worrod's Equator Studios, Ecklas Kawalya and Bonnie Kyambadde continued to release many of their signature songs on the AGS label throughout the early to mid-1960s.

Ecklas "Sitale" Masembe Kawalya's musical journey began in 1937 in the small village of Kasiga, Bulemezi, now part of Luwero District. His father, Israel Masembe, was a respected landowner and farmer, and his mother, Florence Nabawanuka, a nurse who later worked at Mulago Hospital, Uganda's leading medical facility. Raised in a devout Anglican family, Kawalya developed a strong sense of discipline and faith. Recognizing his potential, his parents sent him to live with his aunt, Violet Nakyeyune, in Masulita, where he attended Masulita Primary School, known for its strong music program. Kawalya thrived both academically and musically, actively participating in school and church choirs. His exceptional performance earned him a place at Makerere College School, where he continued to excel in his studies while nurturing his passion for music. At Makerere College School, Kawalya lived with his uncle Charles, a World War II veteran who owned a double-bass guitar, a gift from his British commanding officer. The instrument fascinated young Kawalya, and his uncle began teaching him to play. Kawalya mastered the double-bass, even performing a cover of Neyagalira Ono Omutono Eyava Mu Bitta (I Love the Slender One Back from the War), a popular song at the time.

After graduating from Makerere College School, Kawalya joined a select group of students admitted to the prestigious Kampala Technical College, now Kyambogo University, to train as an automobile fitter machinist. There, he met and formed a close friendship with Henry Wassanyi Serukenya, an engineering student who was also a singer, songwriter, and playwright. Years later, Serukenya would compose several notable songs for Kawalya, including Kulabako Oli Wala (Kulabako, You Are Beyond Pretty) on the Uganda Muwogola label, as well as Yudaya (a female name), Akasolo Mujje (The Squirrel, Come Here), and Omumbejja (Princess).

Despite his technical training, Kawalya realized his true calling was music. In 1959, he left college to pursue his passion, composing his first song, Ebibuulire Bisanyusa (Advice Breeds Joy). With Elly Wamala on guitar, he recorded the track on the Tom Tom label. Fortuitously, Israel Magembe was present at the Opel Gramophone recording company and was impressed by Kawalya's unique voice. Magembe invited him to join his Kampala City Six. As a member of Kampala City Six, Kawalya played the double-bass and often served as lead vocalist. His initial recordings with the band featured Magembe's compositions, such as Milly Gwe Sherry (Milly, You Are My Darling) and Uganda Ddembe (Uganda at Peace). He contributed to several hits, including Abataka Basajja (The Clan Headmen).

Just like Freddie Kanyike and Andrew Kyambadde, Kawalya found himself at a crossroads after the closure of the Opel Gramophone Record and Battery Factory, when prospects of recording seemed to vanish. However, when Kanyike and Kyambadde demonstrated that Nairobi's River Road still offered viable opportunities, Kawalya eagerly joined the venture. Invited by Kanyike, he traveled to the AGS studios and went on to record some of the most memorable music of that era.

Among his recordings were songs that became classics, including Empuuta Kawomera (Delicious Nile Perch), Nakito (a female name), Akasolo Mujje (The Squirrel), Namata (a female name), Etonya (a place),

Omulongo (The Twin), Komawo (Come Back), Minzaani Yomukwano (The Measure of Love), Serina (a female name), Tofayo Rebecca (Don't Mind Rebecca), and Omukwano Bweguba (That's How Love Is). Notably, in Komawo, Kawalya even mentions Vida by name, a gesture that sparked persistent rumors among fans. It was said that Freddie Kanyike had enlisted Kawalya as an emissary to convey his own deep affection for the enchanting Vida:

> What should I do, my darling?
> Now you are filled with anger.
> I call out, but you ignore me.
> Please, come back to me, my love,
> For my heart has grown cold.
> If you accept me,
> I'll break up with Getu,
> I'm tired and done with her.
> Come back to me, Vida;
> I promise, all that is mine is yours.

Despite the controversy surrounding his duet Sifaayo with Yunia, which was widely interpreted as a veiled critique of the Kabaka's indulgent lifestyle, Ecklas Kawalya remained a royalist at heart. In a 1973 interview, he explained that audiences often interpreted his songs in ways that reflected their own views and experiences, sometimes attributing meanings he had not intended. Kawalya did not write most of his material, and especially in the early stages of his career, it is unlikely he would have risked openly criticizing Sir Edward Mutesa, the most powerful figure in Buganda. His loyalty to the kingdom was further underscored by a song he dedicated to Jehoash Mayanja Nkangi, the young Katikkiro of Buganda and father of renowned Ugandan reggae artist Tshaka Mayanja. Nkangi served as prime minister from 1964 to 1966. The song, Nkangi, features Kawalya with backing vocals by Benon Mayambala and praises Nkangi's wisdom and his appointment to the position. Kawalya sings of his desire to have a son as educated as Nkangi, an Oxford-trained lawyer. Nkangi's appointment at the young age of 33 made him the youngest person to hold the position.

One of Kawalya's defining characteristics was his collaborative spirit. Many of his early successes in the 1960s were born from partnerships with fellow Ugandan artists, including Mary Nattima, Benon Mayambala, Yunia Nalwanga, Bonnie Kyambadde, Rose Musoke, and Freddie Kanyike.

In 1963 and 1964, he joined forces with Mary Nattima on Rinie (a female name) and Fumbira Abaana (Cook for the Children), two emotional and romantic serenades that became iconic recordings on the AGS label. This marked the beginning of a long and fruitful musical partnership between Kawalya and Nattima, resulting in numerous hits. Ndifuna Owange (I'll Find My Lover), like Fumbira Abaana, explores the theme of love and longing, a recurring motif in their collaborations. Nze Nkwagala (I Love You) is another beautifully rendered duet on the AGS label, where Kawalya and Nattima express their enduring love in sultry tones. In this song, the AGS Boys provide a mellow and sentimental guitar introduction, setting the stage for Kawalya's opening lines of gratitude as he croons:

> Thank you for your gift
> And for the letter beyond praise
> Which revealed to me that I am cherished
> By the love you hold for me.

Mary Nattima takes it from there in a poised and reassuring voice that drips with sweetness:

> It is of no importance,
> Don't worry,
> That's what love is,
> Even so, honey,
> I love you,
> And babe you make me lose my soul.

Kawalya, however, expresses his doubts and anxieties:

> But I bear the weight of poverty,
> And the meager money that will never grow,
> Still, our love endures,
> And we pray that God will unite us.

Nattima, understanding his concerns, reassures him, dismissing any notion of materialism:

> I'm not greedy,
> Nor do I feel discontent,
> Even if you cannot provide for me,
> But, my dear, my love for you endures.

In the post-AGS period, Kawalya continued to nurture his musical partnerships, offering Mary Nattima additional opportunities to grow and shine. Their collaborations grew stronger over time, and Kawalya's commitment to their partnership opened new avenues for both artists. During this phase, he also joined forces with Hadija Namale and his brother-in-law, Chris Mwebe, further broadening his collaborative repertoire.

Kawalya's musical artistic breadth was evident in his work with Yunia Nalwanga on the AGS label. Their duets Beranga Mwana Mwesigwa (Always Be a Truthful Child), broke away from the typical themes of heartache and longing that marked many of his songs. This track, rich with parental wisdom, offered guidance to a young, soon-to-be independent listener facing life's challenges. Adding another layer to his collaborations, Kawalya teamed up with Rose Musoke and Yunia Nalwanga on Omulongo (The Twin). This song stood as a testament to a love as enduring and unique as the bond between twins, a heartfelt pledge to embrace marriage and shoulder its responsibilities with sincerity.

Kawalya's collaborative spirit extended beyond his own recordings. He, along with Rose Musoke and Yunia Nalwanga, lent their backup vocals to Freddie Kanyike's hit Dorothy and Elizabeth. In this dynamic piece, Dorothy carried a smooth cha-cha touch, while Elizabeth pulsed with the vibrant energy of Twist. Additionally, Kawalya recorded several memorable tracks with Freddie Kanyike, including Sizanyira Kunsimbi (I Don't Play with Money) and Mwesibe Tugende (Dress Up and Let's Go).

What began as a casual friendship between Kawalya, Freddie Kanyike, and Bonnie Kyambadde soon evolved into a creative partnership that would transform the trajectory of their careers. Their decision to leave Kampala City Six and form The Stars Band marked a bold turning point in Uganda's club scene. Initially, Kanyike and Bonnie Kyambadde, known for their fondness for socializing over drinks, viewed Kawalya, who had been raised in a strict Christian household and was a committed teetotaler, as reserved and even dull. His shyness and deliberate distance from female admirers set him apart from his more outgoing colleagues. However, over time, they realized that beneath his cautious exterior lay a fellow songbird with a shared passion for music. Once their differences were set aside, the trio forged a tight bond and delivered some of the most exciting and energetic performances on the Kampala club circuit. Later, at Susana nightclub, Kawalya overcame his shyness and reticence, transforming into an outgoing and gregarious personality.

Kawalya's Christian faith inspired one of his most iconic songs, Gugudde (The Burden Has Fallen), released in 1968 on Chandarana's Wachezaji label. The song drew inspiration from Makerere Full Gospel Church, the first Pentecostal congregation in Uganda, which opened in 1962 just outside Makerere University. Renowned for its miraculous healings, that church became famous for stories of worshippers casting aside their crutches and walking again. Gugudde invited Ugandans burdened by illness to seek out the church's healing power and let their burdens fall away. But in 1971 Kawalya surprised many listeners with Malagadaga (Just Suffer), recorded with James Kigongo on Chandarana's Furaha label. In this song he praises the Mayembe, spirits believed to dwell in horns, gourds or other vessels, and celebrates both their power to heal and their capacity to harm. Within Buganda's belief system two types of Mayembe are recognized. Clan spirits called *ag'ekika* pass down through families and were once carried into battle as talismans. Witchcraft spirits known as *kifalu* act independently and are feared for their ability to inflict harm and even kill. By embracing these traditional beliefs and ancestor veneration, Kawalya ventured into territory long denounced by Christian missionaries and church leaders.

Although some Christian fans were dismayed by his turn toward ancestral worship, Kawalya's reputation remained strong. In 1973 Idi Amin's government ordered all nightclubs and bars to close by 1 am, a decree formalized in 1975. In an April 1973 interview with Taifa Empya, Kawalya explained that the new closing time finally allowed him to be home in time for Sunday worship at St Paul's Cathedral Namirembe, where he was a faithful parishioner. The cathedral's leadership even courted him to join their choir and considered a rare permission to include guitar accompaniment in praise. After careful reflection Kawalya declined their offer, preferring to keep his music outside formal liturgy. To reaffirm his devotion he followed with the buoyant Christian pop song "Yesu Gyali" ("Christ Is Real"). With its uplifting melody and joyous lyrics, the track reminded listeners that above all things Kawalya's life and art were rooted in his belief in Christ.

Another musician that Kanyike introduced to AGS, and one who would go on to join the pantheon of Uganda's celebrated 1960s and 1970s artists, was the young and gifted Steven Sempasa. He was the younger brother of Israel Magembe of the Kampala City Six and was born in 1945 in Mengo to Mr. Samwiri Wamala, a former Prime Minister of Buganda. Sempasa attended Namirembe Primary School, where he sang in the school choir, before moving on to Entebbe High School. At home, the presence of a gramophone in his father's house meant that music was a constant companion. The Wamala home in Mengo was filled with the sounds of many musical genres, and it was within this environment that both Magembe and Sempasa developed their deep love for music.

At just sixteen years of age, Sempasa had already begun composing his own songs. Among his earliest works were Ninda Kabandole (Waiting for the Double-Decker Bus), Namazi (a female name), and Abakazi Tebesigwa (Women Can't Be Trusted). He initially hoped to record these songs with the Kampala City Six, but Magembe believed they were better suited for

Ecklas Kawalya's voice. That decision proved momentous. Had it not been for Kawalya's 1960 recording, Ninda Kabandole might have remained a quiet and overlooked gem. Instead, Kawalya's rich vocal phrasing and polished delivery transformed the song into a major success of the early 1960s. In Kawalya's delivery, Ninda Kabandole became more than a love song. It emerged as a cultural touchstone, evoking the themes of longing, journey, and the sweetness of reunion.

While Kawalya brought his song to life, Sempasa had begun recording as well. In 1961, still only sixteen, he recorded several of his own compositions under the AGS label. Backed by Sarah Namagembe, these included Kampala City, Margaret Nalwoga (a female name), Nafira Ku Jesca (I Die for Jesca), and Omulembe Omutesa (Era of Negotiation). In collaboration with Andrew Kyambadde, he also recorded Malia Cha Cha (Maria Cha Cha), Omukazi Gemaka (A Woman Is the Home), Bulungi Bwa Uganda (The Beauty of Uganda), and Oliva Owe Kitalo (The Amazing Oliva). With support from Kanyike, Sempasa further released Nafuna Owebeyi (I Found Someone Chic), Mama Bena, and Ayimamaye Sofia (Splendid Sofia).

Sempasa was not only prolific but also outspoken in advocating for the rights of Ugandan artists. He repeatedly called on musicians to unite under a common umbrella and push for greater control over their creative work. He was particularly concerned with the exploitative arrangements that Ugandan artists faced when dealing with the Nairobi-based recording studios, which at the time dominated the East African music industry. These studios often imposed unfavorable contracts that granted artists minimal royalties and stripped them of ownership rights over their recordings. Musicians typically relinquished control over publishing, licensing, and distribution. The result was a system in which studios reaped most of the profits, while artists, despite their popularity and cultural significance, saw little financial benefit. This imbalance extended beyond economics. It also constrained artistic freedom, as musicians were pressured to conform to the tastes of producers or imagined market preferences. In many cases, this diluted the authenticity of the music and discouraged innovation.

Recognizing these injustices, and inspired in part by Andrew Kyambadde's earlier formation of the Sweet Voice label, Sempasa made the decision to establish his own independent record label. In 1968, he and his brother Israel Magembe launched Serena, determined to create a platform where Ugandan musicians could retain creative and financial control over their work. Under the Serena label, Sempasa not only recorded his own music but also gave opportunities to other Ugandan artists. He released several acclaimed tracks, among them, Joy Owekitalo (The Amazing Joy), which featured backing from the Vox Nationale band. With Orchestre Melo Success, he recorded Mama Jesca and Tewo, and with the Top Ten Band he produced hits such as Nalunga Fumbirwa (Get Married Nalwanga) and January 25th 1971, a song that celebrated the military coup that ousted Milton Obote and brought Idi Amin to power.

In 1970, Sempasa collaborated with James Kigongo to record the popular Rose Yabasinga (Rose Is the Best of Them All) on the Furaha label. However, his output slowed during the 1970s, a decade during which groups such as the Cranes, Rwenzori, and Peterson T. Mutebi dominated Uganda's airwaves. By 1971, the Serena label had folded. However, Sempasa returned to the studio in 1978, once again partnering with Andrew Kyambadde. For this recording project, the two assembled a studio band they called Orchestre Blue Stars. This was not a regular performing band, but rather a group brought together specifically for the recording sessions held in Nairobi. The result of this one-time collaboration included the hit Ndagire Jangu (Ndagire, Come Over), which marked a final flourish in Sempasa's storied musical journey.

Nelson Sabavuma was another musician of the 1960 to mid-1970s era who significantly influenced Uganda's popular music scene, releasing several hits. His earliest recordings featured the Kampala City Six band, even though he was not a permanent member. This collaboration marked the beginning of a substantial and impactful musical career.

Born around 1940 in Jungo, near Nakawuka township, Sabavuma was the son of a teacher, Mr. A. Musisi. He attended Mityana Junior Secondary School and joined the school choir alongside Fred Masagazi.

His passion for music deepened under the guidance of the influential choirmaster Arthur Bagunywa, who also taught him to play the guitar. After completing his education in Mityana, Sabavuma returned to Jungo and trained as a motor vehicle mechanic in Natete. While his lasting impact would be in music, his early years involved a blend of activities. He served as musician John Bosa's informal driver, worked as a respected automobile mechanic, and performed part-time in Natete bars, where his smooth and melodic voice gained recognition.

In 1960, encouraged by John Bosa, Sabavuma established the Golden Jazz Band, which regularly performed at a bar in Wobulenzi township. His debut recorded song, Olabye Ennaku Kate (You've Had Hard Times, Kate), was released on the Tom Tom label with backing from the Kampala City Six. Other early recordings included Samba Kampala (Kampala Samba) and Bena (a female name).

When Fred Kanyike became a talent scout for AGS Studios, he recruited Sabavuma as one of the initial Ugandan artists to record in Nairobi. His work with AGS resulted in several popular songs, including Nambejja (a female name), Ndi Kumwoto (I Am On Fire), and Kampala Teri Kyabwerere (Nothing Is For Free in Kampala). Sabavuma's 1960s songs were released on various labels, including on CMS, where he recorded a succession of hits such as Mundeke Mbere Nono (Let Me Be With The One), Zikusanze Betty (Woe To You Betty), Nakulabula (I Warned You), and Gwe Kenyini (You Are the Very One). He released Tewali Kirungi Na Kibi (There Is No Good Or Bad) on the Equator label, and the song was met with warm acclaim.

In partnership with his childhood friend Andrew Kyambadde, he co-founded the Sweet Voice label, which produced numerous widely enjoyed tracks. In 1973, supported by the Cranes Band, he recorded Ssenga Nkutumeko (Auntie, Can I Send You?). Like many of his contemporaries, such as Fred Masagazi, Ecklas Kawalya, and Andrew Kyambadde, he also recorded kagutema songs, notable among these was Twalya Namunye (We Ate the Wagtail) on the CMS label. Adapted from a traditional folksong, the piece celebrates the African pied wagtail, a striking black-and-white bird commonly found across much of sub-Saharan Africa. In Uganda, it is often seen in wetland habitats and national parks like Murchison Falls and Queen Elizabeth. Its presence while working in the fields is traditionally regarded as a sign of good luck.

By 1967, Sabavuma had formed a second group, the 7-Up Jazz Band, which performed at the White Nile Club in Kampala. The Congolese-led King Jazz Band also featured at this club. Sabavuma's band typically performed as the opening act before Selemani and King Jazz took the stage. With 7-Up Jazz, he recorded several beloved songs, including Kinnuma (It Hurts Me), Beera Muteefu (Be Humble), and Ono Ye Kampala (This Is Kampala).

Sabavuma's career extended over a decade and involved collaborations with a diverse range of musicians, both well-known and less famous, including Andrew Kyambadde, Sarah Namagembe, Margaret "Mega" Nakayenga, Sendege, and Alice Nambula. Despite his increasing fame, Sabavuma remained known as a soft-spoken and gentle man, appreciated for his warm personality and gracious manner.

Nelson Sabavuma's life was cut short during one of Uganda's darkest chapters. This was the brutal civil war that unfolded between 1980 and 1986. The conflict pitted President Milton Obote's Uganda National Liberation Army (UNLA) against the National Resistance Army (NRA) led by Yoweri Museveni. The Luwero District, especially the area that would become known as the Luwero Triangle, became the heartland of the insurgency. In addition to the NRA, other rebel groups such as the Uganda Freedom Movement (UFM) also operated in various regions, spreading instability and fear. By 1981 and 1982, the UFM was actively present in the Mpigi District, and violence soon followed in its wake.

In such volatile environments, civilians often become the invisible casualties. It is a tragic pattern in many conflicts. When armed groups clash, innocent people are frequently swept up in suspicion, accused without evidence of aiding the enemy. Such allegations, however baseless, can lead to detentions, beatings, and in some cases, extrajudicial killings.

This is what happened in Kasanje, a small township where Sabavuma lived quietly, enjoying peaceful days in the company of friends and family. One day in 1982, UNLA soldiers arrived in response to reports of rebel activity in the area. Unable to find any guerrillas, the government soldiers rounded up several local men at random, marched them to the outskirts of town, and executed them without trial. Among those killed that day was Nelson Sabavuma, a gentle soul whose voice had once soared across Uganda's airwaves and brightened dance floors throughout the country. His death was senseless, and the silence it left behind was profound. While his life ended on that tragic day, his music did not. Sabavuma's voice lives on, offering not only comfort and inspiration but also a poignant reminder of the artistry and humanity that once flourished, even in the shadows of violence.

Chapter 7

Ugandan Pop in the 1960s: Kanyike, Kawalya, and Their Contemporaries

In 1964, after a series of successful hits on the AGS label that had elevated their status to true celebrity, Kawalya, Kanyike, and Kalule, renowned for his work as the drummer with Kampala City Six, made a decisive break from Magembe. Their split paved the way for an entirely new musical venture: The Stars. The band emerged with an exciting lineup that featured a blend of fresh talent and seasoned musicianship. Jimmy Brown led on lead guitar, while Zidolo provided rhythmic support on the guitar. Kawalya contributed both on double bass and as a vocalist, and Batulumayo added a vibrant edge with his trumpet. Kalule kept the beat on drums, and the vocal harmonies were enriched by Fred Kanyike, A. Kapinga, and Tabu. Together, they forged an innovative sound.

The band soon found its home at the White Nile nightclub, a venue that was already a celebrated hub of music and nightlife in the city. Since the club's opening in 1961, White Nile had been the stage for a resident band that was largely composed of Congolese musicians. It has long been suggested that Jolly Joe Kiwanuka was the mastermind behind The Stars' departure from Kampala City Six. Determined to establish White Nile as the heartbeat of Kampala's nightlife, Jolly Joe engaged in an energetic rivalry with competing clubs, drawing top talent to his establishment and transforming the venue into a beacon for music lovers.

White Nile was renowned for its infectious energy and heady, sensual atmosphere. The club's bohemian charm and dynamic performances made it an irresistible destination for those in search of an authentic musical experience. In Jonathan Bower's novel *African Aftermath*, the character Claire vividly recalls her first encounter with the club: "Once inside the door, my first impression was of immense dynamic energy of the place—the thick mass of bodies, the throbbing, cohering rhythm of the music, the band bathed in brilliant light, playing their electric guitars with a practiced nonchalance, and the bustle of people carrying beer bottles from the bar into the dense crowd gathered around." She goes on to remark that she "had never seen any dance hall in England with quite the same scale of intensity." Whether it was The Stars or the resident Congolese band on stage, White Nile and its rival clubs throughout 1960s Kampala offered a level of exuberance and spontaneous joy that was difficult to find elsewhere. Though all the major Kampala nightclubs were modest in design, typically low, boxy structures with minimal ornamentation, they radiated life from within. Their charm lay not in architectural grandeur but in the electric energy of the crowds, the soul of the music, and the sense of freedom they provided. Inside those plain facades, generations danced, dreamed, and defined what nightlife in Kampala would come to mean: a vibrant, communal release where joy was the only true measure of luxury.

Firmly established at the White Nile nightclub and encouraged by Jolly Joe Kiwanuka to pursue an authentically Ugandan sound, The Stars embraced a bold new musical direction. Kawalya, whose passion for traditional music had been kindled in childhood, was equally drawn to native melodies and the lively Kenyan Twist beats emerging from Nairobi's River Road Studios. Growing up in a home with a gramophone, he spent countless hours listening to recordings by traditional artists such as Elizabeth Namale, Mariam Namale, and Sekinomu.

The foundations for the emergence of an authentically Ugandan musical style, which Jolly Joe Kiwanuka actively encouraged, were also laid in Uganda's missionary schools, where the English choral tradition emphasized discipline, multipart harmonies, and European-style hymn singing. These schools trained students in vocal precision and ensemble work. Over time, Ugandan musicians reinterpreted this formal training by blending it with folk melodies and indigenous rhythmic patterns. An important figure in this creative evolution was Elon Bugembe. Drawing from choral technique, he removed much of the rigidity of Western form and infused his a cappella songs with African melodic phrasing and local storytelling. His compositions, including Bulange (Buganda Parliament), Okunayiza (Meddling), Bakatonda B'ebuganda (The Gods of Buganda), and Omutti (The Tree), were released on the Tom Tom and Uganda Rafiki labels. Bugembe's work served as a critical bridge between Western choral structures and the experimental incorporation of traditional Ugandan musical elements. This fusion helped pave the way for what would become known as the kagutema or ding ding style. Bugembe's life, however, ended in mystery. One afternoon in the 1970s, he left his Kampala home and was never heard from again. To this day, his disappearance remains unsolved.

Kawalya and The Stars naturally gravitated toward this emerging kagutema genre, and the band became popularly referred to as the Kagutema Band.. The kagutema rhythm drew from Baakisimba and other traditional dance forms found throughout Uganda, while ding ding was partly inspired by a full moon ritual performed by young Acholi girls. The name kagutema had gained early recognition through a 1950 recording by Semakula & Party, released on the Jambo label. What made the sound distinctive was its ability to blend old and new. Groups like The Stars replaced indigenous instruments such as horns, drums, and gourd rattles with guitars, snare drums, and trumpets, resulting in a vibrant, modern sound that still evoked familiar village rhythms.

The effect of the kagutema rhythms on Kampala's nightlife was immediate. One of Kawalya's breakout songs, Kagutema Bamwongere Endeku (Another Gourd of Drinks for Kagutema), sent crowds at the White Nile nightclub into a frenzy. During some performances, The Stars would appear shirtless with rolled-up pant legs, abandoning their formal suits to evoke the look of rural peasants at work. The crowd responded with exhilaration. Women kicked off their high heels, known locally as *kakondo*, and wrapped jackets around their waists in place of raffia skirts. The dance floor moved with the natural cadence of traditional Ugandan rhythms. Feet pounded the dusty ground while handkerchiefs waved through the air, soaked with sweat and joy. Kagutema became a proud expression of cultural identity. These performances were as much about physical movement as musical composition. Intricate footwork, rhythmic waist motion, and call-and-response vocals created a collective sense of celebration. Women danced with joyful abandon. Men joined them with equal enthusiasm. Together they transformed the club into a space of cultural affirmation and shared belonging. The energetic exuberance of Kagutema music, also known as ding ding, was recognized even in Kenya, where renowned musician Daudi Kabaka paid homage to the genre in his hit song Western Shilo, released in the mid-1960s on the Equator label. In the song, Kabaka croons, "I went to Mbale Uganda and rejoiced in ding ding," a clear nod to the Kagutema dance craze that had taken Uganda by storm.

Kawalya's love for the Kagutema style endured well into the late 1960s and early 1970s. His notable Kagutema tracks include Erindya Empologoma (The Lion Will Eat Me) recorded on AGS, "Nsamba" (Stomp) on the Furaha label, Okuzaala Kujagaana (Parenthood Is Joy) also on Furaha, and Omumbejja (Princess) released on the Serenade label. The appeal of both Kagutema and Ding ding continued to inspire many other artists throughout the 1970s. Notably, the song "Njabala," recorded by Kawalya and Hadija Namale on the Furaha label, drew its title and inspiration from a traditional Luganda folk tale.

The story of Njabala tells of a beautiful young woman, pampered by her parents, who was married off by her relatives at a tender age after their passing. Unfamiliar with household chores and fieldwork, she struggled to meet her husband's expectations. Frustrated, he threatened divorce and sent her back to relatives who had never shown her kindness. Heartbroken, Njabala fled into the open fields, crying and pleading for her deceased mother to return and teach her the ways of home and field labor. In a poignant turn, her mother's spirit appeared to help with the work and cooking. However, when the village folk discovered that a spirit was aiding her, they labeled Njabala a witch and ostracized her. This Luganda narrative bears a striking resemblance to the German fairy tale of Rumpelstiltskin.

When The Stars performed at White Nile, they brought an unexpected mix to their sets, often featuring popular AGS tracks by either Kawalya or Kanyike. One performance that became a highlight was Kawalya's performance of Nalule. Recorded on the AGS label, this song resonated with the audience, earning its place as one of the club's most memorable numbers.

Kawalya composed and performed "Nalule" for a Ugandan woman of Goan origin with whom he shared a secret, brief romance. He affectionately nicknamed her Nalule, a name traditionally associated with the women of the *ngeye* (colobus monkey) clan of the Baganda people. At that time, while a considerable number of Ugandans were of Indian ancestry, social circles were largely segregated. There existed a small but significant group of Ismaili Muslims and Goan men, predominantly Roman Catholic, who were married to Black Ugandan women. In this racially divided Uganda of the 1960s, a union between an African man and an Asian woman was exceptionally rare.

Against this backdrop, Kawalya's clandestine affair with a Goan Christian woman was particularly striking. It is said that Nalule came from a prominent and affluent Goan family in Kampala. Her beauty was accentuated by a distinctively long, narrow nose, a feature also common among the Balalo (singular, Mulalo), a pastoral tribe in western Uganda. Both Kawalya and Nalule understood that their relationship was unlikely to endure. In the wake of their parting, a frustrated Kawalya, with the vocal support of Benon Mayambala, poured his heart out through his music, leaving an enduring impression on those who listened.

Where did Nalule go?
The fair, slender girl of medium height—
the one I love so dearly.
Ah, I am sorrowful.

The other day, while we were dancing,
I did nothing to upset or insult her;
I only watched her walk away from me.
Ah, I am sorrowful.
I fear what I will do
when I return home to Mengo—
who will be there to find her?
Ah, I am sorrowful.
If you were hurt, mama,
please do not suffer;
come back, and I shall marry you.
But from where will the one to find you come?
Ah, I am sorrowful.
Nalule is the one I ask for,
Nalule is the one I seek.
She has a Mulalo's nose
and Goan hair—
Mama, Nalule.

The legendary fallout between Fred Kanyike and Jolly Joe Kiwanuka, the owner of White Nile, over the affections of the enchanting Vida, led The Stars to seek a new home. They found it at the New Life nightclub in Mengo, a move that delighted Kamulu, the proprietor of New Life. Kamulu, much like Jolly Joe, was eager to present top musical talent and draw larger audiences to his club. He was known for his proactive approach, frequenting rival clubs and enticing musicians with attractive offers during their breaks. Despite his persistent efforts, The Stars had previously resisted his advances, drawn to the lively atmosphere of Jolly Joe's White Nile, where special nights featuring ding ding dance competitions drew skilled dancers and influential politicians.

With The Stars now under his roof, Kamulu seized the opportunity, rebranding the group as the New Life Star Band. New Life already had a resident band, led by Kenyan saxophonist and bandleader Charles Calist, and featuring Filipo and Tanzanian Alifunsi on guitars, Hassan on drums, and vocalists Joseph Omali and Pascali. This ensemble primarily performed covers of popular European and Latin American hits. However, the arrival of Fred Kanyike and Ecklas Kawalya marked a significant shift. Kanyike and Kawalya's influence soon led the resident band to incorporate a variety of Luganda songs into their repertoire, creating a dynamic fusion of international and local sounds.

It was at New Life that Kawalya unveiled one of his most enduring compositions, Gwanaggomola (Unforgivable), recorded on the AGS label. His smooth tenor voice, brimming with emotion, delivers a heartfelt plea to a lover who has rejected him. The AGS Boys provide an energetic guitar rhythm and a driving tambourine beat, amplifying the emotional intensity of Kawalya's performance:

> Whatever I did is deemed unforgivable,
> Because you refuse to forgive.
> What are you thinking?
> I loved you more than my own parents,
> but now you shun me.
> What are you thinking?
> You coveted the dresses I bought for you,
> craved the 900-shilling watches,
> and even the television I provided;
> but now you shun me.
> What are you thinking?
> I did nothing but do good for you.
> You enjoyed the dresses,
> desired the 900-shilling watches,
> and feasted on daily meat.
> But you have left me.
> Who am I to be left alone with?
> Perhaps I should kill myself
> and vanish, just as you did.

Gwanaggomola soared to the top of the charts, surpassing even the popularity of Millie Small's My Boy Lollipop, another 1964 favorite in Uganda. Within weeks of its release, the single sold over 7,000 copies, an unprecedented achievement in Uganda's music history. To truly grasp the magnitude of Gwanaggomola's success, it is important to consider the context. While hundreds of thousands of Ugandan families owned transistor radios, record players were a luxury few could afford. Often, only one or two households in an entire village possessed one. This means that selling 7,000 copies likely meant that roughly one-third of Ugandan record player owners purchased Kawalya's song.

The song's immense popularity led to the New Life Star Band being nicknamed the "Gwanaggomola" band for a period. In the mid-1960s, Paul Mukasa Mubiru, who would later join the Cranes band, organized a "Gwanaggomola" concert featuring the New Life Stars at Uganda's National Theater in Kampala. The concert was a resounding success, with tickets selling out completely. Further solidifying its triumph, Gwanaggomola topped the weekly Top Ten chart published by the Ugandan newspaper *The People* in collaboration with AGS Studios, holding the number one spot for the longest duration since the chart's inception.

To further enhance their vocal prowess, Kawalya and Kanyike recruited Bonnie Steven Kyambadde, also known by his stage name B. K. Steven. This pseudonym added a touch of mystique to his recordings, although it was primarily for reasons of setting himself apart from Andrew Kyambadde. Bonnie, a skilled bassist, joined the New Life Star Band in 1964 and became a beloved vocalist and prolific recording artist. His smooth voice and amiable personality charmed the club's patrons, particularly the female audience. It was with the New Life Star Band that Bonnie achieved his national breakthrough.

Like Kanyike and Andrew Kyambadde, Bonnie grew up in the Natete and Busega area. His father, Erisa Kyambadde, was a close friend of Fred Kanyike's father, Henry Kanyike, and both were acquainted with Andrew Kyambadde's father, Kinatama Bulera. Bonnie's musical talent was evident from a young age, as he sang in the local church choir. He attended Natete

Junior School, where he was a few classes behind Freddie Kanyike. The two often rehearsed songs together. Bonnie later attended Kyambogo Demonstration School and completed his secondary education at Pillai's Secondary School. After graduating, he dedicated himself to music full-time.

Bonnie joined Kampala City Six in early 1960, shortly after Kanyike and Andrew Kyambadde. His first composition was Mukyala Jerida (Mrs. Jerida) in 1957, and the song was released on the AGS label in 1961, attributed to Fred Kanyike and the Kampala City Six Band. He stayed with Kampala City Six for six months before joining Fred Masagazi's band in Nakayibi on the outskirts of Masaka town. He continued with Masagazi, playing bass and singing in the newly formed Uganda Kezaala Jazz Band, also known as the UK Jazz Band, in 1962. He was a backing vocalist on most of Fred Masagazi's UK Jazz Band songs. When Masagazi disbanded the UK Jazz Band in August 1964, Bonnie sought new opportunities. Kawalya and Kanyike welcomed him into the New Life Star Band at Kamulu's Mengo nightclub.

The trio collaborated on one of the band's signature songs, Tulo Tulo (Sleep, Sleep), which begins with a playful dialogue between Kanyike and Kawalya:

Kanyike: "Eh, my good fella, those of Kawalya, Kanyike, and Steven, where do you find them?" Kawalya: "Eh, my good fella, you do not know that they are at New Life? Where do you come from?"

The song then delves into the predicament of a female fan who missed out on the fun at New Life due to her pregnancy. Now that she has given birth, she longs to return to the club and asks her husband to take her dancing. However, the baby poses a challenge, and the husband insists she cannot leave the child behind. She then recalls a traditional lullaby to soothe the baby, allowing her to rejoin the festivities she has missed:

Sleep, sleep,
take the baby.
If you do not take her,
then you are a witch.

Sleep, sleep,
take the baby.
After these nine months here,
quiet now, baby, sleep.
I am off to dance,
to have some fun.
Sleep, sleep, baby, sleep,
so I can go to the dance
and move to the music.

Between 1964 and 1966, Bonnie produced a remarkable body of work at AGS Studios, a period that yielded some of his most celebrated recordings. His association with the New Life Star Band proved crucial, as it facilitated his frequent trips to AGS Studios in Nairobi alongside Kanyike. There, he embarked on a prolific recording spree, crafting a series of songs that gained widespread popularity, becoming staples on Radio Uganda's airwaves.

One of his earliest compositions, Taata Ndese Omusajja (Dad, I Brought My Man), originally penned in the 1950s, found new life in a 1964 recording and became an instant sensation. This success was not an anomaly. Bonnie followed with a string of highly regarded tracks, each demonstrating his exceptional songwriting and melodic talent. Leka Ngende (Let Me Go), Lwaki Olwana (Why Do You Fight?), Jimmy Jukira (Jimmy Remember), Masitula (a female name), Ngobuba Sooka Kuloza (Think Before Becoming Resentful), Faisi (a female name), Mwami Tonimba (Husband, Do Not Lie to Me), and Simanyi Kyembade (Do Not Know What Has Become of Me) all found enthusiastic audiences.

Among these, two songs stood out as monumental achievements: Onnemye Okukyawa (Cannot Stop Loving You) and Nkwagale Ntya (How Should I Love You?). With their haunting melodies and beautiful lyrics, these tracks marked Bonnie's emergence as a defining voice in Ugandan music. Beyond matters of the heart, his output also included songs of social commentary, such as David Asome (Let David Go to School), which spoke to the importance of education, and Tetujja Kwekisa (We

Will Not Hide), a song of defiance. This period at AGS Studios marked a time of extraordinary creative output for Bonnie, a time when his talent and artistry reached their zenith.

Uganda's 1962 independence constitution established a complex political structure, granting significant concessions to the Buganda kingdom. Buganda received a unique federal status, distinct from the other three kingdoms of Bunyoro, Toro, and Ankole, and the eleven districts that comprised the Ugandan state. In October 1963, Uganda transitioned into a republic, and a month later, the Kabaka of Buganda was appointed the ceremonial president. Real political power, however, resided with the prime minister, Dr. Milton Obote. The people of Buganda celebrated this arrangement, viewing it as a recognition of their king's stature, placing him at the forefront of the nation's symbolic leadership.

Bonnie, alongside Kawalya and Kanyike, were staunch royalists, expressing their loyalty through songs that praised the Kabaka. This tradition continued in Bonnie's 1964 song Uganda Nebyayo (Uganda and Its Heritage), where he declared: "The most manly of all men/ He accepted to be behind the steering wheel/ Mutesa truthfully swore to steer Uganda/ Why is it that he was accepted in the west and east?/ Because they realized without him at the helm, Uganda was doomed." Backed by the AGS Boys, the song reflected the strong sentiment of many in Buganda.

Following the 1964 referendum on the so-called "lost counties" of Buyaga and Bugangaizi, territories incorporated into Buganda by the British in the late 19th century, tensions escalated between Obote and the Kabaka. The overwhelming vote by the residents to return these counties to Bunyoro infuriated the Kabaka, who suspected that Obote's central government had manipulated the outcome. Feeling deeply betrayed, the Kabaka even contemplated drastic measures, including the possibility of Buganda seceding from Uganda. Allegations that high-ranking officials, including Obote and Idi Amin, were illegally profiting from gold and ivory originating in the Democratic Republic of the Congo only further destabilized the political landscape.

The tension between the two political leaders reached a breaking point in May 1966 when the Kabaka issued an ultimatum, demanding that Obote and the central government vacate Buganda's territory by May 30, 1966. This ultimatum effectively amounted to a declaration of secession. Obote responded by accusing the Kabaka of high treason. The situation escalated rapidly. Obote arrested five ministers, suspended the 1962 Constitution, and dismissed Mutesa from the presidency. The military and police, under Obote's command, were mobilized, and troops led by Colonel Idi Amin besieged and stormed the Kabaka's palace at Mengo. The Kabaka managed to escape and found refuge in exile in London, where he died in 1969.

Following the military assault on the Kabaka's palace, Obote's government declared a state of emergency in Buganda and abolished all traditional kingdoms in Uganda. Widespread violence, including shootings and looting, erupted in Kampala. Kabaka loyalists and opposition leaders were arrested and imprisoned without trial. Among those detained was Jolly Joe Kiwanuka, who remained imprisoned until Idi Amin's coup in 1971. This period of political upheaval deeply affected Bonnie, turning him against the Obote government. Therefore, when Idi Amin overthrew Obote, who was deeply unpopular in Buganda due to his conflict with the Kabaka, Bonnie, along with many other Ugandan musicians from Buganda, welcomed Amin's rise to power.

In 1964, Bonnie's talent for vocal harmony shone brightly through a series of tender and playful duets with Yunia Nalwanga, recorded at AGS Studios. These collaborations included Nga tukyali bato (When We Were Still Young), though Yunia was not credited on this particular track, and Wesige nze (Trust Me). He also partnered with Kawalya and Masagazi for the song Sirina Ampana (Nobody to Admire Me). Bonnie's relaxed and accessible singing style made him a firm favorite among the New Life crowd, who considered their resident band to be among the finest in Kampala. This high regard was evident during the 1966 Sportsman band competition, sponsored by British American Tobacco. The New Life Star

Band, under the direction of Caliste, delivered a strong performance, ultimately securing second place behind the winning Susana band.

Kamulu, the owner of New Life, like other prominent Kampala club proprietors, sought to enhance the entertainment experience at his venue. Recognizing the growing popularity of Congolese rhumba, a genre the New Life band did not specialize in, Kamulu successfully recruited the highly regarded King Jazz Band from the White Nile nightclub. The two bands then alternated performances at New Life. However, by early 1966, both King Jazz and the New Life Star Band became dissatisfied with their working conditions and Kamulu's management. This led to the departure of King Jazz, who relocated to the Rainbow Club in Bwaise. Shortly after, the principal New Life Star Band, led by Charles Caliste, disbanded. Caliste, Omali, and Filipo returned to Kenya, while Alifunsi went back to Tanzania. Pascal joined the Susana band.

Bonnie, Kanyike, and Kawalya then transitioned to the Lorina Nightclub, which continued being known for most part by its old name of Satellite Night Club. Satellite was officially launched in 1964 by the Minister of Finance, Mr. Amos Kalule Sempa, a man known for his refined taste in classical music and for patronizing the growing number of nightclubs that catered to Kampala's African urbanites. At the opening ceremony, Tony Kiberu, the nightclub manager, added a theatrical touch by having the newly recruited barmaids line up in two neat rows. As if officiating a state function, Sempa strolled between them with the measured air of a man inspecting a military parade. Amusing as it was, the scene set the tone for a venue that would blend flair with fun. Given their growing popularity, Bonnie, Kanyike, and Kawalya were soon invited to form their own resident band, which they named the Lorina Stars. This ensemble featured some of Kampala's most talented musicians, including Charles Ginaro, a highly skilled guitarist from Congo, and Kenyan saxophonists Harry Pancho and Surrur Salim. The Lorina Stars performed alongside the long-established Lorina Top Ten Band, which had served as the resident group since the venue's earlier days as the Satellite Nightclub. The Lorina Top Ten Band was managed by Shelton Mazowe who also oversaw the

Susana Band and led the Shelton Trio, a group that regularly entertained guests at Kampala's prestigious Grand Hotel. Although the venue was officially renamed Lorina Nightclub, many locals continued to refer to it as the Satellite, and the Lorina Top Ten Band later adopted the name Satellite Top Ten Band in keeping with that popular usage.

Ever the consummate innovator, Shelton introduced the very popular African Variety Show at the club, which became a signature attraction, drawing in crowds with its mix of rhythm, spectacle, and cosmopolitan flair. Central to the show's appeal were Pennie and Shellie, two highly acclaimed South African dancers whose stage presence embodied both sensuality and discipline. Dressed in feathered headdresses, sequined bodices, and beaded skirts that caught the glimmer of the club's lights, they moved with a precision that blended African dance motifs with the cabaret style popular in Europe and America. Their performances, accompanied by the Lorina Top Ten Band and the syncopated pulse of Kampala's nightlife, transformed Lorina into a magnet for revelers eager to witness a new kind of entertainment that merged local vitality with imported glamour.

During their time at Lorina nightclub, Kanyike, Kawalya, and Bonnie Kyambadde produced a string of successful songs. Notably, Kanyike's Oh Africa became a major hit, paying tribute to the leaders of a newly independent Africa. In this track, Kanyike and the AGS Boys drew inspiration from the Congolese music scene, incorporating the melody and rhythm of Carrefour Addis-Abeba, a popular song by Joseph "Le Grand Kalle" Kabasele's L'African Jazz, a band widely admired in Uganda.

However, the political climate cast a long shadow over the music scene. The state of emergency imposed after the attack on the Kabaka's Lubiri palace and his subsequent exile brought Kampala's nightlife to a standstill. The city was subjected to a strictly enforced dusk-to-dawn curfew, severely impacting the entertainment industry. Some clubs, like Susana, attempted to adapt by introducing daytime dancing on weekends, but these efforts met with limited success.

Lorina, in an attempt to revitalize its business, launched special afternoon dances targeted at Kampala's student population. To cater to this younger audience, they brought in a new band called the Cranes, composed primarily of students. The Cranes had previously performed afternoon shows at the Crested Crane Bar and Restaurant on Kampala Road, but it was their weekend performances at Lorina that popularized the concept of teenage dances in Uganda. The Cranes were not alone. Several other bands formed by teenagers emerged during this period, including the Slingers, the Spears, the Thunderbirds, the Hurricanes founded by Wasswa "Rocky" Birigwa, the Echoes, the Flames (not to be confused with Hanny Sensuwa's 1970s band of the same name), and the Phoenixes.

The year 1966 presented significant challenges for musicians in Uganda, particularly in Kampala. The curfew and the tense political atmosphere led many bands to relocate to towns with less restrictive conditions, while others, lacking financial stability, were forced to disband. In December 1967, facing these difficulties, Kanyike, Kawalya, and Bonnie Kyambadde decided to dissolve the Lorina Stars and pursue separate paths.

After the Lorina Stars disbanded, Kanyike embarked on a new chapter in his life, joining the sales department of the British American Tobacco company. However, his passion for music remained strong, and he continued to perform at various Kampala nightclubs, entertaining audiences with his old hits and introducing new material. The music recording industry in Uganda was undergoing a significant transformation, with new and more accessible recording facilities beginning to emerge. These developments made it increasingly difficult for Fred Kanyike to continue bringing musicians to the AGS studios in Nairobi. The old model was becoming obsolete.

Since the closure of the Opel Recording Company, Ugandan musicians had waited anxiously for the emergence of a new home-grown studio. Promises came in plenty. In the mid-1960s, Charles Ssenkatuka, visiting Kampala from Kinshasa, boldly declared his intention to open a recording studio. Charles Sonko, returning from several years in Kenya and citing his experience at Equator Sound with Charles Worrod, also pledged to fill the void left by Opel. Even respected local musicians like Israel Magembe and Fred Masagazi voiced their ambitions to establish studios.

Appeals were made to the Uganda Development Corporation (UDC), a government parastatal founded by the British in 1952 to drive industrial development, to support these efforts. Despite the pledges and petitions, the dream remained stubbornly out of reach. However, that changed in 1968, when Dutch businessman Paul Kerssemakers established Serenade Recording Studio in Ndeeba, a Kampala suburb. Backed by the Dutch multinational N.V. Twentsche Overzee Handel Maatschappij (Twentsche Overseas Trading Co. Ltd.), which had operated in East Africa since the early twentieth century, Kerssemakers launched both a recording and distribution company. He operated two recording studios, one in Kampala's central business district on Salisbury Road (present-day Nkrumah Road), and another in Ndeeba, where it was housed within his newly opened Peacock nightclub. Kerssemakers brought in Edmund Batte, a well-respected sound engineer and musician, and negotiated with the Philips pressing plant in Nairobi to manufacture records under his Serenade label. At the same time, drummer and instrument repairman Joseph Ndugga, who had formed the Satellite Top Ten Band in 1967, left Satellite and was brought into the Serenade fold. His group, which included talented musicians such as Molile Reny, Pancho, Kalule, and Elvis Sevume, became the core session band for Serenade Studios and was renamed the Serenade Top Ten Band. From the mid-1960s to the mid-1970s, they emerged as the most iconic and influential Ugandan session musicians of the era. Their playing can be heard on many of the rumba-based hit songs released on local labels such as Serenade and Kagaabe. Behind the scenes, they helped shape the sound of an entire generation of popular Ugandan music.

To safeguard both fairness and credibility, Kerssemakers established a small vetting committee to review new recordings, selecting Elly Wamala together with Paul Munyagwa Nsibirwa, then serving as Deputy Minister of Information, Broadcasting and Tourism. He was determined that the committee function independently, mindful of the controversy that had shadowed some Kenyan talent scouts, who were accused of rejecting songs only to rework them later for their own purposes. In principle, Kerssemakers preferred to keep musicians off such bodies to avoid conflicts of interest. However, he made a deliberate exception for Wamala, whose reputation for artistic integrity was matched by a rare degree of financial independence. Unlike many of his contemporaries, Wamala did not depend solely on performance income; his principal livelihood came from his work as a presenter at Uganda Television.

Meanwhile, beyond Uganda's borders, new opportunities were opening up for local artists. Ugandan musicians were increasingly drawn to the A. P. Chandarana studio in Kericho, Kenya. In 1967 its owner, Arvindkumar P. Chandarana, toured Kampala's nightclubs in search of promising talent, presenting musicians with the prospect of professional recording sessions. The Kericho studio was well equipped and efficiently run, but its greatest advantage lay in geography. Closer to Uganda than Nairobi, it offered a journey that was both quicker and markedly cheaper, a decisive factor for artists navigating the realities of limited resources. Combined with his reputation for paying better rates than the Nairobi-based studios on River Road or Victoria Street, Chandaran's operation became a preferred destination for many Ugandan musicians.

After leaving the Lorina Stars, Kawalya returned to Susana Nightclub in 1968, where he continued to attract large crowds. There, he collaborated closely with Martin Munyenga, a versatile Congolese multi-instrumentalist who had been with the band since the early 1960s. Munyenga's influence was crucial in guiding Kawalya towards the burgeoning Congolese soukous sound that was rapidly gaining popularity across East Africa. Susana's lineup during this period was a vibrant fusion of local and regional talent. The band was led by Richard Majola, with Ecklas Kawalya serving as the principal vocalist for Luganda songs, supported by Rose Musoke. Vocals were shared among a diverse and gifted ensemble. Majola and Shelton Mazowe performed popular covers in English, French, and Spanish, while Kawalya took the lead on Luganda numbers. Martin Munyenga and Hyppolithe Kitenzogu Makassy contributed Lingala songs, adding a distinctly Congolese flair. The guitar section was equally impressive. Charles Ginaro and Hamisi played lead guitar, alongside Toby, a Congolese musician also on lead. Richard Shonga from Zambia and Jimmy Kajwanja from Tanzania handled rhythm guitar duties, while Makassy played bass in addition to his vocals. Later additions to the band included Cornelius Mbayo, another Congolese guitarist who contributed on rhythm guitar. On drums were the Ugandans Geoffrey "Mutooro" Nsereko and Magumba. The brass section was led by trumpeters Twalib Mohammed and Haruna, and it eventually included Congolese trumpeter Willy Bartholomew and saxophonist Charles Kaliste. Ugandan vocalists Hadija Namale, Monica Mbabazi and Jolly Rwakanegere would also join in the years that followed. This particular configuration of the Susana Band, which took shape around 1970, is widely regarded as the finest in the band's history.

During his Susana era, many of Kawalya's standout songs were composed by the talented Naiti Nandawula. While managing a day job at the Bat Valley bar and restaurant on Bombo Road, Nandawula found time to compose a series of hit tunes specifically for Kawalya. Among these compositions were Jane, Joyce, Tubireke (Let's Leave It Alone), and Lydia. The relationship between Kawalya and Nandawula extended beyond the professional, as the married Kawalya and the gifted Nandawula were known to be romantically involved. Another woman, Aida Nabacwa, also occasionally composed for Kawalya, and she was the force behind his successful ding ding song Nsamba Nsamba (Stomp-Stomp).

Among his notable hits at Susana nightclub was Ndikulaba (I Will See You Later), released on Chandaran's Wachezaji label. This widely popular song tells the story of a journey to Dar es Salaam on a VC10 to visit a lover. Another success was Tangiwa (Don't Let Me Down), inspired by a woman he encountered at Susana, whose subtle wave sparked a desire to marry her immediately at Namirembe Cathedral. Kawalya's creative endeavors extended beyond music during this period. He also embarked on an acting career, taking on the role of Domazo in a Uganda Television sitcom.

By 1967, Congolese music had firmly taken root in Uganda. A poll conducted by the local *People* newspaper that year revealed that Franco Luambo's OK Jazz and Joseph Kabasele's African Jazz Band were the most popular bands in the country. The River Road two-part vocal harmony style was fading, replaced by the infectious energy of soukous. This genre featured intricate guitar interplay, powerful horn sections, and an irresistible, driving beat, often punctuated by a vibrant instrumental section called the sebene, characterized by hard-driving, undulating guitar lines.

Meanwhile, with the disbanding of the Lorina Stars, Bonnie's rising popularity caught the attention of Nile Breweries, who sought to engage him for a major marketing campaign promoting their Nile and Club beers. Bonnie's youthful appeal, stylish image, and strong following among young urbanites made him an ideal ambassador for their brands. Nile Breweries had recently signed a contract with Vox Nationale, a Congolese band based in Kampala, to perform in major Ugandan towns as part of their promotional efforts. However, Vox Nationale primarily performed in Lingala and lacked fluency in Luganda, the language commonly used in Ugandan popular music. Recognizing the importance of connecting with the local audience, the brewery saw the value in adding a musician who could sing in Luganda, and Bonnie fit the bill perfectly.

The Vox Nationale promotional shows for Nile Breweries proved immensely popular. Bonnie and the band toured extensively across Uganda, bringing their music to towns like Jinja, Mbale, Soroti, Lira, Fort Portal, and Kabale. Following the successful campaign, Bonnie returned to Kampala and continued performing with Vox Nationale at New Life nightclub. By then, the band's lineup had expanded to include several promising Ugandan musicians, such as Philly "Bongoley" Lutaaya, John Mutebi, a highly skilled guitarist, Geoffrey Nsereko, and John Kajura.

In 1969, Bonnie recorded several soukous hits with Vox Nationale on the Serenade label, including Sirina Mulala (Don't Have Another), Emikwano Gigwayo (Love Ends), Ntegedde Onjagala (Understand You Love Me), and Kambotole (I Confess). When Vox Nationale returned to Congo in 1970 due to the inability to renew the work permits for many of their predominantly Congolese musicians, Bonnie was extended an invitation to rejoin the group and relocate to Congo. Despite this opportunity, he chose to stay in Uganda, where he found a new musical home with the Marina Band, performing regularly at Kololo Club, which would later become known as Guvnor.

On January 25, 1971, Idi Amin seized power in a coup d'état, over-throwing Dr. Milton Obote's government. This marked the beginning of a brutal eight-and-a-half-year reign of terror. Initially, many were unaware of Amin's true nature. He presented himself as a champion of law and order, promising a return to democracy and a departure from Obote's increasingly authoritarian rule. Caught up in the wave of optimism that followed the coup, Bonnie joined the Uganda Air Force Jazz Band, based at the Entebbe air base.

For the next eight and a half years, this unassuming and gentle musician toured the country with the Air force band, primarily entertaining soldiers at military bases in Entebbe, Nakasongola, and Gulu. Like other military-owned bands, they occasionally performed for civilian audiences at major events. Bonnie even appears in a well-known photograph of Idi Amin playing his beloved accordion alongside the Air Force band. In the image, Bonnie is the young, handsome man to Amin's left, holding a microphone and wearing a printed shirt. Despite this proximity, Bonnie did not have a personal relationship with Amin. He was essentially an honorary soldier, without formal military training, and unfamiliar with weapons like the Heckler & Koch G3 assault rifle favored by Amin's troops.

At his core, Bonnie was an exceptionally talented musician with a smooth, heartfelt tenor voice that exuded warmth and charm. However, his disillusionment with the Obote regime and his subsequent embrace of Idi Amin set in motion a chain of events that would tragically culminate in his brutal murder in April 1979. During his time with the Air Force Jazz Band, Bonnie did not produce any major hits, his musical output overshadowed by the turbulent political climate.

Another alumnus of Kampala City Six who would go on to dizzying musical success was Fred Hannington Masagazi Muwonge, widely known as Fred Masagazi. Born in 1937 in Mpererwe, a quiet suburb in the northern part of Kampala, he would go on to become a prominent figure in Ugandan music. His early life was rooted in the simple rhythms of rural life, with his father, Paul Matovu, working as a local farmer. Masagazi's formal education began at Mityana Junior School, where he first encountered the structured world of musical instruction under the guidance of Mr. Arthur Bagunywa. This early exposure to music set the stage for his future endeavors. He continued his studies at Lubiri Senior Secondary School in Kampala, broadening his academic horizons.

Mr. Arthur Bagunywa, Masagazi's influential teacher, was more than just a music instructor; he was a mentor who instilled a deep appreciation for the arts. Bagunywa's career trajectory was remarkable, evolving into a distinguished academic and author, contributing significantly to Ugandan literature. His public service extended into politics, where he served as a Member of Parliament for a Mityana constituency during the 1990s. He also served as the Buganda Kingdom's Minister of Tourism, Heritage, and Cooperatives in 2005.

After completing his education at Lubiri Senior Secondary School, Masagazi explored various employment opportunities, but none of these ventures provided him with the sense of fulfillment he sought. The seeds of musical passion, sown by Mr. Bagunywa, had taken root, and Masagazi felt an undeniable pull towards a life dedicated to music. He believed that only through music could he find true satisfaction and purpose.

Masagazi's formal introduction to the music scene came in 1960, at the age of 23, when he joined Robert Kavuma's band, which held a regular engagement at the East African Railways Club in Nsambya. Recognizing the spark in Masagazi's voice, Kavuma took him under his wing, nurturing his talent and giving him space to grow on stage. During this period, Masagazi also briefly collaborated with Simon Kaate Nsubuga, the band's seasoned lead vocalist. The band's performances extended beyond the Railways Club to a venue known as Nkonko, later rebranded as Peacock, located in Ndeeba. At the time, Ndeeba was a semi-urban outpost on the edge of Kampala. It was at Nkonko, beneath a corrugated roof that echoed with the sounds of dance and cheer, that Masagazi's voice began to take root. His music found a devoted audience among mechanics, market vendors, railway workers, shopkeepers, and others who had left their villages for town life. These revelers came not just to be entertained, but to experience something they could truly feel.

In 1961, Masagazi took a significant step in his nascent musical journey by joining Magembe's Kampala City Six, which performed at the popular Planet nightclub in Bwaise. This move placed him in the company of established and talented musicians. With Kampala City Six, he recorded his first songs, Kasonsomolera (Spillover) and Namazi (a female name), marking the beginning of his recording career.

That same year, 1961, saw the opening of Jolly Joe Kiwanuka's White Nile nightclub. Jolly Joe secured Magembe's band for a regular engagement at White Nile. However, Masagazi struggled to find his voice there. The club's patrons overwhelmingly favored Congolese (Lingala) cover songs, a genre Masagazi did not perform. This preference significantly limited his opportunities to appear on stage. Frustration grew as he found himself competing for limited stage time with the band's other talented vocalists, including Ecklas Kawalya, Freddie Kanyike, and B. K. Steven.

In February 1962, Masagazi made a decisive move, parting ways with Kampala City Six. He recognized that to truly broaden his musical horizons and gain greater stage presence, he needed to master the popular Congolese Lingala style. With this in mind, he joined Kampala's Congolese band Rock'en Band, reasoning that this was the most direct path to learning from the "experts" of the genre. He immersed himself in the study of Congolese songs, dedicating himself to mastering the nuances of the style. Within a few months, his diligence paid off, and he achieved notable proficiency in Lingala music.

With Rock'en Band, Masagazi began establishing his reputation as a recording artist. For the AGS label, he recorded tracks such as Kabaka Yekka (King Only) and Fred, Mutesa, both tributes to King Freddie, the Kabaka of Buganda. This marked a bold inflection in his career, as he blended his newly acquired Lingala skills with a deep connection to his cultural roots. During the next recording session, the band rebranded as Rock A. Mambo and continued working with AGS, producing songs like Sente (Money) and Omukyala Omufumbo (A Married Woman).

During a performance with Rock'en Band, Masagazi's talent caught the attention of a wealthy businessman from Masaka. Impressed by Masagazi's musical abilities and stage presence, the businessman approached him with an enticing proposition: to assemble a band for a regular engagement at his bar in Nakayiba, a modest town on the northern edge of Masaka. Nestled along the Kampala–Masaka road, Nakayiba was little more than a single street flanked by a few trading stores, yet it pulsed with enough life to offer a steady audience for live music. Masagazi, seeing this as an opportunity to lead his own musical band, carefully selected a group of young and talented Ugandan musicians. The resulting band proved to be a hit with the revelers at the Nakayiba bar. Their vibrant and innovative music brought a fresh sound to the town, which had never before experienced weekly live rhumba-style performances. Despite the warm reception in Nakayiba, Masagazi, a man of considerable ambition, felt that the town offered a limited platform for his aspirations. He envisioned a much larger stage for his musical talents, dreaming of achieving widespread recognition and stardom.

The year 1962 was a landmark year for Uganda, culminating in the nation's independence in October. During this period of national celebration and optimism, Masagazi and his band were invited to perform in and around Kampala. The atmosphere was charged with excitement and hope, with independence promising a future filled with endless possibilities. Masagazi relished the opportunity to perform in Kampala once again.

The band's return to Kampala proved to be a turning point. Jolly Joe Kiwanuka, who had an eye for great talent, witnessed their performance and was sufficiently impressed to offer them a regular engagement at White Nile nightclub. Consequently, the band did not return to Nakayiba. After a four-month stint at White Nile, Masagazi, driven by a desire for artistic independence, made the decision to leave. He had acquired his own musical instruments and was determined to lead his own band.

Masagazi christened his new band the Uganda Kezaala Jazz Band, also known as the UK Jazz Band. The name, which translates from Luganda to "Born of Uganda," reflected Masagazi's strong sense of national pride and identity. At the time, the majority of prominent live acts in Kampala's nightclubs were Congolese, and there were few Ugandan musicians with the resources and drive to establish their own bands. Ugandan musicians often struggled to gain recognition and relevance in the face of this dominance. This situation led to a degree of tension between Ugandan and Congolese musicians, although there were instances of collaboration and integration, with Congolese bands sometimes incorporating Ugandan musicians into their lineups, as was the case with Masagazi when he performed with Rock'en Band.

Although founded by Masagazi, the UK Jazz Band was not composed exclusively of Ugandans. It brought together a diverse group of talented musicians from various countries. The band featured Ugandan members such as Fred Masagazi (founder and frontman), B. K. Steven (vocalist), Joseph Mutebi (rhythm guitar), Kigozi (bass, who would later join the Prisons Jazz Band), and Katembo (saxophone). The lineup also included Tanzanian Jimmy on lead guitar and Kenyan Ndiri on saxophone.

In December 1962, Masagazi's newly formed Uganda Kezaala Jazz Band secured a significant residency at Miti's Top Life nightclub. This was no short-term engagement, as they signed a comprehensive five-year contract, establishing themselves as the resident band. The band's lineup expanded to include Mary Nattima. Mary Nattima's talent would soon shine, as she gained considerable prominence through her beguiling duets with Ecklas Kawalya.

UK Jazz became known for their dedication to promoting and performing music rooted in the kagutema or ding ding genre. In these early days of his solo career, Masagazi was deeply committed to reclaiming and celebrating Uganda's traditions and customs. His most iconic kagutema song, Nandere, released in 1963 on the AGS label and accompanied by the AGS Boys, became a cultural touchstone. That same record also featured the song that catapulted him to national prominence, Omusolo (Poll Tax). Omusolo served as a musical call to action, encouraging Ugandan adult men to pay their poll tax and highlighting the consequences of non-compliance, which could include imprisonment. The poll tax, established by the British colonial administration through the Poll-Tax Ordinance of 1905, required adult male "natives" to pay two rupees per annum. This tax, along with the hut tax, was deeply unpopular and viewed by some as a form of forced labor.

The years 1963 and 1964 were incredibly productive for Masagazi and the UK Jazz Band. They spent extended periods at the AGS studios in Nairobi, recording a series of popular songs. These included Mutesa Ndaiga (Mutesa in Ndaiga), Mutesa-Obote-UK Jazz, Tewali Kwebaka Uganda (There's No Sleeping in Uganda), and their signature song, Sanyuka Ne UK Jazz (Rejoice with UK Jazz). Masagazi also collaborated with his friend, Bonnie Kyambadde (B. K. Steven), providing backup vocals on tracks like Sente Sente (Money) and Mwatu Nina Kyengamba (Beloved, I Have Something to Share). He also joined Fred Kanyike as a supporting vocalist on B. K. Steven's Sirina Ampana (Nobody to Admire Me), all released on the AGS label.

By 1964, Masagazi had become one of Uganda's most sought-after musicians. He mesmerized listeners with popular songs that attracted a devoted following and achieved enormous record sales. Even at Makerere University, where social gatherings had traditionally been formal affairs dominated by ballroom dancing, Masagazi's live performances with the UK Jazz Band drew significant attention. The university itself had a lively ballroom dancing scene, with the Makerere Ballroom Dancing Association (MABADA) boasting the largest membership of any student club. The university also had its own band, which was especially active during the annual social events organized by the various Halls of Residence. These long-standing events often attracted student nurses from the Mengo and Mulago Nursing Schools, who were brought in by school buses for the occasion.

In the early 1960s, the university band was led by Peter Nazareth, a future novelist and literary critic, who initially called the band Teddy Bear but later rebranded it as the Makerere Jazz Band. Despite this vibrant musical tradition, it was Masagazi's dynamic performances that captivated the university's students. They attended lectures by day and eagerly anticipated evenings at Top Life in Bwaise, a short walk from the sprawling campus. At nightfall, the sleepy daytime neighborhood of Bwaise transformed into a beehive of activity. The area buzzed with a colorful mix of people, including domestic workers, street vendors hawking candy, clothes, *chapati*, *mandazi*, and washing blue, as well as individuals engaged in spirited barter trades, exchanging items like a cake of Sunlight soap for a bottle of *kwete*, a creamy fermented alcoholic beverage made from corn. Men arrived at Top Life with their lovers, and patrons from every stratum of society converged to dance, drink, and socialize. The revelers ranged from newly appointed Uganda police constables to male university students seeking a lively night out or hoping for a chance encounter with local women from Bwaise or Katanga, a corrugated shanty neighborhood in Wandegeya on the eastern edge of the university campus, where there was no piped water or sewage.

In May 1964, Makerere upheld its long-standing tradition when Dr. R. G. Katongole, a senior civil servant in the Ministry of Information and Broadcasting, was invited as guest of honor at a university dance in the Main Hall. The occasion carried the formality of an academic ritual, yet the hall came alive with music and the elegance of students and their guests, capturing the blend of intellect and youthful exuberance that defined campus life in the early years of independence. The evening, however, belonged to Masagazi and his UK Jazz Band, who made their highly anticipated debut performance on campus. Their energetic set ignited the Main Hall, which was packed with an ecstatic crowd. The atmosphere was electric, with some students even standing on chairs, dancing in place, and erupting in cheers for their favorite lines, delivered with fresh vibrancy by Masagazi and B. K. Steven.

This fervent response from the university community was a clear acknowledgment of UK Jazz's burgeoning preeminence on Kampala's vibrant live music scene. Adding to their momentum, 1964 also saw Masagazi release a string of hits that resonated across the nation, including the catchy Sente Eno (Money) and the poignant Mukyala Nga Olabye (Sorry Woman). However, as the year progressed, Masagazi and the UK Jazz Band's contract with Top Life came to an end. Recognizing that he could achieve even greater success without the logistical challenges of managing a band, Masagazi decided to disband UK Jazz. By then, he had already secured significant national recognition and was widely regarded as a leading figure in Uganda's evolving music scene.

In 1965, Masagazi transitioned from AGS Studios to Charles Worrod's Equator Studios. His initial recording session at Equator Studios in Nairobi, backed by the Equator Boys band, yielded four songs: Oh Lovely Night, Fa Ku Mwana (Care for the Child), Luki (a female name), and Obuwuulu (Bachelorhood). Charles Worrod was deeply impressed by Masagazi's vocal talent. Having worked with numerous Ugandan artists, Worrod found Masagazi's voice exceptional. He recognized Masagazi's potential for widespread success and, in an unusual gesture, sent him a letter after the recording session stating, "The company has every confidence that these exceptional numbers will become extremely popular not only in Uganda but in the East African territories as well." Worrod committed to promoting Masagazi's music throughout East Africa and internationally. This marked the beginning of a fruitful collaboration with Equator Studios. Later, Worrod appointed Masagazi as Equator Studios' sales representative in Uganda. Masagazi recorded a substantial number of songs on the Equator label, becoming the most prolific Ugandan artist associated with it. He also achieved the highest sales figures for Equator in Uganda and became closely linked with the label in the public consciousness.

In 1966, Kamulu orchestrated a significant coup by recruiting King Jazz Band, also known as King Jazz d'Equateur, from the White Nile Club to his New Life venue in Mengo. When King Jazz relocated to Jinja to perform at Kamulu's New Life in Bugembe, due to a dusk-to-dawn curfew imposed during the state of emergency, Kamulu recruited Masagazi into the King Jazz band. Around this time, Masagazi had released Mpa Omwoyo (Give Me Your Heart), arguably one of his most popular songs of 1966. The song received extensive airplay on Radio Uganda and was frequently played on jukeboxes, becoming one of the most requested tracks of its time. It soon became popularly known as Alululu after its distinctive refrain, a rolling, onomatopoeic chant that punctuated the verses with warmth and elasticity. Each 'lu' landed like a rhythmic drumbeat, playful yet hypnotic, drawing listeners into a communal call-and-response that echoed oral traditions while resting comfortably within the modern rumba form.

With Masagazi's addition, King Jazz gained a prominent vocalist who sang in Luganda, attracting large audiences. Masagazi rose to become a star within the band. He formed a strong bond with Mario Andre, the band's Congolese vocalist, and together they injected new energy into King Jazz. Upon returning to Kampala around July 1967, Masagazi and King Jazz continued to perform at New Life for a few more months. However, later that year, they returned to performing at the White Nile.

With King Jazz, Masagazi continued recording for the Equator label, releasing popular songs with titles in both Luganda and English, such as Kawa Takyadda (Everybody Blames Eve), Zisimuleyo (Don't Be a Miser), Advice to Lovers (Entanda Yomukwano), and Honour Your Parents (Oku-zaala Kwa Kasandali). In 1967, Fred Masagazi and King Jazz achieved notable success with the song Kola Zizo (Make Your Own Money). The song drew critical acclaim and was broadcast on BBC World Service radio, reportedly becoming the first Ugandan pop song to receive such international airplay. Following this breakthrough, Masagazi, a man of slight build, gained international recognition. He began to envision broader possibilities for the Ugandan music industry, expressing a desire to establish a recording studio to reduce the need for Ugandan musicians to travel to Nairobi. This vision was realized in 1973, when he co-founded Rwenzori Studios with Fred Kanyike and Hadija Namale.

On October 8, 1969, the political landscape of Uganda underwent a significant shift with the presentation of Milton Obote's Common Man's Charter. This landmark document, unveiled at a gathering of ministers, ruling party officials, civil servants, journalists, and diplomats in Kampala, signaled a "Move to the Left" for Uganda. It advocated for the redistribution of political and economic power to the majority, a reduction in foreign economic influence, and the nationalization of key economic sectors. The Charter's goals aligned closely with the "Africanization" policies, which aimed to transfer economic control from foreigners to Ugandan citizens, particularly targeting non-citizen Ugandan Asians. Further demonstrating this nationalistic turn, Obote's government expelled approximately 30,000 Kenyans from Uganda between 1969 and 1970.

This wave of nationalism had a profound impact on the music scene, particularly affecting Congolese musicians in Kampala. Government officials began to routinely harass them, and even before the formalization of the Common Man's Charter, obtaining work permits became increasingly difficult for foreigners, including those from neighboring countries. For Congolese musicians, many of whom had arrived as refugees, work permits became virtually unattainable. Officials argued that they should reside in designated refugee camps. Among those affected was the legendary Congolese musician Apollinaire Kabeya, the frontman of the Diablo band, which had been the first Congolese band to arrive in Uganda in April 1961. The members of King Jazz also faced these mounting challenges. In 1970, Selemani, the leader of King Jazz, made the difficult decision to return to Congo.

Although Masagazi was a member of King Jazz, he occasionally recorded with other bands. The group, made up mostly of Congolese musicians, frequently faced work permit issues, and there were times when the Congolese members could not perform at the White Nile nightclub due to expired documentation. This left the Ugandan members, including Masagazi, without instrumental support. In such moments, he turned to other bands for recording sessions. For instance, when Pope Paul VI visited Uganda from July 31 to August 2, 1969, marking the first visit of a reigning pope to Africa, Masagazi, along with Louise Bagenda and the Florida Fiesta Band, recorded songs to commemorate the occasion. These included Abajulize Mutulabiza Papa (The Martyrs Have Made Us See the Pope) and Tulabirawa Papa Paul (Heartfelt Welcome Pope Paul), both of which were released on the KIP label, owned by Wycliff Kiyingi of Kiyingi Productions. Kiyingi Productions specialized in developing radio commercials, and its founder was also a celebrated Ugandan playwright whose works shaped the growth of theatre in Uganda, including the free traveling theatre initiative at Makerere University in the mid-1960s. In

1970, Masagazi began working with Joseph Ndugga's Serenade Top Ten band, who provided backing for his songs Majoba (a male name), Kwekuba Kwagala (If It Is Love), and Akantu Katono (A Small Matter), all released on the Serenade label.

When King Jazz left the White Nile Club and returned to Congo, the owner, Joseph Salongo Kyeyune, was faced with a vexing and immediate challenge: how to retain the club's regular patrons. To address this, he assembled a new, predominantly Ugandan band, naming them the White Nile Club Band. Although their recording career was brief, this new group enabled Masagazi to release hits such as Lusi Fumba (Lusi Get Married) and Namulanda (a female name). These recordings were produced in Kampala by Kiyingi Productions, while the records were manufactured in Nairobi. The songs were released on the KIP label.

With the curtailment of King Jazz's performances at the White Nile, Masagazi found himself without a regular engagement. Although he had previously recorded with the Florida Fiesta Band, it was not until the latter half of 1969 that he joined them as a full-time member. As the house band at the Florida nightclub, Florida Fiesta became his musical home until 1971. By the latter part of 1970, Masagazi had not released new material that captured the public's attention, leading to speculation that he might retire from music. It was against this backdrop that Mr. Wycliff Kiyingi approached him with a proposal to compose and sing commercial jingles for radio, which Masagazi politely declined. After Idi Amin overthrew Milton Obote's government in January 1971, Masagazi emerged as a prominent artist and vocal supporter of Amin and his policies. During this period, he released significant songs, including Joanna and Minzani Yo Mukwano (The Measure of Love), both of which became radio hits. He continued to perform and record with the Rwenzori Band well into 1975.

Two young musicians in central Uganda, early 1900s, with a drum and flute. *Photograph, early twentieth century. Private collection.*

The Namilyango Boys' School Brass Band, ca. 1912.
Established by the Mill Hill Missionaries, the band is shown here
with Father Toner standing at left, reflecting the early introduction of
Western brass instrumentation in Ugandan mission schools.
Photograph, early twentieth century. Private collection.

Rhino Boys, No. 1 (East African) Entertainment Unit, 11th East African Division of the King's African Rifles (KAR), pictured in Burma during the Second World War. From left to right: Robert, Valentine Muwulya (violin), Fundi Konde, Petro, and Petero. After the war, Muwulya emerged as a key figure in the K-Rhino Boys and also performed briefly with the Mengo African Orchestra. *Courtesy of the Imperial War Museums*

Standing, left to right: Fred Kanyike and Nelson Sabavuma. Seated, left to right: Muliika and Adrew Kyambadde, during a trip to Nairobi to record, ca. 1961. *Courtesy of Andrew Kyambadde*

The Tames band during a staged performance session. In the back row,
from left, Deo Mukungu on bass guitar and Matovu on rhythm guitar.
In the front row, from the extreme right, Bernard Gonza on lead guitar,
followed by Peter Kabale on alto saxophone, and Peterson Mutebi holding
a tenor saxophone. Although Peter Mutebi appears with a saxophone in this
photograph, he did not play the instrument. *Courtesy of Tony Kalanzi*

Andrew Kyambadde (left) with guitar, Charles Sonko (center) with lap
steel guitar, and Moses Katazza (right) playing a melodica during a studio
portrait session in Nairobi, early 1960s. *Courtesy of Andrew Kyambadde*

Fred Kanyike performing with a guitar during a live appearance in1970. *Courtesy of John Luggya*

Andrew Kyambadde ca. 1961
Courtesy of Andrew Kyambadde

The Congolese band Bavy du Zaire, resident at Kampala's Arizona nightclub in the 1970s. *Courtesy of Suismann N'goy*

Seated, from left: unidentified, Frida Sonko, Andrew Kyambadde, Namugenyi, and Margaret Nakibuuka. Standing, from left: Tom Nduga, Louise Bagenda, Christopher Kato (holding an umbrella), and Fred Masagazi. *Courtesy of Andrew Kyambadde*

Left to right: Simon Berunga, Mary Nattima, Adrew Kyambadde, Frida Sonko, David Jingo, and Hadija Namale at the Sheraton Hotel, Kampala, 1994. *Courtesy of Andrew Kyambadde*

The Apolo Jambos, who played at the Apolo Hotel in Kampala in the 1960s. *Courtesy of Louise Bagenda*

Jolly Rwakanegere (left) and Louise Bagenda (right). Jolly performed with the Susana band, while Louise was the first and only female member of the Kampala City Band. *Courtesy of Louise Bagenda*

Live show at the Sheraton Hotel, Kampala, 1994, with David Jingo on drums, Andrew Kyambadde at center holding the microphone, and Margaret Nakibuuka on the left wearing a gomesi. *Courtesy of Andrew Kyambadde*

Louise Bagenda performing at the Apollo Hotel, Kampala, ca. 1970.
Courtesy of Louise Bagenda

Lariki, a vocalist from Tanganyika who performed with Kampala's
Bagatelle Band on William Street. *Courtesy of Louise Bagenda.*

Kagutema dancing at White Nile nightclub ca 1964.
Revelers dancing the kagutema at the White Nile nightclub, Kampala, ca.
1964. In the checkered shirt is Jolly Joe Kiwanuka, the club's proprietor.
Courtesy of Martin Munyenga

Miriam Ssempa, a member of Ivan & Co., which later became
the Mengo African Orchestra, and sister of its bandleader, John Bosa.
Courtesy of John Luggya

211

Charles Sonko and Jamie Candelaria-Greene (Fitch) in a Nairobi recording studio, 1979. *Courtesy of John Kineman*

From left: Hadija Namale on drums, Eva Nanyonga on guitar, and Ssemanda on keyboards. *Courtesy of Jane Frances Kiryangokibi (Hadija Namale)*

Eva Nanyonga with guitar, early 1950s.
Courtesy of Jane Frances Kiryangokibi (Hadija Namale)

Monica Mbabazi (wife of musician Martin Munyenga)
singing at a celebration marking Zaire's independence at the Zairean
Embassy, Kampala, 1973. *Courtesy of Martin Munyenga*

Fred Kigozi, 1967. *Courtesy of Jane Frances Kiryangokibi (Hadija Namale)*

From left: Margaret Nakibuuka, Andrew Kyambadde, Namugenyi.
Martin Muyenga, Hadija Namale and Suismann N'goy.
Courtesy of Martin Munyenga

Odeon shellac record Galimuwagula, recorded in Luganda and issued as part of the first commercial recording session in Uganda in 1930. *Private collection; photograph by the author.*

Original Tames Band lineup, early 1973. Seated: Peterson Mutebi. Standing, left to right: Fred Semwogerere Tebuseke, Fred Kigozi, Billy Mutebi, Frank Mbalire, and John Makubuya. *Courtesy of Frank Mbalire*

Album cover of Jimmy Katumba and the Ebonies.
Photograph by Vaclovas Sakalauskas

Susana Band, ca. 1968. Front row, standing (L–R) Bob, Jimmy Kajanjwa, Rose Namere, Frida Sonko, and Martin Munyenga. Standing at the back Twalib (trumpet). Seated (L–R) Bruno Sereman, Irunga, and Ecklas Kawalya. *Courtesy of Martin Munyenga*

A young Frank Mbalire with a guitar at Mugwanya Preparatory School, Kabojja. *Courtesy of Frank Mbalire*

Cranes, 1968. In front, holding hands, are Louise Bagenda and Moses Matovu. *Courtesy of Louise Bagenda*

Simon Berunga, ca 1967. *Courtesy of Simon Berunga*

Charles Sonko's handwritten draft of song lyrics composed
in Nairobi, 1979. *Courtesy of Jamie Candelaria-Greenee*

A couple competing in the Kagutema dance at the White Nile
nightclub in Kampala, ca. 1964. Dance competitions were a popular feature
of the city's nightlife during the 1960s. *Bwire Family Archive.*

Illustration 34: Rwenzori International. *Courtesy of Frank Mbalire*

CHAPTER 8

The journeys of Andy Kyambadde, Margaret Nakibuuka, and Kaate Nsubuga

Israel Magembe's Kampala City Six served as the premier home for Uganda's leading vocalists during the late 1950s and early 1960s. Among the band's most promising talents was Andrew "Andy" Kyambadde, who joined the group in 1959, on the same day his childhood friend Freddie Kanyike became a member. Born in 1940 in Busega, Andy attended Kyambogo Demonstration School, a renowned institution celebrated for its robust music program. At Kyambogo, where he was two classes ahead of Bonnie Kyambadde, he often joined his peers in spontaneous singing sessions. The music classes emphasized the Tonic Sol-fa system, a notation method introduced by British missionaries, which Andy mastered and later employed in his songwriting.

After graduating from Kyambogo Demonstration School, Andy proceeded to Mengo Junior Secondary. There, he became acquainted with Elly Wamala, who was about five years his senior. Although they were not in the same class, the two developed a bond during their daily walks to school. Elly lived in Bulenga and had to pass through Busega on his way to Mengo, where Andy lived. Many mornings, Andy would wait by the winding, dusty path, shaded by overhanging trees, to join Elly for the rest of the journey. The walk was unhurried and filled with the sounds of nature. Birds called from every direction, their songs ever-present in the morning air, rising above the hum of life stirring in the surrounding homes. Elly's acoustic guitar, always slung over his shoulder like a companion, intrigued Andy and won his admiration. In the afternoons, they often found a quiet spot beneath the canopy of a *mutuba* (Natal Fig) or *mvule* (African Teak) tree, where Elly would strum a few gentle chords as Andy tried out improvised lyrics. It was in these shaded corners, under the embrace of trees that had stood for generations, that Andy's musical curiosity began to take root. Shortly after completing his studies at Mengo Junior Secondary, Andy joined Kampala City Six.

One of the first songs Andy composed with Kampala City Six was Lupiya Zange (My Rupees), a collaboration with Freddie Kanyike released on the Tom Tom label. The track raised their public profile and sparked a shared excitement about recording more music. However, their ambitions soon met an unexpected obstacle. The 1959 boycott of foreign-owned businesses, which severely affected many Asian-Ugandan traders and triggered a wave of capital flight to Kenya, led to the closure of companies such as the Opel Gramophone Record and Battery Factory. With local recording options dwindling, musicians were forced to look elsewhere. Kanyike and Andy turned to Nairobi's River Road studios to fill the void. Their first session took place at AGS, though Kyambadde was only permitted to record a few songs. Hoping to expand their catalog, he urged Kanyike to explore other studios, especially CMS and Equator. However, Kanyike had recently accepted a position as AGS's Uganda talent scout. His new role made him reluctant to branch out beyond AGS, and he resisted Andy's proposal for a multi-studio strategy.

The disagreement quickly strained their friendship. Andy felt betrayed, believing that Kanyike was placing loyalty to AGS and to unfamiliar business contacts above their personal bond. Tensions escalated, and harsh words were exchanged. Kanyike came to believe, whether rightly or wrongly, that Andy resented his appointment as a talent scout for AGS. Eventually, Kanyike agreed to record a few songs on the CMS label, including Ekibuga Katwe (Katwe Town) and Freddie Mwana (Freddie Boy), although he did so with visible reluctance. While the two continued performing with Kampala City Six and even traveled together to Nairobi for further sessions, the disagreement left a lasting fracture. They would never record a song together again.

Andy did not entirely abandon AGS. He continued to record songs on the label, albeit sporadically. Notably, he produced two brisk Kenyan Twist tracks on the AGS Twist label: Damali (a female name) and Mary Twist. Over time, the warmth between him and Kanyike diminished further. This rift became even more apparent when, years later, Kanyike launched his most ambitious music project with the formation of the Rwenzori band, from which Andy was conspicuously absent. Throughout his career, Andy Kyambadde carried himself with the conviction that he was the true musical force. Though he did not play any instrument, he was a prolific composer, proud of his mastery of the tonic sol-fa system, through which he crafted songs with precision and flair. It was a skill he valued deeply, and one that Fred Kanyike, for all his talents, could not match.

Their creative tensions were not confined to music. Undercurrents of rivalry simmered beneath the surface, intensified by a shared affection for the singer Yunia Nalwanga. More than a muse, Yunia was a gifted performer whose voice and stage presence earned admiration across Kampala's music scene. Andy had known her longer, as his brother was married to her cousin, but in the end it was Kanyike who captured her heart. That single turn of fate cut deep, wounding Andy's pride and widening the rift between the two men.

When Kawalya and Kanyike left for the White Nile Club in 1963, Andy remained with Kampala City Six and stepped into the spotlight as the band's central figure. With two of its stars gone, the group leaned heavily on Andy's charisma and vocal presence to carry the weight of its performances. He rose to the challenge, earning accolades in his own right, but the ghost of past tensions lingered. The stage was finally his, yet he remained shadowed by the absence of the men who had once stood beside him.

In 1964, Shankardass & Son Ltd., which had long operated a well-known music store in Kampala, announced plans to record Ugandan artists. Aiming to launch their Uganda SDS label with a recognizable name, they turned to the musicians of Kampala City Six. At that time, many Ugandan bands were bound by loose contracts that permitted solo projects, so it was relatively easy for the label to secure a prominent talent. Shankardass & Son Ltd. signed Andy Kyambadde, making him the first Uganda-based artist to record on the SDS label. His inaugural recordings featured the songs Totya Kunjatulira (Don't Fear to Tell Me) and Edita (a female name). Later, in collaboration with his childhood friend and fellow musician from Busega, Nelson Sabavuma, Andy recorded another single on the SDS label titled Nze Nobwegassi (Unity and I).

Andy also produced several popular songs that paid tribute to the Kabaka. Among these were Kulikayo Kabaka Wange (Welcome Back My Kabaka) and Mutesa Webale (Thank You, Mutesa). Kulikayo Kabaka Wange celebrated the Buganda king's return from exile in Britain, and it was a song that helped solidify Andy Kyambadde's reputation, particularly in central Uganda. In 1965, when Kampala City Six was invited to perform for the Kabaka, Andy's performance struck a chord with the monarch. As a gesture of appreciation, the Kabaka presented him with a British-made Raleigh bicycle, a significant symbol of wealth and status at the time.

As he expanded his musical pursuits, Andy began performing duets on stage at Planet nightclub in Bwaise with aspiring female musicians. During this period, members of Kampala City Six often invited young women with musical talent to rehearse with the band. These guest artists either performed their own songs or joined the male singers in duets. Kampala City Six was among the first groups in Uganda to introduce male and female duets into the Congolese-style rumba popular at the time, although female singers more commonly provided vocal backup. Many of Uganda's promising female musicians of the 1960s got their start with Kampala City Six. Notable names include Margaret "Mega" Nakibuuka, Sarah Namagembe, Mary Nattima, and Rose Musoke. Andy Kyambadde formed a particularly strong musical bond with Margaret Nakibuuka. Her voice provided a distinctive richness and warmth to his songs, blending effortlessly with his own in a way that elevated each performance. Her mellow timbre added emotional depth, while her confident phrasing gave their duets a graceful, conversational intimacy that became a hallmark of their collaboration. Margaret Nakibuuka never overshadowed Andy but instead complemented his phrasing with instinctive timing and gentle emphasis. Their voices danced around each other with a natural, unforced rhythm, making even the simplest melodies feel personal and poignant.

Margaret Nakibuuka began her education at Luwero Primary School before moving on to Nalinya Lwantale Junior School in Ndejje, also in Luwero District. It was at Nalinya Lwantale that her musical gifts began to blossom. As choir prefect, she was known for her confidence and vocal clarity, and found unwavering support from her music teacher, Ms. Joyce Serunkuma. Ms. Serunkuma recognized in young Nakibuuka not just a gifted singer, but a budding artist with the potential to earn national acclaim. Seeking broader horizons, Margaret moved to Kampala for her senior secondary education. She briefly enrolled at Mengo Senior Secondary School, but soon decided that a trade school, where she could learn to become a seamstress, was a better fit for her. The vibrant city life offered her experiences far different from the quiet rhythms of her home district. It was in Kampala that she became a regular at Planet nightclub and developed a keen admiration for Kampala City Six.

During this transformative period, the legendary Ugandan ballroom dancer Christopher Kato took notice of Nakibuuka's potential. At a time when Kampala City Six performed popular English waltzes and foxtrot songs, Kato, renowned for his elegant style and proficiency in western dance, offered to train Margaret as a ballroom dancer and potential dance partner. With her elegant presence, svelte and toned build, Kato envisioned a promising future for Margaret in professional dance. Despite her success on the dance floor, Margaret Nakibuuka's true passion remained singing.

Her breakthrough on stage came in 1963, when she joined Freddie Kanyike as a backup vocalist during a live performance. In a 1974 interview with *Munno* magazine, she credited Kanyike as the mentor who introduced her to the world of music. Later that same year, when Kanyike left Kampala City Six, Margaret found a new musical partner in Andy Kyambadde. The two forged a close working relationship that soon evolved into a profound romantic bond. With Kawalya and Kanyike no longer in the picture, Margaret and Andy became the main attraction at Planet nightclub. Emerging as Uganda's first star couple, they consistently delivered hit after hit, and even as Congolese bands began to dominate the Ugandan music scene, their popularity endured.

Often regarded as husband and wife, although they were never formally married, Andy and Margaret cohabitated for about six years and had three children together. Their relationship was intense and frequently tumultuous, marked by mutual accusations of jealousy and infidelity, as well as occasional physical confrontations. Margaret accused Andy of being overly controlling, while Andy described her as stubborn and jealous. Despite their periodic separations, they always reunited within a few days, each time vowing to work hard to preserve their family bond. The highs and lows of their relationship were vividly expressed in many of their duets, with their songs serving as personal vignettes of both the joy and the strife they experienced.

In the early days of their romance, Andy recorded the song Monica Nkusimye (Monica, I Appreciate You), with Margaret contributing background vocals.

What should I do, mama Monica, to win your love?
I have sent many letters without a reply—
soaked by rain, bitten by mosquitoes,
and even attacked by robbers last Saturday, nearly losing my life.
I cannot sleep, for my thoughts are consumed by you;
I long to see you, to find some peace.
Now I ask you, mama Monica, for a small favor:
Please, find a moment to write back, so I know where I stand.
I will not pretend that I lack means,
but more than that, I am well-behaved and educated.

I cherish you, Monica.
If I am to have you in my life, please tell me,
for I fear you might choose me only to leave me tomorrow.

On one of the few recordings released by the couple on the Assanand label, the song Yatondera Mega (Mega Was Created for Me) leaves no doubt about Andy's deep affection for Margaret "Mega" Nakibuuka. In response, Margaret reaffirmed her love with her own song, Andy Wange (My Andy), a 1965 track in the ding ding genre released on the CMS label. In Andy Wange, Margaret sings of her unwavering love for Andy and her readiness to do anything to keep his devotion. Their mutual feelings are further expressed in the duet Dali Gwenerondera (The Darling I Chose). Even in Komawo (Come Back), where Margaret does not perform, her presence is unmistakable through the lyrics: "My lady, you tell lots of lies / I see no reason for the lies / What should I do, beautiful Mega?" Later in the song, Andy explains why Margaret has left and pleads for her return, promising never to cause her pain again.

When Andy felt that Margaret was being disrespectful, he channeled his frustrations into the song Oba Onjagala Mbulira (Tell Me If You Love Me), which warns of the dangers of habitual drunkenness and the toxic conflicts that can corrode a relationship. In Nzikiriza Nkwetondere (Allow Me to Apologize), Andy adopts a more vulnerable tone, pleading for forgiveness. He sings, "Dear wife, please come back / Allow me to apologize / My darling, beloved / If it is because I went drinking and spent nights out / I will not do it again / I will not beat or insult you." The lyrics continue with poignant self-recrimination: "Mama, look now / How I have lost weight / I now cook for myself / Because you left me / I had other women / Sent them all away / Mama, please accept my apology."

These songs evoke the dynamics of a strained relationship but are also reflective of broader cultural expectations. In many traditional Ugandan settings, women were often expected to remain loyal and forgiving to their husbands, even in the face of infidelity, neglect, or abuse. Through music, Andy explores this tension between personal remorse and societal norms, expressing both contrition and a desire for reconciliation on terms shaped by custom.

Together and individually, Andy Kyambadde and Margaret Nakibuuka ventured into various musical genres of the era. Their repertoire spanned Kenyan Twist and rumba beats. They recorded popular Kenyan Twist songs like Mukyala Wamugaso (A Wife Is Precious) and Abawala mu Kampala (Girls in Kampala). They also had well-received kagutema tracks, including Olumbe Luno (This Pestilence) and Ebyomunju (What Happens at Home), alternatively rendered as Do Not Wash Your Dirty Linen in Public, though they primarily returned to a rumba beat.

By 1967, the Lorina Nightclub had reverted to its original name, Satellite, a reflection of how deeply the earlier name had endured in public memory. That same year, Joseph Ndugga, formerly of Nairobi's Sportsman Cha Cha Band, founded the Satellite Top Ten Band after a brief stint with a Congolese group that had temporarily based itself at New Life. The newly formed Satellite Top Ten Band became the resident act at the revitalized venue. Ndugga recruited many members from the old Lorina band, which had been hit hard by the 1966 curfew on Kampala's nightlife and the departures of key figures such as Ecklas Kawalya, Bonnie Kyambadde, and Fred Kanyike. The Satellite Top Ten Band featured Ndugga on drums, Molile Reny, Pancho, and the virtuoso lead guitarist Kalule. "Elvis" Sevume handled rhythm guitar and vocals, and Ndiri played saxophone. Later additions included Kalistino on lead guitar, D. Nsubuga on rhythm guitar, and Abudala on bass. However, the band lacked a consistently reliable lineup of vocalists. Although Sevume recorded a few songs in the early 1970s, such as Okukola Kilungi (It Is Good to Work) and Cissy (a female name), his frequent absences due to struggles with alcohol weakened the group's overall performance. Ndiri, the saxophonist, despite his own issues with drinking, was a dependable presence when needed.

To strengthen the vocal section, Ndugga brought in Andy Kyambadde and Margaret Nakibuuka. The duo was already familiar to Satellite audiences; in 1964, they had been commissioned by the nightclub to compose and record Ngenda Mu Setilayiti (I Am Going to Satellite), a song that promoted the club. Andy and Margaret spent several months with the Satellite Top Ten Band before Kamulu, always on the lookout for the best musicians in Kampala, enticed them to join New Life. Their time at New Life was short-lived, and by the end of 1967 they had found a new home at Susana nightclub.

At Susana nightclub, Andy Kyambadde was reunited with his former Kampala City Six bandmate, Ecklas Kawalya. The two found themselves performing together once more, this time in the vibrant and competitive atmosphere of the Susana band. Between 1967 and 1970, Andy's time at Susana proved transformative. It offered him a front-row seat to the evolving landscape of Ugandan music and placed him in close contact with some of the era's most influential and innovative performers. Among them was the exceptionally gifted Martin Munyenga, a versatile Congolese multi-instrumentalist whose mastery of guitar, bass, and percussion made him a sought-after mentor for many aspiring Ugandan musicians. Andy also shared the stage with Charles and Frida Sonko, who had recently returned to Uganda after an extended musical stint in Kenya, bringing with them fresh styles and refined performance experience. Other notable musicians in this circle included the soulful Rose Musoke, the dynamic Sarah Namagembe, and the talented young Hadija Namale.

At Susana, Andy Kyambadde and Margaret Nakibuuka reached new heights in their musical partnership. In 1967, they recorded one of their most memorable duets, Ani Alikunkyaya (Who Will Make Me Forsake You?), released on the Philips label. Although Nakibuuka was not officially credited on the record sleeve, her contribution was unmistakable. Her inviting and vibrant vocals added an extra emotional dimension to Andy's impassioned performance, creating a dynamic interplay where tension and tenderness coexisted. Andy's voice, filled with both desperation and determination, pleads for his lover's unwavering loyalty, while Margaret's background harmonies intensify the emotional depth of his appeal.

What should I do now, Mama Milly?
Oh, poor me!
I have walked so far and am utterly exhausted;

I have penned countless letters, but you remain unresponsive.
Though you live miles away in the mountains,
my love for you fears no distance.
If you love me, Mama Milly, even if you are too afraid to say it,
at least send me a picture to brighten my day.
Who could ever make me forsake you?
Where would another come from, my dear Milly?
Only death fails to recognize the beauty of the world.

Andy Kyambadde was the primary composer of the narrative ballads he performed in duets with Margaret Nakibuuka. With the establishment of Serenade Recording Studios in Kampala and access to facilities at A.P. Chandarana's studios in Kericho, Kenya, the duo seized the opportunity to record a broad array of songs. On Chandarana's Furaha label, they recorded memorable tracks such as Bena Yandekawo (Bena Left Me) and Furo Furo (Furo is a female name derived from Florence). Later, on the studio's Wachezaji label, they revived an old Luganda folk song, Kiwalanganga. This song tells the tale of a selfish man who rejected the communal sharing that was a hallmark of local civility. Among their other notable duets was Kangende (Let Me Go), released on the CMS label. Though again uncredited, Margaret's presence elevated the track. Her harmonies softened the confrontation embedded in the lyrics, allowing the song to carry both tension and tenderness. It was this emotional duality that defined much of their collaboration.

They also recorded Kyayera Mbuga (What He Swept the King's Court With). This song is based on a renowned Buganda folktale about Kyewungula, a man who, centuries ago, defied the trend when Buganda and its king faced an existential threat. While many of the king's subjects fled, Kyewungula remained steadfast in his loyalty. As a testament to his devotion, he vowed not to shave his beard until the king triumphed over the threat. When victory was finally achieved, a jubilant Kyewungula returned to the palace, which had long been abandoned and neglected, and swept the royal court clean with his long beard, much like a broom. This story echoes the actions of thousands of Baganda men during British colonial rule, who, in a bold act of defiance, swore not to shave until the exiled Kabaka was restored to his throne. In October 1955, amid great fanfare, approximately 6,000 men gathered outside the palace to parade before the returning king and participate in a mass shaving ceremony. In Kyayera Mbuga, Margaret Nakibuuka draws a parallel between Andy's love for her and Kyewungula's unwavering loyalty to the Kabaka. She sings of his bright, expressive eyes and a voice as sweet as the gentle notes of a piano, and she even takes a moment to thank Andy's parents in Busega. Both Kiwalanganga and Kyayera Mbuga became part of a series of successful kagutema hits that the duo recorded during this vibrant era.

Margaret Nakibuuka also collaborated with other members of the Susana band on several recordings. For instance, Jane Namukasa provided vocal backup on Nakibuuka's tracks Nantume and Frora, the latter reflecting a local Ugandan pronunciation of the female name Flora, itself derived from Florence, and commonly used in that form in certain circles. Sarah Namagembe, revisiting the Kenyan Twist genre on a Furaha label record, produced Ngenda Ntinda (Going to Ntinda) with Nakibuuka as a backup vocalist. The song tells of a woman rushing to meet her lover Sam in the Kampala suburb of Ntinda, while warning rival suitors that she is prepared to fight for him, with only the police capable of breaking up the struggle. Its frenetically ricocheting guitars set the pace beneath the sweetly interwoven voices of Namagembe and Nakibuuka. In blending the Kenyan Twist's propulsive rhythms with near-choral vocal richness, the track achieves a sound both irresistibly danceable and melodically striking.

However, beneath the musical blend of Ngenda Ntinda lay a bitter controversy that ultimately strained the relationship between Nakibuuka and Namagembe. Ngenda Ntinda was composed by Sarah Namagembe, who sought a female backup artist for the recording. Among the many talented regular singers at Susana nightclub, including the teenager Hadija Namale, the seasoned Frida Sonko, the successful Mary Nattima, and the tall, regal Rose Musoke, Namagembe chose Nakibuuka during the session at Chandarana's studios in Kericho. However, when the record hit the stores, Nakibuuka was credited as the primary singer instead of Namagembe. Although such errors were not uncommon, with recording studios frequently misspelling artists' names or song titles, Sarah Namagembe did not accept the mistake at face value. She suspected that these misattributions were not mere accidents, but deliberate shenanigans on the part of Nakibuuka to claim credit for a song she believed was destined to be a major hit in Uganda. Decades later, as she paid her respects at Nakibuuka's funeral in November 2015, Namagembe spoke quietly to fellow musicians about the pain of that loss, recalling how the song she had created slipped from her grasp. Her words, tinged with both respect for the departed and the persistence of old wounds, showed how deeply Ngenda Ntinda remained tied to her memory.

The demands of nightly gigs, coupled with mounting personality clashes, began to strain Andy Kyambadde and Margaret Nakibuuka's marriage. In 1969, Nakibuuka left home without informing Andy, disappearing for two months and leaving him to care for their three children. When she returned, a fierce argument erupted; Andy's anger boiled over into violence, and neighbors called the police. He was briefly arrested, but by the next morning Nakibuuka was at the Kibuye station securing his release, refusing to press charges. The cycle of domestic violence, relentless quarrels, and the pressures of composing, performing, and recording gradually eroded their partnership. Eventually, Andy and Margaret agreed to end their domestic life together, though they would still collaborate musically on occasion. By then Andy had also grown weary of the nightly grind at Susana nightclub and of disputes with management over working conditions. In 1969, he left Susana to concentrate exclusively on recording.

Embracing a new identity as part of the Kampala Fiesta Band, Andy teamed up with Nelson Sabavuma to record songs such as Nkole Ntya Bbosa (What Should I Do, Bbosa) and Nze Nobwegasi (Unity and I). Andy further expanded his musical reach with Vox Nationale, a band of predominantly Congolese musicians based at New Life and led by Johnny "Dr. Soliste" Cleophas. With them, he recorded soukous numbers featuring rapid-fire sebene sections inspired by the kiri-kiri style of Dr. Nico

Kassanda's L'Orchestre African Fiesta Sukisa. Among these tracks were Nabacwa (a female name), Rweza Yekka (Only Rweza), and Nampima Komawo (Come Back, Nampima).

A shrewd businessman at heart, Andy sought to break free from the confines of established Kenyan music labels. He partnered with Nelson Sabavuma to negotiate a deal with Columbia Gramophone Company Greece Ltd., a local EMI subsidiary in Athens, enabling them to press their songs on their own Sweet Voice label. Distributed by Kyambadde & Bros., Andy released songs such as Omulongo Abuze (The Twin [Sweetheart] Is Lost) and Simanyi Gyeyada (Don't Know Where She Went). His Sweet Voice catalog also featured popular tracks like Oba Onjagala Mbulira (Tell Me If You Love Me) and Jeni Gwenalonda (Jane Whom I Chose). On the same label, Sabavuma, backed by Orchestre Melo Success, released songs including Ggoolo Eri Emu (There Is One Goal) and Namazzi (a female name).

However, life without Margaret Nakibuuka left Andy struggling to rediscover his creative spark. He eventually found another woman and remarried, with Ecklas Kawalya serving as his best man. After Idi Amin's overthrow of the Obote government in 1971, Andy relocated to the eastern town of Jinja, where he took on a clerical position at Walukuba Housing Estate. Jinja's nightlife, though spirited in its own way, was far more restrained than the pulsating energy of Kampala. In Jinja, weekend evenings revolved around bars with jukeboxes, their metallic clatter and the crackle of vinyl spilling into the streets as patrons gathered to sway or sing along. It was a cheerful but predictable rhythm. Kampala, by contrast, throbbed with the immediacy of live performance, its venues like the White Nile and Susana nightclubs alive with permanent bands whose music transformed every night into an event.

Nevertheless, Jinja was home to two major military barracks, Magamaga and Gaddafi, each with its own music band to entertain soldiers. Of the two, the Gaddafi Army Band, which was first known as the Central Volcano Band and later renamed the Eagle Jazz Band, was widely regarded as the stronger group. The band was led by the charismatic saxophonist

Isabirye and occasionally performed at Jinja's Town Hall. Isabirye had known Andy for several years and was also a close friend of Bonnie Kyambadde, who had recently joined the Uganda Air Force Band. In reality, neither Isabirye nor Bonnie were soldiers in the traditional sense. They had never undergone military training, never worn uniforms, and never carried weapons. Their connection to the army was purely musical, defined by saxophones and dance tunes rather than drills or combat.

In 1979, however, following the overthrow of Idi Amin, a wave of fear swept Uganda as Tanzanian troops moved through the country, rounding up former Amin soldiers. Rumors of summary executions fueled widespread panic, prompting many to flee. Among those caught in this turmoil were Bonnie Kyambadde and Isabirye. Their attempt to escape the advancing Tanzanian forces ended tragically in Magamaga, a town east of Jinja. Villagers, enraged by the years of Amin's brutal rule, identified and intercepted them. Despite having been soldiers only in name and musicians in reality, both men were subjected to mob violence and beaten to death.

Earlier, in 1973, Andy found modest success with songs such as Mukyala Wattu Agenda (My Dear Departing Lady) and Asingira Abangi Nalujja (More Beautiful Than Most, Nalujja), recorded with the Lewonadi Band. Hoping to replicate the winning formula he had enjoyed with Margaret Nakibuuka, he paired with another female artist, Margaret 'Mega' Nalujja. The collaboration, however, lacked the distinctive musical chemistry he had once shared with Nakibuuka, and the anticipated breakthrough never materialized.

By the mid-1970s, Andy's new recordings had become increasingly rare. One notable exception came in 1976 with Express FC, composed and recorded with Les Kinois, the group associated with Congolese musician Samba Mapangala. A passionate football supporter, Andy wrote the track to celebrate Express FC's victory in the 1974 Uganda National League championship. Soon after, he gradually withdrew from the popular music scene, though he did work with Steven Sempasa on what proved to be his final recordings for Sempasa's Blue Star label.

Meanwhile, Margaret Nakibuuka left Susana shortly after Andy's departure. Their breakup proved to be a painful turning point for her. Disillusioned by the end of their partnership, she quit her regular night-club performances to concentrate on recording music. Working with the Chandarana studio band, she recorded tracks such as Bagonza (a male name), Obugumba (Barrenness), and Mubiru (a male name). Among her compositions was a song she had originally titled Andy. On the evening before a scheduled recording session in 1971 at the Chandarana Studios in Kericho, Hadija Namale, who was sharing a hotel room with Nakibuuka, overheard her rehearsing the piece. Knowing the turbulent and often toxic nature of Nakibuuka's relationship with Andy, Hadija was startled by the personal lyrics and urged her to drop his name from the song. Despite her lingering affection for Andy, Nakibuuka hesitated but agreed to consider the advice. Mary Nattima, who was staying in the next room, joined Hadija in persuading her to remove any reference to Andy or Kyambadde.

In the end, Andy's name was replaced with Frank. At the time, Nakibuuka was dating Frank Makulu, and under this new title the song found immediate popularity. It became widely celebrated as Frank, though few listeners ever knew that it had been conceived as a tribute to Andy, the very man whose name was erased. The lyrics serve as a heartfelt confession of Nakibuuka's lingering love for Andy and her desire to rekindle their romance. In one stirring refrain, she sings:

> How will I feel when you leave me, Frank?
> I love you so much, woe to me
> I love you much and I am sad.

In the song, Nakibuuka praises "Frank", celebrating his handsomeness by comparing it to the brightness of the sun and noting his well-groomed mannerisms. Hadija Namale's deep, resonant voice joins the refrain, adding an emotional intensity that rides atop the powerful sound of bellowing saxophones:

Oh, see, I love you, Frank!
I longed for a wedding ring and marriage,
but you refused, favoring others and despising me.
I cannot be drawn into romantic rivalries, so I rejected that path.
Our love was once incredible and strong.
Oh, see, I love you, Frank!

Nakibuuka returned to collaborate with Joseph Ndugga, whose Satellite Top Ten Band had undergone several transformations, first becoming the Serenade Top Ten Band and later simply the Top Ten Band. With the establishment of Serenade Studios in 1968, the Top Ten Band became the studio's resident group, providing a stable platform for recording sessions. Much like the famed Muscle Shoals session musicians in the United States, they gave artists a reliable and polished backing sound, ensuring consistency across recordings while adapting fluidly to different musical styles. With their backing, Nakibuuka recorded a series of songs that revealed the full color and expressive beauty of her musical gift. Among these were Makulu (her boyfriend at the time), Bera Nange (Stay with Me), Lwanga (a male name), Willy (a male name), Ogumanga (Stay Strong), and Mwagala Nyo Caesar (I Very Much Love Caesar).

During the 1970s, the rising popularity of Congolese music, along with the emergence of prominent Ugandan bands such as Peterson Mutebi's The Tames, Hanny Sensuwa's The Flames, and Fred Kanyike's The Rwenzoris, reduced the spotlight on artists like Margaret Nakibuuka. Her absence from a band that provided regular live entertainment further limited her exposure. Much like Andy Kyambadde, she gradually withdrew from the music scene during the mid-1970s. Outside of music, Nakibuuka discovered a new passion in designing and tailoring clothes. After stepping away from active performance, she found great joy working on her Singer sewing machine, a craft that allowed her creativity to flourish in a different medium. Margaret "Mega" Nakibuuka's contributions to music and her later pursuits in fashion design remain fondly remembered by those who knew her.

Another alumnus of Kampala City Six who recorded numerous songs with the Capitol Music Store studio was Saimon "Sai" Kaate Nsubuga. Born in 1934 in Kitetika, a small hamlet just north of Kampala along the Kampala–Gayaza road, Kaate Nsubuga's early life was shaped by both academic promise and personal hardship. He attended Gayaza Roman Catholic School, where his love for reading and writing earned him a spot on the editorial board of the school magazine. However, orphaned in his early teens and unable to afford continued education, he left school in 1948.

Naturally inclined toward literature, Kaate Nsubuga began his working life as a reporter with the East African Standard, a position he held for two and a half years before moving on to the Kampala and District Bus Service. Evenings were reserved for his growing passion for music. He began taking guitar and singing lessons from Mr. John Sebirumbi, leader of the Kansanga Music Party, a band rooted in Kansanga township. Sebirumbi, a gifted multi-instrumentalist best known for his accordion skills, would later rename his band the OK Jazz Band. His distinctive use of the accordion, melodically, harmonically, and texturally, often made it sound like an ensemble contained within a single instrument. In 1956, Sebirumbi formally invited Kaate Nsubuga to join the band. That same year, in September, Nsubuga recorded his first song, Gwe Mwana (You Are the Babe), on the Tom Tom label. The record sold far better than he had anticipated, and its success convinced him to pursue music full-time. He went on to collaborate with Elly Wamala on Jane, Walumbe Tang'anya Kulya (Death Will Not Let Me Eat), and other tracks released on the Tom Tom label.

Seeking greater opportunities, Kaate Nsubuga left OK Jazz Band in 1958 and joined Robert Kavuma's Robby Jazz Band, the resident band at the newly formed East African Railways and Harbors Club in Kampala. He remained with Robby Jazz until 1960, when he joined Kampala City Six. There, he performed alongside prominent vocalists such as Kawalya, Kanyike, Andy Kyambadde and Bonnie Kyambadde, forming a formidable lineup. Kaate Nsubuga distinguished himself not only through his powerful vocals and commanding stage presence but also as the first Ugandan musician to perform a rumba song in Lingala, the lingua franca of the Democratic Republic of Congo and the language most closely associated with Congolese rumba. For local audiences, hearing a Ugandan voice command the same language as the celebrated Congolese stars was both surprising and exhilarating, affirming that their own musicians could stand confidently on the same podium as their regional counterparts.

In 1963, following the departure of Kawalya and Freddie Kanyike from Kampala City Six, Kaate Nsubuga left the band to form his own group, the Kampala Wanderers Jazz Band. Unlike the established clubs in Kampala, Kaate Nsubuga chose to tour the towns outside the city, where jukeboxes often replaced live bands. This strategy garnered the group a loyal following in the eastern and northern regions. Ahead of the 1962 elections for Uganda's independence, he had released Akalulu ka Kabaka Yekka (The Vote Is for Kabaka Yekka), expressing his support for the Kabaka Yekka party, a monarchist political party dedicated to uniting the people of Buganda under their Kabaka, who was seen as the embodiment of a unique Buganda identity distinct from the rest of Uganda.

Kaate Nsubuga, while leading the Kampala Wanderers, composed and recorded some of the early to mid-1960s' most memorable hits. His repertoire included a string of hits released on the CMS label, including Obuggya Ne Buba (Jealousy And Envy), Bazukulu ba Gabunga (Descendants of Gabunga), Abakyala Mugondere Abami (Wives, Be Obedient to Your Husbands), and Kabiite (Beloved). He also collaborated with Joyce Nalule on Ezakasimo Zagwawo (The Gratuity Money Is Depleted) and Agenes Nkutute (I Have Taken You, Agnes). On the SDS label, Nsubuga recorded Uganda Waragi, Nava (a female name) and Tereza Jangu Ofumbe (Come Marry Me, Tereza).

Kaate Nsubuga achieved national stardom in 1964 with the hit song City Tebola (The City Does Not Perish). With the support of OK Jazz, this track was a brilliant cover of Merengue Scoubidou by Grand Kalle's L'Orchestre African Jazz, rendered in Luganda rather than Congolese Lingala. The same approach was used for Kaate's Mukwano Teza (Darling Teza), which was essentially a Luganda version of African Fiesta National's

Starlefine Ruffy. The OK Jazz band that supported him, composed of CMS session musicians who often adopted creative stage names, should not be confused with Franco Luambo Makiadi's TPOK Jazz or Sebirumbi's OK Jazz. City Tebola featured a lacework of syncopated guitar arpeggios that were both cheerful and energetic, while Kaate Nsubuga's vocals seamlessly drove the rhythm.

Despite his evident talent, Kaate Nsubuga struggled as a band leader. Internal disagreements plagued the Kampala Wanderers Jazz Band, and in 1965, a mass resignation of all band members delivered a devastating blow. Confronted with this crisis and seeing no clear path forward, Kaate Nsubuga made the decision to sell the band's musical instruments and shift his focus entirely to composing and recording.

Kaate Nsubuga was a man of strong opinions with a keen interest in the politics of his time. In the early years after Uganda's independence in 1962, a political alliance between Obote's Uganda People's Congress (UPC) and the pro-monarchy Kabaka Yekka (KY) enabled Obote to secure a majority and form a government. However, from the very beginning, this alliance was marked by internal discord and power struggles within KY. By 1963, the chaos within Kabaka Yekka became intolerable for some of its parliamentary representatives, leading to defections to the UPC. Many Baganda felt betrayed by this internal strife, prompting Freddie Kanyike to compose and record his song Kabaka Yekka, which both praised the king and warned fellow KY members against joining other political parties, namely the predominantly Protestant UPC and the majority Catholic Democratic Party (DP).

At the same time, the Kabaka's own government, distinct from the national government under Dr. Obote, was struggling. Its ministers were seen as inept and corrupt, with funds disappearing at an alarming rate and public services suffering as a result. This situation unfolded against the backdrop of a steep fall in coffee prices, the main cash crop for many rural families in the Kingdom of Buganda. This prolonged crisis, often referred to as the Buganda crisis of 1964, fueled widespread discontent with both the Kabaka's government and the Kabaka Yekka party.

Disillusioned by the duplicity and failure of the Kabaka's government to deliver for the people, Kaate Nsubuga eventually embraced Obote's UPC. Earlier in his career, he had openly praised Kabaka Mutesa II in songs such as Kabaka Mutesa and Sabasajja Awangale (Long Live the King). His wholehearted support for the UPC, and particularly for Dr. Milton Obote, illustrates the intricate ties between political propaganda and popular music during this period. Even when it became clear that Obote was losing favor in Buganda, Kaate Nsubuga recorded several songs praising him. Among these were the 1964 tracks Obote Yekka (Obote Only) and Dr. Obote Wangala (Long Live Dr. Obote). Obote Yekka proved so popular in the country that the Drifters, a boy band of Ugandan Goan descent composed of Michael Rattos, Richard Rattos, Clifton Carrasco, and Magnus Fernandes, covered the song in their 1965 hit single. The Drifters' record also included a cover of Malaika (Angel), the celebrated love song composed by Kenyan musician Fadhili William and later popularized by Miriam Makeba. By the 1960s it had become an anthem across East Africa, cherished as one of the region's most enduring expressions of romance and longing. Its influence soon extended beyond the continent, with international artists such as Harry Belafonte and Boney M introducing Malaika to audiences around the world.

Kaate Nsubuga's President Obote, recorded shortly after Obote's storming of the Kabaka's palace and the king's subsequent flight into exile in Britain, was met with fierce opposition in Buganda. The song painted an image of a benevolent, hardworking leader and urged Ugandans to embrace their new president. For many in Buganda, however, the song was seen as a profound affront, evoking memories of events like the Nakulabye massacre in November 1964, which followed protests over the results of the "lost counties" referendum. This local referendum had decided whether the counties of Buyaga and Bugangaizi should remain part of Buganda, be transferred back to Bunyoro, or become a separate district.

In 1968, Kaate Nsubuga recorded Cabinet Yamba Obote (The Cabinet, Assist Obote). The song opens with a brief narration, "Long live Dr. Obote, lead us Uganda," before Kaate Nsubuga's electrifying voice, backed by King Jazz band, takes over with consuming intensity:

All of Uganda is filled with joy,
all of Uganda is rejoicing.
We remember October 1962,
when we achieved full independence.
Obote is the leader who fought for us,
and has guided us for six years.
Under the banner of the UPC,
long live our elder Dr. Obote,
lead the nation, Dr. Obote!

In Cabinet Yamba Obote, Kaate explicitly names each cabinet minister, including John Babiiha (vice president and minister of Animal Industry, Game and Fisheries), Kalule Settala (Finance), Ojera (Information, Broadcasting and Tourism), Sam Odaka (Foreign Affairs), Katiti (Culture and Community Development), Kalema (Commerce and Industry), Kakonge (Agriculture and Forestry), Felix Onama (Defence), Basil Bataringaya (Internal Affairs), Ochola (Regional Administration), Lubowa (Attorney General), Anyoti (State for National Service), Wakholi (Public Service and Cabinet Affairs), Lwamafa (Health), Babumba (Marketing and Co-operatives), Choudry (Mineral and Water Resources), Nkutu (Works, Communication and Housing), Okae (Planning and Economic Development), and Lakidi (Labour). He also mentions Akena Adoko, head of the formidable and dreaded General Service Unit (GSU), Obote's paramilitary intelligence agency. Kaate himself was accused of belonging to the GSU, but this claim is not credible. He was, however, a staunch UPC loyalist.

There is a bitter irony in Cabinet Yamba Obote. At the time of its recording, Kaate Nsubuga was supported by King Jazz band, the resident band at White Nile nightclub. In a striking twist of fate, Jolly Joe, the onetime proprietor of White Nile, was languishing in Luzira Prison, detained without charge by the Obote government. Kaate Nsubuga's praise songs for Obote found a receptive audience among UPC supporters and received heavy airplay on Radio Uganda. Songs honoring the Kabaka had long been part of Uganda's musical tradition, with both traditional and modern compositions by artists such as Elizabeth Namale, Malyamu

Namale, Fred Kanyike, Ecklas Kawalya, and Christopher Ssebadduka celebrating the monarch. Kaate Nsubuga's work, however, occupied a different moral and political space. Actively promoted by the state as an instrument of political messaging, his songs were widely regarded in Buganda as an act of political apostasy, provoking anger and deep resentment toward a musician many felt had turned against his own people.

Before Kaate Nsubuga's overt displays of loyalty, other musicians had produced songs intended to flatter and appease Obote's government. For instance, Andrew Kyambadde and Margaret Nakibuuka recorded Uganda Independence, a song that celebrated the nation's newfound freedom rather than offering an outright endorsement of Obote. The only other artist from that era whose political praise matched Kaate Nsubuga's was Juma Odundo, a musician based in the Nsambya suburb of Kampala who sang in both Luganda and Luo. Born in Jinja in 1933 to Joluo parents from western Kenya, Odundo grew up in a rapidly changing, multicultural urban environment. He became fluent in several languages, including his native Dholuo, as well as Acholi, Langi, Luganda, Lusoga, Luhya, Kikuyu, Swahili and English.

In the turbulent years after the 1971 overthrow of Obote's government, Kaate Nsubuga's music fell silent. The political winds had shifted violently, and in the wake of Idi Amin's coup, Kaate was arrested and imprisoned at Mutukula, a feared detention center in Masaka District near the Uganda–Tanzania border. What he witnessed there would scar him for life. One morning, dozens of Acholi and Langi soldiers were lined up. They had been told they were going home. Instead, they were marched into the bush and gunned down in cold blood. Kaate watched in horror as men he had spoken to the night before were slaughtered without mercy. The killings, justified by mere suspicion of loyalty to Obote, left Kaate deeply shaken and the echoes of gunfire would stay with him long after the prison walls had disappeared.

By 1974, however, Kaate began to rebuild his career and entrepreneurial spirit. He established GS Partners on William Street in Kampala, launching his own GSP label to release new recordings. Among these were

Jane, a soulful offering in his signature style, Abawala Bangi Obwesigwa Tebalina (Many Girls Can't Be Trusted), and Katonda Bw'akuwa Todulanga (Do Not Curse When Blessed by the Lord). An observant Roman Catholic, Kaate dedicated a number of songs to commemorate the centenary of the Catholic faith in Uganda, blending his spiritual devotion with his art. He also collaborated with other ensembles, recording Robina with the Rwenzori Band, and later joining the Prisons Band for Tya Mukama (Fear the Lord) and Tunyikire (Let's Be Resolute). For Kaate, these post-1974 recordings were more than a simple return to the limelight; they carried the weight of survival, faith, and determination. In finding his voice again, he demonstrated how music could serve as both a refuge and a bridge, linking personal endurance with the wider cultural life of Uganda during one of its most turbulent decades.

CHAPTER 9

The UTV Catalyst: Elly Wamala and the Musicians Who Forged Their Own Path

In the late 1950s and 1960s, a wave of Ugandan musicians gained recognition beyond the country's borders, often embracing styles that departed from the dominant Congolese rumba and Kenyan Twist trends. Among them was Elishama "Elly" Lukwata Wamala, born on December 13, 1935, in Bulucheke, a village nestled in the hills southeast of Mbale in Bugisu. His father, Ignatius Mutambuze, a local government clerk from Buganda, and his mother, Gladys Nabutiti, a homemaker from the Bagisu community, embodied a union of two cultures.

One of nineteen children fathered by Mutambuze, Elly's early years were marked by upheaval. Around the age of ten, his mother left the family. Soon after, he was sent to live with his paternal uncle, Daniel Katunda, in Bulenga, just outside Kampala. The separation left a quiet ache that never quite faded. Years later, when he first heard Ndikuwa Mama Wange (I'll Give You My Mother) by Eva Nanyonga, it was more than a song. It was a cry from the hollow part of his childhood. In its haunting refrain, he heard the echo of the mother he had lost and the childhood that might have been. Wamala would later say that the song stirred something profound in him.

Wamala's early education took place at Bbira Church of Uganda Primary School and Mackay Primary School in Natete. His natural inclination towards music was evident from a young age, a trait recognized by his father. Young Wamala frequently entertained visitors at his father's home with his singing. The move to Bulenga proved fortuitous, as his uncle possessed a gramophone. There, Wamala listened to recordings by Eva Nanyonga, Polycarp Kakooza, and the trio of Ssempebwa, Luyimbazi, and Lumu, artists who profoundly helped ignite his own desire to become a musician.

At Mackay Primary School, under the guidance of the esteemed principal David Livingstone Semyalo, Wamala's musical development accelerated. He joined the school church choir and was introduced to the guitar by an older half-sibling. After completing his schooling at Mengo Junior Secondary School, Wamala secured a position as a receptionist at the Opel Gramophone Record and Battery Factory, located in Kampala's industrial area.

In the 1950s, Kampala's industrial area was a lively center of economic activity. It lay just east of the central business district, downhill from the more elevated Nakasero Hill. This industrial zone had been deliberately planned during the later years of British colonial administration to separate heavy commerce and manufacturing from the residential quarters of Nakasero and Kololo. The area was characterized by wide, paved roads lined with low-slung warehouses, workshops, and newly built factories. The air was thick with the smells of engine oil, fresh timber, and machine grease, occasionally mingling with the scent of brewing coffee from nearby processing plants. Rows of acacia trees lined some of the roads, offering pockets of shade amid an open landscape bathed in sunlight.

Among the establishments that contributed to the area's energy and character was Opel Gramophone Record and Battery, which occupied a solid, rectangular building with simple modernist lines, constructed from cream-colored brick and concrete. The design was functional rather than decorative, with large ventilation windows set high on the walls. A metal signboard bearing the name "OPEL TOM TOM," along with a hand-painted image of a tom-tom drum, hung above the entrance, giving the building a distinctive identity. It was here, in 1956, that Elly Wamala recorded his first songs, released on the Tom Tom label. These early tracks, firmly rooted in the kadongo kamu tradition and arranged for two acoustic guitars with vocal backing and additional guitar work by Simon Kaate Nsubuga, included Nabutono, Josephine, Jane, Walumbe Tang'anya Kulya (Death Won't Let Me Eat), and Amagezi Gakulimbye (Your Cleverness Is Deceiving You). Other recordings on the label included Nkulisa Mu Tawuni (Welcome Me When I'm Back From Town) and Va Mu Kwecakaza (Leave the Pleasure-Seeking). Nabutono and Josephine so impressed Kabaka Edward Mutesa that he invited Wamala to perform for him at the royal palace.

While these songs are often cited as the starting point of kadongo kamu, such claims oversimplify and distort the genre's deeper roots. Similarly, although Christopher Ssebadduka (another notable kadongo kamu artist) is sometimes referred to as the genre's founding father, this too is misleading. His first recordings also appeared around 1956 on the Tom Tom label, with early titles like Omukazi Malaya (A Female Prostitute) and Namwana Nkuku (Namwana of the Missing Fingers and Toes). The latter refers to the symbolic head of Buganda's Kkobe clan, whose totem is the air yam. The reality is that kadongo kamu had been taking shape well before either Wamala or Ssebadduka began recording. Earlier artists such as Edward Seruwagi, John Oryem, Paulo "Machunia" Ojambo, and Eva Nanyonga, whom Wamala himself cited as a major influence, had already been performing and in some cases recording in the style. In fact, Hugh Tracey documented multiple kadongo kamu performances during his field recording expeditions in Uganda as early as 1950 and again in 1952. Moreover, the genre's stylistic foundations were shaped in part by regional influences. Kenyan and Congolese musicians, particularly Jean Bosco Mwenda (also known as Mwenda wa Bayeke), played a significant role in popularizing the fingerpicked guitar style and lyrical storytelling that would come to define kadongo kamu. Rather than emerging fully formed from a single source, the genre evolved organically from a wider

East and Central African musical conversation, locally grounded, but regionally inspired.

Despite the common misconception, particularly in contemporary Ugandan newspapers, that Wamala only recorded two kadongo kamu songs, his output on the Opel Tom Tom label fits neatly into the kadongo kamu tradition. However, these songs did not achieve the same level of popularity as Nabutono and Josephine. Beyond his receptionist duties, Wamala became a trusted advisor to the Tom Tom management. In fact, Georg von Opel handpicked him to evaluate the commercial potential of songs submitted by local musicians. It was in this capacity that he auditioned Fred Kanyike and Andrew Kyambadde's debut song, Lupiya Zange. The two young men walked into the studio unaware that they would be performing before Wamala himself.

The Tom Tom studio was an austere but modern space for its time. Wooden counters stretched around the room, supporting bulky turntables, reel-to-reel machines, and a control panel studded with dials and switches. Record sleeves leaned casually against the wall, and the air carried the faint smell of warm electronics and varnished wood. A low hum from the equipment filled the silence, heightening the nervous anticipation as artists waited for the signal to begin. Many aspiring musicians had stepped into that room only to be turned away by the studio's stringent selection process. For Kanyike and Kyambadde, however, it was a welcome surprise to find their friend Elly Wamala sitting in judgment. On his recommendation, Lupiya Zange was recorded.

Wamala's tenure at Opel Tom Tom came to an end in 1960, as a direct consequence of the prolonged boycott of foreign businesses organized by Augustine Kamya's Uganda National Movement. The boycott forced the Opel Gramophone Record and Battery Factory to cease operations within the country. However, the connections Wamala had forged at Opel proved beneficial. The company recommended him for a position at High Fidelity Productions, a publicity and advertising agency located in Pioneer House, Nairobi. High Fidelity Productions was owned by Peter Colmore, a close associate of Opel Gramophone Record's senior management. Colmore had a background in music, having led the Peter Colmore Band and produced over 250 East African records for Guy Johnson's His Master's Voice (HMV) Blue Label. The co-owner of High Fidelity was Simon Ndesandjo, a Kenyan who would later become the stepfather of Barack Obama's half-brothers, David and Mark, from Barack Obama Sr.'s marriage to Ruth Baker, an American.

In 1960, Wamala relocated to Nairobi, where he performed as a guitarist on numerous commercial jingles produced by High Fidelity Productions for radio and television. High Fidelity was responsible for creating some of the most memorable jingles of the late 1950s and 1960s, including *Aspro ni dawa ya kweli* (Aspro is the real medicine) and the Sanyo radio sets commercial, *Sanyo juu, Sanyo tops* (Sanyo high, Sanyo tops). Wamala also provided vocals for many of these jingles. Alongside this work, he continued to pursue his recording career. During this time, his Amagezi Gakulimbye (Your Cleverness Is Deceiving You) was reissued on the Melodisc record label. This release represented a significant personal accomplishment for Wamala, as it placed him on the same label as his West Indian musical idols, including Lord Kitchener and Francisco Slinger, known as The Mighty Sparrow. In his 1990s song Ebinyumu Ebyaffe (Fun in Our Time), Wamala reminisces about and honors the West Indian calypso music that shaped his early musical development.

When High Fidelity secured a promotional deal with British American Tobacco (BAT) to market their cigarettes, they implemented a marketing strategy unprecedented in East Africa. Sportsman, a budget-friendly cigarette brand, was being aggressively promoted across the region. Beyond crafting jingles, High Fidelity formed a musical ensemble of stylish young men to promote the brand through live music performances. The band, named Sportsman Cha Cha (and also recording as the Hi Fi Cha Cha band), became a powerful advocate for Sportsman cigarettes under the leadership of the flamboyant trombonist Msafiri Morimori. Elly Wamala played rhythm guitar, and Joseph Ndugga, an influential figure in Ugandan music during the 1960s to mid-1970s, was the band's drummer.

The band embarked on extensive tours throughout East Africa, thrilling audiences across the region, including a standout performance in Dar es Salaam in December 1960. By July 1962, the buzz around Sportsman Cha Cha had reached Kampala. At the invitation of entertainment impresario Jolly Joe Kiwanuka, the band performed at the White Nile Club. The excitement in the club was palpable as the resident White Nile Club band, led by the charismatic Michael Yuma, joined forces with Msafiri Morimori's Sportsman Cha Cha for a much-anticipated joint performance. The rhythm took over, rippling through the crowd, and dancers responded instinctively to every beat. Then came the moment that would shift the mood entirely. Members of Sportsman Cha Cha stepped forward and introduced the Twist, setting off a wave of excitement on the dancefloor. That night marked a turning point. The cha cha, once dominant, began to fade as Kampala embraced the Twist.

With Hi Fi Cha Cha, Wamala recorded Ndi Mugunjufu (I'm Civilized) and Rita Nkusanira (I Deserve You Rita) on the Equator label. During this period, he also collaborated with the Five Arrows, a short-lived band led by Geoffrey Ngao, one of the founders of the Kenyan band, the Hodi Boys. With the Five Arrows, he recorded Onjogerako Bwemage (You Accuse Me Over Nothing) and Guma Omwoyo (Keep a Strong Heart), issued on the USA label, an imprint under Associated Sound (East Africa) Limited (ASL).

In 1963, Uganda Television Services (UTV) was established, bringing television broadcasts to Uganda for the first time. Given his experience in the entertainment industry, Wamala saw an opportunity to join the new TV service. He returned to Uganda in 1963, accepting a position as a producer and presenter for light entertainment at UTV. He was tasked with producing and presenting the nightly UTV nightclub show, a popular musical program that aired at 8:15 pm and featured performances by Uganda's leading artists. Wamala remained at UTV until his retirement in 1981.

Even after retiring from UTV, Wamala continued to compose and record music, enjoying a late resurgence in the 1980s with his band, the Mascots. At a time when many of his contemporaries had faded from the music scene, a new generation embraced his sound as a reminder of an earlier era. With the Mascots, he produced some of his most celebrated hits. The Mascots featured Kabuye Ssembogga (vocals), Jane Kayanja (vocals), Robert Mayanja (vocals), Mohamed Musisi (drums), Ekodere (lead guitar), Henry Wairugala (rhythm guitar), Jonathan Kawagga (trumpet), and Peter Musisi (saxophone). Noah Kyeyune later joined on keyboard. Some of their later hits included Sacramento (The Sacrament), Kaama Katono (A Little Secret), and Leticia (a female name).

Wamala's musical output during the 1960s and mid-1970s was less extensive compared to that of other prominent Ugandan artists of the era, particularly alumni of the Kampala City Five, such as Fred Kanyike, Andrew Kyambadde, Ecklas Kawalya, B. K. Steven, Simon Kaate Nsubuga, and Fred Masagazi. This difference can be attributed to Wamala's status as a part-time musician. Nevertheless, he released several songs in 1964, including Omwenge Kyekyokunywa Kyange (Booze Is My Drink of Choice), one of his few tracks to appear on the People newspaper's Top Ten hit list. This list was compiled through collaboration between the People newspaper and leading record stores in Kampala. Another 1964 release was Abawala mu Kampala (Girls of Kampala), featuring Wamala with the Jambo Boys band. When the Apolo Hotel, a premier Ugandan hotel, opened in 1965, the Jambo Boys (aka Apolo Jambo band) became its resident band. The Apolo Jambo band included notable musicians at various times, such as Philip M. Ngoma, Keya, Charles Ginaro, and Hyppolythe Makassy, who served as band leader in the 1970s. Wamala's other songs from this period included Omukyala Mwambaze (Dress Your Woman) and Manyinti Olina Sente (I Know You Have Money).

Despite his part-time musical career, Wamala's name remained firmly associated with music. This association stemmed largely from the popularity of his UTV music program, the UTV nightclub, which granted him national recognition. Musicians also sought his advice and guidance, given his prominent position and his cultivated relationships with influential political figures who could support their interests. Wamala was instrumental in the formation of the Uganda Artists Recording Association in late 1965, determined to succeed where Israel Magembe's Uganda Musicians Union had faltered. The association's initial leadership comprised Ecklas Kawalya (president), Simon Kaate Nsubuga (vice president), Fred Kanyike (secretary), Bonnie Steven Kyambadde (vice secretary), Edmund Sematimba (treasurer), Andrew Kyambadde (vice treasurer), and Paul Mukasa (organizer). The executive committee included Fred Masagazi, Fred Mukasa, Tony Senkebejje, Sammy Kintu, Yunia Nalwanga, and Margaret Nakibuuka. However, the association struggled with fundraising and membership growth. In 1966, Elly Wamala agreed to serve as the association's president. To bolster the struggling organization, he organized a series of fundraising events.

One notable event was a grand dance held at Mbale's Elgon Hotel, just a short drive from his birthplace, Bulucheke. The event featured live performances by association members including Fred Masagazi, Margaret Nakibuuka, Ecklas Kawalya, Peter Mulindwa, Nelson Sabavuma, Vincent Nsubuga, Fred Kigozi, Akiiki Bulegeya, Stanley Kyeranyi, and Charles Kirunda. Their performance, brimming with the vitality of those halcyon days, sent waves of excitement through the audience. These were Uganda's biggest music stars on stage, performing some of their best songs. Their tracks enjoyed heavy rotation on Radio Uganda and were a constant presence on jukeboxes across the country. Despite Wamala's efforts to unite Ugandan artists under one umbrella to strengthen their bargaining power and increase their earnings, the Uganda Artists Recording Association ultimately collapsed due to internal discord and infighting.

On television, Wamala cultivated an image of refinement, characterized by his dignified bearing and graceful mannerisms. He projected the persona of a sophisticated modern entertainer, comfortable in both his local community and Western cultural settings. Wamala, along with news anchor Ronald Katongole, arguably became one of Uganda's first television celebrities. This prominence is unsurprising, given UTV's limited programming featuring local personalities at the time.

A typical UTV program schedule, such as the one from Friday, December 11, 1964, illustrates this point:

- 6:20 pm: Huckleberry Hound – TV cartoon featuring Huckleberry Hound, Yogi Bear, Pixie, and Dixie
- 6:50 pm: Magic Land of Alakasam – A magic show for children
- 7:15 pm: The Common Man Club – Discussion about the role of the common man in Uganda
- 7:45 pm: News – National news in Luganda and English
- 8:05 pm: TV Newsreel – News in pictures
- 8:15 pm: UTV Nightclub – Wamala's popular musical program featuring Uganda's top artists
- 9:00 pm: Boxing from Rainbow – A championship boxing series from the USA
- 9:30 pm: News – International news in Luganda and English

In 1966, UTV introduced the 'Personality of the Year' award, with the inaugural honor going to James Bwogi, UTV's commercial manager and son of Dr. Ernest Kalibala Balintuma, the sociologist and author of the well-known *Wakaima and the Clay Man and other African folktales* published in 1946. The following year, in 1967, Elly Wamala was named 'TV Personality of the Year,' a recognition of his pioneering role as a presenter and producer and of the cultural influence he had already begun to exert through his work on Uganda's national television.

Through his widely popular TV show, Wamala provided a platform for Ugandan musical groups, both established and emerging. An appearance on Wamala's show guaranteed significant exposure and name recognition for bands and artists, particularly those still striving for success. Wamala's show was eagerly anticipated. The TV crew would visit various Kampala nightclubs, broadcasting live performances by resident bands as they entertained patrons in dimly lit halls filled with swirling cigarette smoke, clinking glasses, and the easy rhythm of laughter blending with music. Nightclubs such as White Nile, New Life, Lorina, and Susana were frequently featured, offering home viewers a rare glimpse into the city's after-hours magic, where sequined outfits caught the light, dancers moved in unison, and melodies lingered long after the screen went dark. Renowned Ugandan musicians like Andrew Kyambadde, Margaret Nakibuuka, Fred Kanyike, Ecklas Kawalya, Bonnie Steven Kyambadde, Simon Kaate Nsubuga, Fred Masagazi, and Nelson Sabavuma regularly took the spotlight. The show also served as a vehicle for introducing new dance styles such as the Toyota, which caught on in nightclubs and living rooms alike, rippling through the country with the same ease as the music that inspired them.

In 1966, Wamala was awarded a scholarship by the Thomson Foundation, along with three other Ugandan employees of Uganda Television Service. This scholarship enabled them to study television production at the Thomson Foundation Television College, located at Kirkhill House in Newton Mearns, near Glasgow, Scotland. The other recipients were Dithan Edward Kavuma (program director), Roger Kivule (producer), and Louis Mabaraza (senior technical assistant for outside broadcast). The Thomson Foundation, a UK charity established by Roy Thomson in 1962, aimed to train journalists, television producers, and engineers from developing countries, helping them utilize modern mass communication techniques for educational purposes.

During the 16-week training program, Wamala, like other participants, engaged in practical exercises of increasing complexity, serving as program director, film director, and transmission controller. In Glasgow, Wamala took the opportunity to pursue formal guitar lessons at a center affiliated with the Scotland Banjo, Mandolin and Guitar Foundation. While such centers offering music lessons are commonplace in the UK and other parts of the world, Wamala's pursuit of formal guitar lessons in Scotland often generates considerable interest and admiration in Uganda, where it is sometimes portrayed as an exceptional accomplishment. Although Wamala valued the formal guitar lessons he received both in Nairobi during his time with High Fidelity and later in Scotland, he did not consider it an extraordinary feat for a Ugandan to undertake such training. Following his television production training in Scotland, Wamala took a leave of absence from UTV to pursue a diploma course at Makerere University's School of Music and Drama.

Elly Wamala was not a regular performer in nightclubs, nor was he a member of any established musical groups from the 1960s to the mid-1970s. Instead, he often appeared as a guest at special events at Kampala's upscale Apolo Hotel, stepping onto the stage in a smart suit and bow tie to perform with the resident bands. The Apolo catered largely to wealthy foreigners and a small Ugandan elite, its atmosphere more laid-back than the bustling rumba clubs that animated the rest of the city. Here, the insistent guitar rhythms of Congolese bands were absent, replaced by smooth renditions of Frank Sinatra, Nat King Cole, and calypso standards, as resident bands filled the evenings with polished covers. Expensive and far beyond the reach of most ordinary Ugandans, the Apolo projected an air of exclusivity. It stood in stark contrast to venues such as the White Nile or Susana nightclubs, where rumba beats pulsed through the night and drew mixed crowds eager to dance. Within this rarefied space, Wamala's elegance and poise seemed perfectly at home as he sang alongside the Apolo Quintet and Apolo Jambos, even as the irony remained that his true artistic identity was deeply rooted in the popular sensibilities of ordinary Ugandans who could never afford to hear him there.

Wamala held a deep admiration for the Afro-Caribbean calypso music genre. He was an ardent fan of Trinidadian calypso singer Aldwyn "Lord Kitchener" Roberts and greatly appreciated the work of Harry Belafonte. His performances included covers of songs by both Lord Kitchener and Harry Belafonte, a tribute to the artists who had shaped his musical tastes. The influential Zimbabwean musician Mazowe, who once led the Susana nightclub band, once stated that only three Ugandan musicians were skilled enough to perform for Western audiences. According to Mazowe, these musicians were Wamala, Taib Mutyaba, and himself. However, Israel Magembe later expanded that list, naming himself, Taib Mutyaba, Gonza (distinct from Bernard Gonza of the Tames band), and Gabriel Mukungu, the father of Deo Mukungu. Deo Mukungu, in turn, gained recognition during his time with Afrigo Band from 1987 to 1992 and for composing the popular Afrigo Batuuse II song.

In addition to performing covers, Elly Wamala composed original songs during the latter half of the 1960s that were well-received in Uganda. Among these, the 1966 song Hamadi stood out for its profound lyrics. Performed with the backing of the Apolo Jambos band, Hamadi tells the poignant story of an orphan who finds himself in a foreign setting where even those who should offer familial or communal support, who themselves are outsiders, reject him and deny him the dignity he deserves. Through this song, Wamala explored themes of isolation and the deep yearning for acceptance, reinforcing his reputation as an artist with a sincere connection to the struggles and emotions of his audience:

I came here as a baby, just five months old, with my mother
after my father had long passed.
That's why I sell peanuts—to earn enough to buy clothes,
to dress well, and to be seen as somebody.
Father's death robbed me, Hamadi! If he were alive, I too
might have known happiness.
I face hardship every day, but at least I have my God to help me.
My fellow Arabs treat me as less than human—accusing me of
being a vagabond who brings shame to their tribe.
They chase me away with cries of "Get lost, destitute!"
I have nothing more to say to them; I leave them in God's hands.
But, there's one good thing about me: I know how to make friends.
I have a Muslim friend in Bukoto who gifted me this turban and robe,
who takes me to the hospital when I'm sick,
and even found the woman who rejected me.
I didn't mind her rejection, for I never truly cared for her.
Had she accepted me, I might have caused her pain—marrying
only to spare the matchmaker's disappointment.
I'm not afraid of being single; let me remain so until death.
I'm 40 now, and I refuse to marry someone my own age.
I long for a partner who is 18 or around 20—
they're easy to find back home, where light-skinned Arab

girls are plentiful, so I hear.
Alas, I must stay away from them.
For now, I'll keep hustling with peanuts, saving money for that journey.

Hamadi holds deep personal significance for Elly Wamala, with many interpreting the song as a reflection of his own early experiences in Bulucheke. His childhood was marked by a profound absence of parental affection. His mother left him at a very young age, and his father, who fathered nineteen children, offered little attention or support. Much like the lonely figure in Hamadi, Wamala felt a sense of abandonment when he was sent away to live with an uncle who was a strict disciplinarian. Despite these hardships, Wamala defied the challenges of his early life and eventually achieved considerable success on television while also building an impressive musical career.

A notable highlight in Elly Wamala's musical career came in 1969 when the government commissioned him to compose a song to welcome and honor Pope Paul VI's historic visit to Uganda, which began on July 31 of that year. Wamala recorded Welcome Pope Paul with the backing of the Apollo (Jambo) Band, and the track was produced by M/S Uganda Records Agencies Ltd. The song proved an unprecedented success, selling fifty thousand copies even before the Pope had set foot in Uganda, a milestone no other record in the country had ever achieved. Beyond its commercial triumph, the song captured the spiritual fervor and national pride surrounding the first papal visit to Africa. In the weeks leading up to the Pope's arrival, church choirs rehearsed tirelessly, Catholic congregations prepared elaborate processions, and the nation buzzed with anticipation. Wamala's composition provided a unifying soundtrack to that historic moment, blending faith, music, and civic pride in a way that was embraced wholeheartedly by Ugandans.

Around the same time, another talented musician, Samuel Wamala, also paid tribute to the Pope. Samuel, who worked as a carpenter in the Nsambya area and generally avoided the spotlight, had already earned acclaim with songs like Nalweyiso in 1963 and Tewesiganga Omuntu

(Never Trust a Person) in 1964. His song honoring the Pope, titled 31st July 1969, did not receive the same level of attention as Elly Wamala's Welcome Pope Paul. Although Samuel and Elly were not immediate family, they both belonged to the Buganda Ngabi (bushbuck) clan, linking them through a shared heritage.

After the Pope's visit, from that time until around 1974, Wamala's recording activity slowed as he focused on his responsibilities with UTV. Despite this, he acquired a new stature as Uganda's first television celebrity and a respected figure in the music world. In 1969, when President Milton Obote hosted an international dinner party at the President's Lodge in Nakasero, Elly Wamala was invited to take part in the festivities. He walked the catwalk alongside Miss Uganda, Beatrice Mulera, as the pair modeled what was presented as Uganda's national dress. Wamala wore a bold, striped outfit with vertical lines and a cinched waistcoat design that reflected both tradition and contemporary tailoring. Ms. Mulera appeared in a full-length wrap skirt patterned with a large central floral motif, framed by intricate symbolic designs. Her ensemble combined elegance with a strong sense of national pride. Together, they embodied a vision of cultural identity and modern Ugandan style on an international stage.

Even though he was a regular at official government functions, Wamala maintained a deliberate distance from the turbulent political scene in Uganda. When Idi Amin's regime took power in 1971, he refrained from composing songs that would serve as propaganda for the government. Instead, he conducted himself with the discretion of a traditional civil servant, a stance that earned him respect even among top military officials. In 1973, when Fred Kanyike and several other musicians sought government support to form the Rwenzori band, Elly Wamala played an essential role in assisting them.

In 1974, Elly Wamala enjoyed two major hits: Violet and Akana ka Kawalya (Kawalya's Child). The latter served as a playful tribute to Ecklas Kawalya, a devoted family man known for his gentle, supportive nature as a father. The song specifically highlights his eldest daughter, Rose Wanyana, celebrated for her politeness, selflessness, and commitment to her studies with dreams of becoming a lawyer. At the same time, the song can be understood as a broader symbol of the Kawalya family, with Ecklas Kawalya having sired eighteen children, many of whom have achieved success. Among them, Joanita Kawalya Muganga is notably recognized as one of Afrigo Band's prominent vocalists. Akana ka Kawalya was composed by Edmund Batte, a skilled sound engineer and musician.

Later that same year, Elly Wamala, together with the Jambos, released an LP album titled Akaana ka Kawalya on the URA label of Uganda Record Agencies Ltd. This album, which brought together both new and earlier recordings, featured tracks such as Violet, Talanta (Talent), Kaama Katono (Little Secret), Chunga Mahaba Yetu (Keep Our Love), Welcome Pope Paul, Enkuba Mu Dungu (Rain in the Desert), Akaana Ka Kawalya, May Tontunulira (Don't Look at Me, May), Namuganyi, Lowoze Nkunze (Think About Me), Georgina, and the 1966 hit Hamadi.

Elly Wamala's 1960s television program became an essential platform through which Ugandans were introduced to numerous bands, especially those performing in and around Kampala. The show featured regular appearances by resident bands from venues such as White Nile, Susana, New Life, La Quinta, and Top Life, helping to boost the popularity of stars like Ecklas Kawalya, Fred Kanyike, Andrew Kyambadde, Margaret Nakibuuka, Nelson Sabavuma, Fred Masagazi, Simon Kaate Nsubuga, Mary Nattima, and Israel Magembe. For many viewers who did not frequent the clubs, either because they did not belong to that scene or lived outside Kampala, the program offered a rare opportunity to appreciate the talents of individual musicians and the skills of dynamic dancers.

Musicians from the Congo often provided the instrumental backbone for the nightclub bands, playing guitars, drums, saxophones, and trumpets. Among these, several instrumentalists became fan favorites. Vox Nationale, the resident band at Kamulu's New Life nightclub, featured guitarists such as Pikolo, Doctor Johnny, and Albert. L'Orchestre King's Jazz Band at White Nile, led by Selemani, also gained attention, with Suleman's lively guitar performances earning a legendary reputation. Meanwhile, the Susana nightclub band was noted for the distinctive guitar work of

Charles Ginaro. The program did not limit its focus to musicians alone. Dancers also emerged as prominent figures on the show. Christopher Kato, an acclaimed Ugandan ballroom dancer and former mentor to singer Margaret Nakibuuka, drew considerable admiration. Suisseman Ngoy, an elegant Congolese performer who became a naturalized Ugandan, offered a unique style when dancing to Congolese rumba music, providing a memorable visual experience for viewers.

Elly Wamala's television show was an influential platform for showcasing Uganda's emerging youth bands during the 1960s. Many of these groups were formed by teenagers inspired by international stars such as James Brown, the Beatles, Jimi Hendrix, and Millie Small. Their performances, often covers of European and American pop hits, were a source of excitement for television audiences and helped propel these bands into the public eye. To encourage this musical movement, regular competitions were held to identify the best group. Two major events, sponsored by British American Tobacco (BAT), took place in 1966 and 1967. The first, known as Pop '66, was staged at Norman Cinema in Kampala, while Pop '67 followed the next year at the Uganda National Theatre, attracting bands from Uganda, Kenya, and Tanzania. Wamala and Uganda Television covered the events, broadcasting them into the living rooms of the few households that owned a television set at the time.

One of the standout groups featured on Wamala's show was The Drifters, a predominantly Goan-Ugandan band led by guitarist and vocalist Richard Rattos. His brothers Michael and Eddie Rattos played bass and drums respectively, joined by Magnus Fernandes on vocals and bass, and Clifton Carrasco on drums. Their renditions of songs like Malaika (Angel) and Obote Yekka (Obote Only) won them broad admiration, reflecting a rich blend of East African and global influences. Another popular act was The Vibrations, formed in 1967. Their lineup included the D'Cuhna brothers, Lester and Philip, along with Henry Ola, Caji Dias, and Lawrence Sequeira. The group performed covers of the Rolling Stones, the Beatles, the Spencer Davis Group, and the American soul band The Vibrations, whose hit The Watusi resonated with young Ugandans. Members of the band came from a range of professional and academic backgrounds: Lester, the group leader, was a business executive; Philip attended Kitante Hill School; Henry Ola, then a student at Aga Khan Secondary School, played bass; Caji Dias, the lead guitarist, worked as an engineer with East African Airways; and Lawrence Sequeira, the drummer, was a journalist. Though musically gifted, the group saw their performances as a hobby rather than a profession and had no plans to record original songs.

The Echoes, a boy band from Jinja, broke through Kampala's dominance with two memorable appearances on Wamala's show. Inspired by British rock groups such as the Shadows and the Beatles, the band featured Deepak Khazanchi on lead guitar, his younger brother Siddharth on bass, Sydney Antao on rhythm guitar and vocals, Nicky Visana as a vocalist, and Chandrakant Gajjan on drums. Most of the members were students at Jinja Senior Secondary School, then the largest secondary school in East Africa and a recognized center of academic excellence. Their earliest audiences were drawn from Jinja's vibrant and multicultural student population. Although they did not record original songs, their live performances earned them considerable acclaim, and their appearances on national television gave them visibility few groups outside Kampala ever enjoyed. Years later, Deepak Khazanchi, performing under the name Guru Deepak, recorded disco tracks such as Sahara Girl and Together in Love while living in the United Kingdom in 1982.

Other youth bands that rose to prominence through Wamala's show included The Sparrows (later renamed The Slingers) and The Cranes Band, both of which emerged from a cabaret troupe known as the Crazy Gang. Formed by teenagers for the 1962 independence celebrations, the group marked the start of a vibrant era in youth-driven popular music. The early 1960s saw the emergence of several teenage bands that developed devoted followings and toured widely across Uganda. Among them were The Flames, Orbit Four, and The Hurricanes, all of which helped define the era's youthful energy. The Thunderbirds were also a key part of this vibrant scene. Their lineup changed over time and, at various points, included future stars like Moses Matovu, Sam Kanyike, and Nathan Semalulu.

Another influential group was the Savannah Swingers, a musically adventurous band featuring Prakash Vinod Joshi on vocals, William Fernandez on piano and clarinet, Peter Fernandez on rhythm guitar, Anthony Dantus on bass guitar, Mike de Souza on violin, Lala Patni on drums, and Herman de Souza as sound engineer. The Savannah Swingers stood out for their ability to cross social boundaries. They performed at predominantly Black venues like Susana Nightclub, while also appearing at more exclusive clubs such as La Quinta, which catered to a mostly non-Black clientele.

School bands injected a vibrant sense of youth and energy into Uganda's music scene. Among the most successful was the King's College Budo Band, affectionately known as the Beards. Comprised of exceptionally talented students with an average age of just sixteen, the original lineup featured Michael Mulira on lead guitar, Meddy Mugenyi on rhythm guitar, Jack Sekandwa on bass, Stephen 'Ringo' Lwamala on drums, and Duncan Kibaya as lead vocalist. The Beards became regular performers on Elly Wamala's television show and toured widely, playing at schools such as Gayaza Girls, Nyakasura, and Ntare, and even crossing borders to perform at Kenyatta College in Nairobi. Their success also sparked a fierce rivalry with St. Mary's College Kisubi, where the Skylarks emerged as the school's answer to the Beards. Led by energetic and gifted performers such as Simon Sagala and drummer Jim Rock Lutaaya, the Skylarks matched their rivals in flair and consistently drew equally enthusiastic crowds. Wherever the Beards performed, the Skylarks were never far behind, and together the two groups set the standard for schoolboy bands of the era.

Another notable group, the InCrowd of Namilyango College, owed its formation to the influence of the Cranes. The spark came from a bold and unforgettable act by one of their own: John Ssentamu, older brother of musician Frank Mbalire and a student at Namilyango College. Ssentamu had been playing with the Cranes band during school holidays, but one fateful weekend he received an urgent message from his bandmates. The Cranes were about to make their television debut on Uganda Television, and they needed him. The timing could not have been worse. It was term time, and Namilyango College, a strict Roman Catholic boarding school run by Mill Hill missionaries, enforced a clear rule that no student could leave the school grounds without written permission from a dormitory master. Ssentamu could have asked, but he knew such permission was granted only under exceptional circumstances, and going to perform in a band on Uganda Television was not one of them.

Determined not to miss this rare opportunity, he slipped out quietly that evening. He crossed the compound, heart pounding, and caught a rickety bus to Kampala, about fifteen miles away. It was a dangerous gamble. The consequences for breaking school rules could be severe. But he believed the chance to perform on national television was worth the risk. That night, the Cranes appeared on UTV for the first time. Across the country, students gathered in common rooms, watching on black-and-white screens as they did every Saturday evening. To their shock, there was John Ssentamu on the screen, calmly playing guitar alongside the Cranes. At Namilyango College, word spread instantly. The quiet, rule-abiding Ssentamu had vanished from school and turned up on television.

The following day, he was summoned by the principal, Rev. Father Bernard Kuipers, a Dutch Mill Hill missionary known for his strict discipline. Everyone braced for the worst. But instead of punishment, Ssentamu received something entirely different. Father Kuipers was deeply impressed by his performance. He saw not defiance, but raw talent and potential. Rather than discipline him, the principal chose to support him. He arranged for the school to acquire musical instruments and encouraged students to develop their creative abilities. That single act of understanding and support led to the birth of the InCrowd band of Namilyango College. Unlike the school's long-established brass band, which had been part of its tradition for generations, the InCrowd introduced something entirely new. It featured Namilyango students performing spirited covers of contemporary popular music.

The original InCrowd lineup in 1965 featured John Ssentamu on vocals, Leonard Kabunga on lead guitar, Kamya on rhythm guitar, Kigobe on bass, another member named Mukasa on bass, Samba Mukasa as a vocalist, and Baltazar Fernandes as a vocalist. Notably, the InCrowd was another of the few multiracial Ugandan pop bands, with Fernandes representing the Ugandan Goan community. Much like the King's College band, the Beards, the InCrowd rose to popularity by performing on weekends at various secondary schools around the country. As the years passed, the InCrowd saw new members join its ranks. Later additions included Fred Tebuseke, who would go on to join the Rwenzori band, Bazanye, brother to Alex Mukulu of the Rwenzori band's sister group, River Nile band, and Sammy Muwanga Kasumba, who later earned recognition as a prominent Ugandan surgeon and became a longtime resident of Johannesburg, South Africa. Among the final schoolboy bands of this era to emerge was the Eclipse Rubaga Boys Band, formed in 1974, capping off a decade defined by youthful creativity, media exposure, and the infectious spirit of musical experimentation.

For teenagers still in school, this level of television exposure was extraordinary. National television brought their music into households across Uganda, and their tours demonstrated that youthful bands could command the same excitement once reserved for established adult groups. In their rise, Uganda's schoolboy bands mirrored the global youth movement of the 1960s, where teenagers from Liverpool to Nairobi were seizing guitars and stages, reshaping popular culture with their energy and ambition.

Another notable musician who was first introduced to Ugandans on Wamala's show was Taib Ahmed Mutyaba. A true polyglot, Taib sang in Luganda, Swahili, Arabic, English, and German, a versatility that set him apart from many of his contemporaries. After spending many years overseas, primarily in Egypt and Yugoslavia, Taib returned to Uganda in 1970. In May of that year, he made his debut on the television program, by then known as the UTV show. Accompanied by the Lake Victoria band, the resident ensemble at Lake Victoria Hotel in Entebbe, Taib delivered a striking cover of Sugar, Sugar, the worldwide hit by the American fictional pop band the Archies. The song's global popularity was such that it even traveled to the moon with the Apollo 12 astronauts in 1969. For Ugandan audiences, it was unusual and exciting to hear such a global sensation performed live on national television, and Taib's confident English delivery set him apart from his peers. In a way, his performance linked Ugandan living rooms to the outer space adventure of Apollo 12, as if the same song echoing on the moon had also found new life on Uganda's TV screens. The broadcast thrilled audiences and earned him numerous appearances throughout the 1970s.

Born in 1938 in Nnama, a village to the northeast of Mukono town, Taib left Uganda in the late 1950s to pursue further studies in Egypt. In Cairo, Taib discovered his near-perfect baritone, a voice that could shift from smooth resonance to a hoarse, breathy intimacy. He could effortlessly interpret the songs of crooners like Frank Sinatra and Nat King Cole. His talent did not go unnoticed by fellow students, who encouraged him to audition with several bands in Cairo's bustling nightclub scene. At his first audition, he secured a place in a group and soon became known for his soulful renditions of Cole's classics, including Route 66 and Straighten Up and Fly Right. The Cairo of the 1960s was alive with cafés spilling onto the streets around Tahrir Square, where radios blared a mix of Umm Kulthum, jazz, and imported American pop. Nightclubs catered to cosmopolitan crowds of Egyptians, expatriates, and international students, their air heavy with cigarette smoke and the scent of strong coffee. In this setting, Taib's voice carried easily across the din, winning him admirers well beyond the student community. One performance even earned him an Egyptian television award, a sign of the recognition he had achieved in the country.

In the early 1960s, Taib earned a scholarship to study philosophy at the University of Sarajevo in former Yugoslavia. Much like his experience in Cairo, he established himself as a sought-after artist in Sarajevo, performing at various concerts and on numerous radio stations throughout Yugoslavia. In 1964, he signed a contract with the German SABA label, headed by Hans Georg Brunner-Schwer. This collaboration led to the release of the acclaimed singles Wenn du auch einsam bist (If You Are Too Lonely) and Wasifa, the latter originally composed and sung by Kenyan musician Fundi Konde. It was in Sarajevo that Taib recorded his groundbreaking 1965 EP, a first for a Ugandan-born musician. On this record, he collaborated with the renowned Serbian composer and arranger Kornelije Kovač, whose skills as a pop and rock musician elevated the overall sound of the production. The EP featured four tracks: Mchezo ya Uhuru (Independence Dance), Wasifa (Praiseworthy), Kasafiri (I travelled), and Mchezo Mpiya (A New Dance). In Mchezo Mpiya, Taib expressed the spirit of Africa's independence, linking his personal artistic journey with the continent's broader quest for freedom and renewal:

> We, the people of Africa,
> demand our independence—
> cherishing freedom above all else.
> Europeans, return to Europe!
> Today, Africa's children dance
> to the rhythm of liberty,
> after a long, bitter struggle.

Taib Ahmed Mutyaba's music was marked by a vibrant, jazzy style infused with a strong rhumba influence. His songs revealed a rich baritone that seemed to float, carrying an almost mythic quality. In 1967, he recorded tracks such as Sugar Baby Train (composed by K. Svab, A. Bauer, and D. David) and It's a Long Way to Your Heart, a composition by Jeff Bailey, on the Austrian label Figaro. For these recordings, he was accompanied by the Austrian group Orchester Erik Brig of Konrad Josef Svab, whose contributions added a lush and sophisticated dimension to Mutyaba's recordings.

Soon after his return to Uganda in 1970, Taib briefly left for Nairobi with plans to record two songs, Back Home and Tonkisa Ky'olowooza (Don't Hide Your Thoughts From Me). However, the political upheaval following Idi Amin's overthrow of Obote's government led to the cancellation of those plans. Sensing the need to be part of a rebuilding effort, Taib hurried back to Uganda, determined to help shape a new national future. Once he returned, he became a regular figure on UTV and even joined the Shelton Quintet for a short period. This band, led by Shelton Muzowe with Pinkie Kabahenda as a key member, had its roots in Muzowe's earlier group, the Shelton Trio, which had performed at the Grand Hotel in Kampala in 1967 with members Shelton (vocals and leader), G. Martas (bass), G. I. Assuman (guitar), and Erica Wamba (drums).

While Elly Wamala's TV show played a major role in introducing many Ugandan musical acts during the 1960s, some artists reached audiences through other channels. One such example is Benedict "Benny" Kalanzi, whose folk-rhumba sound developed a large and loyal following in Germany and Switzerland, even though he remained relatively unknown in Uganda. Born in August 1938 in Kyawangabi, a village near the renowned Villa Maria in Masaka, Kalanzi was the son of Matayo Mugalula, a *mutongole* (a local administrative chief) , and Anastasia Namatovu, a homemaker. Growing up in a staunch Roman Catholic family, he was initially encouraged to pursue the priesthood. After completing his elementary education at Villa Maria, he attended Bukalasa Minor Seminary, which first opened its doors on June 9, 1893, and is recognized as the first formal school in Uganda to offer a Western education.

At the seminary, Kalanzi's passion for music flourished. With a father who was a master drummer and a mother celebrated as a traditional dancer, he immersed himself in the seminary brass band under the guidance of the esteemed Rev. Father John Robinson. Recognizing his knack for learning various instruments, including the clarinet, bugle, and cymbals, Father Robinson also trained him on the harmonium. Kalanzi's ability to read music and master the harmonium led to his appointment as the lead organist when he joined Katigondo Major Seminary in Villa Maria. There, he broadened his musical horizons by studying classical works by Handel, Bach, Mozart, and Lothi, among others. His deep passion for classical music, however, led his predominantly missionary professors to conclude that the priesthood might not be the best fit for him. They advised him to leave seminary training and pursue a secular career in music. Though disappointed by this redirection, Kalanzi eventually embraced his new path, taking a job as a court translator for the Buganda Kingdom judiciary, a position that allowed him to support himself while continuing to develop his musical talents.

While working at the court, Benny Kalanzi encountered many prominent officials of the Buganda Kingdom. One influential figure he met was Mr. Kayemba, the Kabaka's chief musician. Kalanzi asked Kayemba to teach him the various traditional musical instruments used to entertain the Kabaka. Kayemba readily took him on, training him on the madinda (xylophone), *ntongooli* (bowl-lyre), *dingidi* (fiddle), and nnanga (bow-harp). Through these lessons, Kalanzi became highly skilled in playing traditional instruments, a training he had missed during his seminary education, where the focus was on Western instruments and Gregorian chants. This combined training in both Western and traditional Ugandan instruments laid the foundation for Benny Kalanzi's distinctive folk-rhumba beat, which he described as Afro-Western pop music.

In 1963, Kalanzi earned a scholarship to study at the University of Fribourg in Switzerland, majoring in music while also taking minors in German, English, and French. After the death of his music supervisor, Professor Brenn, he transferred to the University of Bern and completed his final semester in Germany at Cologne University. In 1966, Kalanzi and his brother John Sendaula, who had moved to Switzerland, staged their first public performance, receiving an enthusiastic response. Their success led to appearances on numerous radio programs, including Radio Deutsche Welle in Cologne, Radio Berne, and Westdeutscher Rundfunk.

While in Switzerland, Kalanzi and Sendaula were joined by their equally talented sister, Margaret Nabyonga, who was also known professionally as Miss Nabi and at times by her other name, Margaret Mugalula. A skilled vocalist and pianist, she brought a distinctive richness to the trio's performances. Together, the three formed The Three Artists, with the brothers on guitars and Margaret singing, and they became familiar to European audiences through frequent concerts and television broadcasts.

In July 1967, the University of Cologne hosted the International Folklore Music Festival contest, drawing artists from 14 countries. Representing Uganda as the Kars group, Benny Kalanzi, John Sendaula, and Margaret Nabyonga performed using traditional Ugandan instruments and an electric guitar. Kalanzi and Sendaula demonstrated exceptional technical proficiency, while Nabyonga provided a gentle, rhythmic support with her maracas, evoking the soft swish of wind through a field of napier grass. Their performance earned them first prize in Cologne, and they subsequently received numerous invitations to appear on radio shows in Germany and Switzerland. They also made four television appearances in both countries, a remarkable achievement for Ugandan artists who had grown up in a small village and were barely known in their home country.

Alongside these live performances, the trio also built a small but notable discography. As the Kars, Kalanzi and Sendaula released Mazina on the Apollo Sound label in 1969, a 16-track album that featured songs such as Obuvubuka Bulungi (Youth is Splendid), Nyikira Nnyo (Perseverance), and Salaam (Greetings). Later, in 1976, Kalanzi collaborated with Miss Nabi, by then a seasoned performer, to record East African-American Pop Music, a 12-track album on the BAK label that included Kazi (Work), Webale (Thank You), and Mukyala (Wife). Sendaula, too, extended his career in Europe. Together with his wife Rose, herself a talented singer, he recorded the album Sanyu on the VDE label in the 1970s, featuring songs such as Ninda Lumu (Waiting for the One Day) and Abajulizi (Uganda Martyrs).

These recordings, produced far from home, were more than personal milestones. They marked the Kalanzi siblings as pioneers who carried Ugandan music onto international stages, weaving the rhythms of their homeland into new cultural settings. In doing so, they laid a foundation for later generations of Ugandan artists, proving that music born in village courtyards and school halls could command respect and admiration in the cosmopolitan concert halls of Europe. Their story foreshadowed the journeys of many Ugandan musicians who, in the dark years of Amin's rule, would be forced into exile, carrying their songs abroad not only in search of audiences but also as a means of survival.

CHAPTER 10

They Sang and Endured: Uganda's Female Artists of the Post-Independence Years

Uganda's post-independence generation of female musicians looked to Eva Nanyonga as their trailblazer. Encouraged by Israel Magembe and members of the Kampala City Six band, they drew inspiration from her artistry and determination. By the early 1960s, Nanyonga herself was stepping back from active performance, though she was still occasionally called upon to appear. One of her last major public performances came during Uganda's independence celebrations in October 1962, and in 1964 she released one of her final hits, Dali Nkwagala (Love You, Darling). As Nanyonga gradually withdrew from the limelight, a new generation of female voices emerged to claim the stage.

Many of these women were affiliated with Magembe's Kampala City Six. Among the first to follow in Nanyonga's footsteps were singers such as Margaret "Mega" Nakibuuka, whose early recordings signaled that women were ready to take a more prominent place in Uganda's popular music. Margaret Nakibuuka was encouraged to take up singing by Fred Kanyike and began her career as a backup artist at Planet nightclub. She occasionally performed duets with Kanyike before establishing herself as a lead singer. Nakibuuka's career spanned nearly fifteen years, during which she recorded dozens of popular songs. Her collaborations with Andrew Kyambadde, her partner and father of her children, played a significant role in popularizing duets in Ugandan popular music.

Another standout artist was Yunia Nalwanga, whose influence far exceeded her brief three-year career in the limelight. During this period, she recorded a series of beloved songs alongside Kanyike, Kawalya, and Bonnie K Steven. Yunia was perhaps the most recognizable and influential female artist of the time. She was also one of the first Ugandan musicians to have a manager. Her manager, Simon Sonko, spoke in 1964 of plans for Yunia to release an LP of her own compositions, generating significant anticipation among fans. However, the project never materialized because Yunia chose a quiet married life over a prolonged music career. Despite her early departure, her contributions to Ugandan music left a lasting imprint across East Africa. David Amunga, a prominent Kenyan musician who recorded at AGS Studios Ltd in Nairobi during the same period, reportedly admired Yunia so much that he named his daughter after her. Yunia and Amunga both had songs featured on the same EP released by the South African Quality label. This EP included Nina Kyembuza (I Have a Question) and Mwami Wange (My Husband) by Yunia and Kanyike, as well as Amunga's Wangonjwa Mwasumbuka (The Hardships of the Sick) and To My Lover Margaret. All these tracks were originally recorded on the AGS label and backed by the AGS Boys.

Numerous Ugandan women performed in Kampala's nightclubs, though most sang covers of popular Western songs and never had the opportunity to record. Many, like their male counterparts, contributed as backup singers on a few tracks before fading into obscurity. Among the few based in Uganda who managed to record their own music in the early to mid-1960s were Margaret Nakibuuka, Sarah Namagembe, Rose Musoke, and Mary Nattima. All of them were scouted by Fred Kanyike, who took them to Nairobi to record for the AGS label with the AGS Boys as their backing band. Others, such as Frida Sonko, also entered the studio during this period, though her career was centered in Nairobi rather than Kampala.

Sarah Namagembe was born in 1947 and began her education at Kibuli Primary School. Though she struggled through her junior and secondary years, her path soon shifted toward music, influenced in part by her uncle Fred Mukasa, a recording artist with the AGS label. Her greatest inspiration, however, was Israel Magembe. A gifted dancer, Sarah Namagembe was a familiar face at Planet nightclub in Bwaise, where the Kampala City Six often performed. Her striking presence and warm personality quickly caught Israel Magembe's attention. When he discovered that she not only wanted to sing but had the talent to match, he invited her to audition for the band. She was soon performing as a vocalist at his side.

Namagembe's breakthrough came in February 1964, when Kamulu launched the New Life nightclub with a glamorous gala attended by cabinet ministers and senior government officials. That evening, Namagembe dazzled the crowd in a sparkling black-blue minidress, singing and dancing beside Magembe, who wore a white tuxedo jacket, crisp shirt, and black bowtie. Their chemistry lit up the stage and left the audience spellbound. Namagembe became one of the most prominent female voices in the Kampala City Six until her departure in 1968. Both protégé and romantic partner, she was always at Magembe's side during performances, their bond evident in every duet and shared glance. Though their relationship was never publicly confirmed, it was widely known in Kampala's music circles and often spoken of with admiration. Despite the similarity in their names, there was no breach of Buganda's clan taboos: Namagembe belonged to the *mbogo* (buffalo) clan, while Magembe came from the mmamba (lungfish) clan. Even after their romance ended, the two remained close, tied by mutual respect and deep artistic connection. Their story was not unusual. Many musicians working in the same band formed emotional bonds that extended beyond the music.

After leaving Kampala City Six, Namagembe became a much-admired figure at Susana in the late 1960s. Her brief stint with the Susana Band earned her a devoted following and made her one of the club's most cherished female performers. However, the demanding schedule took its toll, and she eventually left the band to work at a Kampala record store, where she sold vinyl records and shared her musical knowledge with customers. Though no longer performing on stage, she continued to hold a deep appreciation for Magembe, who had once believed in her talent. In a 1971 interview with the *People* newspaper, she reflected warmly: "Most of what I learnt vocally came from Magembe, who passed on to me the secrets of music." Her words revealed not only his role as a mentor, but also the enduring bond shaped by their shared journey.

Namagembe's recording career stood apart from her stage performances, revealing her talent as both a singer and songwriter. While she was best known for her work with Magembe, she also recorded with his younger brother, Steven Sempasa, producing tracks such as Omulembe Omutesa (Era of Negotiation) and Nafira Ku Jesca (I Died for Jesca) for the AGS label. A few months later, she wrote and recorded Debula (a female name) on the CMS label. Among her most memorable recordings were Abasajja Balumya (Men Are a Pain) and Ngenda Ntinda (Going to Ntinda), both released in 1967 on the Furaha label. Margaret Nakibuuka provided backing vocals for the two songs, but it was Nakibuuka's name that appeared first on the label. Such mistakes were common at the time. Artists' names were frequently misspelled, songs wrongly attributed, or titles printed incorrectly on vinyl. Even so, this particular oversight left Namagembe deeply frustrated, as she felt it had robbed her of the credit she had earned.

Her song, Abasajja Balumya, stood out for challenging prevailing narratives that often portrayed women in a derogatory light. It marked a shift in lyrical themes, offering a perspective that many female listeners related to, as the song expressed frustrations and experiences familiar to them:

Men are such a pain,
and mine is an especially heavy burden.
You will not even give me a bit of sugar;
then what can I offer our children?
You will not buy me clothes,
what am I to do?

All the good things I do, darling,
you scorn them with disdain;
jealousy and beating,
oh mama, poor me!
If I were to leave,
who would take care of the children?
Even if you divorce me now,
husband, you will forget;
even if you marry someone more beautiful,
husband, you will forget;
all the good I have done,
husband, you will forget;
you are abandoning your children,
husband, you will forget.

Namagembe's later compositions included Obwamalaya Kwebuva (The Origins of Prostitution), a doo-wop tune, and Eddy (a male name), a rumba track, both recorded in 1969 under the Furaha label. She also featured as a backing singer on James Kigongo's Ezadde Libonabona (Parenting is Demanding) for Furaha, and on Nelson Sabavuma's Tewali Kirungi Na Kibi (There's No Good or Bad) for the Equator label.

Despite her ability and early promise, Namagembe never quite reached the heights of stardom, her career overshadowed by Margaret Nakibuuka and other prominent women of the 1960s such as Mary Nattima, Frida Sonko, and Mary Frances Kiryangokibi, better known as Hadija Namale. By August 1970 she had shifted her focus to live performance, joining the Florida Fiesta Band at Florida Nightclub. When the club was renamed Arizona in 1971, she stayed on, working with a succession of Congolese bands that drew huge crowds to the venue. Her Luganda songs held their own alongside the Lingala rumba rhythms, but it was her dancing that often stole the spotlight. Revelers thronged Arizona not only to hear her sing but also to watch her glide and sway across the stage with an energy and grace that seemed to suspend time.

Her final stint came with the Congolese resident band Somosomo (later kwon as Moud-MAS-Jily, which was shortened to Mud Mas Band) in 1974. The relentless schedule of nightly shows eventually wore her down. Although she considered returning to Chandarana's studio in Kericho to record new material, the plan never came to fruition. By the end of 1974 she had slowed her performances and quietly stepped away from the music scene. Her story lingers as one of promise unfulfilled, a reminder of how brilliance on stage does not always translate into enduring fame, and how the demands of nightly performance could extinguish a voice that deserved to be more widely remembered.

Another female musician who made her mark starting her musical career in the early 1960s was Mary Nattima. Born in 1945 in the small village of Kikoma in Singo County, Buganda, she came from a family that had migrated from Bunyoro and settled in Kikoma, where her father worked as a primary school teacher. At home, the family spoke Lunyolo, but the children were also fluent in Luganda. Nattima attended Kikoma Primary School and later Mubende Secondary School. At home, the family owned a gramophone, and Nattima's favorite artist at the time was Edward Seruwagi, whose major hits, Enguli (Gin) and Eriso Ly'omwana (Eyes of My Baby), were recorded in 1952. While at Mubende Secondary School, Nattima was actively involved in the school choir and also served as the captain of the netball team.

Around the age of 16, Nattima left school in Mubende and moved to Kampala with the intention of enrolling in a trade school to pursue a secretarial course. However, those plans were set aside when she and her girlfriends, all newcomers to the city, discovered the vibrant nightlife at Planet nightclub in Bwaise and became enamored with the music of Kampala City Six. It was during this time that Kawalya took notice of Nattima. Recognizing her vocal talent, he arranged for her to audition for Kanyike. She impressed Kanyike with her original compositions, including Rin (a female name). Seeing the emotional depth in her voice, Kanyike suggested that Nattima and Kawalya develop Rin as a duet. This marked the beginning of a partnership that would endure for nearly a decade.

However, Nattima's first recorded solo track was in 1963 with her debut single, John Wange (My John), on the AGS label. Yunia Nalwanga provided backup vocals, and the song became a huge success for the young artist:

Come to where I am, my darling John.
Come to me, dear, and keep me company,
for I am all alone here, John!
See how I struggle, see how I suffer.
Come back to me, John, my darling,
you are the sun that shines upon me.
I want you to marry me, so that we may live together.
I am tired of being alone, John,
you are the only one I need.
Who else should I turn to?
Hasten and come back,
what am I to do?
Hasten and return,
with whom shall I laugh?
Hasten and come back.
Come to me, John, my darling,
to calm my aching soul.
What can I give you
to show my love?
What am I to do, dear?
I am dying of love,
I need you here
to keep me company.

Nattima and Kawalya's first recorded works came in 1963, featuring Rin and Fumbira Abaana (Cook for the Children). Fumbira Abaana became an instant hit, propelling Nattima onto the national stage and earning her widespread admiration. The guitar arrangements, provided by the

AGS Boys, were crisp, melodic, and easygoing. The playful but revealing exchange between Nattima and Kawalya in the lyrics framed a conversation in a bar, shedding light on the gender dynamics of a patriarchal society. The song opens with Nattima's character lamenting her struggles:

Woo upon me, mama,
hard times on me,
for my husband is married to booze.
Woo upon me, Mary,
one as handsome as you living on the road.
If you have rejected me,
it is not a big deal,
because I will find another.

Kawalya's character interjects, attempting to pacify her and avoid public embarrassment:

My dear, darling,
what has become of you?
It is not wise to quarrel in public.
If you are upset,
and if I have upset you,
let us go home and not here in the bar.

Nattima's character, however, remains unconvinced: "It is jealousy that haunts me, my husband to be married to the road." In response, the husband lists his marital contributions, asserting his position: "I bring you food, you eat to your satisfaction, for me to just sit around? What do you want me to do?" The wife counters his justification: "What brought me here is to cook, and the food I cook I would like you to eat," to which the husband finally appears to concede: "That is not what I am saying. I want you to cook. First cook for the children and then quarrel." Ultimately, Nattima's character issues an ultimatum, signaling that she has had enough: "If you are dismissive of what I say, farewell, I am leaving.

278

You will find another." In addition to this landmark duet, Nattima also provided backup vocals on other AGS label hits, including Nyumyenge Nani (Who Should I Chat With) and Mukyala Toyomba (Don't Quarrel Woman), where she supported Fred Mukasa.

Mary Nattima continued to compose and perform music, collaborating with Ecklas Kawalya on the AGS label. Their partnership yielded several major hits, including Minzaani Yomukwano (Measure of Love), Sirina Galivumwa (I Will Not Stand for Abuse), and Ndifuna Owange (I Will Find My Love). These songs, characterized by beautifully pensive melodies and their phantasmagorical soft hues, became a hallmark of the Nattima-Kawalya duets. Notably, the melody of Sirina Galivumwa was heavily borrowed from Tabu Ley Rochereau's 1963 hit Bato Ya Congo with Orchestre African Fiesta. Nattima's voice carried a sweet, hypnotic quality, while the AGS Boys provided guitar lines that echoed with emotion.

Despite the popularity of her duets with Kawalya, Nattima faced challenges in securing a position with a nightclub band as a regular performer. Even Kampala City Six declined to offer her a permanent role, instead allowing her to appear on stage without compensation. It was her older brother, Simon Berunga, a rising star with several successful recordings on the AGS label, who introduced her to Fred Masagazi. Masagazi, recognizing her talent, recruited her to the Uganda Kezaala Jazz Band, also known as the UK Jazz Band. Nattima remained with UK Jazz Band until August 1964, when Masagazi disbanded the group. By this time, she had gained enough recognition and financial stability to rent a cottage in Naguru Housing Estate, one of Uganda's oldest public housing projects built during the British colonial era. The estate was a highly sought-after address for Kampala's growing middle class, particularly civil servants and professionals.

After the dissolution of UK Jazz, she joined the Satellite Top Ten Band, where she beguiled audiences with her performances. When Kawalya, Kanyike, and Bonnie K. Steven departed from New Life to join Lorina (Satellite), Nattima reunited with Kawalya, and their duets became a highlight of the club's performances, attracting large crowds. However, in 1967, Kawalya left Lorina for Susanna Nightclub. Around this time, Nattima was recruited into the Uganda Police Jazz Band, which was led by vocalist James Kigongo. Unlike the Police Brass Marching Band, directed by WWII veteran Venancio Okello, the Uganda Police Jazz Band specialized in popular music, particularly covers of Congolese hits. They regularly performed for the police department and were also available for hire at government and private functions, making them one of the most popular entertainment groups in Kampala.

Mary Nattima and Ecklas Kawalya collaborated on dozens of songs, solidifying their place in Uganda's musical history. In addition to performing together, Nattima also wrote songs for Kawalya that did not include her as a singer. One such composition was Kiriba Kiki (Whatever Will Be), which became one of Kawalya's most admired recordings. However, Nattima was frequently involved in his music, either as a duet partner or as a backup vocalist. Beyond their early successes with Rin, Fumbira Abaana, Ndifuna Owange, and Sirina Galivumwa, Nattima composed one of their biggest hits, Ssanyu (a female name). Ssanyu, popularly known as Mbela Kololo (I Live in Kololo), adapted its melody from Eydie Gormé's 1963 single Blame It on the Bossa Nova, and became a major commercial success. While many of their collaborations featured Kawalya in the lead, Nattima also recorded several songs where the roles were reversed, with Kawalya providing backup vocals. Among these were Nayita Ani (Who Will I Call?), Willy (a male name), and Abwoli Ninkusera (Looking for Abwoli). Nattima primarily sang in Luganda, but Abwoli Ninkusera was one of the few songs she performed and recorded in her native Runyoro dialect.

My handsome Abwoli,
I am searching for you;
my dear Abwoli,
I weep for you.
My handsome Abwoli,
know that my tears fall for you,

for your unmatched handsomeness
and the deep love I feel.
I wish for us to wed, dear,
but if you do not consent,
let us leave it
to God's will.

Very early in her recording career, around 1963 to 1964, Mary Nattima collaborated with her brother, Simon Berunga, producing a series of highly lauded songs on the AGS label. These included Nanyonga (a female name), Nkumye Eddembe (I Have Kept the Peace), and Kyekisera (It's the Time).

Throughout the first half of the 1970s, Nattima remained an active performer. However, after marrying a police officer from Amin's Kakwa tribe in northern Uganda and starting a family, she gradually shifted her focus to raising her children. When Idi Amin was overthrown in 1979, Mary Nattima and her family fled Uganda, seeking refuge in southern Sudan. Their departure was driven by the widespread perception that those who shared a tribal or regional background with the ousted leader had either benefited from or were complicit in the atrocities of the fallen regime. In the chaotic aftermath of Amin's downfall, many Ugandans took justice into their own hands, targeting individuals they believed to be affiliated with the previous government. Many innocent people from the West Nile region, in particular, faced persecution, with their homes looted and their lives threatened.

Fearing for their safety, Nattima gathered her children and joined her husband in a perilous journey away from the country she had served so well through her music. Life in Sudan was fraught with challenges, and eventually, with assistance from the United Nations High Commissioner for Refugees (UNHCR), she and her family were relocated to a refugee camp in Kenya. When she finally returned to Uganda in the 1980s, she faced economic hardship and struggled with deteriorating health.

In 1994, Nattima was given a rare chance to step back into the spotlight. She was among the celebrated musicians featured in the Music

Back to the Sixties concert held at Kampala's Sheraton Hotel. Sponsored by Amos Agaba, the proprietor of Kampala Bottlers and the owner of the Waka Waka Band, the show brought together some of Uganda's most renowned artists from the 1960s. The lineup included Hadija Namale, Andrew Kyambadde, Margaret Nakibuuka, Martin Munyenga, and Frida Sonko, among others.

Frida Sonko, born Frida Basuta in 1930, was the elder sister of Charles Sonko. Her mother, Kasalina, was a Mutoro, and though Frida never knew her biological father, she was lovingly raised by her stepfather, Blasio Kasiko, whom she always regarded as her true father. She grew up in the quiet hamlet of Kidukulu in Bulemezi, central Uganda. The year of her birth was also a landmark moment for East African music: in 1930, Siti binti Saad became the first East African to record on gramophone disc, proving that women's voices from the region could be preserved and carried far beyond their communities. Where Siti rooted her legacy in the tradition of taarab on the Swahili coast, Frida would later emerge in Nairobi as part of a new generation shaping the sound of East African pop. In this way, her story became a continuation of a pioneering lineage of women who expanded the possibilities of music across the region.

Music was already stirring in the lives of the Sonko siblings, and when their parents moved to Nairobi in search of better opportunities, the children followed them in 1944. Two decades later, in the early 1960s, Charles Sonko introduced Frida to Equator Sound Studios at a time when the management was looking for a female vocalist to join their resident group, the Equator Boys Band. Frida auditioned successfully and soon found herself swept into the heart of Nairobi's vibrant music scene.

Within the studio she forged close ties with the Equator Boys, relationships that blossomed into lasting friendships beyond the stage. Together with Moses Katazza, she acknowledged these bonds in the song Ndelema (a female name), a lyrical tribute to the camaraderie they shared. Frida frequently joined the Equator Boys in performances around Nairobi and beyond, her presence adding both musical richness and a sense of family to the group's growing reputation.

Fadhili William Mdawida, a musician from the Kenyan coast, introduced Frida to Mombasa, a city she grew fond of and often visited when she was not recording at Equator Sound Studios. There, she contributed as a backup singer on numerous recordings by a wide range of artists. By 1965, she had emerged from her brother's shadow and launched her own career. Alongside Fadhili William and Zambian artist Nashil Pichen, she released two highly successful songs, Love Me Baby and Step Out, Lady, on the Equator label. These energetic Kenyan Twist songs featured Frida's stirring and passionate vocal delivery.

Love Me Baby, sung in both English and Luganda, captured the emotions of a relationship struggling to maintain its spark. Step Out, Lady was a celebration of female empowerment. Though the title was in English, the song was performed entirely in Luganda:

> Baby girl, show your style!
> Baby girl, show your smarts!
> Baby girls, let us confound them,
> Baby girls, let us entertain them!
> Put on those shoes—the frisky ones.
> Wear that tight dress—the alluring one.
> If you have hair, don a comb,
> and add your confident walk
> so that every head turns.
> But to achieve all this,
> you must first have a good heart and manners.
> Men who truly love you are a blessing,
> and trustworthy friendships are worth cherishing.
> Beware of men who habitually lie—they only disappoint.

Frida Sonko was the most recorded female Ugandan artist on the Equator label. Her songs Alojja Omukwano and Gwe Saba Lugaba turned her into a superstar in Uganda, earning her recognition as the undisputed queen of the country's popular music. The inspiration for Alojja Omukwano (also known as Wambuza meaning You Asked Me, or Olupapula Si Mupira meaning Paper Is Not Elastic) grew out of a small, almost playful moment at home between Frida, her brother Charles Sonko, and their close friend Moses Katazza, who was preparing to return to Uganda after a recording session at Equator Sound Studios.

Katazza, the son of John Bosa of the Mengo African Orchestra, had just finished recording Nona Ente Yo (Come Get Your Cow) and Amazima Lona (Sincerely Lona), two duets with Frida. During his stay in Nairobi, he lodged with the Sonkos, and as he packed for his journey back, he asked whether they wished to send a note to their parents in Uganda. They did, but no paper was at hand. Charles, thinking quickly, emptied a packet of Sportsman cigarettes, peeled out the shiny aluminum-backed inner lining, and scribbled a brief message on the blank side. Holding it up, he sighed at how little he could fit onto it. It was then that Frida, with a flash of wit that turned the mundane into poetry, remarked that paper was not like a ball, for it could not stretch to carry more words. That simple observation became the seed of Olupapula Si Mupira, a metaphor that would soon echo across radios and jukeboxes in Uganda, transforming a passing household frustration into one of the most memorable refrains of her career.

Katazza found Frida's remark more than witty; to him it was pure poetry. With a smile, he challenged Charles and Frida to shape her words about the inelasticity of paper into a song. The idea lingered long after he left, and when he returned to Nairobi in 1965, he was eager to hear what had become of it. Frida had risen to the challenge. Waiting for him was Alojja Omukwano, a tender yet spirited song about testifying to love. Over the years, Alojja Omukwano has remained a cherished Ugandan love song, enduring across generations:

Paper is not a ball, it is not elastic, dear; otherwise, I could stretch it.
When you speak of love, saying too little leaves it hollow,
but saying too much turns it into lies.
My pen ran dry, it ran out of ink, and there was nothing I could do.
The supplies were too far away, my dear. Please forgive me
if you still love me.

You asked if I love you. The truth is, I do; you are my number one.
You brought up the matter of the ring, and while we should discuss it,
I am not sure I am ready.
If you truly want a ring, first take time for self-reflection.
Abandon worldly desires, and then, perhaps, have a
wedding with a ring.

Alojja Omukwano continues to receive significant airplay on FM radio stations across Uganda, standing as a quintessential representation of 1960s Ugandan popular music. Moses Katazza contributed his vocals to the song and went on to be a longtime collaborator with Frida Sonko. Their musical partnership was a natural fit, as Frida's velvet phrasing intertwined beautifully with Katazza's mellow baritone. Together, they released some of the most memorable duets of the 1960s, producing love ballads that remain cherished classics. Among these were Ndelema (a female name), Nona Ente Yo (Come for Your Cow), Sirina Gogera (Words Fail Me), Nkoye Ebaluwa (Tired of the Letters), Ye Gwe Weka (You Are the Only One), and Amazima Lona (Truly Lorna). Unlike Charles and Frida Sonko, Katazza was more reclusive and never performed live in clubs. After recording his songs in Niarobi, he returned to his farm in Ssingo County, earning him the nickname *Omulimi We Ssingo*, the farmer from Ssingo.

Released in 1966, Amazima Lona gained significance beyond its romantic theme. The Buganda king had been deposed, and the kingdom was in mourning. The people of Buganda sought a symbol of hope for the king's possible return from exile in London. Amazima Lona, originally a love ballad about a man waiting for his beloved Lona, was repurposed by Kabaka loyalists who saw its refrain, "Be strong, be strong my darling / I am on my way coming / Coming, coming / Be strong of heart," as a message of encouragement and defiance. Many sang the song with enthusiasm, interpreting it as a veiled statement against the Obote regime, which was widely, though inaccurately, believed to be anti-Buganda. In reality, Obote's government opposed the institution of monarchy rather than the Buganda people specifically, aiming instead to promote broader ethnic balance across the country. This ideological stance became official in 1967, when Obote's administration adopted a republican constitution that abolished all traditional kingdoms, including Buganda.

Frida Sonko also collaborated extensively with her brother Charles, recording several iconic hits. One of their standout singles was Gwe Saba Lugaba (Pray to the Lord), which carried the additional English title There is Always Another. Written by Charles, the song featured his vocals and bass playing. Gwe Saba Lugaba is a woman's lament over a painful betrayal. Her lover abandons her at the height of their romance, leaving her emotionally and physically devastated. She describes her dramatic weight loss, saying she has become as thin as a stitching needle and her body is now as pointed as a weed. Her skin, she laments, has turned ashen like that of a chalk factory worker covered in dust.

Other songs by the Sonko siblings included Nga Walaganyiza (Date Night), Wano Tuli Mu Bar (We Are Here at the Bar), Omutwe Gwa Amaka (Head of a Household), Nawuliranga (I Will Be Obedient), and Gwewasobya (You Are to Blame). Gwewasobya stands out for its energetic guitar work and impassioned vocals. The lead guitar plays fluid, interlaced phrases that weave around the melody like threads in a loom, while the rhythm guitar keeps up a steady, lilting pulse that gives the song its gentle sway. In this song, Frida takes on the role of a daughter lamenting her mother's disapproval of her relationship with an older man, whom she saw as an ideal husband. She blames her mother for forcing the breakup, which has left her struggling. She recalls with longing the luxuries of the man she was being forced to leave, the endless supply of sugar, the wax print fabrics (*kitenge*), and the many gifts that had once made her feel cherished. With frustration, she confronts her mother:

> Mama, you made me leave my man
> You wanted me to find someone younger
> But I truly loved him
> Now I struggle
> Where is the tight dress?

> I also want the high-heel shoes
> Do not call me crazy
> It is you who is responsible.

Beyond her collaborations with Charles Sonko, Moses Katazza, and Fadhili William, Frida also worked with Fred Masagazi, one of Uganda's most celebrated musicians of the 1960s and 1970s. Masagazi and Charles Sonko joined Frida on the beautiful ballad I Must Confess. This song, along with Frida's The Story of Love, reflected influences from Jamaican-British singer Millicent "Millie" Small, whose 1964 hit My Boy Lollipop was a major success in Uganda.

Frida Sonko's career often took her beyond Nairobi's clubs to Mombasa, the sultry coastal city famed for its nightlife and its steady stream of Western tourists. The city's clubs pulsed until dawn, drawing a restless mix of locals, global travelers, and seafarers eager for diversion. On one such night, she stepped into the spotlight as if embodying the very spirit of her own song Step Out, Lady. In her frisky shoes and tight, alluring dress, she moved with playful defiance, commanding the nightclub with poise and confidence. Her voice carried across the smoky hall, and even the rowdy group of Italian sailors on shore leave fell silent. One sailor in particular was so taken with her that he pursued her offstage, and over the following days she slipped into a whirlwind romance that mirrored the city's intoxicating rhythm. For Frida, it was a heady moment of thrill and attention, the freedom of reckless joy, and the sense of being desired in a cosmopolitan world far from the village roots she had left behind. The affair, brief as it was, left its permanent trace: she became pregnant and later gave birth to a daughter, her only child.

In 1967, Frida and her brother Charles Sonko returned to Uganda. Charles secured a managerial position at the iconic Susana nightclub, while Frida joined the renowned Susana Band. The band boasted a talented and diverse lineup, featuring musicians from various parts of the region. Richard Majola, a South African Zulu, managed the band. Haruna and Twalib, both Ugandans of Nubian descent, were skilled on the saxophone and trumpet. Charles Ginaro from Congo handled the lead guitar, while Martin Munyenga played bass. Tanzanian guitarist Jimmy Kajwanjwa played rhythm guitar, joined by Congolese drummer Bruno Sereman and conga player Irunga, also from Congo. The vocalists included Ugandans Ecklas Kawalya and Rose Musoke, with Kawalya also skilled on conga drums and bass guitar.

Although Frida contributed as a vocalist, she did not record new songs with the Susana Band. She remained with them until 1972, when she left to join her brother, who had formed the Charles Sonko and Party Band, also known as the Mbuya Army Barracks Band. The group primarily performed songs in praise of Idi Amin, though most of their material was forgettable. However, they did achieve some success with a few kagutema songs, notably Omukazi Wange (My Woman), recorded in 1972 under the Uganda Re-Craft label.

Frida's final recording to gain recognition was her 1974 single Mwami Wange Mwatu (My Man, My Good Friend), released on the state-owned UG label with backing from the General Headquarters Uganda Air Force Jazz Band. The UG label was primarily a vehicle for government propaganda, beginning in the 1960s with songs praising President Milton Obote, such as Simon Kaate Nsubuga's President Obote and Juma Odundo's Milton Obote. After Obote's removal, its focus shifted to Idi Amin, producing works like Rashid Charles Sonko's Darubini Ya Inchi (The Telescope of the Nation), Matia Kakumirizi's Mzee Dada (Our Elder Idi Amin Dada), and Mali Ya Nyoko (It Is Not Your Mother's Wealth), a notorious kadongo kamu track by Christopher Ssebadduka that celebrated the expulsion of Uganda's Indian community and continues to receive airplay despite its racist vitriol. Against such a backdrop, Frida's Mwami Wange Mwatu stands out less as propaganda than as a personal statement, a fleeting reminder of the artistry that had once enthralled her audiences.

After this recording, Frida withdrew from the music scene. When her brother Charles fled to Kenya in 1977, she chose instead to retreat quietly to Kidukulu in Bulemezi, the village of her childhood. There, she endured a life of hardship, often mired in deep poverty, far removed from the glamour of her Nairobi and Kampala years. In 1994, however, she had a brief but powerful return to the stage when businessman Amos Agaba brought together 25 legendary musicians and dancers from Uganda's 1960s music scene. Though visibly aged and worn down by struggle, Frida stepped forward to perform her timeless hit Alojja Omukwano. The crowd erupted in recognition, swept up once more by the voice and presence that had made her a star three decades earlier. In that moment she reminded everyone of who she was and what she had given to Ugandan music.

And yet, history has been unkind. Today, many of her iconic songs are wrongly attributed to others, her name fading even as her melodies endure. Frida Sonko was one of Uganda's most gifted artists, a pioneer whose career bridged Nairobi's golden years of East African pop and Kampala's post-independence ferment. To forget her is to forget a vital chapter of Uganda's musical story. Her name may slip from memory, but her voice still lingers, a reminder that true artistry can never be fully silenced.

Among the other women who helped shape this era was Rose Musoke, née Namere. Rose Musoke was another notable figure in the music scene. A tall, striking woman with a warm smile, she balanced her life between music and her job as a cashier at Susana Nightclub, where she worked the early evening shift. After handling money at the club, she would step onto the stage, joining Kawalya and the Susana Nightclub Band as a backup singer. Encouraged by Fred Kanyike, she ventured into recording, with Kanyike arranging her first sessions on the AGS label. Her debut song, Mulungi Andrew (Handsome Andrew), was well received. Rose recorded several successful duets with Fred Kanyike on the AGS label, including Eddy (a song dedicated to Edisa, the cashier at New Era Nightclub in Natete) and Ndabye Emotoka (I Have Identified a Car). She also provided backup vocals for Simon Berunga on Onkolabingi Dear (You Make Me Do Much, Dear) and Tonumya Bwotyo (Don't Hurt Me Like That).

Additionally, Rose collaborated with Margaret Nakibuuka on Twegasse Wano (United Here). She joined Kawalya and Yunia in providing backup vocals on some of Fred Kanyike's major hits, such as Dorothy, Elizabeth, and Rose Wanyita (You Are Killing Me, Rose), a song said to have been dedicated to her. Kawalya himself honored Rose Musoke by dedicating one of his major hits, simply titled Rose, to her:

Rose, you make things difficult for me, woman—
you hurt me deeply, dear.
Many men desire you;
tell them you already have your sweetie.
I know you long for many things,
but be patient—I will earn money.
The dresses you dream of, mama,
I will shower you with abundance.
Do not be tempted by the rich;
remember that the world changes.
In Makindye, he lives with Getu,
while he abandoned Jane in Kololo.
I know I chose well.
So be strong-hearted, dear—
those men tell you many lies.
Know this, Rose: it is a dangerous world.

Ecklas Kawalya's daughter, Joanita Kawalya, a prominent vocalist with Afrigo Band, paid tribute to her father's legacy in the mid-1990s by recording a rendition of Rose, renaming it Tony. Just as her father's song had left a lasting impression on audiences, Joanita's Tony followed suit, becoming one of Afrigo Band's most successful hits. Since its debut, the song has remained a key feature in Afrigo Band's live performances, continuing to be a favorite among fans up to the time of writing. Though quieter in the public eye, Rose Musoke's contributions were part of a broader wave of women carving out space in Uganda's evolving music scene. Each brought her own voice, style, and story to the stage.

One such musician was Jane Frances Kiryangokibi, widely known as Hadija Namale, born in 1948 in Mitala Maria, Masaka District, to Benjamin Mutumba and Constantina Nanteza. Her father worked at the local cotton ginnery, while her mother was a homemaker. Namale came from a lineage rich in musical talent. Her father was a sought-after traditional folk singer who performed at weddings and beer parties, though his influence remained local. Her brother led a small band of three young men playing self-made guitars, drawing large crowds at village bars. An uncle, a gifted guitarist, was often hired by Mitala Maria's *dukkawallahs* to play outside their shops as a means of attracting customers. Additionally, her granduncle, Simeon Sebuliba, was part of the Kabaka's royal ensemble, performing alongside John Kasirye with Abadongo ba Kabaka. When Namale was barely a year old, her mother left, and her father Mutumba devoted himself to raising the children alone. With unwavering resilience, he became both father and mother, rising early to cook their meals, washing clothes by hand, and keeping the household bound together with love and discipline. The older children helped, but it was Mutumba's devotion that gave the family its center. To Namale, he was not only a parent but a hero, the best she could have ever hoped for.

Music was the heartbeat of Namale's childhood. Born into a family steeped in musical tradition, she grew up surrounded by melodies and stories that seemed to flow in her blood. Each evening the treasured gramophone came to life as her father carefully dusted the shellac records and set them spinning. Namale would sit close by, wide-eyed and mesmerized, dreaming of the day she too would become a star. Even as a young girl, she sang the songs of her idol Eva Nanyonga with uncanny confidence. Her admiration also reached to folk luminaries Elizabeth Namale of Salama and Malyamu Namale of Kasangati, both distant cousins from the Kkobe clan.

Namale's life changed abruptly when her mother returned after years of absence. She was nine. Her father, worn down by the weight of raising his youngest daughter alone, could no longer cope. With little discussion, the decision was made: Namale would go to live with her mother. For the first time in her life, she was enrolled in school. It seemed like a new beginning. But the promise of that moment was short-lived. While still in grade five, barely thirteen years old, her mother arranged her marriage. The groom was a Muslim tailor, thirty-five years older than her. He had six wives and very many children. Many of the children were older than Namale. Upon marriage he gave her the Muslim name Hadija and replaced her birth surname, Kiryangokibi, with Namale, a name drawn from her Kkobe clan. Soon after the wedding she became pregnant.

Namale was still a child. She neither wanted nor understood the pregnancy, and abortion was never a consideration because of tradition, religion, and her lack of knowledge. At thirteen she could not have been expected to grasp the consequences of motherhood in the way even an older adolescent might. Her story sits within a wider, troubling reality: across Africa, adolescent pregnancy among girls aged 10 to 19, often the result of child marriage, is tied to high maternal mortality, low birth weight, and severe neonatal complications.

In her new home Namale faced relentless hostility from her co-wives. Unable to endure the mistreatment, she fled back to her father's house in Mitala Maria. But divorce meant returning the bride price, a cow that had already been sold, and neither of her parents could afford to repay it. Desperate not to return to her husband, Namale threatened to take her own life. Her attempted suicide deeply shook her family and forced them to accept her wishes. She was sent instead to live with her older sister, Samali Nantege, in Katwe, a bustling Kampala neighborhood. At fourteen she gave birth to a daughter, who would remain her only child.

Rumors soon spread that her husband had obtained a police warrant to forcefully reclaim her. To keep her safe, the family arranged for her to go into hiding. Her brother, a long-distance truck driver who frequently traveled to the Congo, had friends in Bunia, a town in eastern Congo. In 1963, Namale left her daughter in the care of Samali and traveled to Bunia. In Bunia, she found employment as a domestic worker and babysitter for a wealthy and kind Congolese woman. It was in this new environment, fluent in Lingala, that she stepped into her first nightclub at the age of sixteen. She was instantly drawn to the energy of the live band performing there. When it was discovered that she could sing flawless renditions of Franco Luambo's T.P.O.K. Jazz songs, she was invited to join the band. The musicians also taught her to play the conga drums and bass guitar.

Her growing musical abilities earned her local fame, and soon she was being compared to Henriette "Miss Bora" Borazima, a Kisangani-born singer who was three years older than her and one of the most prominent female Congolese musicians of the time.

In 1964, after touring Cameroon and Nigeria with T.P.O.K. Jazz in the early 1960s, Miss Bora joined City Five at Kinshasa's Afro Mogambo. Alongside Ugandan musician Charles Senkatuka, she brought a bold and unforgettable dynamic to the venue. Her tenure there was brief, however, as Tabu Ley Rochereau soon recruited her into L'African Fiesta and gave her the stage name 'Miss Bora.' She became widely known for her rendition of Guantanamera, the celebrated Cuban folk song.

Years later, during the 1975 meeting of heads of state and government of the Organization of African Unity in Kampala, Namale experienced her own triumph. She performed Guantanamera before an audience of African dignitaries. In an unexpected highlight, France-Albert René, the Seychelles representative, joined her onstage to sing along, prompting a standing ovation. Even Libyan leader Col. Muammar el-Qaddafi, known for his stern demeanor, was seen breaking into a smile, charmed by the energy of the performance.

In 1966, Hadija Namale returned to Uganda and settled in Katwe with her sister, Samali Nantege. She became part of a group of musicians, most of whom were Kenyan Luos. Among them were John Siso and Juma Odundo, both of whom lived in Nsambya. The band played occasional gigs at White Nile Club, where Namale continued performing covers of T.P.O.K. Jazz songs, as well as renditions of popular Ugandan female artists such as Yunia Nalwanga and Rose Musoke. The band toured extensively, performing in towns such as Mukono and Kayunga. Their travels took them to western Kenya, where they performed in Homa Bay and Kisumu. They also visited several islands on Lake Victoria, entertaining fishing communities. According to Namale, in 1966, the band was invited by Barack Obama Sr., father of the 44th U.S. president, Barack Obama, to perform at his ancestral home in Nyang'oma Kogelo. She vividly recalled seeing Barack Obama's step-grandmother, Sarah, dancing with enthusiasm to their music.

Despite the excitement of performing, the band struggled to earn a steady income. Namale often found it difficult to afford basic necessities. However, she valued the camaraderie within the group and appreciated the opportunity to hone her craft. Her fortunes shifted in 1967 when Ecklas Kawalya discovered her and invited her to join the Susana Band. Performing alongside Kawalya was an opportunity she had never imagined. She strengthened the band's vocal lineup, joining established female musicians such as Frida Sonko and Rose Musoke.

Drawing from her life experiences, Namale composed and recorded songs that left an enduring influence on the late 1960s music scene. Her first recording, Bosa (a male name), was released in 1967 on A.P. Chandarana's Furaha label. This was also the first time A.P. Chandarana had traveled to Uganda with portable recording equipment, capturing performances directly in the field. Bosa was recorded at New Life Nightclub, with Namale backed by the Susana Band. Namale did not initially have high expectations for the song, which was subtly influenced by T.P.O.K. Jazz's Quatre Boutons. Lyrically, it revolved around a love letter written to an adored partner. However, the interplay between Charles Ginaro's fluid and expressive guitar and Twalib's interjections on the saxophone elevated Namale's tender, heartfelt voice, creating an energetic and engaging track.

Namale had hoped another of her songs, Sente Eteganya (Money Struggles), recorded on the same day as Bosa, would be more successful. This song was deeply personal, expressing the hardships she had faced due to financial struggles. In it, she narrated her travels to Congo and Kenya in pursuit of a better life, only to conclude that true success would come by staying in Kampala and focusing on her ambitions. Despite its heartfelt message, Sente Eteganya did not gain traction. Instead, Bosa, a timeless classic, propelled Namale to widespread fame, turning her into an overnight household name.

However, the journey to recording Bosa was fraught with difficulties. The day before the scheduled session, Namale had rejected the unwanted advances of a fellow bandmate during rehearsals. Enraged, the musician struck her, knocking her to the ground. Ecklas Kawalya immediately intervened, reprimanding the assailant and making it clear that any further mistreatment of Namale would have serious consequences. Kawalya held influence in high places, and his warning was taken seriously. From that moment on, Namale was never harassed by her bandmates again. On the day of the recording, the band arrived at New Life Nightclub at 8 a.m., expecting to begin at 10 a.m. with A.P. Chandarana. However, Chandarana did not appear until 5 p.m. In the interim, Namale waited in the recording room for hours. Though a bustling market stood just across the road, nobody thought of offering her food. She recorded her debut songs on an empty stomach. It was a quiet ordeal, and one that would come to embody the strength behind her voice and the resilience that defined her career.

With the Susana Band, Hadija Namale rose to prominence through her many appearances on Elly Wamala's television show, her role in promoting the late 1960s Nanana dance style, and a strong catalog of recordings. She demonstrated her versatility by performing in Lingala, Luganda, and Spanish. Under the management of Shelton Mazowe and Richard Majora, the band emphasized rehearsing popular English, French, and Spanish numbers to appeal to the nightclub's diverse clientele, which drew people from varied cultural backgrounds. It was in this setting that Namale mastered Guantanamera, making the Cuban classic distinctly her own.

Between 1967 and 1973, before joining Fred Kanyike, Ecklas Kawalya, and Fred Masagazi to form the Rwenzori Band, Namale was one of the most prolific recording artists in Uganda, releasing over 30 vinyl records. Many of her songs were recorded at A.P. Chandarana's studios in Kericho, Kenya, and released under labels such as Wachezaji, Furaha, Mambo, and Upendo.

Male musicians had a tradition of using female names for their song titles. Kawalya, in particular, enjoyed this approach with songs such as Annet, Beatrice, and Harriet. Namale also recorded songs with female names, including Eliza (Elizabeth) and Nantege, but she stood out for featuring male names prominently in her titles, among them Saimon, Frank, Lubwama, Lutalo, John, Mutabazi, and Sejemba. In choosing male names, she quietly challenged convention, signaling that her voice would not be bound by the expectations placed on women in music.

Namale's decision to title songs with male names, though unconventional and defiant, sometimes carried unforeseen consequences. At Susana Nightclub her lively performances stirred the crowd, and male patrons, caught up in the music, often leapt onto the stage to dance and show their appreciation by pressing cash into her hands or inside her blouse before returning to their partners. In Uganda, tipping musicians in this way was and remains a common gesture of gratitude. Yet boundaries were not always respected. Some men groped her under the guise of tipping, while others convinced themselves that the songs were personal tributes. This illusion fueled jealousy and confrontations with wives and girlfriends, and Namale was often accused of being a seductress. She was a striking woman, full-figured with luminous black eyes, and her presence made her an easy target for envy. One night, after stepping away for a brief bathroom break, she was ambushed by a group of enraged women. The clash turned violent, leaving faces bloodied and the bathroom floor stained red. It was Ecklas Kawalya, who had long been like an older brother to Namale, who rushed in and pulled her to safety.

Many of her songs were dedicated to people she cared about, including family members and past romantic partners. Nantege was dedicated to her sister, Samali Nantege. In the song, she adopts the perspective of a male admirer praising Nantege's beauty, particularly her curvy figure and charming dimples. The lyrics express the lover's eagerness to be with her and provide for her. In reality, Nantege was a striking woman of slender build. In Saimon (a male name), Namale name-drops another sister, Nalule, who lived in Mbiko, a small town west of Jinja. The lyrics lament: "Woe to me, I am dying, friends / Because of Saimon / I asked Nalule / There in Mbiko where you live / Have you perhaps seen him?"

As a celebrity whose beauty matched her musical success, Namale inevitably attracted the gaze of wealthy and powerful men. Among them was John Kakonge, a towering figure in Ugandan politics who had once been Secretary-General of the ruling Uganda People's Congress (UPC) and later Minister for Agriculture. Their paths crossed at Susana Nightclub, and before long Kampala was alive with whispers. Some swore the two were entangled in a secret romance, while others dismissed it as nightclub gossip. The speculation only deepened after stories circulated of a rendezvous at Masindi Hotel, where Kakonge was said to have asked her to write a song about their love. When the track Kakonge appeared on the Furaha label later that year, many took it as confirmation, though the truth remained tantalizingly out of reach.

Zoozo (a male name), one of Namale's successful songs, was released on A.P. Chandarana's Upendo label. Over time, speculation grew about the identity of Zoozo. Some in Uganda claimed the song referred to Col. Joseph Ozo, a close ally of Idi Amin and commander of the Gonda Battalion in Moroto. Others linked it to Léon Zozo Amba, the lead vocalist of Les Noir/City Five, a Congolese band that toured Uganda in 1970. Namale firmly denied both theories, taking particular offense at the suggestion of a connection with Col. Ozo. She insisted she had never interacted socially with him and that she only knew Léon Zozo as a member of Les Noir, in the same way any devoted follower of the music scene might.

According to Namale, Zoozo was in fact a nickname she had given to a man she deeply loved, a modest store owner in Mitala Maria. Over the years many men whose names appeared in her song titles claimed to be the inspiration behind her lyrics. In one feature published by the *Uganda Monitor*, a man named Christopher Mulumba alleged that her hit Mulumba, released in the early 1970s on the Kagaabe label, was about him. Namale consistently dismissed such claims, describing them as nothing more than wishful thinking. Still, in Kampala's bars and nightclubs, the whispers never faded, and for many the true identity of Zoozo remains one of Namale's most tantalizing secrets.

Many of Namale's songs reflected the hardships and struggles she endured in her early years. Obufumbo Buzibu (Marriage is Difficult), recorded with the Top Ten Band, explores the realities of being trapped in an abusive relationship. In many ways, the song mirrors her own experiences as a child bride in a short-lived and toxic marriage. Throughout her life, there were periods when she barely had enough to eat, and survival was a daily challenge. Her older sister, Samali Nantege, with whom she lived before securing her own place, was a nurturing figure who provided for Namale and her daughter despite facing financial hardships of her own. Samali worked as a cashier at Peacock Nightclub in the Ndeeba neighborhood of Kampala.

Beyond caring for Namale's daughter, Samali extended her support to many of their siblings who had migrated from Villa Maria to Kampala in search of better opportunities. Witnessing these struggles firsthand, Namale composed and recorded songs that spoke to the difficulties of urban life. Themes of poverty and the ongoing search for stable employment were central to many of her songs, reflecting the daily realities faced by those trying to make a living in Uganda's rapidly growing towns and cities.

Ensimbi (Money) was one of several kagutema beat songs in which Namale tackled economic hardships. Another, Nfune Nange Kyendya (I Too Seek Something to Eat), captured the universal challenge of trying to make ends meet. Nfune Nange Kyendya lyrics found a deep connection with audiences, as it mirrored the experiences of countless Ugandans, particularly women, who were navigating the complexities of urban life, struggling to secure a livelihood, and striving for financial independence:

> The good things others enjoy—I would not turn them down,
> but where can I ever find them too?
> And you too, sister, you fancy them as well.
> What can we do, friends?
> Give me a job
> so I can earn enough to eat.
> Maybe I can babysit your children,
> or clean your home—
> anything that puts food on my table.

Namale's fluency in Lingala, a language deeply admired in Uganda due to the widespread influence of Congolese music, played a key role in shaping her musical career. She recorded several songs blending Lingala and Luganda, including Obufumbo Buzibu (Marriage is Difficult), Kasujja (a male name), Joseph Nkwagala (Love You, Joseph), Tondekera Mukwano (Do Not Leave Me, Love), and Mbulidwa Omwana (Lost My Baby). These bilingual compositions reflected not only her linguistic skills but also a deliberate effort to compete with the dominance of Congolese Lingala music in Uganda.

Namale also borrowed melodies from popular Congolese hits. Beyond Bosa, she recorded Omwana Gwe Nalonda (The Babe I Chose), which drew heavily from Tabu Ley Rochereau's mega-hit Mama Ida. Similarly, Mukulike Omwaka (Happy New Year), which remains a staple on Ugandan radio stations during New Year celebrations, adapted its melody from Franco & L'OK Jazz's 1966 song Ata Na Yebi, performed by Michèl Boyibanda.

Although Ugandans were enamored with Congolese rumba, few understood Lingala beyond commonly heard phrases. In many cases, words from popular songs were integrated into Ugandan speech with entirely different meanings. For example, *mobali*, which in Lingala means "man" or "husband," came to be used in Uganda as a synonym for "music." Likewise, *mawa*, meaning "tragedy" or "sadness" in Lingala, was repurposed to mean "awesome." By merging Lingala with Luganda in her lyrics, Namale did not necessarily clarify the original meanings of the Lingala words she sang. Instead, she helped entrench their localized interpretations, reinforcing a musical vernacular in which borrowed words took on lives of their own.

By 1970, at just twenty-two years old, Namale had risen to become arguably the most popular Ugandan musician. Her songs were a mainstay on Radio Uganda, receiving more airplay than perhaps any other Ugandan artist at the time. Through her association with Ecklas Kawalya, she secured a lucrative recording contract with A.P. Chandarana Studios in Nairobi. The contract provided her with financial security, leading her to scale back on regular stage performances. She left Susana Band in 1969 to focus on recording, though she made occasional stage appearances with different Kampala bands. For a brief period in 1969 and 1970, she performed with Joseph Ndugga's Top Ten Band, which was then based at Peacock Nightclub in Ndeeba.

Namale and Kawalya formed a strong creative partnership, producing several memorable duets released on A.P. Chandarana's labels. Their collaborations included Ojakuba Nange (You Will Be With Me), Getu (a female name), Yogera Ekyakunyiza (Say What Upset You), Nalwoga (a female name), and Okuzaala Kujagaana (Parenthood is Joy). Namale also worked closely with Kawalya and Mary Nattima on tracks such as Nsamba (Stomp), and Ndosire Omuhigo (Dream of a Hunt), .

Namale remained one of Uganda's most prominent musicians well into the mid-1970s before stepping away from the entertainment industry for an extended hiatus. Her success marked a high point in the growing visibility of female performers. Around the same period, other women were also carving out space for themselves in the male-dominated music industry. Beyond Nakibuuka, Yunia Nalwanga, Frida Sonko, Mary Nattima, Rose Musoke, Namagembe, and Hadija Namale, several others rose to prominence, building dedicated fan bases and earning widespread acclaim. Their artistry brought new depth to Uganda's popular music and shaped the industry in meaningful ways.

Joyce Nalule joined Simon Kaate Nsubuga to record two highly successful duets, Ezakasimo Zagwawo (The Gratuity Money Is Depleted) and Agenes Nkutute (I Have Taken You, Agnes), which made a strong impression on the Ugandan music scene. Another duo that found success was Nakayenga and Nelson Sabavuma with their hit Gwe Kenyini (You Are the Very One). Following this success, Nakayenga gradually withdrew from the recording industry.

Jane Namukasa, another talented female artist, contributed as a supporting singer on Margaret Nakibuuka's two rumba hits, Frora and Nantume, both released on A.P. Chandarana's Wachezaji label. Namukasa's beautiful voice complemented Nakibuuka's style, but despite her promise, she soon disappeared from the music scene. Jane Nalugya played a significant role as a backup vocalist on two of Kawalya's well-regarded kagutema songs with the Susana Band. These were Kulikayo (Welcome Back) and Okalya Dda (Eaten in the Past), recorded on the Serenade label in 1971. Okalya Dda is a condensed form of a Luganda proverb, '*Okalya dda, kadda dda*,' meaning that past actions have consequences, much like the English phrase "What goes around comes around."

Robinah Nasejje was another talented musician who achieved notable success when she teamed up with the Top Ten Band to record two engaging up-tempo, guitar-driven songs enriched by expansive saxophone arrangements. The songs, titled Geoffrey and Mponya Omwoyo (Heal My Heart), highlighted her distinctive vocal style. Mponya Omwoyo became a surprise hit, and many believed it would kickstart her musical career. However, despite this promising start, she did not achieve sustained success and eventually became known as a one-hit wonder, a label some attribute to the challenges she faced in joining a full-time band. Notably, like her contemporary Margaret Kivumbi, she was exclusively a studio artist and never performed live in the 1970s. Nevertheless, Mponya Omwoyo earned widespread acclaim, with fans praising her impassioned and heartfelt delivery as she sang:

> Willy The Twin, what did I do wrong?
> Tell me, so my heart may find healing.
> I even came to your workplace,
> but I did not see you.
> Your absence leaves me with restless nights.
>
> Your smile—with that alluring tooth gap,
> and your skin, it takes my breath away.
> I ask of you, Willy The Twin,
> to remember me, for I suffer in sleepless longing.
>
> Dear Willy, please speak the truth—do you love me?
> I tell you from the depths of my heart:
> I am determined, even if it means marriage.

My love,
you are the complete package,
and I truly feel, deep within, that I love you.

Margaret Kivumbi emerged as a defining voice in Uganda's vibrant music scene during the early 1970s. She enjoyed a multifaceted career as a gifted singer, a talented actress who ensnared theater audiences, and a passionate advocate for social change and civil liberties. Born in Kiboga, a town in Uganda's Luwero district, she recorded several successful songs between 1972 and 1974 through her fruitful collaboration with the renowned Top Ten Band of Joseph Ndugga. During this brief but impactful period, she released a string of hit songs such as Joseph, Peter, Dominico, and the evocative Nina Omulala (I Have Got Another). Kivumbi also recorded Kyenva Ndilinya (Why I Step on the Ground), a traditional folk song rendered in the kagutema genre. This reflective piece explores the intricate relationship between humanity and the earth, portraying it as both a life-giving provider and an indifferent force that eventually reclaims even the most celebrated among us.

Kivumbi's artistic talents were not confined to music alone. With a fervent passion for the performing arts, she was an invaluable member of Byron Kawaddwa's Kampala City Players, one of the period's most prominent theatrical groups. Her acting prowess shone in productions like the celebrated play Oluyimba Lwa Wankonko (Song of the Rooster), where her performance contributed to the play's acclaim. This dedication later paved the way for Kivumbi's inclusion in the Heartbeat of Africa, a national dance and drama troupe chosen to represent Uganda at the prestigious FESTAC '77. Held in Lagos, Nigeria, from January 15 to February 12, 1977, the Second World Black and African Festival of Arts and Culture (FESTAC '77) was a monumental event that gathered over 16,000 artists, performers, and intellectuals from 55 nations across Africa and its diaspora. Uganda's representation by the Heartbeat of Africa, with Kivumbi as a member of Oluyimba Lwa Wankoko's cast, exposed her remarkable talent to a global audience.

Tragedy, however, soon overshadowed the triumphant return from Lagos. While Kivumbi and her fellow troupe members were reminiscing about their success at FESTAC '77, unsettling news arrived. Unidentified individuals in a vehicle were searching for Byron Kawaddwa, the influential director of the Kampala City Players. Despite urgent pleas to stay with the group, Kawaddwa opted to meet these strangers. He was abducted, and his badly mutilated body was later discovered in the Namanve forest, a horrifying event that sent shockwaves through the artistic community and the entire nation.

After a vibrant but relatively brief career in recording and acting, Margaret Kivumbi embarked on a new chapter in the second half of 1977 when she joined Radio Uganda, the national broadcasting corporation. This move allowed her to continue engaging with the public through a different medium. Her deep commitment to human rights and civil liberties was significantly shaped by the brutal violence of Idi Amin's regime. This commitment was further intensified by the devastating abuses that unfolded in her home district of Luwero during the protracted armed conflict between Yoweri Museveni's guerrillas and Obote's Uganda National Liberation Army (UNLA), a conflict that claimed tens of thousands of lives in the 1980s.

The turmoil that engulfed the Buganda region tragically impacted musicians Kivumbi personally knew and admired. Fred Sebulime, for instance, was shot while performing on stage at a Ndeeba bar in 1981. The bullet lodged in his right wrist and required extraction at Mulago Hospital. This harrowing experience propelled him to join the rebel Uganda Freedom Movement (UFM), fighting to overthrow Obote's government. However, when the UFM faced significant setbacks and its leader, Andrew Kayira, fled the battlefield in 1982 under relentless pressure from the Uganda National Liberation Army (UNLA), Sebulime abandoned the movement and returned to performing music. His attempt to resume his career was short-lived. He was arrested at Namataba while preparing to perform. A former comrade from the UFM, who had become a government informer (colloquially known as a "Computer"), identified him and led soldiers to his capture, resulting in three years of imprisonment at Luzira Prison.

Adding to the vicissitudes of military conflict during this period, Kivumbi also knew and admired Nelson Sabavuma, who was tragically killed by soldiers in 1982. All this profound suffering and loss deeply influenced Kivumbi's unwavering commitment to advocate for justice and societal reform.

These incredible women who made their mark in Uganda's music industry did more than entertain. They carved out a space where their voices, raw and resonant, could not be silenced in a country often choked by prejudice and shadowed by hardship. They defied not just expectations, but the very limitations imposed upon them, forging a legacy that transcends mere entertainment. Their melodies, once whispers against the roar of a patriarchal industry, now thunder through Uganda's musical soul, a testament to their unwavering spirit. They are not merely footnotes in history, but the architects of its most powerful refrains, their influence a living, breathing force that continues to empower and inspire the next generation to sing their own truth.

CHAPTER 11

When Kinshasa Met Kampala: The Congolese Legacy and Global Musical Encounters in Uganda

Beginning in the 1950s, a succession of global and regional musicians visited Uganda. Among the most notable was American pianist and composer Philippa Schuyler, who toured the country in 1958. During her visit, she developed a close friendship with Kabaka Edward Mutesa and performed a private recital at his palace in Mengo. Schuyler also met several prominent Ugandans, including Bishop Joseph Nakabale Kiwanuka of Masaka, the first native African to be ordained a Roman Catholic bishop in modern times, and George Rukidi III, King of Toro. A much sought-after guest, she was deeply moved by Uganda's people, culture, and natural beauty. Her impressions of the country inspired a number of hauntingly beautiful piano compositions, including Fumitta Embogo (Spear the Buffalo), Nile Fantasia (Nile Fantasy), Tweyanze (Thank You), The Uganda Martyrs, and White Nile Suite. She was soon followed by the legendary Louis Armstrong in October 1960.

The Golden Gate Quartet, an influential American vocal group originally formed in Norfolk, Virginia, visited Uganda in March 1962. Known for their close harmony and rhythmic vocal arrangements of Biblical narratives, the group had gained international acclaim and was, by then, based in Paris. Their lineup at the time included Caleb "J.C." Ginyard, Clyde Riddick, Clyde Wright, and Orlandus Wilson. The quartet is widely credited with popularizing songs such as When the Saints Go Marching In, which gained traction in Uganda partly due to their performances. During their visit, they drew rapturous crowds at Kampala's Lugogo Indoor Stadium, the Odeon Theater in Jinja, and the Bugisu Coffee Hall in Mbale. Ugandans were drawn to the group's intricate harmonies and the spiritual energy that infused their gospel performances.

In July 1962, the Nairobi-based Sportsman Cha Cha Band of Msafiri Morimori played at Kampala's White Nile nightclub. The band featured Uganda's own Elly Wamala and Joseph Ndugga. They gave a demonstration of the Twist dance, kick-starting a Twist mania that would engulf Uganda. In August 1962, South African pop star Dorothy "Dots" Masuka arrived in Uganda, accompanied by the Golden Rhythm Crooners, for a performance at Kampala's National Theatre. By then, Masuka had already established herself as a pioneering figure in African popular music. Her distinctive sound blended jazz influences with African rhythms, and she was widely admired for composing songs in indigenous languages that often addressed political and social issues. Her songwriting talents earned her recognition across the continent, with several of her compositions later reinterpreted by fellow South African musicians. One of her most famous works, Pata Pata, was adapted by Miriam Makeba and went on to become a global hit. Masuka's visit to Uganda marked an important cultural moment, introducing local audiences to a powerful African female voice whose music carried influence well beyond the borders of her homeland.

In December 1964, Uganda became the unlikely stage for a Cold War encounter, not of spies or politicians, but of musicians and music lovers. Paul Taubman and his 34-man All-American Big Brass Band touched down in Kampala as part of a sweeping 17-nation African tour sponsored by the U.S. State Department. Officially a musical exchange, the tour was also a strategic effort to project American soft power across a continent that was rapidly decolonizing and navigating competing global influences.

Taubman's ensemble arrived with its own aircraft, a polished repertoire, and a mission to broaden perceptions of American music and showcase the United States as culturally diverse, racially integrated, and artistically sophisticated. In Uganda, they played a free concert at Nakivubo War Memorial Stadium to a packed crowd, mixing Russian classics like Tchaikovsky's Fourth Symphony with crowd-pleasing cha-chas and Sousa marches. The eclectic program challenged expectations, particularly the notion that Americans only exported jazz or rock and roll. The band's racial composition did not go unnoticed. With five Black musicians in its ranks, the group aimed to counter stereotypes and offered a subtle but powerful statement about race relations in the United States, especially at a time when civil rights struggles were still headline news. For many Ugandans, the concert was more than entertainment. It was an opportunity to experience a different kind of diplomacy, one conducted not through treaties, but through trombones, trumpets, and the universal language of music.

In June 1968, the Berlin Philharmonic, ranked among Europe's most respected ensembles, played to a packed hall at Kampala's Apolo Hotel. It was the orchestra's first tour of Africa, and the occasion was marked with great ceremony. The men arrived in tuxedos, and the women wore elegant evening gowns. The atmosphere that evening was overwhelmingly European and Asian, with a sprinkling of Uganda's Black elite, including doctors, lawyers, and government officials. As the orchestra performed, there was much closing of eyes and gentle nodding of heads. The music evoked quiet admiration, and the audience responded with polite applause and reserved standing ovations.

Just six months later, the mood was markedly different when the Ghanaian group Uhuru Dance Band, led by Stan Plange, took the stage at Susana nightclub and Lugogo Stadium. Their lively brand of West African highlife swept through the crowd with an irresistible energy. Formed in the early 1960s, the Uhuru Dance Band had become a cornerstone of Ghana's music scene, helping to define the highlife genre during a time of cultural pride and innovation. Their Kampala performances were anything but restrained. The polyrhythmic beats, lilting guitar lines, and brassy hooks drew people to their feet, dissolving social boundaries in a wave of dance and celebration. Where the Berlin Philharmonic inspired reflection, the Uhuru Dance Band invited release. Their visit was not only a musical highlight, but also part of a growing Pan-African cultural exchange that brought African rhythms to the forefront of the continent's shared artistic identity.

The Morogoro Jazz Band from Tanzania, one of East Africa's most celebrated groups, visited Uganda in March 1970. At the helm was Mbaraka Mwinshehe, a charismatic vocalist and gifted lead guitarist whose influence spanned borders. Morogoro Jazz Band had already built a formidable reputation across East Africa. By the time they arrived in Uganda, their popularity was firmly established. Mbaraka's hit Tina Turidiane (Tina, Let's Get Together Again) was a daily staple on Radio Uganda. In Kampala, the band's performance at the White Nile nightclub drew an ecstatic crowd. Audiences were swept up in the band's rich blend of Tanzanian melodies, Swahili lyrics, and the pulsating force of rumba. Even after Mbaraka left Morogoro Jazz and relocated to Mombasa to form Super Volcano, he continued to enjoy a devoted following in Uganda. Later songs like Shida (Troubles) showcased his extraordinary talent, and Ugandans embraced him as one of their own.

More highlife music from Ghana was brought to Uganda by Jerry Hansen and the Ramblers. They toured Uganda in March 1972, playing some of their signature highlife, jazz, and calypso songs. They performed in Uganda Hotels Ltd hotels across the country, including Tropic Inn in Masaka, Jinja's Crested Crane Hotel, Mbale's Mount Elgon Hotel, and Lake Victoria Hotel in Entebbe.

In June 1973, Uganda played host to one of Africa's most celebrated musical and political figures. Miriam "Zenzi" Makeba, the internationally acclaimed South African singer and fierce opponent of apartheid, arrived in Kampala at the invitation of the Ministry of Culture and Community Development. Her appearance was met with tremendous enthusiasm. Tickets for her concert at Makerere University's Main Hall sold out within hours, and the venue was packed with admirers eager to witness the voice that had become synonymous with African pride and resistance. Beyond the performance, Makeba was accompanied by her husband, the Trinidad-born revolutionary Stokely Carmichael, a key figure in the American civil rights movement and former chairman of the Student Nonviolent Coordinating Committee. Their visit was both cultural and political, drawing attention from officials and citizens alike. Ever attuned to the optics of power and eager to align himself with pan-African causes, President Idi Amin seized the opportunity to present himself as a champion of African liberation. In a well-publicized ceremony that was as much political theater as diplomatic gesture, Amin granted Ugandan citizenship to both Makeba and Carmichael.

For Makeba, the moment held particular significance. She had been stateless since 1960, when the apartheid regime in South Africa revoked her passport after her outspoken criticism of racial segregation on the world stage. Though she had found refuge in Guinea, where she and Carmichael were based, the Ugandan gesture added another symbolic layer to her pan-African identity. Though rooted in spectacle, the granting of Ugandan citizenship to Makeba and Carmichael spoke to a deeper yearning across the continent. Exiled voices, from musicians to thinkers to activists, were seen, heard, and embraced within the dream of pan-African unity.

The relationship between Uganda and the Central African Republic deepened during the 1970s, beginning with a three-day state visit to Kampala by President Jean-Bédel Bokassa on August 31, 1972. It was the first visit by an African head of state since President Idi Amin had come to power, and Bokassa was received with full honors. In recognition of his visit, Kampala's Alidina Visram Street was renamed Bokassa Street, though it would later be changed to Luwum Street. President Amin awarded Bokassa Uganda's highest decoration, the Order of the Source of the Nile, while Bokassa conferred upon Amin the Grand Order of the National Order of the Central African Republic. A joint commission was formed to explore avenues of bilateral cooperation, including military training, although these efforts did not lead to much substantive collaboration.

Five years later, in 1977, Bokassa, who had since declared himself Emperor of the newly renamed Central African Empire, renewed efforts to strengthen ties with Uganda through cultural exchange. As a gesture of goodwill, he sent his Imperial Orchestra to perform in Kampala. Formerly known as Orchestre Tropical Fiesta de Bangui, the ensemble was led by the celebrated frontman Charlie Perrier. The group performed a smooth, rumba-infused style grounded in Congolese musical traditions. Their concerts at the Nile Hotel and International Hotel were warmly received by Kampala audiences, who responded warmly to the group's polished sound and engaging presence. Perrier's mellow voice and commanding stage style gave the performances a refined and memorable atmosphere. The orchestra's visit was further highlighted by several appearances on Uganda Television.

There were many more foreign musicians who visited Uganda. However, none of these international or regional foreign musicians and groups had the musical clout and mass appeal of Congolese musicians and bands. Congolese rumba had conquered the country, and its irresistible chord progressions and intricate harmonic rhythms became the blueprint for many Ugandan songwriters in the 1960s. Almost every major Ugandan artist of that era recorded songs that borrowed heavily from major Congolese hits, often resulting in renditions that sounded remarkably similar to the originals. The enthusiastic reaction from Ugandan audiences to these adapted songs was telling. In many cases, the borrowed versions not only matched but even competed favorably with the original Congolese tracks. By embracing these melodies and beats, Ugandan artists paid heartfelt homage to the Congolese rumba kings, musical idols who had profoundly shaped the regional soundscape. Furthermore, this heavy borrowing from Congolese music served another important purpose. Since most Ugandans did not speak or understand Lingala, the language in which these songs were originally sung, Ugandan artists reinterpreted them in local Luganda. This allowed audiences to connect with the beat and feel the lyricism, even though the translated lyrics were not direct interpretations of the original words. In effect, these adaptations introduced meaning and context to Congolese hits, making the music more accessible and relatable to Ugandan listeners.

The attraction of Ugandans to Congolese music puzzled many observers. Even Shelton Mazowe, credited with turning Susana nightclub into a Ugandan institution, could not understand the infatuation Ugandans had with Congolese rumba. He once derided Ugandans for their unwavering passion for Congolese musicians, believing that they should have been embracing Western music styles instead. A youthful Moses Matovu, by then a member of the Cranes band and later to become a much-celebrated figure with Afrigo Band, expressed similar frustrations. In an interview with the *Munno* newspaper in April 1974, Matovu criticized the amount of airtime Radio Uganda devoted to Congolese music. He acknowledged that it was acceptable to play Congolese songs on Radio Uganda, but argued that local musicians should also be given ample airtime. He further suggested that presenters should adopt the same approach they used with Congolese music, including providing commentary about the songs and the musicians behind them. However, few paid attention to these calls for change.

Congolese rumba delivered an unmatched excitement and joie de vivre that helped shape Kampala's storied nightlife. Its lilting guitars, honeyed vocals, and hypnotic rhythms became the heartbeat of dance halls across the city. So intense was the demand that, at times, Lingala records appeared in Kampala's music shops before reaching stores in Kinshasa. A case in point were titles like Orchestre Veve's Week-end Tobima and Djamile, along with Kanda Mopaya and Zongisela Ngai, all released by Editions Veve, which were first stocked in Kampala before becoming available in Congo. This was remarkable in itself and a clear reflection of the deep and growing Ugandan craze for Congolese music. This passion went far beyond musical preference. For many, it bordered on spiritual devotion. One Ugandan rumba enthusiast once remarked, "Angels standing around the Lord's throne pray in Latin, but the songs of praise are straight up Congolese rumba." Humorous as it may seem, the comment captured just how deeply the genre was deep-rooted in Uganda.

Congolese people were no strangers to Ugandans. The modern-day states of Uganda and the Democratic Republic of Congo share a long border of 545 miles. Despite the national boundaries established by Belgian and British colonial powers, the borders were mostly fluid, allowing for cross-border movement between the two countries. The number of Congolese living in Uganda grew from 1,585 in the 1931 census to over 19,000 (0.4% of the population) by 1948. Many worked on European-owned plantations. Although most Congolese migrants worked as farm laborers, just as many Ugandans did during the colonial period, a distinct group of migrants that included musicians, dancers, and performers left a lasting mark on Uganda's cultural life. Their music, in particular, became a vibrant part of the local entertainment scene.

As Congo moved toward independence on June 30, 1960, Ugandans followed the developments with intense interest. The Congo's liberation from colonial rule stirred hope in Uganda's own anti-colonial struggle. Patrice Lumumba, the newly elected Prime Minister of the Republic of Congo, emerged as a powerful and charismatic figure. His speeches, widely circulated, captured imaginations across the continent. He envisioned a Congo that would stand as a beacon for all of Africa, a nation where citizens could think freely and enjoy the fundamental rights promised by the United Nations Charter.

The wave of independence was matched by a wave of music. Congolese bands, led by Le Grand Kallé's African Jazz, released iconic songs such as "Independence Cha Cha" and "Vive Patrice Lumumba," both of which quickly became nightclub staples in Kampala and beyond. Across Uganda, people gathered around their radios to tune in to East Congo's Radio Bukavu, a shortwave station with exceptional reach. It became a vital channel for broadcasting the latest Congolese hits and introduced Ugandan listeners to the stars behind them. Wendo Kolosoy, known as "Alanga Nzembo" (Song Master), and Grand Kallé became household names. Ugandan musician Frank Mbalire later recalled that one of his earliest memories of music in the 1950s was listening to Wendo's "Marie-Louise" on the family gramophone. The song, with its lilting sensuality and irrepressible joy, became an anthem. However, it scandalized and infuriated Belgian and French Catholic missionaries in Congo, who had Wendo briefly jailed. His brief imprisonment turned him into more than a musician. He became a voice of defiance, embodying the spirit of a continent breaking free.

Jean Bosco Mwenda, also known as Mwenda wa Bayeke, was another Congolese musician well known to Ugandan audiences. His intricate finger-picking on the acoustic guitar, combined with his warm and relaxed singing style, earned him great admiration. His song "Masanga" remains popular. In the mid-1950s, Mwenda and his cousin Edouard Masengo embarked on a brief tour of Kampala. Performing and recording under the name Masengo Katiti Edouard & Groupe Je.co.ke, also known simply as Je.co.ke, they recorded on Kampala's Tom Tom label. Their recordings included "Tucheze" (Let's Play), a celebration of the rumba craze, and "Safari Yetu Kampala" (Our Kampala Journey). Other Congolese musicians who built a loyal following in Uganda during the 1950s included Losta Abelo and rising stars such as François "Franco" Luambo Luanzo Makiadi, Pascal-Emmanuel Sinamoyi Tabu (Tabu Ley Rochereau), and Nicolas Kasanda wa Mikalay (Docteur Nico).

The fundamental liberties and peace that Patrice Lumumba had envisioned for Congo at independence unraveled fast. By the end of July 1960, the jockeying for power between Prime Minister Patrice Lumumba, Chief of State Joseph Kasavubu, and Moishe Tshombe, the president of the mineral-rich Katanga province, threatened to erupt into civil war. On July 11, 1960, Tshombe, with the backing of the Belgians who had retained a sizable military force in the country, declared the secession of Katanga. Lumumba refused to accept this state of affairs. In early August 1960, he declared a state of emergency, threatened to invade Katanga, and broke off diplomatic relations with Belgium. Soon the country descended into chaos, with violence erupting across Congo and thousands of lives lost. On September 14, 1960, Colonel Joseph Mobutu of the Congolese National Army orchestrated a coup d'état, and the country was plunged into turmoil. On January 17, 1961, Patrice Lumumba was assassinated in Katanga. This period of unrest, known as the Congo Crisis, lasted until 1964. It brought incredible suffering and immense displacement, with hundreds of thousands of Congolese seeking refuge in neighboring countries, including Uganda. Entire Congolese musical groups, along with individual musicians, fled the conflict and sought safety abroad.

The Congo Crisis brought groups of Congolese musicians to Uganda, where they hoped to find peace and a conducive environment to continue their creativity. The first Congolese band to arrive in Uganda was the Diablo band, led by Appolinaire Kabeya. They came in April 1961 from Stanleyville (now Kisangani) and consisted of four men and one woman, the 20-year-old Mangaza Mbuyi. The band featured double bass, guitars, drums, and maracas. Jolly Joe Kiwanuka soon brought them to his White Nile nightclub, where they became the resident band. The Diablo band thus became the first all-Congolese band to settle in Uganda. With their rumba rhythms and Kabeya's electrifying lead guitar, the band won over Kampala audiences.

By 1962, Jolly Joe had renamed the band the White Nile Band. In 1963, another Congolese group, the King Jazz band (also known as King Jazz d'Equateur), arrived in Uganda. Hearing of the high demand for Congolese music and musicians, they came hoping to find fame. The King Jazz band was led by Maindo Gabriel-Grison and included members such as Marie Lopes and vocalist Mupende Thodes. Lopes had previously been the bandleader of the Vivian Mambo band, which had recorded on Congo's Ngoma label. They were initially based at Kololo Club in Kampala's industrial area, which, like New Life nightclub in Mengo, was owned by Kamulu. However, Jolly Joe soon approached Maindo, offering better pay and working conditions, and the King Jazz band moved to White Nile nightclub, becoming the second resident band.

With the arrival of the King Jazz band, Kabeya and his Diablo band became free agents, performing at various venues across Kampala and occasionally in other towns. In 1964, the King Jazz band welcomed a talented Congolese female vocalist, Nesele Leonie, from Bunia. More Congolese musicians joined the group, and by 1965, the band's lineup had significantly changed. Led by Selemani, a mild-mannered and urbane figure always immaculately dressed in a suit and tie, the band remained all-Congolese. Selemani was known for his passionate, galvanizing guitar style. Other members included Jaki, Bonny Kazadi, Andrea Safari, Peter Okoko, Mario Andre, Samona, and Bodwe Kazati. Later, they were joined by a Kenyan known only as Steven and Ugandan guitarist John Mutebi, who had earlier played with the New Life band and would later join Safari Six and Le Noir.

The King Jazz band embraced Franco Luambo's T.P.O.K. Jazz's signature rumba style known as odemba, a deep-seated and sophisticated rhythmic beat. Their take on T.P.O.K. Jazz, delivered with thrilling energy, earned Selemani and his group a devoted following in Uganda. In the ongoing rivalry between Kamulu's New Life nightclub and White Nile, the King Jazz band was lured back into Kamulu's fold in 1966, moving from White Nile to New Life nightclub at Mengo. Following the declaration of a state of emergency and the imposition of a dusk-to-dawn curfew after the May 1966 storming of the Kabaka's palace by Prime Minister Obote's troops, Kamulu relocated the group to his club outside Jinja town, the New Life nightclub in Bugembe. The club would later be known as Gay nightclub and served as the home of the Magamaga Army band during Idi Amin's regime in the 1970s. During the two-month curfew, King Jazz stayed in Jinja, performing for audiences who traveled from Kampala to see them.

It was during this period that Kamulu recruited Fred Masagazi into the King Jazz band, a major achievement. Kamulu wanted a lyrically strong Ugandan singer with national name recognition, backed by a sophisticated Congolese rumba band offering greater musical complexity than the River Road beats from Nairobi or the Luganda songs produced by his own New Life band. Fred Masagazi had already achieved immense success and was among the most highly regarded Ugandan musicians, with numerous hits to his name.

It was one thing for a band to secure a spot at New Life, but quite another to remain there for any significant length of time. Kamulu, the club's proprietor, was a demanding and tireless taskmaster who expected long hours from his musicians. Although he was widely believed to offer better pay than his competitors at White Nile, Susana, or Lorina, he was also known for his tough, often unforgiving nature. Despite King Jazz's early success at New Life, their relationship with Kamulu quickly soured. Within a year, the band moved on to the Rainbow Club in Bwaise and eventually returned to their former base at White Nile nightclub in 1967, bringing with them their Ugandan star, Fred Masagazi. Once back at White Nile, Masagazi teamed up with King Jazz's Congolese vocalist, Mario Andre. Mario became a trusted musical partner, backing Masagazi on many of his most celebrated songs. Their collaboration led to the creation of Kola Zizo (Do Your Own Thing), a major hit released on Charles Worrod's Equator label. The label placed high hopes on the song, confident that it could capture the attention of Western audiences. That confidence was buoyed when Kola Zizo received airtime on a BBC radio broadcast. However, the track ultimately fell short of becoming an international success, unlike Fadhil William's Malaika, another release under the Equator label that went on to achieve global acclaim.

In addition to its popular recordings, King Jazz played a prominent role in Uganda's political music landscape. The band backed Juma Odundo on a number of songs in praise of President Milton Obote, including Obote wa Uganda (Obote of Uganda), Obote Nawabeberu (Obote and the Imperialists), Obote na UPC (Obote and UPC), and Milton Obote. These tracks were recorded on the state-run UG label, a vehicle for music that reflected and supported official state ideology.

Another seminal Congolese band that influenced the direction of Uganda's Congolese-style rumba was L'Orchestre Vox National. The band arrived in Uganda around April 1967 from Luluabourg, now known as Kananga, in Congo's Katanga province. The band leader was the 24-year-old Johnny "Dr. Johnny" Cleophas, fondly known as "Doctor Soliste" because of his wizardly guitar skills and stage swagger that was as syncopated as the band's music. Dr. Johnny was Vox National's lead guitarist and had previously played in Congo with Orchestre LUPE, short for Lumumba Patrice Emile Jazz Band. Other members included Andre Picolo (first rhythm guitar), Arthur Alberto (second rhythm guitar and vocalist), and K. Remy (bass), with Andre and Pierre on drums.

Like King Jazz before them, Vox National made their Ugandan debut at the Kololo Club, the gateway to Kamulu's entertainment empire, where technical skill was rigorously tested. But it was at New Life, where they soon relocated, that they truly proved their mettle. Performing before a discerning and demanding crowd, they rose to the occasion. By 1968, they had secured their place as one of the most compelling acts on Kampala's live music circuit. At New Life, they complemented another resident band, the Newlife Africa Success Band, led by Robert Wembo, a Congolese guitarist who had been part of African Jazz's second-tier band. Newlife Africa Success had originally been known as the Newlife Band under Charles Ginaro, another Congolese musician who left New Life in 1966 and joined the Susana Band.

Vox National's rumba style was deeply influenced by Dr. Nico's African Fiesta Sukisa school of music, known for the "fiesta" beat. Unlike Franco and his O.K. Jazz's odemba style, fiesta music wove dreamlike notes that rippled with tenderness and sophistication. Dr. Nico's guitar work, with its long, bell-toned treble lines and shimmering glissandos, served as a model for the band's sound. Vox National stayed at New Life for just over a year before relocating to Florida nightclub in 1968. They remained at Florida, which later became Arizona nightclub, until 1970, when they returned to Congo.

Most Ugandan musicians at the time were vocalists rather than instrumentalists. Those who played instruments often did not compare themselves to the skilled Congolese guitarists or saxophonists. For this reason, many established Ugandan singers enlisted the services of Vox National or King Jazz as session bands during recordings. Vox National even included two up-and-coming young Ugandan musicians as part of their core group: Philly Bongoley Lutaaya and John Kajura. Both were talented vocalists and greatly admired by their Congolese bandmates.

Philly Lutaaya recorded his first two songs in 1969 while with Vox National: Philly Empisazo (Philly, Mind Your Manners) and Flora

Atwooki, a heartfelt ballad about a woman he adored. In Flora Atwooki, Lutaaya's vocals are tender and unguarded, carried by Dr. Johnny's subtle yet expressive lead guitar, whose graceful riffs lend the song its reflective mood. Both tracks were well-received and introduced Lutaaya to a wider Ugandan audience.

Congolese bands in Uganda nightclubs rarely came up with original compositions, often performing covers of big-name artists from Kinshasa such as Franco Luambo and his brother Bavon Marie Marie, Dr. Nico Kasanda, Tabu Ley Rochereau, Jean "Johnny" Bokelo Isenge, and Georges "Verckys" Kiamuangana. However, Vox National had a few original songs that became popular with Ugandan audiences. These included Bus Namakweke (The Namakweke Bus), sung by Alberto with Lutaaya providing background vocals. When Vox National returned to Kinshasa in 1970, they could not imagine continuing without Lutaaya and Kajura. The two young Ugandan musicians readily agreed to join them and stayed with the band in Kinshasa for several years.

Besides spotlighting the young Philly Lutaaya, Vox National served as the studio band for several Ugandan musicians, adding a polished Congolese rhythm to local beats. The songs were recorded at the newly established Serenade Studios in Ndeeba, Kampala. Most were released on the Serenade label, while a few appeared on the Philips and Sweet Voice labels. In these recordings, performed in Luganda, Dr. Johnny and Picolo demonstrated their mastery of Congolese rumba, offering delightful melodic overlays. Their guitars delivered freewheeling, plucky, and scratchy rapid-fire staccato riffs. The sound of the congas was elevated, delivering a syncopated and electrifying booming pulse.

B. K. Steven and L'Orchestre Vox National recorded Sirina Mulala (There Is No Other) and Emikwano Gigwayo (Friendships End). Andrew Kyambadde recorded Nampiima Komawo (Nampiima Come Back), Nabacwa (female name), Rweza Yekka (Only Rweza), and Nina Owange (I Have Mine). The young Fred Kigozi, a rising musical star, recorded Jukira Mwami Wange (Husband, Remember) and Vayo Gyoli Mary (Return from Where You Are, Mary).

Steven Sempasa, who started his career in the early 1960s but remained in the shadow of his more famous half-brother Israel Magembe, finally came into his own with several songs recorded with Vox National. These included Awo Awatali Gumba (Where There Are No Bones), and Joyce We Naguru (Joyce from Naguru). Sempasa released these songs under his own Serena label.

Susana, White Nile, Lorina, and New Life nightclubs each had more than one resident band to ensure that patrons were entertained daily. In 1968, New Life at Mengo had three resident bands: the New Life Band (also called the Newlife Africa Success Band), Superphonics (composed mainly of Kenyan musicians), and Vox National. Even with these bands, which alternated on stage each evening, Kamulu could not resist the temptation of signing on an additional group. So when a team of eight Congolese musicians arrived at New Life in mid-1968, following a circuitous and arduous journey from their home country, Kamulu had them audition the very moment he set eyes on them. The next day, he presented the musicians with a contract, which they eagerly signed. Kamulu named the group the Vipers and offered them food and housing. The band was led by Raphael Kaumba and included Mado (Kaumba's longtime girlfriend), Gaston, Steven, Ngele, Tumba, Monga Ngoyi Sungu and N'goy Suissman, a swashbuckling, charismatic dancer and vocalist known for his impeccable style. A true dandy, Suissman took immense pride in his appearance, elevating dressing to an art form. He soon became a style icon in Kampala, introducing the city to a taste of Congolese sapeur subculture.

The Vipers musicians had originally been members of Mario Jazz in Kamina, the capital of Haut-Lomami Province in Congo. In 1962, the band traveled to Kalemie, a picturesque town on the eastern edge of Congo and the western shore of Lake Tanganyika. At the time, Kalemie appeared to have been spared the violence and killing that had erupted across Congo. Indeed, the Mario Jazz band found five other bands active in the town, creating a vigorous nightlife. However, the Simba rebellion, which began in 1963 and was led by followers of the slain Patrice Lumumba, soon engulfed Kalemie. Fierce fighting broke out in the streets between the

Simbas and the Congolese National Army, who were supported by white mercenaries. The band hastily escaped to Tanzania and established themselves in Mwanza.

Infighting within the band and accusations of poor pay led eight members to quit. The group was led by the sixteen-year-old Raphael Kaumba, a gifted lead guitarist. In Mwanza, Joseph Kiboko Nyerere (a brother of Tanzania's president, Julius Nyerere) managed a band that was struggling to find solid musicians who could play Western instruments. Joseph recruited the group of ex-Mario Jazz members under Kaumba's leadership. The group toured several Tanzanian towns. Always looking out for better opportunities, Kaumba and his team amicably parted ways with Joseph Nyerere and traveled to Nairobi in 1967.

While in Nairobi, the Vipers played a short run at the Starlight Club, the city's premier nightclub since its founding in 1965. The club's English proprietor, Robert Armstrong, was impressed by their act, and the band hoped to secure a residency. However, Starlight operated on a rotating model, booking bands for short engagements rather than permanent contracts. It is Armstrong who encouraged the band to try their luck in Uganda, suggesting top venues like New Life, Susana, and White Nile. Signing the Vipers proved to be a wise decision for Kamulu, especially as Vox National, the main Congolese band at New Life, decided not to renew their contract.

While not as renowned as Dr. Johnny of Vox National, Raphael Kaumba was a skilled and flamboyant guitarist. His band, the Vipers, established a strong presence at New Life in Mengo township, continuing the tradition of hard-driving Congolese rumba. Kaumba and his bandmates felt at home in Mengo, a township that had become a cultural crossroads for Congolese migrants.

Following the Congo crisis, a distinct community of Congolese women, many from Bukavu, Beni, and Goma, had found refuge in Mengo. These women carved out lives in a dynamic but impoverished slum within the triangle formed by Albert Cook Road, Apollo Kivebulaya Road, and Ham Mukasa Road, located near New Life Nightclub and Mengo Market.

For many, survival necessitated engaging in sex work. At the nightclub, their brightly colored cotton dresses and kitenge wrappers accentuated their figures, and their distinctive, spiky hairstyles enhanced their striking presence. Although they drew attention from men of all backgrounds, including local traders, laborers, and government officials, their daily lives were marred by poverty, limited economic opportunity, and the constant threat of violence and exploitation. The challenges of raising children without paternal support were compounded by the ever-present risk of sexually transmitted infections.

By 1969, the Vipers had expanded their lineup to include Ugandan musicians Sammy Kasule on bass and Geoffrey Nsereko on drums (not to be confused with the vocalist Geoffrey Nsereko). Geoffrey came to the Vipers from King Jazz, while Sammy had originally been a member of the Superphonics. Like Vox National, the Superphonics did not renew their contract with Kamulu, and most of the Kenyan band members returned home. Sammy Kasule soon established himself as the lead singer on the Vipers' Luganda-language songs. It was with the Vipers that Sammy Kasule recorded his first songs, Lidia mama (Mama Lidia) and Julie, on the Angel label. These songs, recorded in 1970, marked the start of what would become a storied musical career. Other early Sammy Kasule songs with the Vipers included Betty Jangu (Come Betty), Kimanye Victor (Know This Victor), and Nja Kwagala Enkya (I Will Love You Tomorrow).

The Vipers boasted an impressive lineup of musicians,, however the band's gravitational pull centered around Suissman N'goy, their star dancer and vocalist. His elegant dance styles and athleticism turned him into a national sensation. Suissman embodied the spirit of rumba and soukous with a magnetism few could match. In the slow, lilting rhythms of rumba, he danced with a quiet intensity, each step a study in subtlety, each sway a gentle dialogue with the music. His body seemed to float just above the floor, gliding in smooth, unhurried movements, as if time had slowed to match his beat. When the tempo quickened to the bright, electrifying rhythms of soukous, Suissman came alive with spellbinding energy. His footwork grew rapid and intricate, his hips circling in tight, rippling patterns while his shoulders shimmied, and his arms sliced the air with flamboyant precision. Entire dance floors would stop moving just to watch him, clapping and cheering as he spun, leaped, and twirled with breathtaking ease.

In 1972, Kaumba composed a song praising Amin, "Amin Dada No. 1," released on the Pathé label. However, the song remained largely unknown. Following the expulsion of Ugandan Asians, Kamulu's New Life nightclub was appropriated by Ramadan Mustafa. He changed the club's name to Economic nightclub. Mustafa was widely believed to have been an operative of the dreaded State Research Bureau, Idi Amin's intelligence organization that was reputed to have killed thousands of Ugandans. In 1974, Kaumba fell out with the management of Economic nightclub.

Economic nightclub had purchased the equipment that Orchestre Veve had left behind after their Uganda tour earlier that year. The club's owner, Mustafa, formed a new band called the Economic Band to replace Kaumba's Vipers. The Economic Band included two of Orchestre Veve's vocalists and a saxophonist. Other musicians were recruited from a Congolese group that had been transiting through Uganda on their way to Nairobi to record. This group was the Eboma Safari Band. Additional musicians were recruited from the Rhino Band at White Nile nightclub and Somo Somo, a Congolese band performing at Arizona. The leader of the Economic Band was Ogbomange Anakese, a Congolese vocalist, and the group had fourteen members.

Meanwhile, Kaumba relocated to Arizona, where he helped a new Congolese band, Bavy du Zaire, establish themselves in Kampala. Bavy du Zaire was led by Mwinda Mulondelwa Kiamba. The band had arrived in Uganda in 1974, having left Congo in 1968, and spent time in Tanzania performing in several cities, including Dar es Salaam, Tanga, Morogoro, Tabora, Dodoma, and Mwanza, before moving to Kenya. In Kenya, they mainly performed at Nakuru's Tropical nightclub. In Uganda, Bavy du Zaire was initially based at Lumumba nightclub in Bwaise, then at Economic nightclub, and later spent short periods performing at Rita nightclub in Kibuye, City Bar, and Good Hope in Kibuye. They eventually signed a contract with Arizona. The band featured two female dancers: Margaret Mukwaya from Uganda and Sulie Moses from Congo. Their energetic and sensual performances were often credited with drawing large crowds to Arizona whenever Bavy du Zaire performed. Among the band's popular songs were compositions praising Amin and his policies, such as Amin Webale (Thank You, Amin) and Mafuta Mingi (Those Dripping in Fat). The mafuta mingi phrase entered everyday Ugandan speech after the 1972 expulsion of Asians, when their properties were handed over to Black Ugandans who came to be known as the 'new money' class.

In May 1975, tragedy struck the Vipers when one of their lead vocalists, Monga Ngoyi Sungu, popularly known as Baddwe, died in a road traffic accident shortly after attending his customary engagement ceremony to a woman from Kabale. He was killed on his way back to Kampala following the celebration. Baddwe's death dealt a heavy blow to Kaumba, who found it difficult continuing the band without him. In Kaumba's mind, Baddwe had been an integral part of the Vipers, and continuing to use the name without him no longer felt morally right. A few months later, he renamed the group L'Orchestre Super Kaumba, more commonly known as Super Kaumba. Around the same time, Kaumba persuaded Ramadan Mustafa to allow the newly renamed band to resume performances at the Economic nightclub. Under the Super Kaumba name, the band released the songs Banoko and Zena. The latter featured vocals by Albert Atibu, a Congolese singer who had grown up in the Ugandan town of Arua.

Atibu joined Super Kaumba around 1975 and remained a fixture on the Ugandan music scene until his death in 2003. He became popularly known by his stage name, Amigo Wawawa. Atibu later had a successful stint with Afrigo Band, composing the iconic Vincent, which he sang with Joanita Kawalya. With his own Waka Waka Band, he released the playful and whimsical song Ekikere Kiri Kumbata (The Frog Is on the Duck).

Kaumba's own life ended tragically in 1980 after he consumed adulterated bootleg gin, known locally as waragi. That year, methanol-laced waragi had become a public health crisis in Uganda, with multiple mass casualty events reported across the country. The outbreak was traced to looted waragi distilleries, where thieves had taken half-processed alcohol instead of the fully distilled product. This unfinished waragi contained dangerously high levels of methanol, a toxic compound often mistaken for ethanol but far more lethal. The contaminated liquor spread rapidly, especially in Kampala's outskirts, where it was sold cheaply and without regulation. Methanol poisoning can cause irreversible blindness and death, even in small doses. Kaumba was one of many victims of this epidemic.

Beyond the Congolese bands that had become long-time fixtures at Ugandan nightclubs, a steady stream of visiting Congolese stars kept the excitement alive. In December 1967, Franco Luambo Makiadi and his legendary OK Jazz made their first tour of Uganda. Invited by the Ugandan government, they performed at the grand opening of Kampala's Apolo Hotel, where Franco and Vicky Longomba animated the audience with a performance that left the city buzzing for days. In June 1974, Kazinga Channel Agencies Limited announced that Franco and OK Jazz would be returning for a nationwide tour beginning at the end of the month. The response was immediate and overwhelming. Tickets sold out within days. Fans braced themselves for another unforgettable encounter with the titans of Congolese rumba. But just as anticipation reached a fever pitch, disaster struck. Kazinga Channel failed to raise the funds required to pay the band, abruptly cancelling the tour. The fallout was swift and severe, nearly triggering a diplomatic standoff. Urgent messages flew between the Zairean Embassy and Uganda's Ministry of Foreign Affairs, as well as the Ministry of Culture and Community Development. Franco never set foot on Ugandan soil that year. Nearly a decade later, in 1983, he finally returned. The wait had only intensified the devotion. Franco stepped onto the Ugandan stage like a conquering hero, met with roaring ovations that left no doubt he still reigned supreme.

In May 1970, Joseph Chuza Kabasele returned to Uganda, where he had left behind his Ugandan wife, Gertrude Nabatanzi, and five children who lived in Mengo. He came with his band, Orchestre City Five/Le Noir, at the invitation of the Ugandan government. Chuza had friends in high places, including President Milton Obote and Uganda Army military commander Idi Amin. Chuza led two bands, Le Noir and City Five, with a combined total of sixteen members. City Five performed Western covers, mostly English, French, and Spanish songs, while Le Noir, whose lead singer was Zozo, performed original Congolese compositions.

During their visit to Uganda, the band was based at New Life nightclub but also performed at Lugogo indoor stadium, Apolo Hotel, and appeared on Elly Wamala's television show. At the time, Charles Ssenkatuka, one of the band's founders, had left and was living in Toronto, Canada. Le Noir had already made a name for themselves in Uganda with popular songs such as Mosebelende and Masikini. While in residence at New Life, the band composed several patriotic songs, including Watoto Wa Uganda (Children of Uganda) and Wa Minister wa Uganda (Uganda's Cabinet Ministers), which called on Ugandans to pull together and rally behind President Obote for national development and peace. They also composed one of their most celebrated Ugandan songs, Banange Jangu Tugende Mengo (Friends, Let's Go to Mengo). The song shimmered with the soft pulse of Congolese rumba, featuring supple guitar threads that wove through harmonies both joyous and yearning. Though danceable, it carried a quiet nostalgia, evoking journeys homeward and the warmth of familiar voices calling from Mengo. It was the kind of song that lingered long after the record stopped spinning. The band returned to Kinshasa in late 1970, just before Idi Amin overthrew the Milton Obote government.

Chuza and his Les Noir band were invited back by Amin in January 1972 to celebrate the first anniversary of his coup. Again, they were based at New Life nightclub in Mengo, alternating performances with New Life's resident band, the Vipers of Kaumba. It was around this time that a youthful Sammy Kasule, a bassist with the Vipers, became entangled in a situation that nearly cost him his life.

Adjacent to New Life nightclub lay a sprawling shanty neighborhood, a patchwork of tightly packed homes topped with rusted corrugated iron, haphazardly built but teeming with life. This area, a mix of temporary settlements and makeshift bars, housed day laborers, soldiers, and others seeking respite from urban hardship. Many dwellings also served as informal, unlicensed drinking spots, lively hubs where people socialized over beers or waragi, finding relaxation and a temporary escape from their worries. In this vibrant setting lived Nalongo, known for her hospitality and her daughters' remarkable beauty. Her home was one such makeshift bar, a welcoming gathering place for neighbors and visitors to share stories and camaraderie amidst the city's chaos.

One Friday afternoon, Sammy Kasule walked over from New Life and visited Nalongo's house. He had taken an interest in one of Nalongo's daughters and struck up a conversation. He was accompanied by his fellow bandmate, John Mutebi. During their visit, a soldier walked into Nalongo's bar, glanced at Sammy and Mutebi, then left without saying a word. Less than ten minutes later, he returned with several angry, gun-wielding soldiers. The soldiers immediately attacked Sammy and Mutebi, beating them with gun butts and threatening to shoot them. Nalongo pleaded for mercy, but the soldiers ignored her. Sammy was falsely accused of having an affair with the wife of a senior military officer, even though the young woman in question, Nalongo's daughter, had no such relationship with a military officer.

Sammy and Mutebi were bundled into a military vehicle and locked up at Republic House in Mengo, which served as the army headquarters. Republic House, once the seat of the Buganda Parliament (Bulange), had been transformed into a military stronghold by the Obote government. Rising above the gentle undulations of Mengo Hill, Bulange had once stood as a proud symbol of Buganda's political heritage, an elegant modernist structure completed in 1958 during the reign of Kabaka Edward Mutesa II. During Amin's regime, it was a place where soldiers could imprison civilians that were snatched from the streets, a striking contrast to its former role as the respected administrative hub of Buganda.

Sammy and Mutebi languished in prison for three nights, enduring constant beatings and being denied food and water. When Chuza heard about their plight, he appealed to his contacts in high places, leading to their eventual release. Upon their release, Chuza and Le Noir were preparing to relocate to Mombasa. Chuza offered Sammy and Mutebi a chance to join the band, and they accepted without hesitation. They eagerly left Uganda, seeking a safer and more stable future.

With Les Noir, Sammy Kasule played bass on many of the band's recordings, including their very popular 1973 hit Sikia Sauce, released on the Pathé label. Sammy Kasule went on to achieve great success in Kenya, playing with multiple bands in Mombasa and Nairobi, including African Jambo Jambo and Orchestra Vundumuna Band. In 1978, Sammy teamed up with Elliot "Elly" Adwonga, Shaban Onyango, and Ali Magobeni to form the Somajeko International Band based in Nairobi. With Somajeko, Sammy released several hugely successful Swahili songs, including Riziki Ni Kama Ajali (Fortune Is Like an Accident) and Nimevumilia (I Have Endured). Marie Wandaka, a paean to his Kenyan wife, became one of his greatest successes. He was later among the founding members of the Makonde Band, based in Nairobi.

Makonde toured London in 1979, and after returning to Kenya, Kasule collaborated with Kenyan singer Zembi Okeno to release an English version of the famous Shauri Yako hit song, originally composed by Congolese legend Nguashi N'timbo and his Festival Du Zaire Band. In 1985, Sammy Kasule relocated to Sweden, where he continued his musical journey. He played the killer slap bass on Philly Lutaaya's highly successful Born in Africa. Sammy returned to Uganda in 2013, joining Afrigo Band before teaming up with Frank Mbalire and John Sentamu to form Ziwuuna Band. He remained active until his death in 2021 in Amsterdam, Netherlands, while en route for medical treatment in Stockholm, Sweden, a country he had made his second home. Sammy maintained a long and prolific career, releasing numerous songs and performing across Africa, Europe, and Japan.

General Idi Amin Dada was an avid fan and a knowledgeable connoisseur of Congolese rumba music. He also played the accordion quite well. About six months into his presidency, Amin's government, working through the Congo embassy in Kampala and Uganda Hotels Ltd, invited Orchestre Volcan (also known as Orchestre Volcan Ni-Bett-Ba) to tour

Uganda in celebration of Amin's rise to power and the establishment of what he called the "Second Republic."

Orchestre Volcan was formed in 1969 after the disbandment of Grand Kalle's African Jazz. Among the former African Jazz musicians who joined Orchestre Volcan were vocalists Mathieu Kuka, Jean-Leonard "Rolly" Nsita, Alexis Mayukuta, and Joseph Diasemua. Other ex-African Jazz members included drummer Jean Balu and guitarist Andre Kambite. Mathieu Kuka, in particular, had a large Ugandan fan base. Shortly before the breakup of African Jazz, Kuka had sung the highly acclaimed BB 69, another favorite on Radio Uganda.

The band composed and sang several songs praising Idi Amin and his new government. Orchestre Volcan was hosted at Radio Uganda and appeared on Uganda Television (UTV). They stayed in Uganda for one month, performing to packed audiences. There was a stampede, and a riot almost broke out as fans pushed each other to gain entrance during the band's performances at Susana and Arizona nightclubs. Things were calmer when Orchestre Volcan performed for dignitaries and government officials (civilian and military) at Kampala International Hotel (formerly the Apolo Hotel). Uganda Hotels Ltd (UHL) ensured that the Amin-praising band toured much of the country, arranging stops at UHL-owned hotels, including Lake Victoria Entebbe, Mt. Elgon Hotel in Mbale, Rock Hotel in Tororo, Soroti Hotel, Lira Hotel, Acholi Inn in Gulu, Masindi Hotel, Hotel Margherita in Kasese, White Horse Inn, and Tropic Inn in Masaka, as well as at Nakivubo National War Memorial Stadium in the heart of downtown Kampala.

Tabu Ley Rochereau had first toured Uganda in May 1966 with African Fiesta, playing to a crowd of thousands at Kampala's Jubilee Park. The band helped elevate the soukous genre of music in Uganda. African Fiesta had several songs that became hits in Uganda, including Merenge President, Mi Amor, Suke, and many others. Ugandans were very familiar with the band, and members like Tabu Ley (vocalist), Nicolas Kasanda wa Mikalay (known as Dr. Nico, the legendary guitarist), and Charles "Déchaud" Mwamba (guitarist and elder brother of Dr. Nico) had a cult following in the country. Tabu Ley's voice, a high tenor, was always sweetly urbane, whether singing about love, his Christian beliefs, or social issues. From the 1960s into the 1990s, he led one of the top bands playing soukous. He wrote and recorded thousands of songs, and as a bandleader and arranger, he widely expanded the sound of soukous, infusing it with both local African rhythms and international pop elements.

In 1973, Amos Biryamujura's Ankole Enterprises paid 300,000 Uganda shillings, a considerable amount at the time, to bring Congolese music royalty, Tabu Ley and his famed Afrisa International band, back to Uganda. Tabu Ley's band, Orchestre Afrisa International, was rivaled only by Le Tout Puissant OK Jazz, led by the guitarist Franco Luambo Makiadi. In September 1973, Afrisa International arrived in Uganda aboard a privately chartered Air Congo flight, courtesy of the Congolese (Zaire) leader, Mobutu Sese Seko. Tabu Ley and his band, twelve people in total, including four dancers, were received at Entebbe International Airport by Colonel Ali Waris Fadhul, the commanding officer of the Simba Battalion. Tabu Ley, a superstar in Africa and Congolese music royalty, held a press conference where he advised Ugandan musicians to compose and sing patriotic songs that could help the people rally behind their leader and national policies. He was then whisked to the International Hotel, where a reception in his honor was organized by Brigadier Moses Ali, the Minister of Provincial Administration.

The band embarked on a demanding tour, performing in major towns such as Jinja, Mbale, Masaka, and Mbarara, with their biggest performance at Kampala's International Hotel, attended by almost every cabinet minister and senior army officer. The tour was physically taxing for Tabu Ley, his musicians, dancers, and crew. Every venue on the tour was sold out, and the crowd could not get enough. Afrisa International's show delivered an impressive and rousing set, with Tabu Ley's singing described as magical. He performed some of his flagship songs, such as Sambuluma, Kaful Mayay, Mongali, and Kiwelewele, to much excitement and rapturous applause.

Ugandans had never seen such energetic stage performance and choreography. Afrisa International dancers, four girls in skimpy minidresses, performed their signature sensual dance with energetic, hip-pumping, acrobatic moves. The band elevated stage performance to new heights, a spectacle that most Ugandan audiences had never imagined or experienced. Tabu Ley also dressed elegantly, changing outfits several times, something that Ugandan performers never did. This new experience had the crowd going wild, dancing with abandon, and celebrating the fact that they were fortunate to witness this child of the Congo delivering magic. Writing in the government-run newspaper *Voice of Uganda*, journalist Moses Oguti described the performance as "piercing through every iota of the hall like it were to awaken the dead souls... But it did not awaken them. It only killed them the more as they stared dumbfounded."

Tabu Ley later had a private audience with Idi Amin, who was among his most enthusiastic fans. Amin's love for music extended beyond Congolese rumba. He played the accordion and often joined live bands on stage, most notably the Five Stars Jazz Band based at the Grand Imperial Hotel. On hot weekend afternoons, he was frequently seen lounging by the pool at Kampala's International Hotel before heading down the hill to the Grand Imperial, where he would spend hours jamming with the band. The group featured Livingstone Ddamulira as bandleader, Peter Rogers on lead guitar, Jimmy Ochen on rhythm guitar, Wasswa on bass, and Manvanga "Demave" Manazambi, a Congolese musician who had previously played with the Susana Band. Twalib Muhammad played the saxophone. During these sessions, Amin especially enjoyed performing Kabalagala Gonja (Banana Pancakes and Plantains), one of his personal favorites. In a well-known video clip, he makes a theatrical entrance into the Grand Imperial as the band greets him with a flute performance by Demave, saxophone lines from Twalib Muhammad, and rhythm from a local Ugandan girl on the congas.

Verckys Kiamuangana Matete, also known as Veve, was one of the most influential Congolese musicians of the 1970s, with his band, Orchestre Veve, enjoying near-cult status in Uganda thanks to a string of hit

Lingala songs, including Nakomitunaka, Ndona, Lukani, and Kalala. In January 1974, Orchestre Veve arrived in Uganda aboard Air Zaire. They were brought into the country by Inter Uganda Impexport Ltd and were scheduled to perform across the country for one month. However, this ended up being two months, much to the delight of the band's Ugandan fans. Verckys was received at the airport by top-ranking civil and military leaders, and an enthusiastic crowd of hundreds of fans turned up at Entebbe International Airport to welcome him. He was received with the pomp and ceremony typically reserved for a head of state. The band was huge, consisting of more than twenty musicians. He arrived in time to commemorate Amin's overthrow of Obote on January 25th and was in Uganda for the festivities celebrating this event. Their shows were thrilling; crowds could not get enough of their music.

The band played various venues in Kampala, including the International Hotel, Makerere University Main Hall, Lugogo stadium, Jinja Town Hall, and Elgon Hotel in Mbale. The band ventured to other Ugandan towns, playing at Gulu Town Hall, Acholi Inn, and also venues in Arua, Kasese, Kabale, Mbarara, and Masaka. The finale was at Nakivubo stadium to a sold-out concert. It was something to marvel at. Just watching Veve blow the saxophone was a trip to musical delight. He later played for Idi Amin at State House. Amin had invited county (saza) chiefs to the private show. An impressed Amin asked Veve to train Ugandan musicians so that they too could achieve a high level of musical mastery.

Shama Shama of Mopero wa Maloba was in Uganda around 1975 and were based at the Economic nightclub in Mengo for several months. Shama Shama was immensely popular in Uganda during the 1970s, drawing in audiences with their vibrant cavacha rhythms. Their songs, characterized by a signature two-part structure, beginning with sweetly harmonized storytelling before shifting into a thrilling dance section, were among the most frequently played on Radio Uganda. Hardly a day passed without their music filling the airwaves multiple times. Their repertoire featured catchy, fan-favorite hits such as Vicky Shama, Mama Aye, Pitchouna, and many others, all distinguished by vibrant parallel-harmony vocals, compelling lead melodies, and shimmering guitar work. Cavacha is a Congolese rumba-style drumbeat, said to have been created by Meridjo Belobi of the Congolese band Zaïko Langa Langa. Shama Shama had a huge fanbase in Uganda, and even a mafuta mingi, a woman who owned a store on Kampala Road in central Kampala, was so infatuated with Mopero that she named her store Shama Shama.

Another major Congolese star who visited Uganda was Aimee Françoise M'Pongo Langu, whose stage name was M'Pongo Love. Unlike in Uganda, where several female musicians were popular and considered stars, this was not the case in Congo. Together with Abeti Masikini, she was the only female Congolese musician to achieve major success and gain recognition outside the Congo. She was a courageous woman. She was paralyzed by polio but never let her disability hold her back. She sang in a clear, slightly nasal voice and utilized precise intonations and was described as having an angelic voice. Her song Ndaya, a composition by Mayaula Mayoni, was a huge success in East and CentralAfrica. Bakeke was another beautiful song. She toured Uganda in 1976, giving a series of concerts, with the main performance held at the International Hotel. M'Pongo Love even sang a song praising Idi Amin, though it was likely never recorded. The song was, however, broadcast on Uganda TV, where she was prominently featured during her tour. At the time, Tshala Muana, the "Queen of Mutuashi," was a dancer and backup singer in her band.

Samba Mapangala and his Les Kinois band spent time in Kampala in the late 1970s, and so did Kanda Bongoman and Diblo Dibla when they were with Bana Mambo, having gigs in Kampala in late 1977. Jojo Ikomo and Coco Zigo of Bana Ngenge and Kombe Kombe, respectively, performed at Ugandan nightclubs in Kampala in the late 1970s. The great Michellino Mavatiku, the legendary guitarist, composer, and ex-TP OK Jazz and Afrisa International, was based at the Equatoria Hotel in 1979, mesmerizing Ugandans with his wizardly guitar.

Due to the political instability and insecurity plaguing Congo, many young musicians sought refuge in Uganda. They arrived individually in the country and found their way into the resident bands at Kampala's nightclubs. Some became household names on the Kampala music scene. Hyppolythe Makassy, a celebrated bass player, arrived in Uganda around 1962 from Kinshasa. He first joined the New Life band before switching to the Susana band in 1965. He would leave the Susana band for the Apolo Jambo band, based at the Apolo Hotel (currently the Sheraton hotel). Makassy was the bassist on many 1960s Susana band songs, and he also played on Elly Wamala's Hamadi and Welcome Pope Paul. His desire was to form his own band, an opportunity that he got in 1975. He managed to acquire musical instruments and left for Dar es Salaam that year, starting what became a widely known band, Orchestra Makassy. They took up residence at the New Africa Hotel, where they were joined by guitarists and singers such as Mose Se Sengo (aka Fan Fan) and Remmy Ongala (aka Doctor of Super Matimila).

Some other notable Congolese musicians who made their home permanently in Uganda include N'goy Suisemann and Martin Munyenga. Munyenga, a polished gentleman with a contemplative manner, married the Ugandan musician, Monica Mbabazi. Mbabazi and Jolly Rwakanegere were the two leading female musicians with the Susana Band in the early 1970s. On the Serenade label, Mbabazi had moderate success with her 1973 song Manyanga Nkwagala (Know that I love you), while Rwakanegere's Patrick and Kisalu (a male name) remained largely unknown. However, Rwakanegere was a favorite at Susana, and the audience would go crazy when she covered John Denver's Leaving on a Jet Plane and other English songs. And there were many more Congolese musicians who opted to remain in the background, content with playing the guitar or drums or the horns without becoming a household name.

After the overthrow of Idi Amin in April 1979, the Nairobi-based Congolese band Mangelepa was invited to perform at Lugogo Stadium in Kampala. Widely admired for their popular songs like Embakasi, Dracula, and Nyako Konya, Mangelepa had built a strong following in Uganda, where their records were played in bars, dance halls, and on radio. The concert at Lugogo was seen as a major event, one that would mark a cultural reawakening after years of silence and fear. Ugandans had longed for a return to the vibrancy of earlier years, and Mangelepa's appearance promised just that. On the night of the show, Lugogo Stadium filled to capacity. Hundreds turned out, eager to hear the music that had defined a generation and to feel, even briefly, the rhythm of a city finding its feet again.

But what was expected to be a joyous evening quickly took a different turn. Before Mangelepa could take the stage, the audience was presented with an opening act by an unknown Tanzanian band. Their set consisted of songs extolling the Tanzanian soldiers who had helped remove Amin from power. Although many Ugandans were genuinely grateful for the role played by the Tanzanian army, the mood that evening was not one of political remembrance or a celebration of a military conquest. The audience had come for Mangelepa. They had come to dance, to lose themselves in music, and to momentarily step away from the uncertainty of the times.

As the patriotic performance wore on, restlessness spread through the stadium. Grumbling turned to protest. Chants began to rise from the crowd, calling for Mangelepa to perform. The tension escalated quickly. The Tanzanian soldiers stationed at the venue responded with force. Shots were fired into the air, and chaos followed. People screamed and scattered in panic. Several were injured in the rush to escape. Fortunately, no lives were lost. Mangelepa, shaken by the violence, never performed that night.

This violent spectacle deepened the rift between the Ugandan public and the Tanzanian forces, who had been seen as liberators just months earlier. Tensions were already rising, as the Tanzanian army, focused on military objectives, struggled with the complexities of post-conflict stabilization. Some accounts allege that rogue elements within the Tanzanian forces contributed to the rising insecurity and violence witnessed around the country, including reports of looting and excessive force. However, the subsequent increase in insecurity and violence at that time is part of a broader, more complex narrative of post-conflict transition, state collapse, and the struggle for power among various factions within Uganda. For Mangelepa, the memory of Lugogo lingered. It would take more than thirty years before the band returned to Uganda. That night in 1979, filled with so much hope and anticipation, had ended instead in confusion and fear. And for many who were present, the sound of gunfire at a concert remained an enduring reminder of how fragile peace and joy could be in the aftermath of war.

The presence of Congolese musicians and music in Uganda had long been a dynamic and influential force, shaping the country's musical identity and leaving a deep and lasting imprint. From the early pioneers who arrived during the colonial era to the celebrated bands and individual artists who toured or made Uganda their home, Congolese music reverberated with Ugandan audiences across generations. This exchange between Congolese and Ugandan musicians broadened artistic expression, introducing new rhythms, instrumentation, and performance styles that blended seamlessly with local traditions. Though political upheavals occasionally disrupted this thriving musical movement, the sounds of Congolese rumba, soukous, and their Ugandan adaptations continued to uplift spirits, bring people together, and define social gatherings.

CHAPTER 12

Kampala's Youthful Sound: The Cranes and the Era of Change in Ugandan Music

Uganda's independence on October 9, 1962, was a joyous affair, with celebrations of Uhuru continuing for days. The Swahili word "Uhuru" resonated across the African continent, symbolizing the hard-won liberation from colonial rule and the aspirations for self-determination and a brighter future. In Uganda, the euphoria of independence was palpable. Black, yellow, and red flags, the new national colors, fluttered proudly from government buildings, while buildings in major towns were adorned with colorful bunting that reflected the nation's newfound identity.

Uganda's independence festivities began on September 30, 1962, and unfolded over three weeks of pomp, ceremony, and joyous celebration. One of the most memorable events was the grand state ball at Kampala's Lugogo Indoor Stadium, attended by 850 invited guests. Representing the Queen, the Duke and Duchess of Kent added royal gravitas to the occasion. In a poignant gesture of unity and transition, Sir Edward Mutesa II, Kabaka of Buganda, danced with the Duchess of Kent. He was followed by the newly appointed Prime Minister, 37-year-old Milton Obote, striking in a white tuxedo and black tie, who also took a turn with the Duchess. The evening radiated optimism and conviviality, capturing the hopeful spirit of a nation awakening to its future.

Music played a central role in the festivities, with traditional folk music ensembles and "new" pop musicians entertaining the crowds. Eva Nanyonga, a trailblazing female artist, took to the stage with her guitar, performing at the main independence celebration venue at Kololo airstrip. Other notable performers included Magembe's Kampala City Six, a popular band known for their catchy tunes, and Fred Masagazi with his Uganda Kezaala (UK) jazz band, adding a touch of sophistication to the celebrations. The joyous atmosphere extended beyond the official events. Salaried workers received bonuses or advances on their wages to further enhance the celebration of Uhuru. The workers flocked to bars and nightclubs around the country, dancing and drinking with abandon, reveling in their newly attained freedom. Street parades were held in all major towns, with the most spectacular one being the independence float parade in Kampala City. The parade, a colorful procession of beautifully decorated trucks, a marching band, and dancers, wound its way through the city streets, starting from Wandegeya and passing through Kampala and Jinja roads. One of the floats featured a group of energetic teenage boys known as the National Youth Dancers, also affectionately referred to as the "Crazy Gang." Dressed in white shirts and black pants, they danced with remarkable vitality and precision. Their movements combined rapid steps, synchronized kicks, and playful gestures that drew cheers from the crowd. Unlike formal traditional dancers, the Crazy Gang embodied a modern, expressive style rooted in urban youth culture. Their performance not only energized the parade but also signaled the arrival of a new generation eager to define Uganda's post-independence identity.

The Crazy Gang was a cabaret group, part of the National Youth Club founded by John Mukasa and his brother Paul Nick Mubiru. The National Youth Club also included the National Youth Players and the National Youth Singers, showcasing the diverse talents of Uganda's youth. The brothers John Mukasa and Paul Nick Mubiru were from a relatively well-to-do family in the Luwafu, Makindye, neighborhood of Kampala. John

Mukasa developed an interest in music early on, attending Namilyango Boys Primary School, Mengo Junior Secondary, and Old Kampala Secondary School. His family was among the few Black Ugandan households that owned a piano, and his father, A.K.S. Mukasa, a skilled pianist, had hoped his son would become a prodigy through piano lessons. Although John became proficient at the piano, he found his true calling in playing the drums. In 1961, he participated in a music contest at Kampala's National Theater, securing third place. Bolstered by his performance, John persuaded his younger brother, Paul Nick Mubiru, to form an entertainment group that would perform plays and cabaret acts during Uganda's independence celebrations on October 9, 1962. This effort led to the formation of the National Youth Club in 1961, with the cabaret and singing segment known as the Crazy Gang. In addition to John and Paul, the original Crazy Gang roster included Philip Ngoma (who later became the band leader of the Susanna nightclub band), Richard Shonga (later the rhythm guitarist for the same band), John Clyde Mayanja, Tony Williams Ssenkebejje, Francis Odida, Sammy Kawuma, Billy Mbowa, Frobisher Ssenkubuge, and Charles Kamanyi. Notably, Charles Kamanyi, along with his older brother Dan Kamanyi, played a historic role by driving the car that whisked the Kabaka away from Kampala into exile in England after Obote loyalists, led by Colonel Idi Amin, stormed the Kabaka's royal palace in May 1966.

In 1963, the Crazy Gang evolved into the Sparrows, a group that featured John Mukasa, Paul Nick Mubiru, Charles Kamanyi, Ted Sensalo, Julius Kiwana, Sammy Mukasa Kintu, and a member known simply as Joe. This new formation was built on a shared admiration for Slinger Francisco, better known as The Mighty Sparrow, a Trinidadian calypso singer, songwriter, and guitarist whose lively songs struck a chord with Ugandan youth during the late 1950s and 1960s. The Mighty Sparrow's playful tunes, including Good Morning Mr. Walker, Teresa, and The Short Little Shorts, were particularly popular, and his influence was so strong that a dedicated Sparrow fan club emerged in Uganda, led by John Mukasa himself. It was even said that Mukasa was the only person in the country who could correspond with The Mighty Sparrow in Trinidad and receive a personal reply. His passion for the artist helped establish the Sparrow's music as a lasting favorite, one that would inspire later generations when soca music became a major trend in the early 1980s.

By 1967, the Sparrows had adopted the name the Slingers, directly reflecting the real name of The Mighty Sparrow. At that time, the band lineup consisted of John Mukasa, who served as the leader and drummer, John Sebana on lead guitar, Daphne Alex Bwanika on the rhythm guitar, and Charles Ssekyanzi as the vocalist. This rebranding marked a new chapter for the group as they continued to perform and entertain audiences with their energetic style.

In 1964, a new musical venture emerged when four former members of the Crazy Gang joined forces to form the Darling Brothers. These were John Clyde Mayanja, who played maracas and organized the band, Tony Williams Ssenkebejje on rhythm guitar and vocals, Sammy Kawuma on drums and as band leader, and Billy Mbowa Kawoya as the lead vocalist. They expanded their lineup by recruiting Paul Nick Mubiru on bass guitar and vocals, along with Eddy Masembe on lead guitar and vocals. With prior recording experience, Billy Mbowa, Paul Nick Mubiru, and Eddy Masembe rose to teen idol status.

Fred Kanyike recognized their potential and connected them with the AGS studio, leading to the release of several well-received songs under the AGS label. Paul Mubiru, in particular, recorded two successful duets with Kanyike: Grace Ndiwuwo (Grace I Am Yours) and Gumira Kunze (Stay By Me), with Kanyike providing vocal support. Adding to the group's growing creative output, Mbowa and Ssenkebejje, who were neighbors in Kampala, collaborated on the track Eva, inspired by Ricky Nelson's 1960 duet You Are the Only One with Lorrie Collins. Nelson and Lorrie's song struck a chord with Uganda's educated urban youth.

Meanwhile, Eddy Masembe built a strong following with hit songs such as Nayitani (Who Shall I Call?) and Rose Gwenonze (Rose My Chosen). The former was delivered in the familiar AGS Boys twist beat style, while Rose Gwenonze offered a mellow, relaxed sound, featuring playful shoutouts to members of the Darling Brothers and performed in the style of Congolese rumba.

> Looking into your eyes,
> I appreciate your love,
> and I promise
> to keep you forever.
> One thing brings tears to my eyes—
> the feeling of being controlled.
> But it doesn't hurt too much,
> for I know it will pass.
> Recalling all that we shared,
> I find the strength
> to ask you
> to honor our promise.
> Mama, I make a promise about my beloved:
> Rose is the one I've chosen.
> When others see you,
> they say, "Rose is the best."
> Rose, my chosen one.
> Paul (Mubiru) tells me so,
> John (Mayanja) agrees—
> Rose is the best,
> Rose, my chosen one.
> Billy (Mbowa) was upset,
> and Sammy (Kawuma) swore
> when they both heard it:
> "Rose is the one you chose!"
> Oh, Rose!

In 1965, the Darling Brothers officially transformed into the Cranes, a name which honored the Crested Crane (*Balearica regulorum*), which was Uganda's national bird. And in May 1965, the band welcomed its first and only female member, Louise Bagenda. The Cranes made their debut on Wamala's TV show that same year and soon became a regular feature on the program. The Cranes were determined to establish themselves as a professional musical outfit, unlike many youth bands of the time that treated music as merely a pastime.

Uhuru was seen as a major victory, a triumph over the shackles and chains of colonialism. Uganda was free, led by a democratically elected prime minister, Apollo Milton Obote. His party, the Uganda People's Congress (UPC), had won the most seats in Uganda's new legislature during the April 25, 1962, parliamentary elections. However, the UPC did not win an outright majority and formed an alliance with Kabaka Yekka (KY), meaning "King Only," a royalist political party aligned with the Kabaka of Buganda. This UPC/KY alliance enabled Obote to form a government, marking the beginning of a complex and often tumultuous political landscape in post-independence Uganda.

In the first two years of Uganda's independence, the relationship between Prime Minister Obote and Sir Edward Mutesa II was remarkably good. The two men, both well-educated, cosmopolitan, and worldly, shared a genuine friendship. They frequently socialized, enjoying scotch and cigars while listening to European classical music. However, beneath this veneer of camaraderie lay profound political differences that would soon test the fragile unity of the newly independent nation. The kingdom of Buganda, historically dominant within Uganda, viewed the newly independent country with suspicion, fearing that its power and the authority of the Kabaka would be diminished. To address these concerns, the 1962 independence constitution granted Buganda special federal powers, not extended to the other four kingdoms of Bunyoro, Toro, Ankole, and Busoga. When Uganda became a republic in 1963, further concessions were made to Buganda, with Sir Edward Mutesa II appointed as the ceremonial president.

These concessions, however, did not fully resolve the underlying tensions. Nonetheless, the country appeared to be on a path of success, creating opportunities for its people in an environment of peace and political stability. Freddie Kanyike's Oh Africa praised Obote and other African statesmen leading the continent's resurgence after decades of colonial oppression. Andrew Kyambadde and Margaret Nakibuuka's 9 October commemorated Uganda's independence and lauded Obote's cabinet for its perceived commitment to the common good. But a simmering conflict persisted between Obote's central government and the kingdom of Buganda. A major point of contention was the so-called 'Lost Counties,' specifically the areas of Buyaga and Bugangaizi in Bunyoro. The rivalry between the Buganda and Bunyoro kingdoms had stretched back centuries. It was a fierce and often bloody struggle over land, resources, and political dominance. In the late 1800s, this long-standing animosity took a decisive turn when Buganda allied itself with British colonial forces to help subdue Bunyoro. As a reward for its support, Buganda was granted control over these contested counties. This move left deep scars in Bunyoro's collective memory and laid the groundwork for future political agitation. As Uganda approached independence, Bunyoro demanded the return of these annexed territories, and the British sought to rectify this historical injustice. Buganda, however, remained unyielding, asserting its rightful claim over the "Lost Counties."

This ethno-political dispute was a contentious issue during Uganda's Independence Conference at Marlborough House in London. While the conference aimed to resolve long-standing problems, the "Lost Counties" issue remained unresolved at independence. The British proposed a referendum to let the people in the "Lost Counties" decide their future, but it was deemed impractical to hold it before independence. In the interim, the British recommended that the central government administer the counties until a referendum could be held under peaceful and secure conditions. In 1964, despite fierce protests from Buganda, Obote's government held a referendum. The residents of the 'Lost Counties' voted overwhelmingly to return to Bunyoro.

Another point of contention between Obote and Edward Mutesa was the issue of direct elections. Buganda's parliament, the Lukiko, opposed direct elections for the national parliament, favoring instead the right to select Buganda's representatives. The central government considered this undemocratic and unrepresentative of the people's will. Israel Magembe's Kampala City Six released Abataka Basajja (The Clan Headmen), a song supporting the Lukiko's stance. With Ecklas Kawalya as the lead vocalist, the song rejected the main political parties not affiliated with the Kabaka and endorsed the Lukiko's rejection of direct elections, urging the people of Buganda to unite behind the King and the Lukiko.

These political tensions, simmering beneath the surface of early independence celebrations, would soon erupt into open conflict, casting a shadow over Uganda's promising future. The escalating political feud between the central government and Buganda reached a point where the alliance between the UPC and Kabaka Yekka could no longer be sustained. Obote, determined to consolidate his power, used persuasion and, some allege, bribery to sway Kabaka Yekka parliamentarians to join his UPC. By mid-1964, Obote's UPC had increased its seats in parliament from 37 to 60, rendering Kabaka Yekka politically expendable. In August 1964, Prime Minister Obote formally dissolved the UPC/KY alliance and dismissed the two KY members of his cabinet: Amos Ssempa, the finance minister, and Mayanja Nkangi, the minister of commerce and industry. Also removed was Florence Alice Lubega, who had been serving as parliamentary secretary in the Ministry of Planning and Community Development. However, Lubega would later return to government service, becoming Uganda's first female deputy minister when she was appointed to the Ministry of Community Development and Labor.

Buganda, with its history of separatism, had long harbored ambitions of independence. Prior to Uganda's independence, the Kabaka had personally appealed to the British for Buganda's secession from the Uganda protectorate. These sentiments lingered after independence, and the growing political rift between the Kabaka and Obote's government fueled Buganda's belief in its right to self-determination. In 1965, the Kabaka even requested military assistance from the British in the event of Buganda's secession, a request politely declined by the former colonial power. The political tensions culminated in a constitutional crisis in February 1966 when Obote suspended the constitution, claiming it was necessary to prevent the overthrow of his elected government. In April 1966, an interim constitution was adopted, recognizing Obote as president and granting him sweeping powers. The Kabaka and his loyal subjects were outraged by these actions, viewing them as a direct assault on Buganda's autonomy.

In May 1966, the conflict reached a boiling point. The Kabaka issued a bold ultimatum to Obote, ordering him to remove the central government from Kampala and Buganda territory by May 30, 1966. Obote responded swiftly and decisively, accusing the Kabaka of high treason and ordering the arrest of three Buganda chiefs perceived as leaders of the secessionist movement. The arrest of the chiefs ignited widespread riots and violence in Buganda. Businesses, primarily owned by Ugandans of Indian and Pakistani descent, were looted and their owners attacked. Illegal roadblocks were erected throughout Buganda, and anyone suspected of disloyalty to the Kabaka was arbitrarily harassed. The kingdom rapidly descended into chaos and anarchy.

Against this backdrop of escalating unrest, the central government, convinced that the Kabaka was stockpiling weapons at his palace in preparation for armed resistance, initiated a preemptive strike. On the morning of May 24, 1966, government troops, under the command of Colonel Idi Amin, stormed the Kabaka's palace, laying siege to the sprawling compound. For two days, fierce battles raged between government forces and the Kabaka's poorly equipped royal guards. The sound of heavy artillery and gunfire echoed through Kampala as the asymmetrical battle unfolded. A dark and ominous plume of smoke rose from the Kabaka's compound, visible for miles and serving as a stark symbol of the kingdom under siege. Hundreds were reportedly killed in the attack. Miraculously, the 41-year-old Kabaka managed to escape and fled to England, seeking political asylum.

Following the attack on the Kabaka's palace, Obote's government imposed a state of emergency and banned the opposition Democratic Party, led by Benedicto Kiwanuka. Hundreds of people, including five cabinet ministers, were arbitrarily arrested. Uganda experienced unprecedented levels of violence, with soldiers and military hardware becoming a common sight on the streets, a grim reality that continues to haunt the country to this day.

In 1967, Obote took the drastic step of abolishing all traditional monarchies in Uganda, including the Buganda kingdom. This move further eroded his popularity, especially among the Baganda people, who deeply resented the exile of their beloved Kabaka and the climate of fear created by the state of emergency. Arbitrary arrests and extrajudicial killings by the General Service Unit (GSU), the government's secret police, became rampant, targeting those perceived as loyal to the Kabaka. These political events cast a long shadow over Uganda's music scene, creating an environment of fear and censorship that would stifle creative expression and force many musicians to adapt or quit the music scene altogether.

The political crackdown extended to Uganda's music scene, with the government censoring any songs that praised the Kabaka or the Buganda kingdom. Radio Uganda, the sole radio broadcaster in the country, was prohibited from playing these songs, and the physical records themselves were marked with a red letter "X" and the words "not to be played." This censorship reached into people's homes, instilling fear and prompting many to destroy their records out of concern for being labeled anti-government and risking detention or worse at the hands of the GSU.

The state of emergency declared in 1966, coupled with the imposition of a dusk-to-dawn curfew, brought Kampala's once-thriving nightlife to an abrupt halt. The city's dance halls, which had pulsed with energy night after night, were suddenly enveloped in silence. From Susanna in Nakulabye to White Nile in Katwe, nightclubs, once the heartbeat of Uganda's burgeoning popular music scene, now stood eerily empty, their doors shut long before the evening's festivities could begin. The economic fallout was immediate and severe. With no patrons to fill their halls and no revenue from nightly performances, nightclub owners struggled to pay their in-house musicians. Many bands, unable to sustain themselves without steady gigs, disbanded, leaving the city's once-flourishing music scene in a state of uncertainty.

Faced with mounting financial pressure, club owners sought alternative ways to keep their businesses alive. The solution came in the form of daytime "teenager dances" held on weekends. By shifting their focus to Kampala's rapidly growing population of urban youth, particularly secondary school students, they hoped to create a new musical culture that could sustain them in this restrictive environment. However, catering to this younger audience required a shift in musical style. The traditional Congolese rumba bands, which had dominated Kampala's nightlife for years, were seen as less appealing to teenagers who had developed a taste for Western pop and soul music.

As a result, club owners turned their attention to a fresh and exciting trend: bands composed of teenage students. These Kampala youth bands mostly performed covers of popular English-language hits, delivering impressive renditions of James Brown's electrifying funk, the Beatles' harmonic melodies, and Elvis Presley's rock-and-roll swagger. Two groups in particular stood out, The Cranes and The Slingers, both of which traced their origins to the National Youth Club, an initiative created by siblings John Mukasa and Paul Nick Mubiru. These young musicians instantaneously became the new darlings of Kampala's entertainment scene, filling the void left by the now-struggling nightclub orchestras.

In late 1966, Lorina nightclub enticed the youthful Cranes band away from La Quinta nightclub, where they had briefly played weekend afternoon gigs. Around the same time, New Life nightclub at Mengo signed the Slingers. The Slingers' covers of West Indian calypso songs, particularly those by Slinger Francisco, helped them gain a loyal following among secondary school students. When they joined New Life in 1967, the Slingers lineup consisted of John Mukasa as leader and drummer, John Ssebaana on lead guitar, Daphine Alex Bwanika on vocals and rhythm guitar, and Charles Ssekyanzi on vocals. Ssekyanzi's exceptional performances of Slinger Francisco's songs earned him the nickname "Francisco." The band's Saturday afternoon shows at New Life were packed with teenagers, drawn to their energetic covers and youthful appeal.

The Slingers were arguably the most popular youth band of Black youths in Uganda at the time. However, with the lifting of the curfew in early 1967 and the return of Congolese resident bands to New Life, the club's owner, Kamulu, relocated the Slingers to his Kololo nightclub in Kampala's industrial area. There, they continued to perform to enthusiastic crowds of teenagers. Despite their popularity, the Slingers never recorded any songs. John Mukasa had envisioned the band as a part-time endeavor, not a path to full-time musical careers. Consequently, members who aspired to pursue music professionally decided to leave the group. Daphine Alex Bwanika joined the Apollo Jambos and later played with the Lake Quintet, where he recorded one of his most famous songs, Mukwano Rose (Darling Rose). Charles Ssekyanzi joined the Cranes band, where he became one of Uganda's most influential singers and songwriters. The departure of these core vocalists led to the disbanding of the Slingers.

The Cranes' initial foray at Lorina nightclub in 1966 proved disappointing. Unlike the Slingers, who enjoyed success at New Life in Mengo, the Cranes struggled to attract a sizable audience for the "teenager dances." Most of the students targeted by these clubs resided in the Mengo, Rubaga, and Lungujja areas, home to upper and middle-class Baganda families, many of whom had amassed wealth through their service to the Buganda kingdom. Lorina, located in the Najjanankumbi area, was considered out of the way for these affluent Mengo youngsters, who preferred patronizing New Life, situated closer to their neighborhoods. Moreover, the Cranes were still relatively unknown, lacking the established reputation of the Slingers. Determined to reach this audience of "rich" children of the Buganda aristocracy, the Cranes decided to bring their music closer to them. They left Lorina and relocated to Susana nightclub, a short walk downhill from Mengo. However, the large crowds of teenagers continued to elude them. After a few months at Susana, the band relocated again, this time to White Nile nightclub around February 1967.

White Nile's proprietor, Salongo Kyeyune, sought to enhance the club's offerings of daytime "teenager dances." Following the lead of Lorina and New Life, White Nile had also recruited a musical group of students, mostly from Pillai Secondary School (later renamed Nakasero Secondary School), called the Thunderbirds. The Thunderbirds lacked their own instruments and had to hire them for performances. At White Nile, Salongo Kyeyune allowed them to use the house band's instruments. The Thunderbirds' lineup consisted of Moses Matovu on vocals and congas, Geoffrey Nsereko on vocals, Bosco Bumozi on bass and drums, Frank Nnaggenda on bass, Richard Mutebi on rhythm guitar, and Sam and Eddy Kanyike on lead and rhythm guitars, respectively. Notably, Eddy and Sam were the younger brothers of Fred Kanyike.

When the Cranes arrived at the White Nile Club, they shared the stage with the Thunderbirds, alternating performances. Unlike the Thunderbirds, however, the Cranes owned their own instruments, giving them a significant advantage. In 1967, the lifting of Kampala's dusk-to-dawn curfew signaled the end of the Thunderbirds' run at White Nile. The adult musicians who had lent the young band their instruments needed them back. Without equipment of their own, the Thunderbirds were forced to disband. This left the Cranes as the main act for the club's daytime "teenager dances," a role they quickly turned into a springboard for wider success.

Their reputation soared among Kampala's secondary and tertiary school students, and their growing popularity culminated in a landmark moment on April 1, 1967: a sold-out Cranes concert at Nakivubo War Memorial Stadium in the heart of the capital. It was the first time a Ugandan band had headlined the stadium, and they became only the second musical group to perform there after Louis Armstrong and his All Stars Band. The Nakivubo concert was a turning point that catapulted the Cranes to national stardom. They cultivated a devoted fan base, especially among young urban audiences who followed them with enthusiasm. Emmy Faith, one such admirer, founded the Cranes Fan Club and served as its first president. Cellie Sempala, who would later join the band as a trumpet player, was vice president. Membership cost five Uganda shillings annually, a notable sum at the time. Within months, hundreds had signed up, gaining benefits such as discounted concert entry and occasional picnic outings with band members, which deepened their connection to the group.

However, the Cranes' journey to stardom began with far more modest steps. Their very first public performance took place in May 1965 at the Agha Khan Sports Club in Old Kampala. At the time, they lacked the means to buy their own instruments and had to borrow guitars and drums from the better-equipped Uganda Police Band. This was made possible through Clyde Mayanja's friendship with Ahmad Oduka, the Police Band's generous and supportive bandmaster.

Ahmad Oduka, though born in northwestern Uganda, spent his early childhood in the Busega-Natete neighborhood of Kampala, a fertile ground for many Ugandan musicians of the 1950s and 1960s. A multi-instrumentalist trained at the Royal Military School of Music in London, Oduka became the first Black bandmaster of the Uganda Police Band after independence, succeeding the British officer John Moon. He was also a founding member of Heartbeat of Africa, Uganda's national dance troupe, and occasionally played saxophone with the Susana band. Oduka was enthusiastic about the Cranes' ambition and generously offered them the use of the Police Band's instruments for their debut performance free of charge.

The Cranes considered their Agha Khan Sports Club show a major success. Although they hadn't recorded or released any songs as a group at the time, most members had individually traveled to Nairobi's AGS studios with Fred Kanyike and released successful singles. At the Agha Khan concert, the Cranes entertained the predominantly multiracial audience of secondary school students with covers of popular songs by Elvis Presley, Roy Orbison, Richard Cliff, Ricky Nelson, and the Rolling Stones. Louise Bagenda charmed the crowd with her rendition of Millie Small's My Boy Lollipop, a song that would become a staple of her three-year career with the band and earn her encores at every performance.

Louise Bagenda, affectionately known as Louise the Ladybird, was born in 1948 in Namirembe, Kampala. She attended Gayaza High School and later Old Kampala Secondary School, where she developed her vocal skills in the school choir and an a cappella group. In 1965, while still a student at Old Kampala, she was discovered by Eddy Masembe, who was struck by her beautiful voice and invited her to join the Cranes. Louise built a loyal following among Kampala students with her near-flawless renditions of English pop hits, her voice carrying a mellifluous timbre that set her apart from many of her contemporaries. She was particularly admired for her interpretations of songs by Millie Small, as well as for her graceful renditions of Sandy Posey's two hits that were popular in Uganda, Single Girl and Born a Woman.

In August 1965, the Cranes finally acquired their own instruments, thanks to Elly Wamala, who vouched for them to secure a loan from Mr. Ahmed Hussein, an Ismaili Ugandan businessman who owned the Crested Cranes Restaurant and Bar on Kampala Road. In exchange for the loan, Hussein asked the band to perform at his establishment every weekend. Their first performance there was a resounding success, with a standing-room-only crowd. As a gesture of gratitude to their benefactor, the band briefly changed their name to the Diamond Cranes, a nod to Hussein's ownership of Kampala's iconic Diamond Trust Building. However, this arrangement ended abruptly in early 1966 when Kampala City authorities cited Hussein for hosting live music without a proper license. Unable to continue performing at the Crested Cranes Restaurant and Bar, the band reverted to their original name and moved to La Quinta nightclub. A few months later, in December 1966, they relocated to Lorina nightclub, where they pioneered the "teenager dances" that would become a defining feature of Kampala's music scene.

The early years of the Cranes were marked by significant changes in their lineup. In 1965, Tony Ssenkebejje joined St. Mary's College, Kisubi, an elite Catholic secondary school, where he excelled in the school's Kisubi Percussion Band. Despite his academic commitments, he continued to perform with the Cranes whenever possible. That same year, Paul Nick Mubiru was expelled from the band for repeatedly violating their strict code of conduct, which prohibited band members from smoking and drinking. He was replaced by Rock Luganzi, a first-year student at

Makerere University who had honed his bass guitar skills in the Kisubi Percussion Band. Even before arriving at Makerere, Luganzi had already made a name for himself as a recording artist. Still in his teens, he had captured public attention in 1962 with a string of beautifully crafted Kenyan twist songs, including Ssabasajja Luwangula Twist (The Great King and Conqueror Twist), Musayi Muto (Youthful One), and Omulungi Amata (The Beautiful As Milk), all released on the CMS label. He also recorded Njagala Ontegeze (Want You to Let Me Know) and Petula (a female name) on AGS's Super label.

Eddy Masembe also left the band to focus on his job at Uganda's Treasury Department in Kampala. His position as lead guitarist was filled by Joy King Mungaya, another Makerere University student and alumnus of St. Henry's College, Kitovu, where he had been a prominent member of the school band. Billy Mbowa also left the Cranes and briefly partnered with Ssenkebejje to record as "Billy Tony Cousins." They released two mellow ballads, Honey Mpuliriza (Honey Listen to Me) and Suzan. Honey Mpuliriza tells the story of a girl determined to love her boyfriend despite opposition from her parents due to his poor background. Suzan is a love song about a young man declaring his unwavering affection for the woman he intends to marry:

> Dad, please allow me to marry Suzan
> to live with the only one I have chosen.
> None of the other girls you suggest please me.
> Suzan is the only girl in my heart.
> Suzan is the flower among all girls.
> She is my beloved, my twin.
> I want you to know she is the one—
> the one I have chosen and who truly deserves me.

Billy Mbowa's departure from the music scene followed the recording of Honey Mpuliriza and Suzan. His passion for music had waned, and he decided to prioritize his studies. He enrolled in a five-year automobile mechanic training course offered by the Uganda Company, a British-founded enterprise established in 1900 that played a crucial role in developing Uganda's infrastructure, including roads, railways, and communication lines. In an August 1966 interview with Uganda's *People* newspaper, Mbowa explained his reasons for leaving the Cranes despite his success as a musician and songwriter: "My time for rehearsals is very limited, and I do not want to commit myself to anything I cannot fulfill."

Born in 1949 in Luwafu-Makindye, Mbowa was neighbors with the brothers Paul Nick Mubiru and John Mukasa. His father was a respected medical practitioner in the area. Mbowa attended Aggrey Memorial School and Bishop Tucker College, Mukono. His compositions included commercially successful recordings made with the AGS Boys, such as Jane Wange (My Jane), Aida, Guma Dear Wange (Be Strong My Dear), and Mirembe Wange (My Mirembe). However, none of his songs were ever recorded with the Cranes.

Despite Mbowa's departure, his close friend Tony Ssenkebejje remained with the Cranes, albeit intermittently, and became one of the band's most influential members. Born in 1949 in Jinja to Paul Kitata, a World War II veteran who served in Burma with the King's African Rifles, and Joyce Nalubega, Ssenkebejje later moved with his family to Kampala. He attended Mengo Primary and Junior School, St. Mary's College, Kisubi, and Lubiri Secondary School. He sang in the Mengo Primary and Junior School choir and the Saint Paul's Cathedral Namirembe choir. Although a bright student who excelled academically and could have pursued higher education at Makerere University, Ssenkebejje opted for a career in music after completing his studies at Lubiri Secondary School. A multi-instrumentalist, he played lead, rhythm, and bass guitars, as well as drums, having learned to play the guitar around 1964 from fellow teenager Sulaiman Mayanja.

Rock Luganzi is credited with revitalizing the Cranes after the departure of Mbowa, Masembe, and Paul Nick Mubiru. A first-year student at Makerere University, Luganzi brought a strong pan-African and anti-colonial perspective, common among university students at the time. He was critical of Ugandan bands that focused on covering English songs and shifted the Cranes' emphasis towards composing and performing original songs in the Luganda language. He was instrumental in defining the band's distinctive sound, blending rock and roll with Congolese rumba. Luganzi's influence was evident at one of the Cranes' most memorable performances, held at Makerere University's Main Hall as Kampala's nightlife began to recover from the curfew. The university was hosting its annual independence dance, a popular event attracting a diverse audience of students, faculty, politicians, civil servants, and prominent members of the military and business community. The guest of honor was Sir Egbert Udo Udoma, the Nigerian-born, Oxford-trained Chief Justice of Uganda.

The Cranes delivered a high-energy performance, unveiling their original Luganda compositions, which had yet to be recorded. The Cranes' first recording session took place in 1968 at Chandarana's studio in Kericho, Kenya, where they recorded for the Wachezaji label. Unlike many other musicians who relied on Chandarana's studio house band, the Cranes used their own instrumentalists. The lineup for this session included Joy King Mungaya on lead guitar, Rock Luganzi on bass and vocals, Tony Ssenkebejje on rhythm guitar and vocals, Sammy Kawuma on tumba drums, Wasswa "Rocky" Birigwa on vocals, Louise Bagenda on vocals, and Clyde Mayanja on maracas. This talented ensemble produced a collection of memorable songs. Ssenkebejje and Luganzi shared lead vocals on Njagala Nkuwane (I Want to Celebrate You). Luganzi sang lead on Beera Mwesigwa (Be Truthful). Louise Bagenda joined Ssenkebejje and Luganzi on Getu, Yogera Kyoliko (State Your Intentions), and Olabye Okuswala (Shame on You).

Despite their initial recording success, the Cranes faced persistent internal struggles and lineup changes that threatened their existence. Throughout their more than ten years of activity, the band was plagued by internal frictions and teetered on the brink of collapse on numerous occasions. One of their biggest challenges occurred in June 1968 when Sammy Kawuma, the bandleader, left to join Kaumba's Vipers band at New Life nightclub. That same year saw the departure of Louise Bagenda and Bumoze. Louise joined the Apolo Jambos, the resident band at the Apolo Hotel, where she teamed up with Taib Mutyaba and Joy Lehai Kanyarutokye (the 1968 Miss Uganda) to form a formidable musical force. She continued her recording career primarily as a backup vocalist through numerous collaborations. In 1968, Louise achieved significant success with a duet alongside Fred Kanyike and Eddie Kanyike on the track Otegese Ki (What Arrangements Are in Place?), backed by a group of session musicians that Kanyike referred to as the Nile Band, not to be confused with the River Nile Band he would later form in the mid-1970s.

Ssenkebejje, who had returned to the Cranes after his brief departure with Mbowa, also decided to leave and pursue a solo career. Meanwhile, the demands of academic life at Makerere University forced Rock Luganzi to leave the band. With the departure of these key members, Clyde Mayanja remained as the sole original member of the Cranes, struggling to hold the group together. Adding to the challenges, a dispute arose between Mayanja and Sammy Kawuma over the ownership of the band's instruments and the Cranes brand. This dispute threatened to fracture friendships and remained unresolved for a time. The instruments were kept in storage while the band explored ways to resolve the disagreement and satisfy both parties. Despite these setbacks, Mayanja was determined to revive the Cranes' fortunes. With his charm and exceptional organizational skills, he set about recruiting new members. By the end of 1969, he had assembled an impressive group of talented musicians. To fill the void left by Bumoze and Ssenkebejje, Mayanja recruited several teenagers from Kampala's secondary schools, including Jessy Gitta Kasirivu on bass guitar and the shy 15-year-old Eddy Ganja on rhythm guitar. Ganja was a student at Kololo Senior Secondary School and the youngest member of the band.

Mayanja also strengthened the vocal section by bringing in Charles Ssekyanzi, the former lead vocalist for the Slingers, and the teenage phenom Moses Matovu, one of the lead vocalists of the Thunderbirds. Both Matovu and Ssekyanzi had been students at Kampala's Pillai Secondary School, and their shared musical ideas and experiences fostered a strong bond between them. This musical chemistry led to a fruitful partnership that would see the duo compose and record some of Uganda's greatest hits over the next thirty years. In 1970, both Ssekyanzi and Matovu released highly acclaimed songs that became instant sensations. Ssekyanzi had hits with Tokweka Kwagala (Don't Hide Love) and Beera Mwenkanya (Show Fairness), while Matovu's popular songs included Katonda Yakola Omukwano (God Created Love) and Ndaagana Kululwo (I Suffer Because of You).

The reconstituted Cranes lineup from August to December 1969 featured Jessy Gitta Kasirivu on vocals and bass guitar, Joy King Mungaya as bandleader and lead guitarist, Eddy Ganja on rhythm guitar and occasional vocals, Moses Matovu on vocals, Charles Ssekyanzi on vocals, John C. Ssentamu on vocals, Paddy Kamya on vocals, and John Clyde Mayanja on tumba drums. In late 1969, Clyde Mayanja successfully persuaded Sammy Kawuma to return to the Cranes from Raphael Kaumba's Vipers at New Life nightclub. Kawuma's return brought a truce and allowed the band to retrieve their instruments from storage. With this lineup, the Cranes renewed their contract with White Nile nightclub, continuing to entertain audiences at the "teenager dances." They also recorded several hit songs, including Charles Ssekyanzi's Onemye (Can't Manage You) and Paddy Kamya's Womerwa Emere (Savor the Food), both released on Shankar Dass's SDS label.

In addition to their own performances, the Cranes served as a popular backup band for various Ugandan musicians. They backed Jackson Mutesasira on his songs Okuffa (Dying) and Abawala Bansobedde (Girls are Incomprehensible) (Serenade label), Nelson Sabavuma's Ssenga Nkutumeko (Can I Send You, Aunt?) and Afuuwa Gugwe (Blow Your Own Trumpet) (USG label), Simon Kaate Nsubuga's Enywera Yerima (Endurance Tills the Land) and Gwenasima (The One I Chose) (Serenade label), and Charles Tibihika and Francis Mwirima's Jjaja Ndeba (Come and I See) and Ngenda Kweroha (Serenade label). Tibihika and Mwirima sang in the Runyankole-Rukiga language, and their songs drew on the folk rhythms of the Banyankole and Bakiga people of western Uganda.

The Congolese band King Jazz Band had been the main resident band at White Nile nightclub. However, by 1970, they faced persistent challenges renewing their work permits in Uganda. The government's increasing hostility towards foreign musicians, including threats to confine some of King Jazz Band's Congolese members to a refugee camp, led the band to return to Congo. This presented an opportunity for the Cranes. Joseph Kyeyune, the manager of White Nile nightclub, signed a new contract with the band, making them the principal in-house act. The Cranes continued playing the daytime weekend "teenager dances" while also entertaining the regular adult clubbers in the evenings. This demanding schedule proved unsustainable, and in October 1971, the band decided to stop performing the "teenager dances" and leave White Nile. They began performing as free agents at various nightclubs in Kampala and occasionally ventured into upcountry venues.

That same year, the Cranes introduced a new sound to their rumba repertoire: the tenor saxophone. Moses Matovu had completed his saxophone apprenticeship under the guidance of Mansur Akiki Bulegeya, an accomplished saxophonist with the Police Jazz Band. Matovu, in turn, trained Jeff Sewava on the tenor saxophone. Sewava made his official debut as a member of the Cranes in 1972 and would later play a crucial role in the formation of the Afrigo Band. Among the first Cranes songs to feature the saxophone were Matovu's Jimmy Sasira (Forgive Me Jimmy) and Jessy Gitta Kasirivu's Omukwano Gwa Lero (Love in These Days).

Around April 1972, the Cranes relocated to Arizona Nightclub. Their time there was brief, and by mid-1973, they had moved on to perform at the Silver Springs Hotel. The band's lineup during this period featured Sammy Kawuma, Tony Ssenkebejje, Eddy Ganja, Jessy Gitta Kasirivu, Moses Matovu, Charles Ssekyanzi, Jeff Sewava, and John Clyde Mayanja. The year 1973 proved to be the Cranes' most productive and commercially successful period. The band secured a deal with Serenade studios to release their records under their own eponymous label. The first releases under the Cranes label in 1973 were all major hits, receiving significant airplay on Radio Uganda. Tony Ssenkebejje released Twagalane (Let's Love One Another) and Aisa (a female name). Charles Ssekyanzi had hits with Rose Guma (Be Steadfast Rose) and Tubyerabire (Let's Forget It). Jessy Gitta

Kasirivu departed from romantic themes, focusing instead on celebrating family stability with songs like Amaka Kikulu Nnyo (A Home is Very Important) and Amaka Kyamuwendo (A Home is Priceless). He also composed and recorded songs promoting good moral and work ethics, such as Todulanga (Never Ridicule) and Omunafu (Slacker). Moses Matovu's contributions included Sifayo (I Don't Care), Wapi Sofiya (Where is Sofiya?), Mundeke (Leave Me Alone), and the tongue-in-cheek Ekadde (Sugar Momma), a perennial favorite that humorously extols the virtues of a sugar momma over the youthful beauty of a young girl:

You have pretty looks—
you're a youthful girl, even dazzlingly so.
I know you're young and always neat,
but you lack those essential qualities.
You tease me because I'm with a sugar momma,
but you don't understand why—
even though I'm as youthful as you,
I chose a sugar momma because she treats me right.
You've abandoned our heritage;
when we see a stunner, we should be excited.
But no—
leave me be with my sugar momma,
for she's the one I truly love.

In August 1974, the Cranes suffered a devastating loss, the biggest tragedy in the band's history. Jessy Gitta Kasirivu, the bassist and vocalist, was a charismatic young man who stood at an impressive 6 feet 2 inches tall. Born in Nakwero village on Gayaza road on January 27, 1952, to Mr. Gitta, an attorney, and Kasalina "Kate" Nakagwa, a businesswoman in Mengo township, Jessy spent much of his childhood with his grandmother. He attended various schools, including Namirembe Primary School, Norman Junior Secondary School, Kololo Secondary School, Mityana Secondary School, and finally back to Kololo Secondary School, where he graduated in 1968.

From a young age, Jessy developed a deep love for music. One person who particularly influenced him was Michael "Mike" Mulira, a close family friend and member of the Beards, the school band at King's College, Budo. Mike Mulira had recorded a song called Counting the Stars, which, though not widely known in Uganda, was one of Jessy's favorites. In 1967, Jessy joined the Love Birds, the Kololo Secondary School music band, which briefly performed at the "teenager dances" at Florida nightclub. After a short stint working for a soya company in 1969, Jessy went to Nairobi to attend a railway training school, where he excelled.

Jessy's musical influences included Christopher Ssebadduka, Tabu Ley Rochereau, and Curtis Mayfield. Although Ssebadduka is generally remembered as a kadongo kamu artist, his repertoire was broader than often assumed. In the early 1960s, he also ventured into Ugandan pop, releasing songs like Mwami (Husband) and Birungi (a female name) on the CMS label. These tracks, melodic and accessible, expanded Ssebadduka's appeal beyond traditional audiences and left a mark on younger musicians like Jessy. In the first half of 1974, Jessy released one of his greatest and, tragically, last hits, Byetulaba (What We See). This breezy and defiant song used the metaphor of dressing to describe love that could be changed on a whim, lamenting the betrayal of a deceitful lover who showed little regard for their partner's feelings. Jessy had also spoken about other compositions he was working on, including two English songs, Mama Turn On and Don't Blackmail Me. The Cranes had occasionally experimented with English-language recordings, such as Eddy Ganja's funk-inspired songs Hurry On Down and I Have Got a Feeling in 1972, but these had not gained much popularity in rumba-obsessed Uganda.

Jessy's English songs were never recorded. Don't Blackmail Me was listed on the band's 1974 LP, recorded by Uganda Record Agencies Ltd., but was ultimately replaced with Tony Ssenkebejje's What's Love. The LP included other notable tracks like Yiga Muno (Learn Your Partner), Musa (a male name), Bakusiima (Accepted), Byetulaba, Wananchi (Ordinary Citizens), Nakugondera (Will Be Obedient), Ekitiibwa Kyo (Your Dignity), Joy, and Betty. Byetulaba became a massive hit, receiving extensive airplay on Radio Uganda, particularly from the popular DJ and presenter Charles Korokoto. The Ugandan public, always eager to interpret song lyrics, began to speculate that the song was about Idi Amin's 18-year-old girlfriend, Sarah Kyolaba, who had also been Jessy's lover. Sarah was one of the two go-go dancers in the Army's Revolutionary Suicide Mechanized Regiment Band based in Masaka, southern Uganda. The other dancer was Zuena, from Mbale in eastern Uganda.

Rumors circulated that Amin was displeased by the song and Jessy's continued relationship with Sarah. The rumors grew darker by the day, heavy with dread. On the night of Sunday, August 4, 1974, Jessy and fellow Cranes bandmate Charles Ssekyanzi finished a set at the Little Flower nightclub, where the band held a standing residency. Just past midnight, the two musicians took a taxi back to their shared apartment in Old Kampala. The streets were quiet. The city slept. What they did not know was that they had been followed. Lurking in the shadows were men from the State Research Bureau, Amin's feared secret police, known for making people disappear without a trace. As Jessy reached for the door to their apartment, the silence shattered. The operatives struck with brutal precision. In the scuffle that followed, Jessy was seized and thrown into the trunk of a white Peugeot 504. He was never seen again. Though no official explanation was ever given, it is widely believed that Jessy Gitta Kasirivu met his end that night at the hands of the regime's enforcers, punished for a love affair and a song that went too far. The Dutch journalist Michiel van Oosterhout documented the haunting events surrounding Jessy Kasirivu's disappearance in the film Bwana Jogoo: The Ballad of Jessy Gitta.

Despite the beautiful music they made, the Cranes were continually bedeviled by challenges that made it difficult to maintain a stable lineup. The band experienced a constant turnover of personnel due to various factors. Some members were not full-time musicians and had to prioritize their academic pursuits or day jobs in the civil service or private sector. Others left due to disagreements over rules they perceived as restrictive or unreasonable, or because of conflicts with management. While financial compensation was a factor, the musicians' primary motivation was not monetary. They found greater reward in the joy their music brought to tens of thousands of adoring fans and in the national and regional recognition they received for their creativity and hard work.

In October 1973, just months after launching their most ambitious recording project, Tony Ssenkebejje, Moses Matovu, Charles Ssekyanzi, and Jeff Sewava left the Cranes. Sewava began laying the groundwork for what would eventually evolve into the Afrigo Band. This presented a challenge for Clyde Mayanja, as the band was contractually obligated to entertain guests at Silver Springs Hotel, and he was concerned about the potential reputational and financial repercussions of breaking the contract. To fulfill their obligations, Mayanja turned to another Ugandan band, The Tames, who had previously played at Silver Springs for most of 1972 before moving to Nile Hotel. The hotel management welcomed The Tames back as the official house band, allowing the Cranes to temporarily regroup.

With several key members having departed, Mayanja brought in new musicians to strengthen the group. These included Edward Kajura on bass guitar, Paddy Banks Nsubuga on rhythm guitar, and vocalists Philly Bongole Lutaaya, Moses Kaggwa Kilyango, and Kiyingi Davies, also known as 'King Davies.' The new recruits complemented the existing core of Eddy Ganja on lead guitar, Sammy Kawuma on drums and bandleader duties, and John Clyde Mayanja himself. Throughout the 1970s, several other notable Ugandan musicians also played with the Cranes, including Anthony Kyeyune on trumpet, Fred Luyombya Sendaula on bass guitar, George Mulindwa on rhythm guitar, and Fred Muyanja Sebulime on vocals.

In March 1974, the "defectors", Tony Ssenkebejje, Moses Matovu, Charles Ssekyanzi, and Jeff Sewava, returned to the Cranes. However, Jeff Sewava left for good three months later to pursue his dream of forming his own band, which materialized in 1975 with the official launch of the Afrigo Band. The decline of the Cranes was gradual, marked by a series of high-profile departures that weakened the band's cohesion and creative output. Around the same time that Sewava left, the Cranes also lost Philly Lutaaya, who had been with the band for nine months, and Eddy Ganja, who opted to join the newly formed River Nile Band, managed by Fred Kanyike's Rwenzori Studios. Both Lutaaya and Ganja maintained that their decision was not driven by discord but by a desire to explore new musical directions. However, Ganja's tenure with the River Nile Band was brief; when the group disbanded in April 1975, he returned to the Cranes.

Meanwhile, in February 1975, Tony Ssenkebejje left Uganda for Kenya, seeking new opportunities in Nairobi and Mombasa. He played for various bands, including the Spartans and the Vikings, the latter with whom he spent seven years performing at the Reef Hotel in Mombasa before returning to Uganda in 1990. Even outside the Cranes, Ssenkebejje remained a sought-after musician, recording several solo projects in the early 1970s, including Nsoyiwa (Forgive Me), Ensi Netolovu (The World is Round), and Cissy. Earlier in his career, he had collaborated with Simon Kaate Nsubuga on Eva (distinct from Eva by Tony and Billy Mbowa). In 1968, at the request of Israel Magembe, he and Geoffrey Nsereko recorded renditions of Magembe's Omukwano Gwaffe Guffe (Let Our Love Die) and Sherry Wange (My Sherry), released on the Serena label. Ssenkebejje and Nsereko were not credited for the songs. Over the years, Ssenkebejje played with various bands, including Lake Quintet and Joseph Ndugga's Top Ten Band, but it was with the Cranes that he became a household name.

The frequent reshuffling of members began to undermine the Cranes' cohesiveness and creative momentum. By 1975, however, the band experienced a brief revival with the release of several successful tracks. Former River Nile Band members Fred Muyanja Sebulime, Eddie Ganja, and David Kiyingi emerged as strong vocalists, each contributing to the group's renewed energy. Their experiments with the Congolese cavacha rhythm yielded notable hits. Sebulime's Monica, Ganja's Nzena Nkoze (The Whole of Me Wasted), and Kiyingi's Marcellinah (a female name), featuring infectious rhythm guitar and syncopated snare drums that produced a giddy, pattering beat, were all recorded on the Cranes Edition label in 1975 and became major successes. For a brief moment, with the band now based at Little Flowers, the Cranes appeared to recapture their earlier popularity.

However, they continued to struggle in regaining the creative spark that had once defined them.

However, Jessy Gitta Kasirivu's disappearance and presumed death cast a dark shadow over the band. His fate, part of the systematic terror that defined Idi Amin's regime, was a chilling reminder of the dangers faced by Ugandans under the military dictatorship. The Cranes had initially welcomed Amin's ascent to power in 1971, celebrating his ouster of Milton Obote, who was deeply unpopular in central Uganda, with the song Twawona Okufa (We Escaped Death). The song denounced the state of emergency imposed in 1966, condemned Obote's arbitrary arrests of political opponents, and lauded Amin as a savior. Ironically, just a few years later, the very same regime they had praised was responsible for the disappearance of one of their own. Between 100,000 and 300,000 Ugandans were tortured or murdered under Amin, and Jessy's vanishing was a tragic embodiment of the era's brutality.

The economic turmoil of the mid-1970s compounded the Cranes' struggles. Uganda's economy was in freefall, with soaring inflation, a collapsing export sector, and a severe foreign exchange crisis. Revenues from key cash crops like coffee and cotton had dwindled due to government mismanagement, and what little foreign income remained was funneled into Amin's military apparatus rather than productive industries. The infamous 'whiskey shuttle' flights, which used Uganda Airlines Boeing 707s and a Lockheed Hercules C-130 to transport luxury goods for the military elite between Entebbe, Melbourne, and London, became a potent symbol of the era's deep economic inequalities, as ordinary Ugandans faced mounting hardship.

This economic downturn also affected the music industry. Recording studios faced production delays, and access to musical equipment and records became scarce. A frustrated fan of the Cranes voiced his concerns in *Munno* magazine on October 21, 1974, lamenting, "Between 1965 and 1972, they released a record almost every week, and it was still difficult to buy their records as they sold out quickly. But now they have not released any new songs since Omunafu and Rose." Band leader Sammy

Kawuma responded, assuring fans that new material had been recorded and was awaiting release. However, the harsh reality was that the country's economic collapse had crippled the production and distribution of music.

As 1975 progressed, Uganda's music scene was evolving. Peterson Tusibira Mutebi and his Tames Band had become the dominant force in rumba, while new bands such as the Flames, led by former Cranes member Moses Kaggwa Kilyango and the flamboyant guitarist Hanny Sensuwa, were gaining prominence. The Cranes, now performing at John Gombya's Topaz nightclub in Najjanankumbi, found themselves not far from other popular establishments of the time, including Emmanuel Ntananga's Green Bar and the Happy Land nightclub. Despite the proximity to this vibrant nightlife, they struggled to draw crowds. Morale was at an all-time low, and the band was running out of options. Desperate to stabilize the lineup, the Cranes recruited Fred Luyombya to replace Jessy Gitta Kasirivu on bass guitar. Luyombya's tenure was brief, and his departure forced the band to make an unprecedented decision. They hired a Congolese bassist, the first and only non-Ugandan musician ever to join the Cranes, a group that had always taken great pride in being a fully Ugandan band competing with the Congolese. However, this move did little to salvage their fortunes. The constant departures had eroded the band's creative core, and their inability to produce new music became glaring.

By January 1977, it was clear that the Cranes could no longer sustain themselves. Clyde Mayanja and Sammy Kawuma made the heart-wrenching decision to officially disband the group, marking the end of a journey that had spanned over a decade and left an indelible imprint on Uganda's popular music heritage. The Cranes had weathered political upheaval, economic instability, and internal discord, yet still managed to produce some of the most beloved songs of their era. In many ways, the dissolution of the Cranes mirrored the broader state of Uganda, a country that had once brimmed with promise but was now grappling with uncertainty and despair.

Another significant figure among the teenage musicians who shaped Uganda's music scene in the aftermath of the turbulent 1966 Uganda Crisis was Geoffrey Nsereko. Born in 1948, he was the older half-brother of musician Wasswa "Rocky" Birigwa, sharing the same mother, Mrs. Aida Nantongo. Growing up in the Kampala neighborhood of Katwe laid the foundation for their early musical experiences. Following the 1966 crisis, when nightclubs began hosting daytime dances for teenagers, this vibrant environment nurtured a new generation of Ugandan musicians, including Nsereko.

Growing up in Katwe, a rapidly urbanizing and multi-tribal community, Nsereko was exposed to a diverse range of musical influences, including Kenyan, Ugandan, Congolese, and Western styles. Katwe, characterized by its challenging living conditions and burgeoning population, became a hub for rural migrants seeking opportunities in Kampala. Residential areas, particularly those along the railway tracks, were often overcrowded and lacked basic infrastructure. Despite these conditions, Katwe pulsed with ingenuity. It was the beating heart of "Made in Uganda," where locals improvised, invented, and got things done.

Nsereko's musical journey began in his childhood, as he sang in both his elementary school and church choirs. This early experience helped him develop an ear for melody and rhythm. In 1966, he joined the Thunderbirds, who held a daytime residency at the White Nile Club. During his time with the Thunderbirds, Nsereko shared the stage with future musical luminaries such as Moses Matovu. During his time with the Thunderbirds, Selemani, the bandleader of King Jazz, had been deeply impressed by Nsereko's vocal talent. He noted the brightness and clarity of his tone, as well as his ability to deliver lyrics with genuine emotion. Comparisons to the renowned Ecklas Kawalya were frequent, with many predicting Nsereko would become his successor. Both artists were celebrated for their deliberate and precise diction in their native Luganda.

In the latter half of 1966, Nsereko and his brother Wasswa Birigwa embarked on a defining journey to Nairobi to record at the AGS studio. This session became a signature moment in their musical careers, as their work, released on the AGS Super label, achieved widespread popularity and firmly established them as emerging stars in Uganda's evolving music scene. Their notable hits included Joy Tonyiga (Don't Get Mad Joyce) and Rocky Tonenya (Don't Blame Me Rocky). Joy Tonyiga borrowed its melody from Alphonso Epayo's Negro Congolese hit Mobio Margo, which he performed with Orchestre Negro Succes. Nsereko also released solo hits such as Nakwagala Obwedda (Loved You For A Long Time) and Okunenya Teriba Bbogo (Blame Me, But Don't Shout at Me) on the same label. These songs, fierce and delicate, won the hearts of Ugandan audiences, offering both emotional solace and vibrant rhythms. It is around this time that Selemani, recognizing Nsereko's exceptional talent, recruited him into King Jazz in 1967. This placed Nsereko among a select group of Ugandan musicians to join the prestigious Congolese band, which also included Fred Masagazi and guitarist Mutebi.

Geoffrey Nsereko became a highly sought-after backup vocalist, lending his talents to Fred Kanyike's series of songs released in 1968 on the HMV label. These included hits such as Sister Calorina, Abayekera (Rebels), and Wasala Magezi Kyi (What Cunning Plan Did You Hatch?). He also collaborated with Tony Ssenkebejje on renditions of Israel Magembe's songs, Millie Gwe Sherry (My Sherry) and Omukwano Gwaffe Guffe (Let Our Love Die). His 1969 solo releases, Ester and Owalana Nze Lwaki (Why Must You Fight Me), backed by Sonko's Orchestre Melo Success and released on the Serenade label, were also well-received.

In 1970, when King Jazz returned to the Congo, Nsereko briefly joined the Florida Fiesta Band at the Florida Nightclub. However, he soon returned to the White Nile Club when Joseph Salongo Kyeyune, in need of a replacement for King Jazz, formed the White Nile Band. Nsereko reunited with guitarist John Mutebi, who had briefly followed King Jazz to the Congo before returning to Uganda. During this period, Nsereko played a crucial role in maintaining the White Nile band's momentum, attracting audiences with his vocal prowess.

Despite his efforts, the absence of Selemani and King Jazz was keenly felt by the White Nile's patrons. Nsereko continued to produce hits, releasing Onumbiraki (Why Attack Me?) and Grace Kyengaamba (Grace, Hear Me Out) on Chandarana's Furaha label, and Abantu Ba Uganda (The People of Uganda) and Winnie Nkwagala (I Love You Winnie) on the Philips label in 1971. Winnie Nkwagala was a deeply personal track, it was a heartfelt tribute to a beloved Kampala young lady named Winnie, whose grace and charm had won him over completely. The song's tender lyrics and soulful melody conveyed a sense of sincerity and vulnerability, and the public experienced his genuine affection and enduring love for Winnie. In 1974, Nsereko joined the short-lived River Nile Band, where he recorded what would be his final song, Kabaseke (Let Them Laugh).

In the post-1966 music scene, two brothers emerged as recording stars: Charles Kirunda and Eddie Rodgers Kabuye. Born into a well-to-do family in Kampala, they enjoyed a privileged upbringing, with a home attended by servants, and received an excellent education at Bukoto Primary School, St. Jude's Naguru, and Kampala Grammar Secondary School. Their musical journey began unexpectedly on their family's countryside farm. One of the laborers, a gifted guitarist, sparked their fascination with Congolese popular music. Under his informal guidance, the brothers learned to play the guitar, setting them on a path toward musical discovery. Charles Kirunda's talent was evident early on; his teachers even appointed him school choir prefect due to his aptitude for music.

As teenagers, they formed a close bond with Fred Kigozi, a popular teen idol who embraced a rock-star lifestyle from an early age and later became an influential mentor. Kigozi helped shape their musical careers and even took Kirunda to Nairobi's Vedis Recording Company. There, Kirunda recorded his debut song, Madina Nsoyiwa (Forgive Me Madina), which paved the way for further hits such as Ntegenza Kyoliko (Tell Me What You Are Up To) and Nkwatira Ekisa (Have Pity On Me) in 1969 on the Philips label. Kirunda continued to score hits with tracks like Molly Omwagalwa (My Sweet Molly), Agnes, and Tewesiga Engambo (Be Wary of Gossip).

Eddie Rodgers Kabuye also made a significant impact. In 1969, he released one of the era's most successful songs, Enaku Ye Kisajja (The Suffering of Men), on the Lamore label, alongside Mon Amie Louiza (My Love Louiza). Later, Eddie pursued a career in the Uganda Army, rising to the rank of major, but he continued his musical endeavors by releasing Enaku Ye Kikyala (The Suffering of Women), although it did not achieve the same popularity as his earlier hit. Both brothers focused primarily on recording their music rather than performing live and distrusted the environment of nightclubs. In particular, Charles Kirunda was wary of singing in clubs. He believed that club owners exploited musicians by demanding long hours for meager pay.

As the influence of the Cranes began to fade, and artists such as Geoffrey Nsereko and the siblings Charles Kirunda and Eddie Kabuye were no longer the musical forces they once were, other artists solidified their presence, taking firm hold of Kampala's nightlife with commanding performances and enduring popularity. Musicians like Peterson Mutebi and his Tames band pressed forward with confidence, drawing devoted crowds and lighting up dance floors with some of the biggest hits of the decade. Their success proved that Uganda's popular music scene was far from dwindling. The disbandment of the Cranes marked not a conclusion but a shift in the musical landscape, as audiences turned to new favorites who continued to carry the torch of innovation and entertainment.

CHAPTER 13

Peterson Mutebi and the Tames: Dancing Through a Decade of Nyegenya

The Squares were a Ugandan band composed of teenagers and young adults, founded in June 1968 by brothers Sam Kigozi (band leader and vocalist) and Jimmy Mayambala (bass guitar). After initial struggles to form a cohesive band, they had their breakthrough in 1969 by recruiting several up-and-coming young artists, many of whom hailed from comfortable middle-class backgrounds. The talented lineup included Peterson Tusubira Mutebi (also known as Amata Agataffa – Milk That Never Dies) as vocalist, Billy Herbert Mutebi on lead guitar, Frank Mbalire on rhythm guitar, Fred Kigozi as vocalist, Henry Musisi as vocalist, Fred Tebuseke on trumpet, and John Makubuya on drums. The Squares gained a reputation for their skill and were considered strong contenders against other prominent bands like the Cranes. They began performing at teen dances in Kamulu's Kololo Club before relocating to Kampala's Silver Springs Hotel in 1970.

Among the Squares' members, Fred Kigozi stood out as a notable talent. Born in Bukasa, just a few miles from Kampala, in 1952, Kigozi came from a prominent Christian family. His father, Rev. Ssempala, was an ordained Church of Uganda minister, while his mother took care of the household. Because of his father's vocation, the family frequently moved, leading Kigozi to attend various schools, including Luwero Secondary School, Bishop Tucker in Mukono, and Saint Francis's Tutorial College in the Kampala suburb of Natete. Kigozi's resolve to pursue music took firm root in 1967 while he was studying at Saint Francis's Tutorial College.

Fortuitously, Fred Kanyike, the revered Ugandan musician and talent scout for AGS Studios in Nairobi, lived nearby the school. Kigozi pitched his first song and auditioned for him, leaving a strong impression. Kigozi, an easygoing but ambitious young man, was determined to succeed in a music scene largely dominated by Congolese music. Convinced of Kigozi's exceptional abilities, Kanyike took him to AGS Studios to record his first single featuring Effumbe (Civet Cat) and Kate (a female name). Released on AGS's Rock label, the single sold respectably. However, it was Kigozi's collaboration with Nairobi's Hodi Boys, with his close friend Herbert Musisi providing background vocals, on the songs Onkyayideki (Why Do You Rebuff Me?) and Mega Jukira (Remember Mega – a female name) that gave him his first major break. Ugandans took notice, and Kigozi's reputation as a serious musician was firmly established. Both Onkyayideki and Mega Jukira, originally recorded on the AGS label, are featured on the 1990s LP titled The Kampala Sound – 1960s Ugandan Dance Music, which highlights popular Ugandan hits from the 1960s.

Even after joining the Squares in 1968, Fred Kigozi continued his solo and collaborative projects. In 1968 and 1969, he teamed up with Orchestre Vox Nationale for support on tracks like Sirina Mpalana Nawe (I Have No Grudge Against You), Jukira Mwami Wange (My Hubby, Remember), and Vayo Gyoli Mary (Return From Where You Are, Mary), released on the Serenade label. Additionally, backed by the Orchestre Kampala Fiesta, which consisted mainly of Top Ten band musicians, Kigozi worked with the Paradise label, a small Kampala-based label, on songs like Cate Jaali (Cate Is There) and Bivudde Mukukola (It's From Working). It is no surprise that Kigozi sought opportunities to record his own compositions with other bands while he was a member of the Squares.

The Squares primarily performed covers of Congolese songs, alternating with English rock and roll hits by the Beatles. The band owners,

Sam Kigozi and Jimmy Mayambala, treated music more as a pastime than a serious pursuit. Coming from a wealthy family and holding well-paid day jobs, they were not concerned about their artists, including the band's standout vocalist, recording with other groups. As a result, the Squares had only a few recorded songs to their name. In 1971, after Idi Amin's overthrow of the Obote government, they released Twawona Ezike (We Survived the Ogre) and Mpulira Nyo Byongamba (I Truly Comprehend Your Words) on the Serenade label. Twawona Ezike was one of several songs that praised Idi Amin, portraying him as the benevolent liberator who had rescued Ugandans from Obote's oppressive regime.

While the band's founders were content to treat music casually, the rest of the group had far greater ambitions. Fred Kigozi, Billy Mutebi, Peterson Mutebi, Frank Mbalire, Fred Tebuseke, John Makubuya, and Henry Musisi shared a deep commitment to their craft. They longed to break away from the routine of performing covers and explore their own musical ideas through composition and recording. Among them, Fred Kigozi, Peterson Mutebi, Billy Mutebi, and Frank Mbalire had already built up an impressive portfolio of original songs, waiting for the right moment to bring them to a broader audience.

During the latter half of 1971, the Squares disbanded. Subsequently, in January 1972, Peterson Mutebi, who had obtained a loan from one of his sisters, Mary Sunday, to purchase instruments, invited Fred Kigozi, Billy Mutebi, Frank Mbalire, Fred Semwogerere Tebuseke, and John Makubuya to join him in forming a new band called the Tames. According to Peterson Mutebi, the name was chosen to challenge public misconceptions about musicians, who were often stereotyped as hard-drinking, drug-using, promiscuous individuals. He sought to erase the prevailing image of insouciant debauchery that many Ugandans associated with musicians, arguing instead that they were as decent and harmless as domestic animals. Shortly after the band was formed, Peterson secured a lucrative contract for the Tames to perform at Kampala's Silver Springs Hotel, where they played for most of 1972.

Not only was Peterson Tusubira Mutebi a gifted vocalist and songwriter, he was convivial by nature and had an uncanny ability to network and establish good relationships with important people. Peterson Tusubira Mutebi was born in 1951 in Salaama, then a sleepy village outside Kampala. His father was a Church of Uganda minister. Peterson pursued his education at Ndejje and graduated from Bombo Sudanese Secondary School in 1968. He came from a musical family: his grandparents, parents, and several siblings were musicians. His oldest sister, Mary Sunday, sang in church and performed with the Edden Jazz Band in Bombo. Recognizing Mutebi's vocal talents, Mary Sunday introduced him to public singing. During his student years at Bombo, Mary Sunday brought him along to her performances with the Edden Jazz Band, and when the band members discovered Mutebi's natural talent, they allowed him to join them on stage, covering beloved songs by Uganda's acclaimed artists such as Elly Wamala, Andrew Kyambadde, and Fred Kanyike.

Eseza Victoria, another sister, embarked on her own musical journey, pursuing music studies at Makerere University's famed Department of Music, Dance and Drama. Meanwhile, Mutebi's older brother Ssempala studied music at an American university. The family's strong musical roots inspired and fueled Mutebi's passion for music. Following his graduation from Bombo Sudanese, Mutebi embarked on a new chapter of his life. He secured a job with the Bata Shoe Company, where he worked as a salesman. Although the job paid well, Mutebi found himself increasingly drawn to music. He spent his evenings practicing, his weekends performing, and his days dreaming of a future where music took center stage. In 1969, he briefly joined forces with Andrew Kyambadde's short-lived Nova Jazz Band as a vocalist, all while juggling his responsibilities at Bata. Ultimately, Mutebi parted ways with the Nova Jazz Band and joined the Squares in 1969, stepping into the spotlight as the band's lead vocalist.

In early 1973, the Tames left Silver Springs after signing a contract with Uganda Hotels Limited, which saw them playing at Nile Hotel and Fairway Hotel in Kampala. Nile Hotel, in particular, offered exposure to a much larger crowd. By this time, the Tames had become a household name and enjoyed immense popularity throughout the country. During this short period, the original lineup of the Tames had recorded several chart-topping hits on the Kagaabe and Serenade labels, a remarkable feat that placed them at the center of the Ugandan music scene. Most of their songs paired romantic, emotionally layered lyrics with bright melodies. But in contrast to the rapid-fire pulse of Congolese soukous, the Tames settled into a steadier, medium-paced rhythm that soon became their defining sound. Some of their most beloved songs from that period included Peterson's Omukwano Gwewala (Long Distance Love), Kankutwale (Let Me Take You), Rose Sembera (Get Closer Rose), Leka Tusanyuke (Let's Be Happy), Tezali Mbiro (It Wasn't A Rush), Ekiwala (The Girl), and Regesie (a female name).

Meanwhile, Fred Kigozi continued to draw wide acclaim with a string of memorable compositions released on the Serenade label. These included Obuwomu Bw'omukwano (Sweetness of Love), Flavia (a female name), Omuwala Omulimba (Deceitful Girl), Cissy Komawo (Come Back Cissy), and Obe Wange (Be Mine). In his song Taxi, Kigozi's voice is fraught with urgency, bemoaning the absence of his sweetheart who has him worried:

> I swear this is my truth:
> I grow restless when she isn't near,
> so I'll hail a taxi just to reach her—
> to see my love and soothe my soul.

"Taxi" evokes a mood of profound longing, accentuated by Fred Tebuseke's saxophone, a luxuriant blend of bliss and euphoria. Towards the end of the song, Kigozi calls out to several taxis, but none stop to pick him up. One can imagine Kigozi flapping his arms in frustration at not being able to see his sweetheart. Notably, Kigozi also penned one of Mutebi's major hits of 1972, Funa Akujamu (Find One That Fits You), which featured a beautiful horn section and dazzling guitar work by Billy Mutebi, Frank Mbalire, and Fred Kigozi.

Within the Tames band, Frank Mbalire stood out as a dynamic presence, crafting rhythm-driven compositions charged with raw energy and relentless momentum. These songs included Etabu Y'emikwano (Trouble With Friendships or Fairweather Friends), Veronica (a female name), Muveko (Leave Her Alone), and his 1973 breakthrough hit, Bamulete (Bring Her). Interestingly, the melody of Bamulete bears a resemblance to Ndombe Opetum's Kamulete, a Lingala song recorded a few years earlier with Tabu Ley's Afrisa International. However, Mbalire insisted that the similarity was merely an uncanny coincidence.

The story of Bamulete begins not in a studio, but in a single, fleeting moment. It begins with a seventeen-year-old girl named Sarah Nsangi. In 1972, Sarah was a student at Tororo Girls School in Eastern Uganda, young, poised, and on the cusp of adulthood. During a short school break, she and three friends traveled to Kampala and found their way to Kololo Club, where the Tames were performing. The night pulsed with music, laughter, and the restless electricity of youth. From the stage, Frank Mbalire noticed them.

Among the group, Sarah stood out. There was something about her composure, something luminous yet reserved. She did not demand attention; she drew it. To the twenty-year-old Mbalire, who was shy by nature and more comfortable behind his instrument than in conversation, she seemed almost untouchable. Yet during a pause in the set, he did something uncharacteristic. He stepped down from the stage and approached the girls. Their exchange was brief. A few words, and a few smiles. Perhaps nothing more than polite conversation. And then it was over.

Sarah returned to school. Life moved on. Mbalire never saw her again, not for decades. But the moment lingered. It settled quietly in his memory, refusing to fade. The image of the girl at Kololo, radiant and self-contained, remained with him long after the music of that night had dissolved into silence. It is from that memory that Bamulete was born. The song was not merely about a school girl. It was about the ache of a moment that never had time to become anything more. It was about youth, possibility, and the quiet power of a single encounter to mark a heart forever. In writing Bamulete, Mbalire did what musicians so often do: he turned a passing glance into permanence, and a fleeting meeting into melody. In the song, Mbalire croons:

> Go, bring her—
> I haven't slept since the day she left our place.
> Food has lost its flavor,
> and even my tea no longer comforts me.
>
> It's all because of Sarah Nsangi.
> Go, bring her—the slender, tall one—swiftly.
>
> Listen carefully:
> I vowed that day never to change my heart,
> and that's why I urgently ask—bring her swiftly.

Frank Mbalire was born in 1952 in Natete to Joseph Yawe, the first Black Uganda postmaster general, and Dorothea Nakibuule Nambi. He attended the all-boys Mugwanya Preparatory School Kabojja, a Catholic boarding school founded by the Brothers of Christian Instruction on the outskirts of Kampala. Kabojja had a strong music program, and one of the prominent teachers was Rev. Brother Cornelius Onega. Frank graduated from Old Kampala Secondary School, where he played guitar in the school band, which predominantly consisted of Indian-Pakistani students. After graduating, Frank joined the Squares and reunited with his childhood friend, Billy Mutebi. Mbalire and Billy had attended Mugwanya Preparatory School together, and, though self-taught guitar players, their skills were greatly improved by Rev. Brother Cornelius Onega's guitar lessons. Another of their former schoolmates was Dede Majoro, a gifted solo guitarist whose path soon diverged from theirs. Majoro went on to play with the resident band at the International Hotel restaurant, where he performed alongside Herman Ssewanyana. Both would later rise to fame in Afrigo band, with Ssewanyana on conga drums and Majoro as lead guitarist, becoming key figures in shaping the band's distinctive sound.

Billy Herbert Kibuka Mutebi was born in 1950 in Kinaawa, a Natete subdivision. He grew up in a relatively affluent Ugandan family. His father, John Mukasa Lukwata, was a magistrate in the Buganda Kingdom government. His parents were keen on music, and his father bought him a guitar as a birthday present when he turned six. Billy would spend hours in his bedroom practicing. He attended Mugwanya Preparatory School Kabojja. Billy Mutebi graduated from Kampala's Lubiri Secondary School. He would later become one of the Tames' influential lead guitarists, arrangers, and songwriters, composing several of the band's successful and memorable songs. Billy Mutebi was also the lead vocalist on Prossy (a female name), Jalia (a female name), Munno Mu Kabi (A Friend in Need), and Ana Maria.

The original lineup of the Tames achieved phenomenal success and were arguably the first Ugandan group to release an extraordinary run of songs that appealed to the public in an incredibly short period. The Tames were a force of nature, and the sky appeared to be the limit. The band released numerous notable hits that consistently made the weekly top 10 charts compiled by Ugandan newspapers, including *Munno* and *The People*. The Tames songs that made the chart, and at times stayed on the list for many weeks, included Love Enzigumivu (Rock-hard Love), Ekikulu Zempisa (Character Is Everything), Oli Omu Jennifer (Only One Jennifer), and Byali Bya Kito (Youthful Ways). Peterson's 1973 Nyongera Ku Love (Show Me More Love) was a monster hit. A *Munno* newspaper journalist described the song as having "turned Kampala crazy." It was indeed constantly played on Radio Uganda:

> Wowo, wowo, Mama,
> My heart is overwhelmed,
> and my soul grows restless
> because of the babe I chose,
> whose face I haven't seen since daybreak.
> Mama, don't hurt me so,
> my dearest, wherever you are,
> your absence is a deep heartache.

My soul explodes, miya, miya;
my heart thuds, du, du.
Give me more love,
don't hold back;
show me more affection.
Lately, your love seems distant;
it appears you're not into me.
Please, show me the love you once gave.
Life is so delightful when you're by my side,
with Harriet next to me as we chitter-chatter.
But when you leave, I catch a fever,
and my love burns and swells.

In early 1973, Peterson announced plans to take the Tames to Nairobi to record an LP album. The project was widely touted as the first LP recorded by a Ugandan artist. However, the distinction of 'first' is subject to debate. Before the Tames, there had already been at least two LPs by Ugandan artists. One was Folk Songs and Dances of Uganda, performed by the Uganda Army Jazz Band and released as the inaugural album on the state-owned UG label. The other was Sanyu, an LP of traditional folk music by John and Rose Sendaula, issued in the late 1960s on the Swiss imprint VDE-Gallo Records. Arriving in Nairobi to record the album titled Love Enzigumivu (Rock-hard Love) were Peterson Mutebi, Fred Kigozi, Billy Mutebi, Frank Mbalire, Fred Semwogerere Tebuseke, and John Makubuya.

For the LP jacket, the band chose a photo featuring Peterson Mutebi seated on a stool, exuding confidence. Around him stood the remaining five band members, forming a tight semicircle of allegiance and quiet defiance, projecting swagger and ambition. Apart from Mutebi, the musicians wore tight-fitting long-sleeved shirts and knotted bandanas, their look unmistakably echoing the spirit of Jimi Hendrix. The photo projected a united front, with Peterson Mutebi positioned at the center to symbolize his prominent role within the group. However, beneath the surface, it concealed the internal struggles that were deeply affecting the band and threatening its very existence.

Despite the public perception of unity, tensions simmered within the Tames. From the start, band members had grown increasingly frustrated with what they saw as Peterson Mutebi's autocratic management style, which left them sidelined from important decisions about the band's direction. They felt ignored and disconnected, never granted access to the details of the contracts that Mutebi unilaterally signed with the venues where they performed. This lack of transparency amplified their sense of alienation and eroded their belief in the band's shared vision. Whispers and rumors circulated among the band members, suggesting that the contracts, particularly those with Uganda Hotels, were lucrative. Nonetheless, they found themselves barely scraping by in Kampala, where the cost of living had escalated following the expulsion of Ugandans of Indian-Pakistani heritage by Idi Amin. These murmurs fueled their growing disillusionment and reinforced the notion that they were being deprived of their rightful share of the band's success.

Shortly after returning from Nairobi in March 1973 from recording their debut LP on the Kagaabe International label, the band members resigned en masse and severed ties with Peterson Mutebi. Around this time, Fred Kanyike, Fred Masagazi, and Hadijja Namale were in the final phases of forming the Rwenzori Jazz Band. They were aware of the discontent within the Tames, and Fred Kanyike had been actively courting the disgruntled musicians for months to abandon Peterson Mutebi and join his new band. After parting ways with Peterson Mutebi, Frank Mbalire, Fred Kigozi, Billy Mutebi, John Makubuya, and Fred Semwogerere Tebuseke immediately joined the Rwenzori Jazz Band.

As a result, Peterson Mutebi found himself the sole remaining member of the Tames, left to navigate the uncertain future of the band on his own. The once-promising unity depicted on the intended jacket sleeve for the band's first LP had crumbled, revealing the underlying fractures and challenges that had ultimately torn the band apart. However, Peterson Mutebi was not one to easily give up. He refused to quit, vowing to breathe new life into the band and emerge stronger than ever. Through his networking ability and good fortune, he soon succeeded in assembling a spectacular lineup of new talent.

Before embarking on restoring the Tames, however, a sense of schadenfreude tinged his actions. As the production of the band's first LP was still underway and the artwork for the jacket sleeve had yet to be initiated, he deliberately erased his former bandmates from the jacket sleeve. This decision came despite his acknowledgement that they had contributed to what was arguably the band's best collection of songs up to that point. The original jacket sleeve photograph was replaced with one featuring the new band members.

The band's first LP was a huge success, featuring eight tracks from their earlier singles, including Love Enzigumivu, Oli Omu Jennifer, Ekikulu Zempisa, Bamulete, Ekiwala, Muveko, Byali Byakito, and President Amin. With his new band members and the success of the Tames' first LP release, Peterson Mutebi stood poised on the precipice of opportunity. He saw it as a chance to prove himself and display his artistic talent, which had been the driving force behind his decision to rebuild the band. The stage was set for a new era, one in which the band's future would be shaped not by past struggles but by the determination of its bandleader and the music he hoped would capture the hearts of the Ugandan public,

The newly formed Tames welcomed a group of talented musicians into its ranks, each bringing their own unique experiences and musical backgrounds. Christopher Mayanja, known for his drumming, had previously played with the Flames, White Nile Band, and the Afro Band. Deogratius "Deo" Matovu, a rhythm guitarist, had been mentored by the legendary Elly Wamala and had also been a member of the Afro Band alongside Christopher Mayanja. Fortuitously, the mass resignation of the Tames aligned perfectly with the Afro Band's recent splintering, allowing Peterson Mutebi to recruit both Mayanja and Matovu. Peter Kayiwa, a bass guitarist, had performed with the Marines at the Bonanza nightclub in Kitintale, as well as with John Sebirumbi's OK Jazz, Vox Fiesta, and the Flames. Charles Kalyokya, an up-and-coming vocalist, was brought on board directly from Kololo Secondary School, where he had made a name for himself as an influential member of the school band. Bernard "Simple" Gonza, a talented lead guitarist, honed his skills at St. Henry's College, Kitovu, where he starred in the school band. Persuaded by Mutebi, he dropped out of school to join the Tames. Peter "Super Ka'stone" Kabale, a vocalist and tumba player, would later reveal an exceptional command of the saxophone, earning a reputation for unmatched skill. He had also played with the Marines and, earlier in his career, with Mzee Bukenya's BKG Band.

The Tames performed at the Economic nightclub, former New Life, for a brief period. They also secured regular gigs every Saturday on the African Queen, an exclusively designed yacht for Lake Victoria. At the time, the yacht was operated by the profligate Ugandan tycoon, Mathew Odoki Opoka, who had made his fortune running a car tire business. The yacht set sail from Jjaja Marina in Munyonyo, bound for various islands. As the boat glided through the water, the band entertained guests with their music, lending a touch of enchantment to the journey.

By June 1973, Peterson Mutebi felt ready to elevate the band's success by traveling to Nairobi to record a series of songs with his new musicians. The band embarked on a successful tour of Nairobi, where Peterson Mutebi had negotiated gigs at various venues, including Hallians nightclub, Acadea nightclub, Woodly Club, and the Nairobi YWCA. They also released several singles in early 1974 on The Tames label. Notable releases were Mutebi's Ntwala Nfumbe (Take Me, Marry Me), Akawungeezi (The Evening), Mangalita (a female name), and Babra Harriet (a female name).

Upon returning from Nairobi, the Tames embarked on a tour of Ugandan towns, bringing their music to fans outside Kampala. In August 1973, they traveled to eastern Uganda, staging concerts at Soroti Hotel and Mt. Elgon Hotel in Mbale. This was followed by concerts in other towns, including a show in Masaka and another live concert in Mbarara. At every stop, the Tames were welcomed by enthusiastic crowds, and the venues were sold out.

In 1974, the Tames expanded their ranks even further. Tom Babi joined as a rhythm guitarist, Lawrence Sayiga took on the drums, and Francis Kigundu enriched the band's sound with his tumba skills. Musa and Willy Muwanga were added to the brass section, playing trumpets, while Sam Nsubuga joined as the band's technician. Tony Kalanzi, who had been with the Marines at Bonanza, was added as a vocalist and saxophonist. Other artists who were part of the Tames included Godfrey Kizito (drums), Deo Mukungu (bassist), Charles Kanaabi (vocalist), Ronald "Ringo" Ndema (vocalist), Willy Mubiru (vocalist), and George Mukasa (vocalist).

In addition to the new musicians, Peterson Mutebi also sought to enhance the band's stage presence by introducing a number of skilled dancers: Massy Nakiyingi, Hady Nakawuka, Edith "Edisa" Nansubuga, Balaba "Crazy-man" Matovu, Norah Bayiga, George Kyambadde, and Lazalo Lubega. The addition of these dancers infused a new energy into the Tames' performances, transforming the concerts into a dynamic visual spectacle and amplifying the crowd's exhilaration.

The dancers pioneered distinctive styles of dance, such as *Yeyo Nnyegenya*, *Digida*, and *Kabinubinu*, which were ingenious and cohesive fusions of traditional dances from various regions of Uganda. Their movements were synchronized with the band's music, seamlessly blending rhythm, melody, and choreography into a harmonious whole that expressed Uganda's cultural richness through its exquisite choreography.

The dancers were at their best when dancing to any of the band's kagutema genre songs, such as Peterson Mutebi's Munno Mulimu Oweddalu (There Is a Crazy One in Here) and Omugole Kimyula (Gorgeous Bride), or Bernard Gonza's upbeat and thrilling Kagutema. The latter was a rendition of Albert Ssempeke's 1953 recording. Ssempeke was a musician at the palace of Kabaka Mutesa II. Peterson Mutebi also released another kagutema song, which, like all their kagutema songs, was extremely popular. The kagutema songs brought out the very best in the dancers. Massy Nakiyingi, Norah Bayiga, Hady Nakawuka, and Edith Nansubuga led the charge, displaying their mastery of the Baakisimba and Nankasa dances. Hips quivered, arms were raised in spear-throwing gestures, bodies moved in graceful undulations, and feet struck the ground with remarkable agility and precision.

Balaba, George Kyambadde, and Lazalo Lubega, meanwhile, circled the stage on stilts while executing intricate Baakisimba and Nankasa movements. When the men finally descended from their stilts, they joined the women for one of the evening's most electrifying sequences. Their pas de deux unfolded in a playful exchange of rhythm and movement, exhilarating and sensuous at once, and it often sent ripples of laughter and delighted murmurs through the audience. Commenting on the Yeyo Nnyegenya dance, a journalist writing in the *Voice of Uganda* newspaper in February 1975 observed that "it demands a strong will and determination to carry out such an acrobatic performance." Indeed, yeyo nnyegenya was an exacting, dynamic dance routine that required remarkable agility and precision.

In 1974, the Tames secured a temporary haven at Silver Springs Hotel, which granted them rehearsal space in exchange for occasional performances. However, their search for a permanent home continued, and they found themselves signing short-term contracts to play at various venues throughout Kampala. City Bar, Standard Hotel, Pearl Afrique Club on Rashid Khamis Road (now Martin Road) in Old Kampala, and Equatoria Hotel were just a few of the venues where the Tames staged their performances.

By 1975, the Tames had solidified their position as one of Uganda's leading musical acts. Sensing the momentum and growing demand for their music, Peterson Mutebi made a strategic decision to embark on countrywide tours and stage shows while maintaining an ambitious recording schedule. To establish a dedicated space for rehearsals and artistic exploration, Peterson Mutebi constructed Tamesland in Makerere-Kavule.

In the 1970s, Makerere-Kavule was a working-class neighborhood tucked between Makerere University Hill and Mulago Hill, sitting astride Bombo Road, which was lined with small shops, informal markets, and clusters of brick and timber houses. Students from Makerere, hospital workers from Mulago, and traders from nearby Bwaise and Kawempe passed through daily, giving the area a lively, rough-edged energy. Despite its modest appearance, Kavule thrived with the daily hustle of Kampala's growing population. Tamesland in Makerere-Kavule became the band's home base, a hub of musical activity where the band members could rehearse, compose new songs, and experiment with different sounds and styles.

Unlike many Ugandan artists such as the Cranes, who struggled to secure foreign exchange for recording trips to Nairobi, Peterson Mutebi and the Tames enjoyed a more favorable position. This was largely due to Mutebi's connection to Bombo town, where he had attended Bombo Sudanese Secondary School. In Bombo, residents proudly claimed Mutebi as their own; he was regarded as a hometown hero. Bombo town was home to a vibrant Nubian community, and Mutebi, being a polyglot, was also fluent in the local Bombo Nubian dialect.

It is worth noting that Idi Amin had spent a significant part of his childhood in Bombo town. Although Amin's father hailed from the Kakwa tribe and his mother from the Lugbara tribe, Amin closely identified with the Nubian community. Just like him, the Nubians were predominantly Muslim, setting them apart from the Kakwa and Lugbara tribes, who were primarily Christians. During his presidency, Amin heavily relied on the Bombo Nubian community for his security needs, including staffing the infamous State Research Bureau with its members. However, it is important to recognize that the majority of the Nubian community strongly disapproved of Amin's excesses and abuse of power and did not support his authoritarian regime, just like many of their fellow Ugandans. Nevertheless, the association between the Bombo Nubian community and Amin's security forces granted them a disproportionate influence over political and economic power.

With his debonair presence and fluent command of the Bombo Nubian dialect, Peterson Mutebi developed a strong network of influential Nubian friends. These relationships proved invaluable. They helped him access scarce foreign exchange to finance the Tames Band's travel and recording sessions in Nairobi, and they led to invitations that were rarely extended to civilian musicians. Because of his rising fame and ties to the Bombo

Nubian military elite, Mutebi achieved what few civilian musicians ever did. He and the Tames Band were invited to perform at military venues typically reserved for army ensembles. For example, in November 1973, they played at the Army Hall in Masaka, entertaining soldiers in a space long considered off-limits to non-military performers. Under Idi Amin's rule, such venues were the exclusive preserve of army bands. However, Mutebi was cautious about entangling himself with Amin's toxic rule any more than he had previously done. Aside from the Amin praise songs recorded in 1972, namely President Amin and Alukeseeza, the Tames refrained from producing further music glorifying the brutal dictator.

In the latter half of 1974, the Tames began releasing hit singles on their own UTMS label at an unprecedented frequency. Several of the songs, which were usually lengthy with the singles featuring Part 1 and Part 2, climbed the charts and landed on the much-anticipated weekly *Munno* magazine top ten list. Some of the top hits to emerge from Tamesland included Charles Kalyokya's heartfelt Maimuna (female name) and Kimuli Kyange (My Flower), which bore witness to his soulful vocals and emotive delivery. George Mukasa's Fina (a female name), with its graceful melodies and irresistible rhythms, which found favor with audiences. Ronald Ndema's more subdued Totutabula (Do Not Confuse Us) offered a contemplative counterpoint to the band's more upbeat offerings. Willy Mubiru's fast-paced Kambabulire (Let Me Tell You) injected a jolt of energy into the dance floor, while Grace (a female name), which was written, sung, and recorded by Deo Mukungu, captured the expressive depth of his musical voice.

Meanwhile, Peterson Mutebi's vocals propelled a string of chart-topping hits. In Tozanyisa Love (Don't Play With Love) and Abawala Bimuli (Girls Are Flowers), he brought a playful lyricism that connected instantly with listeners. When performing these songs live, his lively charisma and irresistible rhythm pulled audiences into his orbit, making every Tames concert a moment to remember. Salah Aninze (Sarah Waits for Me) and Eno Ye Weekend (This Is the Weekend) became instant favorites, their catchy melodies and danceable rhythms earning widespread affection from fans across the country. In Eno Ye Weekend, Kabale's saxophone swells like a gathering afternoon storm, bursting forth in an expansive and lavish display that seems endlessly delightful. Solome (a female name) features naughty and playful lyrics sung by Peterson Mutebi and prominently expressed Kabale's saxophone prowess. His saxophone solos, together with Bernard Gonza's inviting and heart-warming solo guitar, provided a complex set of labyrinthine rhythms with a powerful dynamism. The song's catchy melody and contagious beat made it a hit in Uganda, and it soon became something of an anthem. The song's lyrics also helped to popularize a new lexicon in urban slang. The word *Solome* came to be used as a synonym for a perky and plump booty, often used in sexually suggestive contexts:

I want you to know, oh Mama,
that I'm in a difficult place.
Your beauty, Solome,
has turned my heart upside down—
a single glance at you, seated there,
ignites a flame in my soul.

Solome, I want you to understand how I feel,
for you have captured my very being.
I tell you I love you,
but how does your heart feel?

From where I stand, I long for us to be inseparable,
just as we are now—feeling you so close in my chest.
My life is where you are, dear,
and I would be broken if you rejected me.

Wow, wow, Solome,
Eeh, eeh, Solome—
I love you so much, Solome.
You look beautiful, oh Mama, Solome.

Allow me to take your hand, Solome;
allow me to wed you with this ring.
You are so youthful, Solome—
your curves are bold and striking.
Smile for me, Solome,
for you are a princess, Solome.

Twerk, twerk, Solome—
twerk that booty for me to see, Solome.

The Tames enjoyed remarkable success and, unusually for a Ugandan band at the time, built a large following in both Kenya and Rwanda. Their 1976 tour of Rwanda was a triumph, with audiences thrilled by their performances. One standout was Karaga, sung in Kinyarwanda by Peterson Mutebi, which became especially beloved in Rwanda. The song is a sophisticated blend of Ugandan band aesthetics and Rwandan traditional rhythms. It opens with the soft elegance of the *Umushayayo* dance, characterized by graceful arm movements and serene melodic lines that evoke joy and harmony. As the song progresses, the tempo shifts, building into a lively section inspired by the *Intore* dance, known for its bold, athletic steps and ceremonial vigor. This smooth transition from calm to celebration made Karaga a staple at weddings and festive gatherings across Uganda and Rwanda, reliably drawing crowds to the dance floor.

By this point, Peterson Mutebi and the Tames seemed unstoppable. Their songs dominated the airwaves, regularly playing on Radio Uganda and becoming part of the national soundtrack. But on October 30, 1978, the country was jolted by a dramatic political move. President Idi Amin, likely seeking to distract from growing unrest within the army, sent roughly 3,000 Ugandan troops into Tanzania's Kagera Salient, a contested 700-square-mile region he claimed belonged to Uganda. This reckless invasion triggered a chain of events that culminated in the collapse of his regime on April 11, 1979.

Tanzania began mobilizing to drive Amin's forces out of the Kagera region. As Tanzanian troops pressed forward, intent on toppling the Amin regime, they drew closer to Kampala. In response, Amin's government imposed a strict dusk-to-dawn curfew, bringing nightlife in major Ugandan cities to a halt. The once-vibrant music scene fell silent as venues closed and musicians were confined to their homes. In early 1979, with the curfew still in place and no way to perform for live audiences, Peterson Mutebi decided to take the band on a tour of Kenya. This strategic move allowed the Tames to remain active creatively and continue recording during a time of deep uncertainty. They were still on tour in Kenya in April 1979, when Amin's government was finally overthrown.

Unsure of the unfolding security situation in the immediate aftermath of Amin's overthrow, the Tames decided not to return to Uganda in the short term. Instead, they secured a residency at the Small World Country Club in Athi River, a serene haven located just outside Nairobi, approximately 30 minutes away. Here, they sought solace and stability, continuing to entertain their Kenyan fans in a safer environment.

With the gradual improvement of the security situation in Uganda, Peterson Mutebi was eager to lead the band back to their home base, Tamesland. However, some of the leading band members found Kenya to be a comfortable and secure place to pursue their musical endeavors. While Mutebi returned to Uganda in mid-1979, Bernard Gonza (lead guitar), Peter Kabale (saxophone), Tony Kalanzi (saxophone), Deo Mukungu (bass guitar), Godfrey Kaggwa (vocals), Medi Matovu (vocals), and Lawrence Sayiga (drums) chose to stay behind. They formed a new group called the Horizon Band, with Bernard Gonza assuming the role of band leader. The Horizon Band later relocated to Mombasa. Between 1980 and 1982, the band recorded four singles and an album, Obufumbo Kyamuwendo (Marriage Is Priceless). The songs all appeared on their own Horizon label and included Bernard Gonza's Ensi Madala (The World Is a Stairway) and Obufumbo Kyamuwendo, Medi Matovu's Salima (a female name), Tony Kalanzi's Suleiman (a male name), Godfrey Kaggwa's Ndekera Eddembe (Leave Me in Peace), and Deo Mukungu's Rita (a female name).

The separation of the Tames marked a significant turning point for the band, as their musical family, forged over a period of years, splintered and pursued different paths. Meanwhile, back in Uganda, Peterson Mutebi faced a challenging journey in finding his musical groove amidst a country grappling with the aftermath of Idi Amin's overthrow. The anticipated calm and security that the populace had hoped for failed to materialize, and Uganda continued to be plagued by insecurity and lawlessness even after the tumultuous reign of Amin came to an end. Senseless acts of violence and random killings shocked and paralyzed the nation, leaving Kampala far from safe and certainly not ready for the return of its famed nightlife.

Life at Tamesland, once a thriving hub of creativity and camaraderie, became mostly quiet. Peterson Mutebi, who had previously praised Idi Amin in songs such as Alukeseeza and President Amin, maintained a low profile. Those associated with Amin's government faced public scrutiny and were subjected to vigilante justice, with some being lynched or summarily killed without trial. The Tames' songs were barely played on Radio Uganda, and the country had shifted towards the rhumba sounds of Kenya-based musical groups. These included Congolese bands such as Les Mangelepa, Orchestra Super Mazembe, and Shika Shika. Tanzanian musicians based in Kenya had also made an impression on Ugandans, and songs by Les Wanyika, such as Pamela (a female name) and Paulina (a female name) were played around the clock on Radio Uganda and could also be heard booming from radio cassettes that were carried by the Tanzanian soldiers. The soldiers had mostly looted the radio cassette players from Ugandan stores and in most cases played Pamela, and Paulina on a loop. Many Ugandans who were old enough during the Uganda-Tanzania war of 1978 and 1979 probably associate these songs with that war period and the eventual overthrow of Idi Amin.

Ugandans even came up with their own substitute lyrics to the melody of Pamela's refrain, replacing the Swahili, *Jambo la Muhimu* (An Important Matter), *Nakuwomba Mama We* (I Request You, Mama), and *Twende Kwa Wazazi Nyumbani* (Let's Go Home to the Parents), with the following Luganda words: *Kampala Muwambe* (Kampala Is Captured), *Namadukka Masibe* (Even the Stores Are Closed), and *Tunajawa Sukali No Munyo*

(Where Will We Find Sugar and Salt). When indiscipline began surfacing among Tanzanian troops, with a disturbing number of soldiers alleged to be involved in acts of violence, Ugandans soon changed the Pamela refrain to reflect the pains of a liberation that appeared to have gone wrong, singing: *Kampala Mulimu* (There Is in Kampala), *Abakombozi Mama We* (Liberators, My Mama), and *Abakuba Amasasi Nyumbani* (Who Fire Bullets at Homes).

When Peterson Mutebi finally resumed recording, it was under a changed political climate. In 1980, he recorded a few singles on the TAMSIC label, another label owned by the Tames. The songs included Charles Kanaabi's Gorret (a female name) and Oli Kiwala Fit (You Are a Fit Girl). Meanwhile, Peterson Mutebi's songs released during the period were decidedly political, a departure from the romantic themes that had made him and the Tames famous. These included Twagala Mirembe (We Need Peace), DP Chama (DP Party), and Amazima N'obwekanya (Truth and Equality). Twagala Mirembe served as a plea for peace and a return to civility, decrying the political factionalism, tribalism, corruption, and economic hardships that had engulfed the post-Amin period. On the other hand, DP Chama and Amazima N'obwekanya were songs in which Peterson Mutebi took political sides and declared his support for the Democratic Party (DP) following the reintroduction of multiparty politics in the country after a hiatus of about twenty years.

On the Tames' 1980 album, Kanvugenvuge (Step on the Gas), Mutebi exhorted his fellow Ugandans to embrace the return of multiparty democracy and seriously respond to their civic duty in electing their representatives to parliament through the songs Voting Time and Tugende Tulonde (Let's Go Vote). The 1980 elections featured two main parties: the DP, once led by Benedicto Kiwanuka and now headed by Paul Kawanga Semogerere, and the Uganda People's Congress (UPC), led by Milton Obote, a divisive and disliked figure in much of central Uganda. Obote, during his previous tenure as president, had ordered the invasion of the Kabaka of Buganda's palace, forcing the Kabaka into exile in Britain, where he died in November 1969. Obote had also abolished opposition parties, effectively turning Uganda into a one-party state where political adversaries were held in preventative detention under emergency provisions. Many of the people of Buganda, including Mutebi, were profoundly opposed to Obote and his UPC party. Peterson Mutebi's DP Chama and Amazima N'obwekanya, which embodied the DP motto, were his public demonstrations of support for Paul Semogerere and the DP.

However, despite the widespread support for Paul Semogerere and the DP, the December 1980 presidential election ended in controversy. The UPC, led by Milton Obote, was declared the winner after the Electoral Commission announced on state radio that his party had secured 66 of the 126 parliamentary seats. The declaration was met with disbelief and anger across much of Buganda, where support for Semogerere had been particularly strong. In other parts of the country, however, many still viewed Obote as the legitimate winner. Even so, the disputed results deepened political divisions and reignited old suspicions between regions, political parties and religion. For artists, the uncertainty was palpable, as the return of Obote's government meant renewed caution in what one could say or sing in public.

Amid this tense political climate, Peterson Mutebi faced a dilemma. He feared that his songs praising the DP might expose him to scrutiny or harassment under the new UPC regime. Unwilling to take chances, he left the country around 1981 and briefly settled in Britain. He returned to Uganda in the mid-1980s and made several attempts to revive the Tames' fortunes, but none succeeded in restoring the group's earlier prominence. By 1982, the Tames had effectively ceased to exist as a formidable band.

Despite their eventual decline, the Tames left behind an impressive collection of work, mostly written by Peterson Mutebi. In their ten years of active performance, the Tames released more than thirty singles, with many of their songs appearing on the *Munno* magazine's top ten list. Peterson Mutebi and the Tames also boasted of recording six studio albums, a feat that no Ugandan band had ever achieved. The six albums were the 1972 Love Enzigumivu, followed by Ekirabokyo (A Present to You) in 1975. The two albums Abawala Bimuli Volume 1 and Volume 2 were released in 1977 and 1978, respectively. Kanvugenvuge (released 1980) (Step on the Gas) and Le Voyage de Orchestre Tames a Rwanda (released in 1982) (Orchestra Tames' Journey to Rwanda) completed their discography.

CHAPTER 14

Military Bands and the
The Rwenzori Era

On January 25, 1971, a watershed event unfolded in Uganda's history as Major General Idi Amin orchestrated a military coup, overthrowing the civilian-led government of President Milton Obote. Amin assumed control of the country's 6,000-man army and positioned himself as Uganda's new military leader. The reasons cited by Amin for his actions were manifold, including accusations against Obote and his administration of suppressing democracy, neglecting to hold elections, engaging in corruption, promoting tribalism, and failing to maintain law and order. Amin further asserted that Obote had long disregarded the Army's appeals for improved living conditions, instead favoring his cronies. Moreover, he accused Obote of indulging in drinking, smoking, and womanizing, in addition to maintaining an idle life at the expense of the Ugandan taxpayer.

In a declaration to the nation, Amin emphasized that he was a professional soldier, not a politician, and proclaimed his intention to establish a military caretaker government. He claimed that his objective was to promptly transfer power to a democratically elected civilian government. The news of the coup sparked elation among the populace, and jubilant crowds flooded the streets of Kampala and other towns, extending a warm welcome to Amin. The military intervention was widely interpreted as a rejection of Obote's increasingly authoritarian leadership and undemocratic policies, particularly his decision to abolish Uganda's centuries-old monarchies, suspend the constitution, dissolve parliament, and arbitrarily detain political opponents.

Ugandans were hopeful for a new beginning, one that would represent a stark departure from Obote's policies. A segment of the population, especially royalists in Buganda, also hoped that Amin would restore the Buganda monarchy. The future held promise, with Ugandans hoping for an accountable form of government that would respect human rights and bring an end to the Obote-era one-party rule. However, there was also uncertainty, with reports of purges and killings of soldiers and politicians deemed loyal to Obote's overthrown government. Additionally, there was trepidation about Amin's intentions, as his new military government avoided providing an exact date for transitioning the country to civilian rule.

As Uganda entered a new era under Amin's leadership, the country stood at a critical crossroads, and the nation awaited the dawn of a new political era with a mixture of anxious hope and quiet dread. The rise of Idi Amin gripped Uganda with uncertainty, and musicians, like many others, watched the unfolding events with bated breath. Despite private apprehensions, artists from diverse backgrounds and musical styles responded to the new regime by composing and releasing a multitude of praise songs dedicated to Amin. These songs, often born out of a complex blend of genuine admiration, opportunism, and political expediency, exalted both Amin as an individual and the policies he championed. Amin was often cast as a benevolent father figure, Big Daddy, a fearless defender of Uganda's sovereignty against Western imperialist forces accused of seeking to divide the country and plunder its natural resources. The nickname Big Daddy caught on through Western media, which used it to underline the flamboyant and unpredictable side of his character.

During the first three years of his rule, there was an astounding number of songs composed in praise of Amin and his military rule. Radio Uganda, the only radio station in the country at the time, regularly played songs that portrayed Amin as a gracious and warmhearted leader. The top artists of the day participated in singing Amin's praises, flattering the general with a vigor and enthusiasm that had not been extended to his predecessor, Milton Obote. Moses Katazza, known for his beautiful 1960s ballads with Frida Sonko, joined forces with Top Ten Band to release President Amin under the Kagaabe label. Hadija Namale and Chandarana's Kericho studio band, Orchestra Kericho Jazz, recorded Amin Jajafe (Our Grandfather Amin) on the Furaha label. Peterson Mutebi and the Tames extended their gratitude to Amin with their song President Amin, which was released on the Kagaabe label. The Cranes, on their track Twawona Okufa (We Overcame Death), extended a warm welcome to Idi Amin who, they crooned, had freed the country from the jaws of death under the Obote regime. The song was released on the Serenade label.

One particular event that significantly bolstered Amin's popularity among the people of Buganda was when he brought back the body of Kabaka Edward Mutesa II from Britain for burial at the royal tombs in Kasubi in March 1971. This momentous act elevated Amin's standing in the sub-region to unprecedented heights, and his role in attacking the king's palace in the first place and sending him into exile in Britain was completely disregarded. The musician Israel Magembe, a close friend and confidant of the late Kabaka, emerged from semi-retirement and collaborated with Fred Kabuye and Paul Kasozi to record two songs that thanked Amin for facilitating the return of the Kabaka's body and bestowing upon the deceased king a state funeral. These songs, titled Bana Uganda Mwebale (Thank You Ugandans) and Amada Genjole (The Royal Homecoming), were released on the Serena label. Steven Sempasa joined the chorus of praise for Amin and his coup d'état, recording and releasing January 25 on the Serena label, which he co-owned with his brother Magembe.

During Amin's eight-and-a-half-year reign, an astonishing number of over 120 songs were composed to extol his leadership and endorse his rule with gusto. This musical phenomenon reflected the unique blend of adulation and propaganda that characterized Idi Amin's regime. While most musicians contributed just one or two songs dedicated to Amin before moving on to entertain their fans on other subjects, a select few artists emerged as standout examples of unabashed obsequiousness and unwavering loyalty to the dictator. Their simpering sycophancy and bigoted nationalism were largely justified by the overthrow of the Buganda kingdom's nemesis, Apollo Milton Obote. One of these notable artists was Fred Masagazi, whose collaboration with the Top Ten Band resulted in the 1971 release of Amin Tuli Naawe (Amin We Are With You) and Ani Yali Amanyi (Who Would've Known?).

Ani Yali Amanyi's lyrics represented a new and sad low in Uganda's cultural and political commentary. Like most Amin praise songs, Masagazi's Ani Yali Amanyi started off by commending Amin for overthrowing Obote's government. The song beseeched Amin never to retreat in his stated mission and to seize the historical moment to propel Uganda forward. However, the lyrics soon pivoted, taking on a more sinister turn. In the song, Masagazi accused Milton Obote, the ousted leader, of diverting government resources and taxpayer funds to favor his ancestral village, Akokoro, in the Lango region of northern Uganda, to the detriment of the rest of the country. This accusation, although absurd and untruthful, was pushed by Amin and his lieutenants and cited as one of the justifications for overthrowing Obote's government. Indeed, the Amin government often cited a fictitious document, the so-called "Lango Development Master Plan of 1967," which allegedly outlined a nefarious scheme by which Uganda's political, military, and economic institutions would be dominated by Obote's tribesmen from Akokoro. This fictitious document only existed in the minds of those who loathed Milton Obote.

Despite its promotion of inter-tribal animosity, Masagazi's Ani Yali Amanyi received extensive airplay on Radio Uganda. Tragically, for some Ugandans, it became a license to torment and harass people from the Lango region, the birthplace of Milton Obote, accusing them of driving the country into the ground. The episode stands as a sobering example of how music, when aligned with power, can be weaponized to inflame ethnic resentment rather than heal it.

This pattern deepened after Amin's 1972 expulsion of Ugandans of Indian and Pakistani ancestry. Masagazi's Lekerawo Akanyomonyomo (Stop the Contempt), recorded with the Rwenzori Band, openly celebrated the expulsion, portraying Asians as a community driven solely by greed and disdain for Black Ugandans. Such caricatures erased a far more complex and humane reality. For generations, Ugandans of Asian descent had been woven into the fabric of the nation's social and economic life. Many had participated in the independence struggle, contributed to civic life, and helped build the commercial infrastructure of towns that Ugandans still take pride in today. They were prominent in professional, intellectual, and cultural circles, and their philanthropy supported schools, hospitals, and community institutions across the country. Their commitment to Uganda was, for many, not transactional but deeply rooted and sincere.

Masagazi's song expressed no empathy for the approximately 80,000 people who were given just 90 days to abandon their lives because of their racial identity. Many were permitted to carry only a single suitcase and small amounts of cash. Homes, thriving businesses, close friendships, and cherished memories were left behind as these Ugandans began uncertain new lives abroad, with many resettling in the United Kingdom and Canada. In celebrating their removal, Lekerawo Akanyomonyomo ignored both their humanity and their enduring contribution to their country.

Another musician who stood out for her extreme loyalty to Idi Amin and his military regime was Annette Ddamulira. Ms. Ddamulira had been a member of Uganda's Prisons Jazz Band, where she stood out as the respected queen of sentimental and lovelorn ballads. Her song Njagala Mbe (I Want to Be), recorded with Orchestra Kericho Jazz, Chandarana's Eldoret studio band, was among the leading popular songs in Uganda just before Idi Amin's 1971 coup. With Amin in power, Ddamulira made a significant career move, departing from the Prisons Jazz Band to become one of the main vocalists in the Bombo Army Band. In 1971 and 1972, Ddamulira recorded a series of songs that celebrated Amin and his policies.

These tracks included Muve Ku Uganda (Leave Uganda Alone), Fuga Uganda (Reign Over Uganda), Amin Ne Uganda (Amin and Uganda), and Mwesimiwa Amin (His Excellency Amin), all released under the Re-Craft label, owned by kadongo kamu musician, Gerald Mukasa.

Amin took notice of Ddamulira's performances. She even had a stage photo opportunity with Amin, with the president playing the accordion and a smiling Annette Ddamulira looking on approvingly. In this context, Annette Ddamulira's transition from the Prisons Jazz Band to the Bombo Army Band and her dedication to creating songs that celebrated Amin exemplify the broader phenomenon of musicians aligning themselves with the regime to gain favor and recognition. Through the proliferation of Idi Amin praise songs, musicians knowingly or unknowingly contributed to the construction of a personality cult and the cultivation of an aura of invincibility around Amin. These songs played a crucial role in shaping Amin's image as a revered, almost mythical figure. Music became a potent tool for propaganda, bolstering Amin's public stature and reinforcing his grip on power.

However, this association with the regime came at a cost for many musicians. Some, like Ddamulira, may have genuinely believed in Amin's promises and policies, while others were driven by opportunism or fear. Yet their visible alignment with the government often alienated sections of their audience, who saw them as sell-outs or regime loyalists. At the same time, Amin's unpredictability meant that even those who once praised him were not immune from persecution if they later fell out of favor with him or his associates. Regardless of their motivations, their participation in the regime's propaganda apparatus helped to legitimize Amin's rule and sustain his cult of personality.

During Amin's rule, the three main sectors of Uganda's security forces were the army, police, and prisons. However, he prioritized the Uganda Army, showering the military with the most resources and attention. Recognizing the power of music as a tool, Amin employed it for two key purposes: propaganda and troop morale. Music could be used to spread messages praising his regime and demonizing his enemies, while simultaneously boosting the spirits of his soldiers. This was not a new strategy. The Rhino Boys, many of them Ugandan servicemen, had played a similar role during World War II by entertaining and uplifting East African King's African Rifles troops deployed in the Far East, bolstering their morale amidst the hardships of war. By resorting to this tactic, Amin aimed to create a similar sense of loyalty and enthusiasm within the military ranks.

At Uganda's independence and shortly thereafter, the security forces bands consisted entirely of marching bands. The most prominent of these was the Uganda Police Band, led by Mr. Ahmad Oduka. The security forces began forming popular music bands in the mid-1960s, shortly after the visit of the Congolese Police Band. The Congo Police Band had a successful tour of Kampala, performing popular Congolese rumba songs. The Uganda Police Jazz Band was the first security forces group to play popular music, venturing beyond the brass band genre that had come to define the regular marching bands associated with the uniformed services. The Uganda Police Jazz Band boasted notable members such as James Kigongo and Mary Nattima, who also recorded individually with the backing of other groups. However, the Prisons Jazz Band was generally regarded as the best of the security services' popular music bands in the country. Simon Berunga and Annette Ddamulira were among the top musicians on the Prisons Jazz Band lineup.

The Prisons Jazz Band was formed in 1968. It was a large ensemble, consisting of twenty-six members at its formation. The vocalists included Simon Berunga, Annette Ddamulira, and Kiwanuka Sozi. Senkuba, Ojok, and Mutebi played saxophone. Ojera and Wasswa were the trumpet players. The lead guitarists were Elliott Adwonga and Odoi. The band had three rhythm guitarists, namely Bukenya, Okwi, and Musisi. Magoba played the bass, Semakula was the drummer, and Kigozi (not to be confused with Fred Kigozi) played the egg shakers. The band also backed up different artists, such as Andrew Kyambadde and Margaret Nakibuuka on their 1967 hits Uganda Ekuze (Uganda Has Come of Age) and Uganda Is Independent.

In the swinging 1960s, Kampala's nightlife pulsed with energy, and Susanna nightclub was its heart. Like several high-ranking military officials and prominent political figures, Amin was a regular patron of Susanna nightclub and could be found there on most Saturday evenings. To the Ugandan elite, Susanna held a special allure, akin to an exclusive, members-only social club where invaluable networking opportunities abounded. Amin's deep love for music, particularly rumba, helped usher in a remarkable era that saw the expansion of military rumba bands across the country. However, the roots of these bands go back further, emerging in the early to mid-1960s before Amin's rise to power. In that period, the first army popular band, the Uganda Army Jazz Band, was formed under the leadership of Captain Abednego Orech Okot. In 1968, the band recorded the album titled *Folk Songs and Dances of Uganda*. The back of the album cover featured three photographs. One photograph showed President Milton Obote and his wife, Miria, dancing. Two other photographs showed Major General Idi Amin, then commander of the Uganda Army, wearing a tidy suit and tie while performing a traditional dance flanked by soldiers. Another photograph showed Idi Amin and Constantine Baranga Katiti, the Minister of Culture and Community Development, joining traditional dancers in a Baakisimba dance.

The government aimed to boost morale by expanding entertainment options for soldiers, including the establishment of popular music bands at every major army barracks. A key figure in this initiative was Ali Fadhul, a flamboyant non-commissioned officer in his mid-twenties who had first joined the King's African Rifles in 1953. In the mid-1960s, Fadhul was stationed in Moroto Barracks and was tasked by Captain Orech Okot with assisting him in creating the army bands. Known for his love of Congolese rumba, Fadhul seemed the perfect fit. He did not disappoint. Starting with the Echo (or EKO) Moroto Armed Forces Jazz Band in Moroto, Fadhul oversaw the establishment of popular music bands in every major army barracks across the country.

By the 1970s, the Ugandan Armed Forces boasted an impressive network of army bands. Some notable ones included the Malire Orchestre Capitale (or Malire Jazz Band) stationed at Malire Barracks, formerly the Kabaka's palace, in Kampala; the Suicide Revolutionary Jazz Band in

Masaka; the Simba Jazz Band, also known as the Simba Air Borne Jazz Band, in Mbarara; and the Masindi Army Jazz Band in Masindi town. Others included the Tiger Army Band in Mubende, the Air Force Jazz Band in Entebbe, the Mbuya General Quarters Band, and the Eagle Jazz Band stationed in Jinja's George V Barracks, the former home of the prestigious pre-independence 4th Battalion King's African Rifles. This last barracks was renamed Gaddafi Barracks by Idi Amin in 1972.

Unlike the polished performances of the Police and Prison jazz bands, the army bands were known for their lack of musical refinement. Filled with amateur musicians who would not qualify for a reputable nightclub band, they paled in comparison to their more skilled civilian counterparts. This weakness stemmed from the military's fearsome reputation for brutality and intimidation. Musicians, wary of association with the regime, avoided joining the military bands. Public opinion mattered, and aligning oneself with the military could damage a musician's career. As a result, while the Police and Prison bands flourished, exhibiting impressive talent, the military bands mostly remained mired in mediocrity.

However, there were a few exceptions. The Echo Jazz Band stationed at Moroto Barracks stood out. Unlike its counterparts, Echo Jazz relied heavily on skilled Congolese musicians such as Jose, Jido, Bolingo, and Apolinari. Echo also managed to attract some talented Ugandan musicians, which set the band apart from their less musically proficient counterparts among the military rumba bands. Interestingly, the story of the Echo Jazz Band intersects with that of future Ugandan music legend Philly Bongoley Lutaaya, whom some admirers dubbed the "Bruce Springsteen of Africa." The comparison stemmed largely from the title of his celebrated song Born in Africa, which invited parallels with Springsteen's iconic Born in the U.S.A.

Although Lutaaya had a brief stint with Echo Jazz in 1971, his rise to national prominence came in 1974 when he took over as bandleader for the Kampala-based River Nile Band, owned by Fred Kanyike's Rwenzori Band. Despite his earlier efforts, Lutaaya remained relatively unknown outside Uganda until his sensational reggae hit Born in Africa exploded in 1987, making him a star across Africa. However, Lutaaya's legacy transcended music. In a time of silence and stigma surrounding AIDS, he became the first prominent Ugandan to publicly declare his HIV-positive status, a pioneering move for the entire African continent. This courageous act was a watershed moment, sparking vital conversations and bringing much-needed attention to the AIDS epidemic that was devastating Uganda. Lutaaya is remembered not only for his musical talent but also as an emblematic figure in the fight against AIDS and a beacon of hope for those facing similar challenges.

The Echo Jazz Band was not the only military band with star potential. By the early 1970s, the Mbuya General Quarters Band had gained a reputation not just for its lively performances but also for its impressive lineup of talent. Among its standout members was Charles Sonko. Equally gifted was his older sister, Frida Sonko, whose powerful voice and commanding stage presence made her one of the band's defining figures. Adding to the band's appeal was teenage dancing sensation Frida Namuddu, whose mesmerizing performances left audiences spellbound with her signature moves. She crouched low, swiveled her hips with precision, and trapped time in a furious crossfire of rhythm. The sheer vitality of her movements made her performances unforgettable, drawing thunderous applause wherever she danced. A few years later, Namuddu married Dan Mugula, a leading figure in kadongo kamu. Their marriage became more than a personal bond; it evolved into a creative partnership that produced some of the genre's most enduring songs. Among their best-known compositions was the 1980s hit Bulijjo Card (No Invitation Is for One Alone), a song released on cassette. Lyrically, Bulijjo Card used the metaphor of an invitation card sent to a couple, symbolizing the importance of mutual participation and shared experiences in a marriage. The song emphasized the value of unwavering support, respect for individuality, and the delicate balance that allows both partners to grow while strengthening their relationship.

Meanwhile, at Jinja's Gaddafi Barracks, the Eagle Jazz Band, formed in 1968, featured a crowd favorite in soldier Isabirye, whose soaring vocals made him a standout performer. His impassioned rendition of Congolese rumba covers stirred audiences to their feet, carried along by the driving, jubilant riffs of the Eagle Jazz Band. His ability to channel the spirit of Kinshasa's most beloved rumba icons guaranteed him a place of honor among Jinja clubgoers. The band regularly performed at the Intercontinental Nightclub in Bugembe, a popular venue that drew large crowds eager to hear their lively rumba covers.

Across the country, the Ugandan Air Force was actively scouting for musical talent to elevate its own ranks. In 1971, Brigadier Smuts Guweddeko, the Air Force Commander, personally recruited B. K. Steven, already a well-respected musician, to spearhead the newly formed Air Force Band in Entebbe. Recognizing that a successful band needed top-tier musicians, B. K. Steven set out to lure promising young artists from Kampala's music scene. However, despite the Air Force's reputation for discipline and intellectual rigor compared to the regular army, his attempts to recruit rising stars such as Frank Mbalire and Billy Mutebi were unsuccessful. Even the assurance that they could perform as civilians failed to persuade them.

Further east, near the Kenya border, the Rubongi Barracks, just a few miles northwest of Tororo town, was home to another military-backed band, led by the accomplished Congolese musician Safro Mazanga. Among the standout members was the gifted Ugandan vocalist Smart Simbwa, whose smooth yet expressive voice made him a local sensation. Simbwa eventually found success beyond the barracks, recording two widely popular songs, Muganwa (a female name) and Ensimbi (Money), with the Serenade Top Ten Band.

Despite the military's efforts to cultivate local talent, recruiting elite Ugandan musicians remained a challenge. Authorities soon turned their attention to a more reliable solution by enlisting seasoned Congolese musicians into the ranks of the army bands. The Military Police Band, based in Kampala's Makindye neighborhood, became a prime example of this strategy. The ensemble was predominantly composed of Congolese musicians, with its leaders, Siko and Dido, hailing from the renowned Orchestre Bella Bella of Kinshasa. This band, founded by Soki Vangu, was already a household name in Uganda, making Siko and Dido invaluable additions to the Ugandan military's musical corps.

To motivate and improve the quality of performance among security service bands, the Amin government introduced a highly publicized competition in January 1973. This unprecedented event had all the hallmarks of a grand state function, except for the fact that it was not officially declared a public holiday. The competition took place at the iconic Entebbe Cricket Ground, drawing an audience of high-ranking military officials, diplomats, and government dignitaries. The guest of honor was President Idi Amin himself. The competition's judging panel was led by Lt. Col. Charles Arube, then commandant of the School of Infantry at Jinja's Gaddafi Barracks. Also in attendance was Lt. Col. Ozo, the acting commander of the Uganda Army, alongside other senior officers.

The contest crackled with energy as military bands from the various branches of the security forces took the stage, each determined to outshine the other. The police and prison bands delivered tight, polished performances that many in the audience quietly agreed had surpassed those of the army. However, few were under any illusion about how the evening would end. When Lt. Col. Arube and his panel announced the army band as the winner, the decision was met with silent murmurs rather than surprise. The outcome, it seemed, had been settled long before any of the bands had set foot on the stage. Amin, keen to project the army's dominance, strode forward to present the prize himself. The victorious band received five cows and several cases of beer and soft drinks, while the police band, relegated to second place, was awarded three cows and twenty cases of beer. In his closing remarks, Amin hailed the large turnout as proof of unity and harmony under his leadership. For many present, however, the carefully choreographed spectacle felt less like a celebration of music and more like a performance of power, staged in a country already groaning under the weight of repression.

Beneath the festive mood at Entebbe Cricket Ground, fault lines were already forming. The easy laughter and public camaraderie between Amin and Arube concealed a rivalry that would soon explode into violence.

Within the barracks, resentment simmered. Many Ugandan soldiers bristled at the growing influence of foreign mercenaries recruited from neighboring countries, men widely feared for their brutality and believed to be used to intimidate and crush dissent. Arube emerged as a focal point for this discontent.

In March 1974, that tension erupted. Determined to reclaim the army's pride and purge it of what he saw as corrupting influences, Arube launched a bold coup attempt against the very man he had once stood beside. Gunfire crackled across Kampala as rebel units advanced, and for a brief, electric moment, it seemed the balance of power might tilt. The confrontation reached its climax at Amin's official residence in Kololo. Arube pressed forward, convinced he had cornered the president. But he underestimated his opponent. As Arube approached, Amin lay in wait behind a door. In a sudden burst of gunfire, the president opened fire, cutting down his challenger at close range. Arube fell, and with him the rebellion collapsed. Leaderless and outmatched, the insurgent troops were quickly subdued. The failed coup did more than eliminate a rival. It tightened Amin's grip on the military and deepened the atmosphere of fear that defined his rule. The message was unmistakable. Loyalty was not optional, and dissent would be answered with lethal force.

Amin's government eagerly exploited security service "jazz" bands as part of its public relations campaign, hoping to win over a public that was growing increasingly disillusioned with his regime's economic mis-management and rampant human rights violations. By 1974, Uganda was grappling with severe economic hardship, exacerbated by Amin's 1972 expulsion of Ugandans of Indian and Pakistani heritage, an act that had crippled the commercial sector. As public frustration mounted, Amin sought to harness music as a tool of distraction and display. In March 1974, he issued a directive requiring all jazz bands within the Uganda Armed Forces, as well as the Police and Prison Forces, to stage free public concerts in major towns every weekend from 5 to 7 pm. The objective was clear: to entertain and calm a restless population while projecting the image of a confident and benevolent regime.

In Kampala, the order was carried out at City Square, the symbolic and geographic heart of the capital. The Square lay framed by imposing government buildings, including the High Court, as well as banks, offices, and commercial buildings. Manicured lawns stretched beneath tall palms, flowerbeds lined curving pathways, and the open green expanse functioned as a civic stage. On those late afternoons, taxi drivers slowed along the surrounding roads and pedestrians gravitated toward the swelling sound of music. The Malire Jazz Band became the centerpiece of these performances. For two hours each weekend, music echoed across the lawns and into the surrounding streets. Crowds gathered out of curiosity, duty, or simple love of music. Yet even in that carefully tended space, under the watchful gaze of the High Court and the machinery of state, melody could only temporarily mask unease. After several weekends, attendance thinned and the concerts gradually lost their force as instruments of persuasion.

Despite the state-sponsored push, most of the army bands relied heavily on cover versions of popular Congolese songs, drawing from the rich catalog of Franco Luambo Makiadi, John Bokelo, Verckys Kiamuangana, and Tabu Ley. Their performances mimicked the lilting guitar rhythms of Kinshasa's leading orchestras, but they rarely introduced original compositions. A few army bands and musicians attempted to record original material, but much of it was overtly propagandistic, glorifying Amin and his military government. Even B. K. Steven, once a dazzling force in Uganda's music scene during the 1960s, struggled to produce any compositions of national significance after joining the Air Force Band.

Among the military bands, Simba Jazz Band produced the largest body of recorded material. Their repertoire was overtly propagandistic, with titles such as Terehe 25 (The Date of 25th), commemorating January 25, 1971, the day Amin overthrew Obote's government; Katonda Kuma Dada (God Protect Dada), invoking Amin by his self-bestowed title "Dada"; Tukusabira Idi Amin (We Pray for You, Idi Amin); and Tunatowa Sifa (We Give Praise), yet another anthem of devotion. These songs were saturated with praise not only for Amin himself but also for his senior military officers and close confidantes, whose names were woven into the lyrics as loyal pillars of the new order. Between 1971 and 1973, these recordings received heavy rotation on state-controlled Radio Uganda. However, their lifespan was tied to the volatile fortunes of the regime. As Amin's rule grew increasingly unpredictable, many of the very officers celebrated in these songs fell out of favor, were dismissed, arrested, or eliminated. In such an atmosphere, it became politically dangerous to broadcast music that immortalized men who had been declared enemies or traitors. To praise a fallen officer in the same breath as Amin risked implying divided loyalties. Gradually, the songs disappeared from the airwaves. Even at the height of their official promotion, these recordings failed to resonate in nightclubs or with ordinary music lovers. Outside the echo chamber of state radio, audiences gravitated toward music that spoke to romance, hardship, humor, and everyday life rather than to the shifting loyalties of power.

Few army band compositions genuinely resonated with the wider public. One notable exception emerged in 1972, when the Echo Jazz Band, the army band based at Moroto Barracks, released Kirumya Ememe (It Hurts the Soul) on the state-run UG label. Unlike most military band recordings, which were saturated with political messaging, Kirumya Ememe departed from overt propaganda. Instead, it revealed an unexpected emotional depth, giving listeners something more personal and reflective than the usual anthems of praise.

The track was credited collectively to the Echo Moroto Army Jazz Band, with no individual musicians named. However, it was both written and sung by Charles Sonko, who at the time had a brief stint with the Echo band before ultimately finding his artistic home with the Mbuya General Quarters Band. Kirumya Ememe offered listeners a poignant lyrical narrative:

> I had never known such soul-wrenching pain,
> my love, who shattered my spirit.
> I believed we would never part,
> but she left, capturing my thoughts in her wake.

Now I suffer, filled with regret over my choices,
such is the maze of love in our daily lives.
You have truly moved on, while my soul slowly heals.
In this vast world, I will find love again,
with someone worthy of true commitment.
Once, anger consumed you,
but that fury no longer resides in my heart.

In the immediate aftermath of Idi Amin's overthrow of Milton Obote's government, few Ugandan artists grasped the political utility of music as shrewdly as Fred Kanyike. In 1972, he embarked on an unusual musical course, composing and recording a series of songs that openly and lavishly praised General Amin. Rather than working independently or with an established civilian band, Kanyike strategically aligned himself with army ensembles, a calculated move that later proved central to his ambition of assembling Uganda's first true "supergroup," modeled on the expansive formations of Congolese giants such as Franco's O.K. Jazz and Tabu Ley Rochereau's Afrisa International.

With the Simba Jazz Band, Kanyike released Uganda Ekyyuse Nnyo (Uganda Has Changed Much), a song that reflected his belief that the country was undergoing a period of transformation under Amin, and that the change was for the better. He followed this with Tumusime President Barre (We Should Be Grateful to President Barre), a tribute acknowledging the role of Somalia's President Siad Barre in defusing a potentially explosive situation between Uganda and Tanzania. The backdrop to this song was the September 1972 invasion of Uganda by anti-Amin guerilla forces based in Tanzania, who, with tacit support from the Tanzanian government, sought to topple the Amin regime. As tensions escalated, President Barre intervened diplomatically, preventing a full-scale war and facilitating the signing of the Mogadishu Accord in October 1972. This agreement saw Uganda and Tanzania formally agree to end hostilities and restore peace.

With Malire Orchestra de Capitale, Kanyike continued his pattern of lyrical devotion to Amin and his policies. He released Government

Esobola (The Government Is Capable), Yewuyo Salongo Amin (The One and Only Amin, the Father of Twins), and Abayindi Bagende (Indians Leave). The latter song crossed into dangerous territory, spewing racist rhetoric that demonized Ugandans of Indian descent, an ugly stain on the reputation of an otherwise significant Ugandan musician. During this period, Kanyike had become little more than a mouthpiece for Amin's propaganda machine, replacing the heartfelt love songs that had once defined his artistry with nationalistic anthems of loyalty to the regime. For many of his longtime fans, it was a bewildering transformation for an artist who had once serenaded audiences with some of the most poignant Ugandan love songs of the 1960s.

However, beneath the patriotic fervor and his apparent devotion to Amin, Kanyike harbored a deeper ambition. Ever since parting ways with The Stars, the band he had co-founded with Ecklas Kawalya in 1964, Kanyike had nurtured the dream of leading his own powerhouse musical ensemble. He envisioned a band that would not only be the most formidable in Uganda but would also rival the legendary Congolese orchestras in size, melody, and rhythmic complexity.

In January 1973, Kanyike reached out to Hadija Namale, pitching the idea of forming a band together. Namale was, at the time, Uganda's leading female artist, with a string of successful releases to her name. In 1972, she had recorded several chart-topping hits, including Kasujja (a male name), Lubwama (a male name), and Nantege (a female name), all recorded with Orchestre Kericho Jazz on the Furaha label. Nantege was a deeply personal song, a dedication to her older sister who had raised her after their mother abandoned the family when Namale was still a child. In early 1973, she scored yet another hit with Mulumba (a male name), recorded with Top Ten Band and released on the Kagaabe label. By the time Kanyike approached her, Mulumba was one of the most frequently played songs on Radio Uganda and a staple in nightclubs across the country.

Namale shared Kanyike's enthusiasm for the project, but both faced a significant hurdle: neither had the financial means to acquire the musical instruments needed to launch a full-scale band. Then, an unexpected opportunity emerged. At the time, the Ugandan military was modernizing its army bands in preparation for the 1975 Organization of African Unity (OAU) summit, which Uganda was set to host. As part of this effort, the government was importing new instruments for the military "jazz bands," leaving a surplus of older equipment.

Kanyike and Namale were quick to recognize this as their chance. If they could secure some of the military's redundant instruments, their dream of forming a supergroup could become a reality. What they needed, however, was a well-placed ally within the regime. That ally came in the form of Colonel Ali Fadhul, one of Amin's most trusted confidants. Fadhul had played a central role in the 1971 coup that ousted Obote, earning him rapid promotion to commander of the Simba Mechanized Brigade in Mbarara. Although stationed outside the capital, he retained considerable influence over the army's logistical and administrative affairs, including oversight of the military bands.

Neither Kanyike nor Namale had any personal connection to Fadhul, so they turned to a mutual friend, Elly Wamala. A household name, Wamala was one of Uganda's first true entertainment icons, a gifted musician and television personality admired across tribal, religious, and political lines. His reputation for integrity and sophistication gave him rare access to people in power. He could walk into almost any government office and be received with admiration and deference; officials were often flattered simply to meet him.

When Kanyike and Namale approached Wamala to help them reach Fadhul, he was impressed by their vision and agreed to assist. Although he did not personally know Fadhul, his endorsement carried great weight. Through his intercession, Fadhul agreed to provide Kanyike and Namale with some of the army's surplus instruments. He went even further, pledging financial assistance toward the establishment of a recording studio, a long-held dream of Kanyike's.

However, Fadhul's support came with conditions. He insisted that the band must consist exclusively of the finest Ugandan musicians, a requirement that aligned with Amin's broader Economic War policy. Following the 1972 expulsion of Ugandan Asians, Amin had launched a sweeping campaign aimed at empowering Black Ugandans to dominate the country's institutions, businesses, and cultural spaces. Ensuring that this new band featured only Ugandan talent was, in Fadhul's view, a fitting extension of that agenda. Additionally, Fadhul made it clear that while he was willing to fund the venture, he had no interest in managing its day-to-day operations. As a high-ranking military officer, he had little time to oversee a band or a recording studio. Instead, he appointed a trusted representative to handle his business interests in the music industry, his first wife, Sylvia Kosa. With Fadhul's backing and Kosa's administrative oversight, Kanyike and Namale's dream of forming a supergroup was now within reach.

In February 1973, on the recommendation of Colonel Ali Fadhul, the Ugandan government funded Fred Kanyike's trip to West Germany to procure the equipment necessary to establish a state-of-the-art recording studio. On March 15, 1973, amidst much fanfare, Kanyike and Hadija Namale officially launched the Rwenzori Jazz Band and inaugurated Rwenzori Studios, strategically located on Kampala's bustling Kimathi Avenue. Kanyike took the helm as the studio's managing director, while his longtime associate and former bandmate, Ecklas Kawalya, was appointed studio manager. Namale, an integral part of the project, was recognized as a founding member of both the band and the studio. The event attracted considerable media attention, befitting Kanyike's affable, larger-than-life persona.

The Rwenzori Jazz Band was meticulously assembled in line with Fadhul's directive that only the finest Ugandan musicians be selected. Kanyike's ambitious vision required an all-star lineup, and he was determined to recruit the most talented artists available. The initial roster of Rwenzori Jazz Band members included Fred Kanyike (vocalist), Hadija Namale (vocalist and tumba drums), Fred Masagazi (vocalist), and Ecklas Kawalya (vocalist). To inject youthful energy into the band, Kanyike embarked on a lightning advertising campaign aimed at recruiting musicians into its ranks. The demand to join Rwenzori Jazz Band was overwhelming. According to Kanyike, over eighty musicians expressed interest in becoming part of the group, necessitating a rigorous selection process to ensure only the best talents made the final cut. Kanyike successfully enlisted a group of promising young musicians who had recently left Peterson Mutebi's Tames Band. These included Billy Mutebi (vocals and lead guitar), Frank Mbalire (vocals and rhythm guitar), Fred Kigozi (vocals and bass guitar), Fred Semwogerere (saxophone), and John Makubuya (drums). A few months later, the band further strengthened its horn section with the addition of saxophonists Mansur Akiki and Saul Kaliba.

Beyond creating a musical group, Kanyike was equally determined to turn Rwenzori Studios into a haven for aspiring Ugandan artists. The studio welcomed musicians from across the country, providing them with the opportunity to record and refine their craft. The first group to record at Rwenzori Studios was the Air Force Band, led by Kanyike's close friend B. K. Steven. Their tracks, Air Force and Mariana (a female name), were released on the newly established Rwenzori label. To further unearth new talent, Rwenzori Studios initiated monthly auditions, offering a platform for musicians to bring out their skills. Those who impressed the selection panel earned the opportunity to record their songs with Rwenzori Jazz Band. As word of this initiative spread, a wave of aspiring musicians flocked to the studio, hoping to secure a recording deal.

However, as Kanyike later observed, while many hopefuls submitted songs with compelling lyrics, only a handful demonstrated the vocal ability required for recording. Among the few artists fortunate enough to record at Rwenzori Studios was Katana Bossa, who released Sarah Kintu (a female name) and Panga Amaka (Organize Your Home), both backed by Rwenzori Jazz Band. On Panga Amaka, Hadija Namale lent her voice as a backup singer. Another successful recording artist was Charles Musisi, who recorded Abawala Begwanga (The Girls of the Nation) and Nanfuka (a female name), further establishing Rwenzori Studios as a vital force in Uganda's evolving music landscape.

Despite the studio's early success, it soon faced significant challenges. The ripple effects of Amin's Economic War led to a severe shortage of foreign currency, making it increasingly difficult for Rwenzori Studios to send its recordings to Nairobi for vinyl pressing. By August 1973, the studio was inundated with artists eager to record, but mounting financial pressures brought Kanyike to a stark choice. He could no longer provide the Rwenzori Jazz Band as a backing group for new recordings, and artists were henceforth required to bring their own bands for rehearsals and sessions. Aware of the financial burden this placed on many aspiring musicians, Kanyike offered to cover the cost of hiring external groups. It is believed, however, that Colonel Ali Fadhul, acting quietly behind the scenes, persuaded the authorities to subsidize these expenses. For Fadhul, the initiative represented more than artistic encouragement: it provided employment for idle youth and helped project the image of a government committed to cultural development.

Even as Rwenzori Studios became a hub of musical innovation, Rwenzori Jazz Band was making waves in Kampala's live music scene. Initially, the band held a regular gig at Kampala's International Hotel before relocating to Equatoria Hotel, where they became the resident band. With their dynamic sound, rich melodies, and introspective lyrics, the band won over audiences. Their music tackled themes of love, unity, and the aspirations of the Ugandan people. In March 1974, the band celebrated its first anniversary with a grand event at Bat Valley Club, a popular entertainment venue on Kampala's Bombo Road. The occasion was graced by Major Juma Abdalla Oris, then acting Minister of Foreign Affairs, who served as the guest of honor.

By this time, Rwenzori Jazz Band had firmly established itself on Uganda's music scene. Within their first year, the band had released an impressive thirteen singles, displaying the diverse talents of its members. These included by Fred Masagazi, Johnny and Herbert by Hadija Namale, Sabira Omuzukulu (Pray for the Grandchild) by Fred Kigozi, Vicky by Billy Mutebi, and Senjobe (a male name) by Frank Mbalire. With a growing discography and a thriving live performance circuit, Rwenzori Jazz Band had brought Fred Kanyike's vision to life. However, Kanyike was not one to settle for mere dominance of Kampala's music scene. Resting on his laurels was never an option. Driven by an unrelenting ambition to expand the band's reach beyond Uganda's borders, he set his sights on an even greater milestone.

In early 1974, Rwenzori Jazz Band announced a groundbreaking U.S. tour, an unprecedented move that would make them the first Uganda-based popular music group to perform on American stages. The tour followed in the footsteps of Benny Kalanzi, John Sendaula, and Margaret Nabyonga, three Ugandan musicians who had won over U.S. audiences in the late 1960s and early 1970s with stirring performances of folk songs, accompanied by guitar, lyre, and traditional drums. Unlike those earlier performances, however, Rwenzori Jazz Band was set to introduce an electrifying new sound, Ugandan rumba and jazz-infused dance music crafted for a contemporary international audience.

The U.S. tour was made possible through a deal Kanyike brokered with the Francis brothers of the African Record Center in Harlem, New York. The Francis brothers agreed to promote the band's performances in the U.S. and signed Rwenzori onto their Editions Makossa label, giving them a crucial foothold in the international music market. This partnership positioned Rwenzori Jazz Band as a major force in East African music, setting the stage for their anticipated American debut.

To ensure their performances met the highest international standards, Rwenzori took inspiration from the exhilarating stage shows of some of the biggest names in Congolese music. In the early 1970s, Tabu Ley Rochereau and Kiamuangana "Verckys" Mateta, both renowned for their dynamic live performances, had toured Uganda, leaving audiences mesmerized with their spectacular choreography and high-energy dance routines. Determined to match the level of professionalism displayed by their Congolese counterparts, Rwenzori recruited a talented troupe of dancers to add flair and dynamism to their stage presence. The group included Elizabeth Naggayi, Morgan Musisi, Michael Luzinda, and Margaret "Maggie" Nampiima Kulubya, all of whom brought a combination of agility, grace, and rhythmic precision to the band's performances. Beyond their skills as dancers, Elizabeth Naggayi and Maggie Kulubya also proved to be exceptional vocalists, earning them roles as backup singers on several Rwenzori recordings. Their inclusion strengthened the band's vocal section, adding lush harmonies to their already rich sound. Hadija Namale also took on a new role, contributing to the group's traditional Ganda dance performances. With its expanded lineup and a sharpened focus on stagecraft, Rwenzori Jazz Band was ready to take on the world. The upcoming U.S. tour was not just about presenting their music. It was a bold statement of Ugandan cultural excellence, a declaration that the country's distinctive musical identity deserved a place on the global stage.

Before embarking on their American adventure, Rwenzori Jazz Band felt a deep obligation to properly bid farewell to their loyal Ugandan fans. Since they had announced that they would be out of the country for several months, the band embarked on a nationwide tour, a grand prelude to their historic U.S. trip. The announcement generated immense excitement, with media outlets covering every detail of what promised to be a spectacular farewell.

Throughout April and May of 1974, the band temporarily left behind their familiar home at Equatoria Hotel and set off on a whirlwind tour that took them across the country. Over the course of two months, they crisscrossed Uganda, performing in more than ten towns. From Mbale in the east to Mbarara in the west, Arua in the north to Masaka in the south, every performance drew enthusiastic crowds, with sold-out halls becoming the norm. At each stop, the band delivered riveting performances, their exhilarating rhythms and charismatic stage presence bringing audiences to their feet and erupting in applause. In every venue, devoted fans eagerly anticipated one final show before the group's departure. Crowds pressed closer to the stage, straining for a better view of their stars, and some even climbed up, handing wads of money as tokens of appreciation.

A particularly unforgettable moment came when Rwenzori Jazz Band took the stage at Makerere University's Main Hall. Hundreds of college students crammed into the hall, transforming the concert into a raucous celebration. The excitement reached a fever pitch as students sang along and danced wildly in the aisles, turning the venue into a pulsating sea of music and movement.

However, the undisputed highlight of the farewell tour was the grand International Music Show, held at Nakivubo Stadium on June 6, 1974. Sponsored by S.P. Tools & Machinery, Uganda Ltd., this highly publicized event promised to deliver "songs and dances prepared to thrill the vast audiences anxiously waiting to see their performance in the USA," as the government-owned newspaper *Voice of Uganda* put it. The concert lived up to every expectation, drawing an enormous crowd that included foreign diplomats, prominent civil servants, and high-ranking military officials. As the band took to the stage, a wave of excitement swept through the stadium. The audience erupted in cheers, the sheer energy in the air making it clear that this was no ordinary concert. The show featured dazzling performances, particularly the breathtaking Baakisimba dance routines executed by Elizabeth Naggayi, Margaret "Maggie" Kulubya, Michael Luzinda, Morgan Musisi, and Hadija Namale. Their intricate footwork and perfectly synchronized movements created a spectacle that left the audience in awe. Fred Kanyike and the concert's sponsor, S.P. Tools & Machinery, hailed the event as a preview of what American audiences could expect in the months to come. Even Peterson T. Mutebi of The Tames Band, one of Uganda's most revered pop culture icons, was in attendance. Despite being a competitor, Mutebi openly acknowledged that the performance had elevated live entertainment in Uganda, setting a new benchmark for stagecraft and musical excellence.

With the U.S. tour fast approaching, Kanyike had one more crucial matter to address: the Rwenzori Jazz Band's contractual commitment to Equatoria Hotel, where they were the resident band. Rather than abandoning the venue, Kanyike came up with a solution. He would form an entirely new group to carry on the band's legacy while they were away. This new outfit, River Nile Band, was officially unveiled in July 1974 at Equatoria Hotel.

Though owned by Rwenzori Jazz Band, River Nile Band featured a fresh lineup of young, talented musicians eager to make their mark. The original members included Kalyango, a bassist who worked at Bata Shoe Co.; John Mukasa, a lead guitarist and student from St. Henry's College,

Kitovu; Edward Serunjonji, rhythm guitar and formerly of Kampala City Five; and drummers Lawrence Kato and Edward Musoke, the latter of whom worked as a waiter at New Legal Restaurant in downtown Kampala by day. The band also featured vocalists Edward Kyeyune, Jimmy Nsamba, and Paulo Munyagwa, each of whom brought their own unique style to the group.

With River Nile Band firmly in place to maintain Rwenzori's presence at Equatoria Hotel, Kanyike and his bandmates could now turn their full attention to their next great challenge: introducing Ugandan music to American audiences. But it didn't take long before Kanyike grew dissatisfied with River Nile Band's commitment and felt that the musicians lacked the distinctive musical magic he was looking for. Doubting their ability to adequately uphold Rwenzori's legacy at Equatoria Hotel, he made the sweeping decision to overhaul the entire lineup by the end of July, replacing them with more seasoned professionals.

This new iteration of River Nile Band was anchored by two key recruits from Cranes Band: Edman "Eddy" Ganja on lead guitar and Philly Bongoley Lutaaya as the lead vocalist and trumpeter. Lutaaya became the band's frontman and official bandleader, while Ganja assumed the role of acting bandleader. They were joined by a talented ensemble, including Alex "Django" Mukulu (also known as Asiita) on bass, Roger Musisi on vocals and drums, Johnny "Negro" Kiwanuka on vocals and saxophone, and Nathan Semalulu on drums. The core lineup later expanded to include Andrew Tamale, Geoffrey Nsereko, Henry Kasaasa (Kanyike's younger brother), Miti, Michael "Mike" Lubega (formerly of The Marines, the resident band at Bonanza Nightclub in Kitintale), Freddy Sebulime (another Cranes Band recruit), and Paul Sserumaga, a student from St. Henry's College, Kitovu.

With River Nile Band firmly in place to handle Rwenzori's commitments at Equatoria Hotel, Kanyike and his group, now rebranded as Rwenzori International Band, a nod to their global ambitions, departed Uganda for New York on September 14, 1974. Their U.S. trip was primarily sponsored by Colonel Ali Fadhul, but additional financial support came from Uganda's business and political elite. Several companies, including S.P. Tools & Machinery, Fabricano, and New Flexfoam, made contributions, while Kampala businessman Jack Kasato Kironde also provided sponsorship.

Seventeen members of Rwenzori International Band landed in New York, forming a formidable ensemble that included Fred Kanyike, Ecklas Kawalya, Fred Kigozi, Billy Mutebi, Hadija Namale, Frank Mbalire, Fred Masagazi, Mansur Akiki Bulegeya, Hussein Bruhani, Saul Kaliba, Fred Ssemwogerere, John Makubuya, Elizabeth Naggayi, Morgan Kibirige Musisi, Maggie Kulubya, Michael Luzinda, and Teo Bukesa. For the first few months, the tour appeared to be a resounding success. The promoters upheld their agreements, booking Rwenzori for lucrative performances at venues in and around New York City. The band consistently delivered energetic, high-quality shows, thrilling audiences with their blend of Ugandan and Congolese musical influences. Their most significant performance took place at Manhattan Center, 311 West 34th Street, before an audience of hundreds. Notable attendees included Uganda's Ambassador to the United Nations, Khalid Younis Kinene, UN Secretary-General Kurt Waldheim, and several high-profile diplomats.

During the show, an unexpected call from Idi Amin prompted Kanyike to step off stage and speak with the president. Amin expressed his admiration, noting that he had heard the band performing exceptionally well and emphasizing their duty to elevate Uganda's name. Even Amin and his lieutenants held deep respect for Kanyike and Rwenzori. It was a proud moment for Kanyike, a towering figure in Ugandan music who had rubbed shoulders with top politicians and royalty. A particular highlight of the Manhattan Center show was the band's intricate Kiganda traditional dance performances. The well-rehearsed routines of Elizabeth Naggayi, Margaret "Maggie" Kulubya, Michael Luzinda, Morgan Musisi, and Hadija Namale thrilled the New York audience, as they seamlessly executed the three movements of Nankasa, Baakisimba, and *Muwogola*. This performance took place just weeks after Bob Marley and the Wailers had graced the same stage, a fact Kanyike often cited as evidence of

Rwenzori's growing international recognition and as proof that the band deserved to be taken seriously.

Then, on October 24, 1974, the band made history again with a well-attended concert at the legendary Apollo Theater in Harlem. To perform on that stage was no small achievement. The Apollo was more than a venue; it was an institution that had shaped the sound and spirit of twentieth-century popular music, having hosted icons such as Ella Fitzgerald, Duke Ellington, Count Basie, Sam Cooke, Mahalia Jackson, Marvin Gaye, and The Supremes. For the members of Rwenzori, stepping onto that stage was both humbling and exhilarating. It marked a defining moment not only for the band but also for Ugandan popular music, which now found itself represented on one of the world's most revered stages. The performance affirmed that Rwenzori's journey from Kampala to Harlem was more than a tour; it was a bridge between cultures and a declaration that Ugandan musicians could take their place among the greats of global music.

As Rwenzori gathered momentum in the United States, their recording ambitions began to crystallize. The Francis brothers, who had successfully distributed Fela Kuti's Afrobeat records across the American market, urged the band to cultivate a sound that blended Afrobeat's driving pulse with their own East African sensibilities. They believed Rwenzori could achieve the kind of international recognition Fela enjoyed, and perhaps even rival it. That vision soon took tangible form in the studio. A pivotal contribution came from the band's saxophonist, Mansur Akiki Bulegeya, who had recently fallen in love with a Caribbean woman shortly after arriving in New York. Inspired by the romance, and encouraged by the Francis brothers' call for an Afrobeat-inflected release, Bulegeya composed Handsome Boy, a track that fused personal sentiment with the band's evolving transatlantic sound. Released under Editions Makossa, the track featured backup vocals by Maggie Kulubya and Elizabeth Naggayi and became one of Rwenzori's most celebrated hits. It would, however, remain the only record the band released under Editions Makossa during their 1974–75 U.S. tour.

By December 1974, cracks began to show in Rwenzori's American adventure. Kanyike fell out with the Francis brothers over financial disputes. He believed the promoters were underpaying the band, considering the large crowds they were attracting at their shows. Convinced that cutting out the middlemen would allow the band to keep a greater share of their earnings, Kanyike severed ties with the Francis brothers. However, the reality of operating independently in the U.S. music scene was far harsher than he had anticipated. Without a well-connected American promoter, Rwenzori struggled to secure consistent gigs. Unlike in Uganda, where their reputation guaranteed packed venues, New York was a fiercely competitive market. While they managed to book some shows, there were not nearly enough to sustain the seventeen-member group financially.

Band members soon found themselves working odd jobs in restaurants and hair salons to make ends meet. The Uganda UN Mission provided occasional assistance, but it was not enough to keep morale from sinking. With few performances and dwindling resources, frustration mounted within the group. Many longed to return home to Uganda, but Kanyike remained hopeful, continuously promising that better opportunities lay ahead. He did manage to arrange a few gigs outside of New York, including well-received performances at Howard University and Holiday Inn in Washington, D.C. However, most concerts were poorly promoted, leading to disappointing attendance.

The band later traveled to Chicago, where they played at local colleges such as Roosevelt University, Illinois State University, Malcolm X College, and Kennedy-King College. Despite these scattered successes, the band mostly performed in smaller venues, a stark contrast to the grandeur they had experienced in their early months in New York.

Determined to leave a lasting musical legacy, Rwenzori International Band booked studio time in Chicago, resulting in two albums, The Best of Rwenzori Vol. 1 and Vol. 2. Released under their self-owned Africanza label, the albums were sonically cohesive, capturing the spirit of their Ugandan roots while incorporating elements of their American experience. The albums included tracks such as Beat by Ecklas Kawalya; Adam ne

Eva (Adam and Eve) by Fred Kigozi; Anyese (a female name) by Frank Mbalire; Herbert by Hadija Namale; and Cox Pachanga by Mansur Akiki Bulegeya. Some of these songs were also released as singles.

The track Herbert is especially personal for Hadija Namale. Before the band's U.S. tour, she had been romantically involved with her bandmate, Billy Herbert Mutebi. Their relationship was short-lived. It ended painfully when Billy began seeing Hadija's cousin. The betrayal cut deeply, and from that wound came Herbert. In the song, Namale bares her anguish with striking vulnerability. She sings of disbelief that the man she trusted and loved could abandon her for another woman, Eva. At the same time, she searches her own heart, asking forgiveness if she had wronged him and pleading, almost tenderly, for a second chance. In what appears to be a riposte to Hadija's raw confession, Billy later released a track titled Ebyomukwano Byakabi (Friendship Hurts), suggesting that romantic entanglements are fleeting and that heartache is an inevitable part of life.

Despite the recording studio achievements of the Rwenzori band, financial hardships persisted. Paying for daily necessities, hotel bills, and studio sessions became an ongoing struggle. Tensions among the band-mates grew, and many openly expressed their desire to leave the bitter cold of Chicago and return to the familiar warmth of Uganda. This grow-ing disillusionment with their American adventure was best captured in Rwenzori's song Chicago America, a melancholic reflection on their hardships. Sung by Fred Kanyike with backing vocals from Billy Mutebi and Elizabeth Naggayi, the track embodied the band's frustration with their faltering dream. The once-promising U.S. tour had turned into a difficult, humbling experience:

> I have seen much in America—
> I will not lie, I speak the truth.
> Some say overseas brings happiness,
> but what kind of happiness is that?
> I am a Black soul from Africa, a great land.
> In America, many weep from hunger,

and many shiver in the bitter cold.
People care little for one another.
Visit Chicago to experience America,
to see what it truly offers.
Bundle up, or you will get frostbite—
Ah, Chicago is truly interesting.
Let me return home,
back to my birthplace.
I have been in America,
playing music for my country and Rwenzori.
The biting wind assails me—
why must I endure this cold?
It is all for the sake of my children.

The Rwenzori returned to Uganda in the spring of 1975, but their home-coming was marked by sorrow and uncertainty. During their year-long absence, much had changed both in the Ugandan music scene and within their personal lives. Frank Mbalire returned to the devastating news that his younger sister had passed away while he was on tour. His family had deliberately kept the news from him, fearing it would distract him while abroad. The loss hit him hard, and years later, in the 1990s, he would channel his grief into Ndikusanga (I Will Find You), a deeply personal and emotional tribute to his late sister.

Adding to the band's woes, just three days after their return from the U.S., tragedy struck again. On the evening of May 14, 1975, drummer John Makubuya and saxophonist Saul Kaliba were riding a motorcycle when they collided head-on with an oncoming car near the Queen's Clock Tower roundabout in Katwe. Makubuya was pronounced dead at the scene, while Kaliba suffered serious injuries and spent several weeks recovering. The sense of misfortune surrounding the band deepened further when, just days later, dancer Morgan Musisi was involved in a serious road acci-dent. Though he survived, the string of tragedies cast a dark cloud over Rwenzori's return.

Despite the U.S. tour not yielding the success the band had anticipated, Fred Kanyike insisted on portraying it as a triumphant journey. He claimed that as a result of their acclaimed performances abroad, Rwenzori had received invitations to tour several African countries, including Kenya, Rwanda, Burundi, Tanzania, and Zambia. He also falsely boasted that an American promoter had extended an offer for the band to return to the U.S. for another tour.

The Ugandan music scene had also undergone significant changes during Rwenzori's absence. Peterson Mutebi and the Tames had solidified their position as the country's undisputed pop culture icons. Their music dominated the airwaves, and their live performances were major events. Mutebi, a gifted performer and showman, had an undeniable charisma that made him difficult to compete with. Although Rwenzori still boasted some of the finest musicians in Uganda, the void they had left had been filled by new groups, many of which had risen from relative obscurity to prominence. Struggling to reclaim their former glory, Rwenzori found themselves in a precarious position.

While the band viewed their U.S. trip as a mixed experience, valuable for exposure but financially disastrous, Ali Fadhul, who had bankrolled much of the trip, saw things differently. He had heard about the large crowds at their New York shows and took Kanyike's exaggerated claims at face value, assuming the tour had been lucrative. He was particularly enthralled by Kanyike's fabricated accounts of meeting legendary American artists like James Brown. In reality, Rwenzori was financially worse off than when they had left Uganda. However, Fadhul believed they had made substantial money and demanded a share of the profits. This created a tense and distrustful relationship between him and Kanyike.

Back in Uganda, Rwenzori resumed their performances at the Equatoria Hotel. However, the magic was gone. The band struggled to recapture its past appeal, and while their musicianship remained strong, they no longer commanded the same level of excitement. In late 1975, a surprising new opportunity emerged. A Japanese music promoter, who had heard about the band's traditional dance routines, approached Kanyike with an offer for Rwenzori to perform in Japan. The plan was for them to replace a Kenyan traditional music group at a Nasu Machi hotel, a popular tourist destination in Nasu, northeast of Tokyo, known for its natural hot springs. Unlike their U.S. tour, where they had to cover their own expenses from ticket sales, this arrangement offered far greater financial security because the Japanese hotel would handle all travel and living expenses.

To prepare for the tour, Kanyike placed newspaper advertisements inviting young performers to audition for the band. Over the next few months, Rwenzori intensified their rehearsal schedule, sharpening and expanding their traditional dance routines in anticipation of Japanese audiences who were expected to relish spectacle as much as sound. In a move that surprised many, Kanyike chose not to include Ecklas Kawalya and Fred Masagazi on the tour. The irony was hard to miss. All three men were in their mid to late thirties, and yet Kanyike concluded that the physically demanding choreography required for the tour would be too strenuous for his two colleagues. Determined to present a visibly youthful and agile ensemble, he left them behind. To inject fresh energy into the group, he recruited Philly Lutaaya, who had been leading Rwenzori's River Nile Band.

When Rwenzori arrived in Japan in early 1976, they were warmly received at their Nasu Machi hotel, where they performed almost daily for local Japanese tourists. Although the financial rewards were far superior to those of their failed U.S. tour, band members later admitted that they felt more like an exotic curiosity than a respected artistic act. Nonetheless, the trip was a much-needed success and allowed them to regain financial stability.

The band returned to Uganda in May 1976. However, the challenges of re-establishing themselves in Kampala's evolving music scene proved overwhelming. They managed to record only two new tracks, both of which became hugely popular. Rwenzori, an anthem celebrating their tours of the U.S. and Japan, positioned the band as cultural representatives of Uganda, while Zaliwango (a female name) became one of their standout recordings.

The song Zaliwango was written by Frank Mbalire's older brother, Adrian Lwere, who had also composed several of Frank's other songs. Zaliwango featured an all-star lineup, including Frank Mbalire (rhythm guitar and vocals), Philly Lutaaya (trumpet), and Saul Kaliba (trumpet), with Eddy Ganja (lead guitar) and Andrew Tamale (bass). Backup vocals were provided by three young Makerere University students: Grace Musoke, Oliver, and Vicky Luyima. Longtime friends of the band, they had already served as muses for several compositions, including Grace, written by Andrew Tamale and performed by Philly Lutaaya and Freddy Sebulime; Oliver, composed by Frank Mbalire; and Vicky, written by Billy Mutebi.

Meanwhile, tensions between Kanyike and Ali Fadhul intensified. Fadhul remained convinced that Rwenzori had earned substantial profits from its overseas tours and continued to demand his share of what were, in reality, nonexistent proceeds. Matters were further inflamed by Fadhul's suspicion that Kanyike had been involved in a tryst with one of his wives. Their exchanges soon turned acrimonious, with raised voices and open hostility replacing any semblance of civility. Both men possessed formidable temperaments and expansive egos. Kanyike regarded himself as the éminence grise of Uganda's popular music scene, a strategist shaping its direction from behind the curtain. Fadhul, by contrast, drew authority from proximity to power, never hesitating to remind others that he could summon the formidable apparatus of the state against those who defied him. Unwilling to concede, Fadhul ultimately exercised that leverage by repossessing the band's instruments, an act that brought Rwenzori's activities to an abrupt halt. For Kanyike, the implications were chilling. In an atmosphere where detention without charge was commonplace, he feared that imprisonment on concocted accusations could easily follow.

One afternoon in 1976, as the feud with Fadhul continued to smolder, a stranger slipped quietly into Kanyike's office at Rwenzori Studios. The visitor wasted no time on pleasantries. He carried a warning. Kanyike's name had surfaced in dangerous conversations, and if he valued his life, he should leave Uganda at once. The message was unmistakable. In a climate where arrests could come without explanation and disappearances required no justification, hesitation could be fatal. Kanyike acted swiftly. Within days, he had slipped out of the country and into exile.

Kanyike eventually resettled in Poughkeepsie, a modest town in upstate New York, worlds away from the intrigue and menace that had come to define his life in Kampala. The irony was profound. The man who had once been one of Amin's most ardent musical champions, composing praise songs that echoed across Radio Uganda, now underwent a striking metamorphosis. From court troubadour of the regime, he evolved into one of its outspoken detractors, turning his voice and reputation against the government he had once exalted.

Few former members of Rwenzori went on to record memorable music after the band's dissolution. Hadija Namale, Fred Masagazi, and Ecklas Kawalya effectively retired from Uganda's music scene. Others, restless and unwilling to let the music die, sought new beginnings. Among them were Frank Mbalire and Billy Mutebi, who joined forces with a group of Ugandan and Congolese musicians to create the Kampala Black International Band. Taking over the stage at the International Hotel, they carried the torch of live music in the capital after the previous resident group had folded. Their group blended talents from Uganda and the Congo: Hussain Boyes on drums, Simon Bosa on trumpet, Albert on saxophone, and Sam Mulungi on keyboard, together with the Congolese players Balibel on bass, John Ogbomange Akinase on vocals and drums, and the vocalists Matondo and Tambwe. Not long after, Philly Lutaaya and Fred Kigozi swelled their ranks, giving the band fresh energy. Of note, Philly Lutaaya had initially tried his luck with Elly Wamala's Mascots, but he did not stay long as he preferred performing rumba-style music, which was not the Mascot's forte. For a brief moment, these ex-Rwenzori members at Kampala Black International seemed to promise a new chapter of Ugandan music.

However, one afternoon, Fred Masagazi arrived at a Kampala Black International rehearsal accompanied by an official from the president's office. Amin, he announced, wanted the musicians to vacate the International Hotel and relocate to Cape Town Villas in Munyonyo, on the shores of Lake Victoria overlooking Murchison Bay. The property had once been a private British-owned estate but was expropriated by Amin in the mid-1970s and converted into a lakeside resort that included one of his personal residences. Masagazi's message from the president was less a request than a command, and the band had no choice but to comply.

Rebranded as the Villas, the group found itself in a new home, where they attracted fresh talent. Vocalists Barbara Kyolaba and Cathy Mukasa, lead guitarist Dede Majoro, and bassist Andrew Tamale joined the group. At Cape Town Villas, whispers soon circulated about Cathy. It was said she was one of Amin's girlfriends, and that the president had even gifted her a gleaming car, a Honda Accord, that turned heads wherever it appeared. Whether true or not, the rumor added an air of glamour and danger around the Villas, where music, politics, and power seemed to mingle in equal measure.

The Villas benefited from state support, with reliable pay and a high-profile venue that offered musicians a level of stability few others enjoyed. Despite these advantages, some artists still chose to move on in search of greater artistic freedom or international exposure. In late 1976, Philly Lutaaya left Uganda for Nairobi, where he reunited with fellow Ugandan musicians Johnny Kiwanuka and Paul Sserumaga in L'Orchestre Les Muzikans. With this group, he recorded Asaba on the Kenyan Musiki du Zaire label and Zongela on another Kenyan label, City Boom. Meanwhile, the Villas' tenure as the resident band at Cape Town Villas came to an end with the overthrow of Idi Amin.

In the mid-1980s, Lutaaya, along with Billy Mutebi and Frank Mbalire, relocated to Sweden. It was there that Lutaaya's defining moment arrived. In 1986, he released Born in Africa, an album that became a runaway success and catapulted him to superstardom across Uganda and beyond. Lutaaya continued to build on this momentum in Sweden, recording a string of critically acclaimed albums, including Merry Christmas, Tumusinze, and Alone. In 1988, he made headlines as the first prominent Ugandan to publicly reveal that he was living with HIV. This courageous act broke a cultural silence and gave a human face to a devastating epidemic that was tearing through Ugandan communities. At its peak, the AIDS crisis was claiming tens of thousands of lives, leaving behind grieving families, orphaned children, and entire villages reeling from loss. In this climate of fear, stigma, and misinformation, Lutaaya's public declaration was nothing short of heroic. Lutaaya's album Alone, released shortly after his announcement, carried a powerful message of personal struggle and resilience. Its title track was a deeply moving testimony in which Lutaaya reflected on the isolation, fear, and social rejection he faced. The song became a rallying cry for AIDS awareness and prevention, and was widely used in public health campaigns. By turning his diagnosis into a platform for advocacy, Lutaaya not only changed the national conversation about HIV/AIDS but also became one of Uganda's most influential and beloved artists. His legacy endures not just in music, but in the countless lives his honesty helped to save.

The dancer Michael Luzinda took a different path, joining Afrigo Band, which had become the resident band at Cape Town Villas alongside the Villas. Known for his warm and easygoing nature, Luzinda befriended Amin's wife, Sarah, who had once been a dancer herself and admired his performances. Then, without warning, he disappeared. Some Ugandans speculated that he had been murdered by Amin's State Research Bureau, possibly because of his association with Sarah. To this day, the circumstances of his disappearance remain shrouded in mystery, a haunting reminder of the silence and fear that enveloped so many lives during Amin's rule.

After Amin was overthrown in April 1979, Fred Kanyike returned to Uganda and attempted to resurrect Rwenzori. Billy Mutebi, Frank Mbalire, and Fred Kigozi embraced the idea and rejoined the band. Kanyike also recruited new members, including Gerald Nadibanga (drums), Florence Sebalu (vocals), Norah Kasirye (vocals), and Florence Okurut (vocals). In 1980, the band released two songs openly supporting the Democratic Party under the Africanza label: D.P. Egumire (D.P. Is Strong) and D.P. Chama Changu (D.P. Is My Party). By this time, Uganda had returned to multiparty politics. The 1980 elections saw four parties competing: Milton Obote's Uganda People's Congress (UPC), the Democratic Party (DP),

Yoweri Museveni's Uganda Patriotic Movement (UPM), and Mayanja Nkangi's Conservative Party (CP). Kanyike and Rwenzori publicly aligned with the DP. The return of party politics also sparked a brief resurgence for several musicians from an earlier generation who had spent years in relative obscurity. Though not nationally prominent, they were deeply admired in their regions and remembered for songs that had once echoed through local markets, bars, and village gatherings.

Among them was John Oryem from the Acholi region in the north. Known for his sharp wit and social commentary, Oryem had recorded multiple tracks for His Master's Voice label in the 1950s, including Auma, Lawiny Pa Nyako Odongo, and Lapwony Ruku Laci. Oryem followed in the tradition of Acholi musician-poets like the blind nanga player Lakana Omal (also known as Adok Too) and the poet Okot p'Bitek. During the 1980 campaigns, Oryem performed at rallies for UPC candidate Otema Allimadi in Gulu East, drawing large crowds wherever he went. Allimadi would later serve as Prime Minister in the Obote II government.

Paulo "Machunia" Ojambo, a respected figure from the Samia region in eastern Uganda, enjoyed a similar revival. In the late 1950s, he recorded several songs on the Mzuri label, including Balimboya Emikoye (I'll Be Tied With Ropes) and Abalayi Bakhirana (Some Are More Beautiful Than Others). With his humorous lyrics and unmistakable vocal delivery, Ojambo had built a loyal following across eastern Uganda and western Kenya. During the 1980 elections, he joined the UPC campaign trail and performed for candidate Romano Emmanuel Masiga, who contested and won the Iganga South East constituency. Masiga would go on to serve as chairman of the Busoga Growers Cooperative Union, which under his leadership grew into one of the most successful agricultural cooperatives in the country. These campaign performances gave Oryem and Ojambo one final moment in the national spotlight. Sadly, Oryem's life ended in tragedy when he was bludgeoned to death by his wife during a domestic dispute.

When Obote's UPC was declared the winner and Obote returned to power, Fred Kanyike suddenly found himself in a precarious position.

Having spent much of the early 1970s glorifying Amin and vilifying Obote in his songs, he feared retribution. This dramatic reversal, though striking, must be understood within the context of Uganda's evolving political and social landscape. Unwilling to gamble his safety under the new administration, Kanyike left Uganda once again and returned to Poughkeepsie. There, far from the limelight he had once commanded, he took up work as a janitor at Dutchess Community College. It might have been the quiet end of a once-prominent career, were it not for a chance encounter with a group of students who discovered his musical gifts. Invited to join their band, alongside Bob Lehane on drums, Michaela Friest on bass, Adrian Maier on rhythm and lead guitar, and Paul Sheridan on saxophone, Kanyike returned briefly to the recording studio. The resulting album featured tracks such as Jambo Lady, Jesus, and Wonderful World, bringing a final, understated close to his recording journey.

Thus ended the story of Rwenzori, a band that had risen with grand ambition, dazzled audiences both at home and abroad, and fallen victim to the turbulent tides of Ugandan history. Its members scattered across different continents, their paths shaped by politics, exile, and personal tragedies. Some, like Philly Lutaaya, achieved legendary status. Others, like Kanyike, faded into quiet exile. But for a brief, unforgettable time, Rwenzori had embodied the dreams of a generation, dreams of music, success, and international recognition.

Afrigo, the Ebonies, and the Rise of Uganda's Post-Rwenzori Bands

As the Rwenzori Band pursued recognition in the United States, the music landscape at home was quietly undergoing a transformation of its own. A new wave was gathering momentum in Uganda, shaped less by established bandleaders and more by restless, ambitious youth determined to define their own sound. The groups that began to surface in the mid-1970s were fueled by raw creativity, experimentation, and a hunger to break from older templates. Many of their members were barely out of school. They rehearsed in modest neighborhood spaces, drawing inspiration from Congolese rumba and local rhythms.

What makes this surge all the more striking is the context in which it unfolded. Nightlife in Kampala and other towns was increasingly constrained by curfews, political uncertainty, and economic hardship. Venues opened and closed unpredictably. Equipment was scarce. Public gatherings were often shadowed by suspicion. But rather than extinguish musical expression, these pressures seemed to intensify it. Out of restriction came reinvention. In an era when stages were fewer and freedoms narrower, a generation of young musicians found new ways to be heard, setting the tone for a vibrant and resilient chapter in Uganda's musical story.

Historically, Uganda's nightlife was vibrant and freewheeling, with little or no enforcement of regulations governing the operation of bars and nightclubs. As a result, nightspots catered to patrons from the early evening hours until well into the morning. The first real test to this laissez-faire approach came after Milton Obote's government declared a State of Emergency following the suspension of the Ugandan constitution in 1966. What followed was a withering of nightlife, especially in Kampala. After Amin's 1971 coup, the State of Emergency became irrelevant, despite never being formally lifted, and nightlife made a tentative comeback with unrestricted operating hours for bars and nightclubs. This newfound freedom, however, was short-lived. As Amin's regime consolidated power, the fear of encountering violent soldiers at impromptu roadblocks deterred many from venturing out at night. These roadblocks became infamous for the brutalization of civilians.

In 1975, the government issued a decree limiting nightclub hours from 7 pm to 1 am, and restricting drinking times to 12:45 pm to 2 pm and 5 pm to 10 pm. These rules were rigorously enforced by often inebriated soldiers who roamed the streets on the lookout for any violations. Punishments for offenders ranged from severe beatings to imprisonment and even extrajudicial killings. This clampdown on nightlife was part of a broader pattern of terror that characterized the Amin regime.

The Uganda-Tanzania War in 1978 ushered in a nationwide curfew, further suppressing nightlife and emptying streets after dark. Despite this, the indomitable spirit of Ugandan musicians persevered. Their music became a beacon of hope, offering solace to a nation suffering under Amin's oppressive rule. New musical groups emerged, while others, long overshadowed by established bands like Peterson Mutebi's Tames, Mayanja and Kawuma's Cranes, and Kanyike's Rwenzori International, found their time to shine. The period from 1974 to 1980 saw a surge of creativity, with these groups recording a string of hits that would become the most memorable songs of the era.

In a strategic move, Kanyike and his Rwenzori International formed the River Nile Band in July 1974 to fill the void left by his impending

United States tour with Rwenzori International. The goal was to maintain their residency at the Equatoria Hotel, a coveted spot in Kampala's music scene. To ensure the new group would rise to the occasion, Kanyike enlisted Philly Lutaaya, a rising star from the Cranes band. At the time, the Cranes were playing at Silver Springs every day except Sunday, when they were at Pearl Afrique on Martin Road in Old Kampala. Lutaaya had joined the Cranes in October 1973 following his return from Kinshasa. Lutaaya, however, set a condition for joining and leading the River Nile Band. He demanded complete creative freedom in crafting the band's music. He told Kanyike that their music would likely be distinct from Rwenzori's established beat. Kanyike, recognizing Philly's immense talent and potential, granted him his wish.

Under Lutaaya's charismatic leadership, the River Nile Band established a unique identity. Lutaaya, with his flamboyant fashion sense of wide bell-bottoms, slim-fitting flowery shirts, four-inch platform shoes, and his signature black beret, became the band's iconic frontman. His exceptional vocal range and musical versatility on the trumpet, bass, and drums underscored his status as an extraordinary musical talent. Other members of the River Nile Band were equally formidable. In addition to Philly Lutaaya, the group included Eddy Ganja on lead guitar, Alex Mukulu on bass, rhythm guitar, and trumpet, Musisi on drums, Johnny "Negro" Kiwanuka on saxophone and trumpet, John Sembera on trumpet, Mwebe on saxophone, Nathan Semalulu on drums, Andrew Tamale on bass, Geoffrey Nsereko on vocals, Henry Kasaasa Kanyike on rhythm guitar (he was Fred Kanyike's younger brother), Roger Musisi on drums, Michael "Mike" Lubega on lead guitar, Freddy Sebulime on vocals, and Paul Sserumaga on vocals.

The River Nile Band exceeded all expectations, impressing both the Equatoria Hotel's management and its discerning patrons. With Philly Lutaaya at the creative helm, the band's performances began drawing new and curious audiences, eager to experience their distinctive sound. Brimming with talented singers and songwriters, the band dedicated themselves wholeheartedly to their craft. When not performing, they could often be found at Rwenzori Studios, tirelessly honing their sound and recording new material. There was much experimentation with musical styles, and the sheer musical ingenuity within the band was palpable. Members constantly pushed and inspired one another, resulting in a vibrant musical style that stood distinctly apart from the sound of Rwenzori International Band. It was clear that the River Nile Band was poised to usher in a new chapter of Ugandan popular music, even as the country itself continued to grapple with uncertainty and change.

It was this collaborative synergy, with Philly Lutaaya firmly at the center, that propelled the River Nile Band into producing their crowning achievement, the LP Ashita, a remarkable testament to their musical innovation and spirit. Released in 1975 on Rwenzori's Africanza label, the eight-track album captured the energy of the times, particularly the nation's fascination with the Congolese cavacha beat. This fast-paced, syncopated drum rhythm had become a national sensation in Uganda, largely through Mopero wa Maloba and his Orchestre Shama Shama from Kinshasha. Lutaaya and the River Nile Band seamlessly integrated cavacha into their own songs, creating a fresh sound that felt both contemporary and distinctly Ugandan.

The Ashita album was met with widespread acclaim. It featured standout tracks such as Philly Lutaaya's Nkowoola (Heartfelt Plea), Johnny Kiwanuka's Kamale Galeke (I Will Just Give Up), Alex Mukulu's Senga Mpa Eddembe (Auntie, Give Me Freedom) and Ashita (a female name), Geoffrey Nsereko's Kabaseke (Let Them Laugh), and Fred Sebulime's Gida. In Gida, set against a blissfully alluring cavacha beat, Sebulime delivered a heartfelt ballad in his characteristic falsetto:

> I have but one love,
> she outshines them all.
> I adore her grace—
> her eyes and perfect teeth, wonders to behold.
> How can I bridge the distance between us?
> Though we are far apart, just say the word,
> and I will journey to you.

> I am not swayed by finery,
> nor by fair skin or lofty height.
> My heart is set on one, my Gida,
> my chosen one,
> Mama Gida, extraordinary Gida.
> How can I bridge the distance between us?
> Though we are far apart, just say the word,
> and I will journey to you.
> My love for her knows no bounds;
> she captivates me completely.
> She is my chosen one, my babe,
> in her flared pants, she is a vision,
> as if born to dazzle.
> Gida, I yearn for your closeness,
> for I have declared my love for you openly.

Although the River Nile Band was primarily based in Kampala, performing regularly at Equatoria Hotel, they occasionally ventured beyond the capital to reach new audiences. In November and December 1974, the band embarked on a memorable tour of Eastern Uganda. Their first stop was Soroti, where they performed at the Soroti Hotel. The concert was a resounding success, drawing a sold-out crowd that packed the venue and responded with unrestrained enthusiasm to the band's cavacha-style rhythms, alive with trembling sensuality and delicate overtones. Following their triumph in Soroti, the River Nile Band continued to Mbale, staging performances at both the prestigious Elgon Hotel and the lively Nandutu Nightclub. In both venues, the band was met by large, passionate audiences who could not get enough of their spirited beat and lively stage presence. The River Nile Band also frequently played at smaller, more intimate venues around Kampala, keeping their connection with the capital's nightlife vibrant.

The River Nile Band's meteoric rise left a lasting mark on Kampala's music scene, its inventive spirit embraced by Ugandan audiences as a welcome breath of fresh air. The success of the River Nile Band owed much to Philly Lutaaya, its bandleader known for his tenacity and strong work ethic. Born on October 19, 1951, to Tito and Justin Lutaaya in Mengo, Kampala, Philip Bongoley Lutaaya hailed from a family of educators; his father was a teacher at Kasaka Boys Primary School, and his mother was the headmistress of Kasaka Girls Primary School. Lutaaya began his education at Kasaka Boys Primary School and later attended Budo Kabinja Junior School in Kampala before joining Kololo Secondary School in 1969, where he played in the school band.

Lutaaya's musical journey as a recording artist started early. In 1969, singing with Vox Nationale based at New Life Nightclub, he released his first single titled Philly Empisa Zo (Philly Mind Your Manners), followed by hits like Flora Atwoki (a female name), Tugila Tulinda (Let's Wait), and Bwo'oba Osimye (If You Are Appreciative). During this time, he also contributed vocals to Vox Nationale's hit Baasi Namakwekwe (The Namakwekwe Bus). In 1970, when Vox Nationale left Uganda to return to the Congo, Lutaaya was invited to join them in Kinshasa, marking a significant milestone in his career. His stubborn streak and relentless work ethic would prove instrumental in his future successes, shaping him into the iconic musician and HIV/AIDS activist he would become.

Despite its success, the River Nile Band folded when Rwenzori International returned from their U.S. tour in May 1975. However, the influence of cavacha persisted. After a brief stint with River Nile, guitarist Fred Sebulime joined the Cranes Band and released Monica in 1976. This track is arguably the most iconic Ugandan cavacha hit. The success of Monica inspired the Cranes to continue integrating the cavacha beat into their music. Struggling to maintain relevance in the Ugandan music scene, the Cranes recorded and released more songs driven by the cavacha rhythm in 1976 to wide praise. Notable among these were Eddy Ganja's Anifa (a female name) and Nzena Nkoze (All of Me Emaciated), as well as Davies Kiyingi's Marcelinah (a female name), all recorded under the Cranes Edition label.

Another band that emerged in the wake of Rwenzori's absence was the Flames, formed in 1974 following the disbandment of the Marines Band. To understand the Flames' impact on Uganda's popular music scene, it is necessary to trace back to the origins of the Marines Band in 1971. Initially based at Bonanza Nightclub in Kitintale, a bleak shantytown on the edge of the more affluent Mbuya neighborhood of Kampala, the Marines gained popularity as a spirited group of young men who gave their all on stage, thrilling patrons of the newly opened bar. The neighborhood had a semi-rural feel, with dirt paths, small garden plots where residents grew maize and beans, and goats and chickens roaming the yards. Bonanza was owned by renowned politician and trade union leader Humphrey Lwande, a Kenyan Samia who played a significant role in Uganda's struggle for independence.

The Marines Band, comprised entirely of high school students, included notable members such as David Mukasa (bandleader, vocalist, and rhythm guitar), Peter Kayiwa (bass guitar), Hanny Sensuwa (lead singer and lead guitarist), Fred Muwonge, Godfrey Isingoma (tumba drums), Peter Kabale (later transitioning to saxophone), Michael Lubega, Gerald Kabogoza, and John Kakoza. Like many young musicians at the time, they relied on rented musical instruments. In their case, they rented from Mzee Bukenya of the BKG Band, also based in Kitintale. This youthful band of musicians transformed Bonanza into one of Kampala's premier nightlife spots.

By 1972, the Marines had started recording and swiftly achieved commercial success with hits under local labels GLK and BMP. Their repertoire ranged from upbeat numbers to poignant songs exploring themes of human fragility and death. Their notable songs included David Mukasa's Jenifa Wange (My Jennifer) and Mbeera Eno (This Is Where I Live), Hanny Sensuwa's Remember Hanny, and Gerald Kabogoza's Abazadde Mbebaza (Thanking Parents). They excelled particularly in poignant tracks like Hanny Sensuwa's Kandye Ebyange (Eating What Is Mine) and David Mukasa's Okufirwa (Bereavement). Despite Okufirwa's somber lyrics, the

Marines managed to pull everything together on this mournful cut. The song's sebene section was grounded in the uniquely Ugandan kagutema music tradition.

In early 1974, following the disbandment of the Marines Band, which was prompted in part by the defection of members such as Peter Mukasa and Peter Kabale to Peterson Mutebi's Tames, Hanny Sensuwa briefly joined the Susana Band at the once-renowned Susana Nightclub. During its heyday in the 1960s, Susana had been one of the epicenters of Kampala's nightlife, a glamorous venue where stars like Eclas Kawalya and Hadija Namale ruled the stage. Its rise to fame was supported by a powerful group of fun-loving patrons: Sam Odaka, Elizaphan "Phan" Ntende, Roger Mukasa, and Sam Mukasa. By the time Sensuwa arrived, however, Susana's golden age had already passed. The original financial backers were no longer involved. Sam Odaka had gone into exile in Dar es Salaam following Idi Amin's overthrow of the Obote government. Roger Mukasa had lost his position as Chairman of the Coffee Marketing Board, and while Phan Ntende remained at the Lint Marketing Board, he had shifted his focus away from the nightclub to concentrate on building and expanding the Rotary Club in Uganda. Without their support, Susana struggled to maintain its former sparkle.

Determined to breathe new life into the venue, Sensuwa joined forces with two longtime members of the Susana Band: the Congolese vocalist and guitarist Ginaro and the celebrated musician Martin Munyenga. A natural showman, Sensuwa thrilled audiences with his electrifying guitar solos and theatrical flair. He would lie flat on his back, one leg raised, strumming his guitar as it rested on his chest. The pose always drew wild applause. At other moments, he slung the guitar behind his neck and leaned forward to pluck out sharp, lyrical melodies with startling precision. His technique was both acrobatic and expressive, effortlessly weaving Congolese rumba lines with rhythmic flourishes that gave his performances a pulse and personality all their own. Whether upright or upside down, Sensuwa played with total command, a whirlwind of sound, movement, and sheer charisma.

Sensuwa, Ginaro, and Munyenga managed to lure back loyal patrons from the 1960s while attracting a new crowd eager to experience the club's storied past. Their partnership injected fresh energy into Susana, sparking a modest revival. But the resurgence was fleeting, and Sensuwa's stint at the club ended almost as suddenly as it had begun. The pull to reunite with his former bandmates from the Marines grew stronger, and by the latter half of 1974, he gave in to that call. He left Susana and teamed up with David Mukasa and Davies Kiyingi, a former member of the Cranes Band, to form The Flames. The birth of The Flames marked a fresh turning point, not only for Kampala's nightlife but also for the musicians who would go on to enchant listeners with their music. At the center of this new chapter stood Hanny Sensuwa, a magnetic performer whose rise to stardom was as bold and unforgettable as the music he created.

Born in 1954 to Nsanja Muloddokaayi and Mary Namuddu, Sensuwa was raised in a household steeped in music. His father sang in the church choir, while his mother occasionally graced the stage at Susana Nightclub, performing alongside icons such as Ecklas Kawalya and Martin Munyenga. His uncle, Sserubugo, also became a well-known figure in Kampala's street music scene during the 1970s, often seen performing lively folk songs with his daughters.

Sensuwa's own musical journey began in earnest in 1971, at the age of 17, when he joined a band performing at Baseesa Nightclub in Bwaise. His remarkable confidence and commanding stage presence were evident from the very start. That same year, his breakthrough arrived with the hit song Asimwe (a female name), backed by the Top Ten Band. The following year, just before joining the Marines Band at Bonanza Nightclub, he recorded Nkoye N'ensi (Tired with the World) with Peterson Mutebi's Tames Band, although this track failed to capture widespread attention.

Throughout his early career, Sensuwa evolved through a series of collaborations with various groups, refining his craft and sharpening his skills. However, it was with the Flames that he truly took Uganda by storm, unleashing a wave of raw vibrancy that generated a remarkable buzz across the country. The Flames initially performed at VIP Night Club in Zana on the Kampala-Entebbe Road, before relocating to Rita Night Club in Kibuye by the end of the year. The core group of the Flames also recorded under different names, calling themselves the B.S.L Boys when recording for the Busula record label, and taking on the Satana Band moniker for records released on the Satana label.

Hanny Sensuwa's honey-toned vocals and irresistible guitar lines became the recognizable sound of the Flames' beat. He cleverly blended the folksy ostinato of kadongo kamu with the vigorous and sparkling soukous guitar-driven rhythm, crafting a melodic and rhythmic idiom that became his hallmark. This fusion was evident in the songs recorded under the Satana label starting in 1976, including hits such as Muleke Anna (Leave Anna Alone), Debula (a female name), and Oyitangayo (Swing By). Margaret "Meega" Nakintu, who would become a longtime collaborator, backed him on these recordings.

Among all his compositions, Oyitangayo, colloquially known as Robina, captured the hearts of Ugandans with its lush romanticism. Sensuwa's signature guitar notes bent and convulsed before building into a frenzied rhythm, creating an irresistible anthem. Oyitangayo propelled Sensuwa to the forefront of Kampala's live music scene and transformed Rita Nightclub into a must-visit destination for a night of revelry. The song echoed endlessly through the streets of Ugandan towns, played in bars, broadcast daily on Radio Uganda, hummed by farmers in the countryside, and sung by schoolchildren in playgrounds. Robina, the song's protagonist, became part of Uganda's popular lexicon, synonymous with beauty and grace. The story behind the song, as recounted by a confidant of Sensuwa, lends it an intimate dimension. Sensuwa had a close friend who was not only an ardent admirer of his music but also a devoted presence at every Flames performance at Rita Nightclub. The friend was deeply in love with a young woman named Robina Nalwoga, a striking beauty from Makindye. Eager to celebrate their romance, he asked Sensuwa to compose a song in her honor. Sensuwa agreed, crafting a melody and lyrics that distilled tenderness, longing, and the exhilaration of new love. The lyrics reflected the romantic longing of the moment:

Don't hesitate to find a moment to visit—
swing by Ndeeba, come see me, Robina.
These days I'm at home on vacation;
I would come to you, but I'm afraid of getting in trouble.
Your workplace might seem better, but you're always busy.
Robina, open your heart and understand:
I am the only boy who truly loves you,
with all my mind and one sincere heart.
This isn't mere fancy—it's the truth.
Please reject those who pursue you,
for they don't deserve your love.
Robina, be wary of their falsehoods;
though many girls may desire me,
my heart yearns only for you.
When can we meet to plan our future?
I've earned enough, so worry not.
Robina, I'm not like those worthless men
who tarnish the meaning of manhood—
their actions are not the way to be.
They abandon women after conquest.
If your soul is with mine,
that is the path we should follow.

Although Sensuwa's subsequent works never quite matched the towering success of Oyitangayo, he continued to record songs that were well-received by fans. Among these was the 1978 Harriet Ensobi Tewali (There Was No Fault, Harriet), released on the Busula label. During this time, Sensuwa and the Flames emerged as a dominant force in Ugandan music. Bands that had once reigned supreme, like Kanyike's Rwenzori International, found themselves eclipsed by the Flames at Rita Nightclub, as the new generation of musical energy captured the imagination of a country still searching for joy amidst hardship.

Upon their return from their U.S. tour in 1975, the members of Rwenzori International were stunned by the dramatic shift in Uganda's music scene. In their absence, the Flames had surged to prominence, igniting Kampala's nightlife and stealing the spotlight they had once effortlessly commanded. Rita Nightclub, which had previously been just another venue on the circuit, was now the epicenter of the city's after-hours glamour. Hadija Namale recalled the moment it all hit home. She and Kanyike, still riding the high of their American tour, arrived at Rita expecting the usual nods of recognition and open doors. Instead, they found themselves at the back of a long, snaking queue of eager revelers. For nearly an hour, they stood there, anonymous and ignored, inching forward with the crowd. There was no special treatment, no front-row welcome, no waved entrance fee. It was a stunning fall from grace. Just a year earlier, their names alone would have turned heads and opened doors. Now, they were waiting in line like everyone else, hoping to see the very band that had taken their place.

In the 1960s and 1970s, Ndeeba, a Kampala suburb just south of the Kabaka's Lake, thrived as a vibrant hub of nightlife. Among its standout venues was a large dance hall nicknamed Nkooko, celebrated for its jukebox that played the latest hits of the day. Jukeboxes had become a fixture in bars across Uganda, largely due to the efforts of Dutch entrepreneur Paul Kerssemakers, who built a successful business installing and maintaining them nationwide.

In early 1968, Kerssemakers acquired Nkooko and renamed it Peacock Nightclub. His interests in Kampala's entertainment scene ran deep. He also owned the Bat Valley Bar and Restaurant on Bombo Road and Jajja Marina in Munyonyo. Jajja Marina featured a dock for the African Queen, a yacht he co-owned at the time with Don Gordon, a British businessman enriched by copper mining in Kilembe, and a Danish investor. To ease public concerns over foreign dominance, entrepreneurs like Kerssemakers often partnered with well-known Ugandan figures. For some of his venues in Kampala, he joined forces with Leonard Mugwanya, grandson of Stanislaus Mugwanya, one of the three Regents who ruled on behalf of the young King Daudi Chwa in 1897.

In May 1968, Kerssemakers transformed the rear of Peacock Nightclub into a recording studio and launched Serenade Studios along with its associated label. He later added the URA label, which focused on kadongo kamu music. To manage daily operations, he brought on Simon Beine and Edmund Batte. Batte, Uganda's first indigenous music producer, was also a prolific songwriter. As early as 1961, he had recorded celebrated tracks like Kulomukwano Guno (Because of This Love) and Norah under the AGS label. He also sang on Regina, a collaboration with Elly Wamala, Ginalo, Makassy, and Philip Ngoma.

Later, Kerssemakers opened a second studio behind the Serenade Record Shop on Kampala Road. And in 1969, he created an in-house group, the Serenade Top Ten Band, led by drummer and bassist Joseph Ndugga. Eventually known simply as Top Ten, the band became a pillar of Uganda's recording industry. They provided backing for nearly every major artist who recorded at Serenade Studios. Their polished performances rivaled Kenya's top studio bands, and once under contract, they focused almost entirely on studio work, rarely appearing on stage.

The climate shifted dramatically in 1972 when President Idi Amin launched his Economic War. This sweeping campaign aimed to dismantle foreign control over Uganda's economy and shift ownership to Black Ugandans. Amin positioned the initiative as a blow against colonial dependency and an effort to reclaim the country's wealth. Asians holding British, Indian, Pakistani, or Bangladeshi passports were expelled, and their businesses were seized. Even well-established foreign enterprises were not spared. Amin declared that all assets would be handed over to Africans, regardless of foreign objections. By December 1972, British-owned plantations and factories had been nationalized or banned. Within months, the state had absorbed nearly all remaining British investments. Alongside these economic changes, Amin renamed colonial landmarks to reflect African pride. Queen Elizabeth National Park became Rwenzori National Park. Lake Albert was rechristened Lake Mobutu Sese Seko.

Streets such as Queens Road and Salisbury Road were renamed Lumumba Avenue and Nkrumah Road, respectively.

For businessmen like Kerssemakers, the writing was on the wall. In 1974, he handed over control of Serenade Studios to Simon Beine, while Leonard Mugwanya retained ownership of the Peacock and Bat Valley nightclubs. That same year, tragedy struck Serenade's Top Ten Band. A serious road accident left bandleader Joseph Ndugga physically incapacitated. Without his leadership, the band lost its cohesion and spark. When Kerssemakers exited the music business, Serenade Studios fell silent. With no clear path forward, the Top Ten Band dissolved, marking the end of Uganda's most influential studio ensemble.

In the wake of Serenade's decline, a new sound began to echo from Peacock Nightclub. Inspired by the success of resident bands elsewhere, Leonard Mugwanya introduced a new house group in 1975. He called them the Peacocks. Bold and full of promise, the band stepped into the void left by Top Ten. Its members included gifted young musicians such as Tom Ssengendo on lead guitar, Joseph "J.J." Otieno Adamson on bass, Kasule Mopepe on conga drums, Godfrey Kaggwa on vocals and percussion, and Stephen Mark Kajjubi. The Peacocks quickly made their mark. In the same year, they released several popular tracks under the self-titled Peacock label, including Ensi Temanyirika (The World Is Incomprehensible), Adyeri, and Yesu Mudungu (Jesus in the Desert). It was the release of Yesu Mudungu that eventually brought the group into conflict with Idi Amin's government.

The turbulent political climate in Uganda shaped its music, powerfully intertwining art, hardship, and resistance. Yesu Mudungu (Jesus in the Desert) appears at first to be an innocuous and pleasant song, hardly the kind that would ordinarily provoke controversy. Its lyrics draw inspiration from the New Testament, particularly Matthew 14, which recounts how Jesus, after the beheading of John the Baptist, withdrew to a solitary place. However, the crowds followed him. As hunger overtook the people and the disciples found themselves without sufficient provisions, Jesus performed the miracle of feeding the multitude with five loaves and two fish. Later, he walked upon the water, further affirming his divine authority.

Many Ugandans, however, came to view Yesu Mudungu as a veiled critique of Idi Amin's regime. Just as the hungry crowd in Matthew 14 gathered in search of sustenance, Ugandans were starving under the devastating effects of the Economic War. The forced expulsion of Asians and the seizure of European enterprises had plunged the country into a state of chronic shortage. Essential goods such as salt, cooking oil, toiletries, and grain became scarce. Even sugar, a beloved staple, was in short supply. After the government took over the Indian-owned Madhvani and Mehta sugar estates, a lack of foreign currency to repair or replace broken machinery forced Uganda to import sugar. Inflation soared and unemployment reached unprecedented levels, intensifying the public's despair.

In this climate of desperation, the people longed for new leadership, someone who could liberate them from Idi Amin's brutal excesses and the economic decline that had devastated their lives. Thus, when Tom Ssengendo sang the line, "And the people wanted Jesus to be their king," it was widely interpreted as a rejection of Idi Amin and a call for a new savior. While it remains uncertain if Idi Amin himself saw the song in the same light, elements within his government were clearly displeased. Soldiers were dispatched to threaten members of the Peacock Band, and the pressure eventually forced Tom Ssengendo, Stephen Kajjubi, and others into exile in neighboring Kenya.

In an unrelated but equally tragic incident, Leonard Mugwanya, owner of both the Peacock Nightclub and the Peacock Band, was gunned down by Obote soldiers around February or March 1981. Milton Obote had returned to power on December 17, 1980, and his second term was marred by extreme violence perpetrated by poorly trained and undisciplined security forces, echoing many of the brutal practices seen under Idi Amin's rule.

In the shadow of political repression and curfews, as Kampala's once-vibrant nightlife faded into silence, a spark of artistic revival was unexpectedly lit. One night in 1975, veteran musicians Andrew Kyambadde and

Steven Sempasa, pillars of Uganda's golden music era, sat nursing drinks in a dimly lit bar, trading memories of a vanished time. They spoke of full dance floors, midnight jam sessions, and clubs that pulsed with life until dawn. The conversation turned wistful, then urgent. How had it all disappeared?

Across the room sat two elegant women. As the musicians invited them over, nostalgia turned electric. One of them, Frances Namukwaya, accepted their offer to sing. When her voice rose, it was clear, soulful, and haunting. She seemed to conjure the very spirit of the old Kampala. It was more than a song; it was a revelation. Kyambadde and Sempasa looked at each other with recognition. They would go to Nairobi, far from the constraints of military rule, to reclaim their musical voice and introduce the country to Namukwaya's astonishing talent.

Following this spark of inspiration, Kyambadde and Sempasa spent several weeks crafting songs they hoped would enthrall Ugandan audiences and affirm that their creative peak was far from behind them. Eager to mark a new chapter, they launched a new label, Blue Star. They assembled a talented group of musicians, some based in Nairobi, and convened in the city to rehearse for several days before heading into the studio. This impromptu group, named Orchestre Blue Stars Kampala, featured a diverse lineup. The vocalists included Andrew Kyambadde, Steven Sempasa, Freddie Ntare, Joseph Kateregga, Frances Namukwaya, and B. Mugerwa. The instrumentalists were Meddy Matovu, formerly of Peterson Mutebi's Tames, on rhythm guitar, Sammy Kasule on bass, Dede Majoro on lead guitar, and saxophonists Elliot Adwong and Johnny "Negro" Kiwanuka. The band released a number of highly acclaimed songs, including Frances Namukwaya's Empisazo Zirongose Lwebuga (Mend Your Ways, Lwebuga) and Ndagire Jangu (Ndagire, Come Over), and Freddie Ntare's Susan.

On April 11, 1979, Amin's regime was overthrown. Orchestre Blue Star captured the spirit of this momentous event with the Swahili song Shukurani Kwa UNLF (Gratitude to the UNLF). This track served as a musical tribute to the Uganda National Liberation Front (UNLF), a coalition of Ugandan exiles who, in collaboration with the Tanzanian

People's Defense Force (TPDF), successfully ousted Amin. The song not only celebrated the liberation but also reflected the collective hope and optimism that swept through Uganda during this period of transition. Another memorable song that marked Amin's downfall was Saba-Saba by Kenyan musician Sichangi Wambilianga, who had enjoyed considerable success in Uganda during the early 1960s. Saba-Saba was a humorous yet vivid retelling of the Tanzanian military's defeat of Amin's forces. The narrative began with the expulsion of Ugandan troops from the Kagera Salient and followed the advance of the Tanzanian army through to the fall of Kampala. At the center of the story was the feared saba-saba, the Soviet BM Katyusha rocket launcher, whose thunderous barrage sent Amin's soldiers fleeing in panic. The song also described Amin's escape from Kampala and his frantic journey through a series of towns in eastern and northern Uganda. With its sharp wit and compelling storytelling, Saba-Saba became another major hit for Sichangi, capturing both the absurdity and significance of the regime's collapse.

Afrigo Band emerged in 1975 as a rising musical force, capturing the attention of Ugandan audiences. The group originated from a split with the renowned Cranes Band, with its roots tracing back to January 1974 when a handful of musicians broke away to form the Afrego Jazz Band. Founding members included Jeff Ssewava (appointed bandleader), Moses Matovu, Charles Ssekyanzi, Tony Ssenkebejje, and Jessy Kasirivu. The name "Afrego" reflected Pan-African ideals and a desire to liberate African identity from colonial influence. As Moses Matovu explained, it was short for "Africa Go!", a rallying cry for the continent to move forward unchained. Determined to carve out a unique space, the band positioned itself as a bold alternative to dominant groups like the Cranes and Peterson Mutebi's Tames.

After splitting from the Cranes, the group lacked the funds to purchase musical instruments, a critical setback during Uganda's economic difficulties under Idi Amin, when foreign currency was scarce. In fact, there were no local stores selling musical instruments; even major outlets like Shankar Dass & Sons, which also operated the SDS music label and was run by Ugandans of Indian descent, had shuttered in 1972 following Amin's expulsion of Ugandan Asians. However, Fred Kanyike stepped in and promised to secure the necessary instruments. He arranged for the Afrego Jazz Band to rehearse at Rwenzori Studios, offering full access to the studio's instruments and equipment. Kanyike was rumored to have a vested interest in undermining the Cranes, whose core members included Jeff Ssewava, Charles Ssekyanzi, Tony Ssenkebejje, and Moses Matovu. He had a reputation as a man who could not resist the temptation to shiv a musical rival. Viewing both the Cranes and Peterson Mutebi's the Tames Band as formidable rivals, he had already lured some of the Tames' finest talent into his Rwenzori Band and now allegedly plotted to break the Cranes apart, piece by piece. His ambition, according to those close to the scene, was nothing less than to crown Rwenzori as Uganda's unrivaled musical powerhouse.

The Afrego Jazz Band began as little more than a name. It was held together by the hope that Kanyike would eventually supply the instruments they desperately needed. Rehearsals at Rwenzori Studios were infrequent, with members forced to compete for time on borrowed equipment. Frustrated by the limited opportunities to practice and perform, the group quietly paused its ambitions while awaiting Kanyike's promised support. During this period of uncertainty, Ssalongo Kyeyune, at the White Nile Nightclub, learned of their frustration. Hoping to restore the venue's former glory from the 1960s, when it flourished under Jolly Joe Kiwanuka, he recognized promise in the group's talent. He invited several members to relocate to the White Nile Club where they began performing under a new name, the Rhino Band. Mr. Joseph Kyeyune viewed the Rhino Band, and particularly the talents of Charles Ssekyanzi, Moses Matovu, and Tony Ssenkebejje, as the perfect opportunity to achieve that vision.

The Rhino Band's tenure at White Nile was brief. In April 1974, Moses Matovu returned to the Cranes. But the momentum did not fade. By January 1975, the remaining members regrouped and adopted a new name, Afrigo. Once again, Jeff Ssewava was chosen to lead. This time, the band approached the venture with renewed purpose. They had learned from the frustrations of the Afrego Jazz Band, which had stalled due to broken promises and lack of resources. Although Afrigo still had no instruments of their own and no steady venue, the group was now better coordinated and determined not to repeat past mistakes. Ssewava, in particular, pushed hard to ensure the new band would succeed where they had previously faltered.

For a time, Afrigo existed only in name. But their fortunes began to change when they approached Leonard Mugwanya, proprietor of the Bat Valley Bar and Restaurant. Although the venue was not widely known for hosting resident bands, it had seen performances in the past, including a stint by the Rwenzori Jazz Band from July 1973 to around June 1974. Mugwanya was already enjoying success with the Flames at his Peacock Nightclub and saw potential in Afrigo's pitch. He agreed to support the band and promised to buy them instruments if they could locate the equipment. This commitment laid the foundation for Afrigo to begin regular performances at Bat Valley.

Afrigo's ascent gained momentum in July 1975, when Uganda hosted the 46-nation Organization of African Unity (OAU) summit in Kampala. Delegates were accommodated in top-tier hotels managed by Uganda Hotels Ltd (UHL), a government parastatal responsible for overseeing the country's premier hospitality establishments. In preparation for the summit, UHL undertook extensive renovations and upgraded the musical equipment used by its resident band, Safari Six.

Formed in 1969 as part of UHL's effort to promote tourism and cultural entertainment, Safari Six toured extensively, performing at leading hotels across Uganda. The band, led by G. Mayanja, featured vocalists B. Jessy and J. Moke, with Joe Ssesanga on lead guitar, John Mutebi on rhythm guitar, J. Ndojjo on saxophone, and J. Miti on drums. After UHL acquired new instruments for Safari Six, Afrigo approached the agency and secured an agreement to purchase instruments from the surplus stock.

Leonard Mugwanya honored his earlier promise by funding the acquisition. With instruments finally in hand, Afrigo was ready to step into the national spotlight.

The band officially debuted on November 1, 1975, at Bat Valley Bar and Restaurant, later known as Little Flowers. Their performances quickly attracted attention. Soon after, Tendo Kabanda, manager of Cape Town Villas in Munyonyo and a longtime fan of the Cranes and several Afrigo members, invited the band to play Sunday sets at Amin's lakeside resort in addition to their Bat Valley shows. Cape Town Villas, a retreat frequented by senior army and secret police officers, was largely off-limits to ordinary Ugandans. It was not uncommon to see Bob Astles, one of Amin's most trusted aides, dining with the president himself, who maintained a villa on the premises.

At the time of their debut, Afrigo's lineup included Moses Matovu, Jeff Ssewava, Charles Ssekyanzi, Paulo Sserumaga, Paddy Nsubuga, Fred Luyombya, Anthony Kyeyune, and Geoffrey Kizito. In early 1976, the band recorded its first single, Bwekanya (Equality), composed and performed by Charles Ssekyanzi. That same period saw the release of several other tracks, including Paddy Nsubuga's Omukwano Muzibu (Friendship Is Difficult), Moses Matovu's Werabidde (You've Forgotten), and Njatulira (Disclose to Me), a duet between Ssekyanzi and Matovu. All were released on the Uganda ABP label. During this early period, the group used both Afrigo and Afrego Black Power as band names. The latter, echoing the political mood of the mid-1970s, appeared on some of their initial releases. However, the name Afrego Black Power was eventually dropped in favor of the shorter and catchier Afrigo. By 1978, they had fully adopted Afrigo as their sole identity, a name that would become synonymous with Ugandan popular music.

At Cape Town Villas, Afrigo's fortunes became closely intertwined with Idi Amin. From his villa at the resort, the president first heard the band performing one Sunday and was instantly drawn to their sound. He had played alongside bands like the Five Stars and Air Force Jazz Band, but none had stirred him quite like Afrigo. A representative of the president approached them with an invitation to become Amin's personal house band. Although the group recognized that such close ties to power could be problematic, they felt compelled to accept. From 1976 onward, Afrigo Band was under contract to the president, with its members receiving a fixed monthly salary. Amin also instructed his aides to purchase new musical instruments for the band.

In 1977, Jeff Sewava left the band to form Afrigo Waves in Germany, and Moses Matovu then assumed the role of bandleader. The group continued performing at Cape Town Villas until Amin was deposed in April 1979. During this period, they composed many songs and regularly appeared on Mike Sebalu's Sundowner program on Uganda Television (UTV), which aired every Saturday at 5 p.m. However, as a presidential band, their performance schedule was tightly controlled by the state. They were limited to playing exclusively for the president and at state functions, and they were prohibited from traveling abroad to record. With Uganda lacking proper recording facilities, and with the nearest option being neighboring Kenya, which the government would not permit, most of their new material went unrecorded while under Amin's patronage.

In April 1979, Idi Amin was overthrown by Tanzanian troops aided by Ugandan exiles. In the days leading up to his fall, the air was filled with the relentless roar of artillery and small arms fire. The streets were eerily deserted as residents barricaded themselves at home, fearful of encountering Amin's retreating troops. On Radio Uganda in Kampala, martial music played nonstop, while Radio Uganda International Service in Butebo in Eastern Uganda repeated a few select songs, one of the most memorable being Tabu Ley's Sorozo. As the sound of gunfire faded and Amin's regime collapsed, Uganda's musicians, including the Afrigo Band, were left to navigate an uncertain future, forced to rebuild their lives and careers in a country still reeling from years of fear, loss, and silence.

In the aftermath of Amin's deposition, Uganda descended into a period of widespread looting. Desperate residents scavenged voraciously, plundering everything from basic items like toilet paper at the Army Shop in

Mengo to designer bathtubs they had no practical use for. This looting took on an almost festive air, undeterred by the grim sight of scores of soldiers loyal to Amin lying dead in the streets or the occasional crackle of machinegun fire as remaining loyalists were flushed out of hiding. As Amin's former house band, the Afrigo Band was not spared. They were robbed of all their instruments and forced to start anew. After several months of inactivity, three individuals stepped in to fund the replacement of most of the stolen equipment: Omar Mattar, a Makerere University–trained economist; Samwiri Kapera Tamale, an official with the Sports Club Villa soccer team; and James Wasula, a Kampala businessman.

By October 1979, the band began playing regularly at the Slow Boat Restaurant on Kampala Road, performing every Saturday and Sunday from 2 p.m. to 6 p.m. This schedule was dictated by a government-imposed curfew at 7 p.m., aimed at curbing the insecurity that gripped post-Amin Uganda. In early 1980, the Afrigo Band traveled to Nairobi for their first recording session since 1976, resulting in the album Afrigo Batuuse (Afrigo Has Arrived). The 1980 lineup included Moses Matovu (tenor saxophone, flute, vocals), Charles Ssekyanzi (trumpet, vocals), Paul Sserumaga (lead guitar, vocals), Fred Luyombya (bass guitar), Paddy Nsubuga (rhythm guitar), Eddy Ganja (lead guitar, vocals), Said Kasule (tenor saxophone), James Kibuuka (drums), Saulo Kaliba (trumpet), and Godfrey Mwambala (keyboard). The album featured songs that had become staples during their performances at Cape Town Villas, including Afrigo Batuuse, Enneyisa (Your Manners), Zainabu (a female name), Tondeka Awaka (Do Not Leave Me at Home), Olimujjawa (Where Will You Find Someone Like Me), Christina, Oswadde Nnyo (Shame on You), Yalinze (Waiting for Me), Owe Sente (Omugagga) (The Rich), and Abasajja Tulabye Nnyo (Men Suffer Much). Released on the band's self-established Afrigo Batuuse label, the album marked the first time their music bore the official "Afrigo" name, a name they have proudly maintained ever since.

Although Afrigo was not a major band before 1980, it eventually emerged as the biggest and most impactful band of its generation. In 2025, the group celebrated 50 years of existence, earning its reputation as one of

Uganda's most popular and enduring musical acts. Moses Matovu, in particular, has enjoyed remarkable success with a career spanning more than five decades. While their music is primarily rooted in rumba, Afrigo has also comfortably recorded reggae, kagutema, and a variety of other music genres. Over the years, the band has delivered memorable hits with a beat recognizable to multiple generations. In the process, Moses Matovu built a lucrative business that ensures band members are well cared for. Today, Afrigo is the go-to act at major celebrations when the joyous gravitas of rumba music is required. Unlike many artists who fade from the spotlight, Moses Matovu's name has become virtually synonymous with Uganda's signature rumba beat, the "semadongo" beat.

As of the first half of 2026, the band continued to perform with a strong lineup of seasoned musicians and vocalists. The ensemble included Moses Matovu (vocals and saxophone), Joanita Muganga Kawalya (vocals), Rachel Magoola (vocals), Sarah Namulondo (vocals), Herman Ssewanyana (percussion), Eddie Ganja (lead guitar and vocals), Frank Mbalire (rhythm guitar and vocals), Charles Busuulwa (bass guitar and vocals), Daniel Kaggwa (keyboards), Isaack Zzimbe (drums), Matia Muwonge (vocals), Prince Kazone (vocals), Sarah Ttendo (dancer), Francis Kyeyune (dancer), and Herbert Kiggundu (saxophone). Together, they represent a blend of veteran experience and newer talent that has allowed Afrigo to carry its distinctive sound well into a new musical era.

Moses Matovu was born on June 18, 1949, in Kawempe, a northern suburb of Kampala, Uganda. His early life was steeped in music through a unique blend of cultural influences. His mother, Solome Nakitto, a Christian and dedicated member of the Anglican Church, played a central role in his early exposure to music by taking him to church regularly. At the tender age of four, Matovu joined the Namirembe Church choir, setting him on a lifelong musical journey shaped by hymns and songs of faith. Meanwhile, his father, Abdalla Bukenya bin Adam, a respected member of the Kibuli Mosque, introduced him to the rich traditions of Muslim culture. This fusion of Christian and Muslim influences instilled in Matovu a deep respect for people from all walks of life, a value that has defined both his personal life and his music.

Matovu initially attended Namirembe Primary School, where Sundays were especially significant as he participated in church services and sang in the choir. His passion for music blossomed further when he transferred to Kibuli Demonstration Primary School, bringing him closer to his father. Influenced by popular artists such as Fred Masagazi, Elvis Presley, Jim Reeves, Elly Wamala, and Christopher Ssebadduka, Matovu's early experiences set the stage for a promising musical career. He continued his education at Kibuli Junior Secondary School before moving on to Pillai Secondary School, an institution that was owned and managed by Ugandans of Indian descent. However, political turmoil in 1966, culminating in the fall of the Buganda government, abruptly disrupted his education. Matovu had received a Buganda kingdom scholarship to attend Pillai Secondary, but with the Kabaka deposed and exiled to England, these scholarships were cut, leaving his family to struggle with financial difficulties.

Undeterred, Matovu ventured into music with a teenage band called the Thunderbirds in 1967, which performed at the White Nile Club. Although the band disbanded around 1968, this setback opened new opportunities. Later that year, Moses joined the Uganda Police Band, where he met saxophonist Mansur Bulegeya, a mentor who helped him hone his musical skills, particularly his mastery of the saxophone. In 1969, Matovu left the Police Band to join the Cranes Band, marking a turning point in his career. It was here that he composed and recorded his first major songs, including Bulijjo Ndaaga (Struggling Each Day) and Katonda Yakola (God Made), which were warmly embraced by the Ugandan audience. Known for his humility and infectious modesty both on and off stage, Moses Matovu went on to release numerous iconic tracks such as Emiziro (Totems), Ekadde (Mature), Wapi Sophia (Where Is Sophia?), Mundeke (Leave Me Alone), Jimmy Sasira (Jimmy Forgive), and Katalina (a female name).

Before committing himself to music full-time, Moses Matovu also had a successful career in soccer. He played for notable Ugandan clubs such as Lint Marketing Board, Nakivubo Boys, Express FC, and Police FC. As a right-winger, he wore shirt number 9 and became a fan favorite for his speed and agility on the field.

By the late 1970s, Ugandan musical groups had firmly established themselves with a sound heavily rooted in Congolese rumba, a style that underpinned their compositions and electrified their live shows. Just as Ugandan music seemed securely anchored in the traditions of rumba and dance-driven rhythms, a new and unexpected force was quietly rising. With his rich baritone voice and easy stage magnetism, Jimmy Katumba introduced a sound that marked a departure in popular music in Uganda, offering a gentler gospel-influenced alternative mostly featuring translations of popular American country-music songs rendered in Luganda.

Jimmy Katumba was born on December 9, 1955, to Blasio Katumba, an Anglican priest, and Alice Nakyagaba. Growing up in a musically enriched household, he began his singing journey at the age of eight in the Mukono Church choir. The family's gramophone frequently played records by American country singer Jim Reeves, a sound that would profoundly influence his musical style. Due to his father's frequent transfers, Katumba attended several elementary schools, including Kira, Kakoma, and Mpumu, before pursuing his secondary education at Makerere College and Mengo Senior Secondary School in Kampala. Later, he enrolled at Namutamba Teacher's Training College and began teaching at Buloba Teachers' Training College (TTC).

At Buloba TTC, Katumba's life took a decisive turn when he met Dr. Abbey Kibalama, a devout born-again Christian and charismatic leader who had founded the a cappella gospel group, the Jordan Crossers, in 1962. Recognizing Katumba's talent, Kibalama invited him to join the group, thereby setting the stage for his future in music. In 1975, after Kibalama relocated to Jinja to work with Olivetti Company Uganda and launched another successful gospel group, the Eschatos Bride, Katumba formed his own ensemble, Jimmy Katumba and the Light Bearers. That same year, he recorded his debut songs, Basumba Bakuma (The Shepherd's Protect) and O Little Town (Bethlehem), in collaboration with John Dixon, the organ technician at St. Paul's Cathedral, Namirembe. During his tenure at Buloba, Katumba was also an active member of the historic Masooli choir at St. John's Church of Uganda, led by pharmacist Andrew Samuel Bogere Lubega, who had been nurturing some of the finest Anglican voices since 1964.

The early promise of Katumba's musical journey caught the attention of Perez Bukumunhe, general manager of the Cooperative Bank. Impressed by the group's a cappella gospel repertoire and Katumba's resonant baritone during a modest performance in Kampala, Bukumunhe encouraged them to stage larger shows. However, despite their evident talent, the group had little ambition for national stardom, preferring instead to perform primarily at church functions.

A turning point came when Kampala lawyer John Winston Katende, known by his nom de guerre J. W. K. Ssembajjwe, became captivated by a performance from Katumba and his group. An art enthusiast with a background in theater, Katende was deeply impressed the first time he saw them on a children's television program. Their energy, vocal blend, and stage presence left a lasting impression. Then, in a moment of serendipity, he crossed paths with Katumba on one of Kampala's busy streets. The encounter proved pivotal. Moved by their harmonies and flawless pitch, Katende encouraged Katumba to form a secular music group and pledged to support the effort financially. Knowing he lacked the resources to acquire the expensive instruments on his own, Katumba readily agreed. In 1976, Jimmy Katumba with the Ebonies was born, sealed with a simple handshake between the two men.

To broaden the group's horizons, Katende brought in Yeko Mukasa, formerly of the Rhino Boys (and later the K-Rhino Boys), as a co-founder, and enlisted famed folk musician Evaristo Muyinda to help transition their sound from strictly gospel to a more secular, folk-infused style. Many of the original members hailed from the esteemed Masooli choir and included talents such as Stella Nanteza (who later became Katumba's common-law wife), Mangalita Muwanga, Tina Kigongo, Patrick Dambia, Damali Kyeyune, Isaac Kasasa, and Joy Nakimuli. Over time, the group expanded further, welcoming additional members like Andy Sewanyana, Henry Mpologoma, Peter Clive Lwanga, Jack Muwanga, Kezia Nambi, and Fred Kunya.

Their breakthrough public appearance came during a fundraiser at the Fairway Hotel in support of the construction of the Church House, a project of the Anglican Church of Uganda. The event, which raised $15,000 that was presented to Bishop Dunstan Nsubuga during a ceremony on Buganda Road, won the group widespread admiration and established their reputation among influential well-wishers. In 1978, further support arrived when Yafesi Sabiti, later a deputy minister of Technology and Industry, injected funds into the group, which were used to purchase a state-of-the-art sound system. Demonstrating his commitment, Katumba even took his first flight to London to acquire the audio equipment. Additional financial backing came from Charles Nyonyitono Kikonyogo, then deputy governor of the Bank of Uganda.

The group eventually established a rehearsal space in Kampala's Najjanakumbi neighborhood, affectionately known as "Ebony Village." With a chic and trendy reputation, Jimmy Katumba with the Ebonies became the talk of Kampala and, eventually, the entire nation. Although their primary performances were held in Kampala, the insecurity of the late 1970s forced them to stage shows in safer locales outside the city. This strategy broadened their audience and built a loyal following. Their music, a departure from the dominant Congolese rumba, blended gospel influences with an American country twang, enriched by electric keyboards and synthesizers. Most of the repertoire was composed by Peter Clive Lwanga, who also played keyboards, with additional contributions from Wassanyi Serukenya, Fred Ibanda, and John Katende. Although many Ebonies records list Katumba as the composer, he did not write the music. His role was as a vocalist, bringing his distinctive baritone to songs crafted by the group's talented composers.

Jimmy Katumba with the Ebonies soon became an institution in Ugandan music, renowned for sold-out concerts and a string of hit songs. Early tracks such as Zizinga (a male name), Twalina Omukwano Ne Gufa (We Had A Love That Died), Jesus Save My Soul, and Drums of Africa became anthems embraced across the country. Twalina Omukwano Ne Gufa emerged as a major hit, receiving regular airplay on Voice of Kenya's English service, an unusual feat for a Ugandan song at the time. In 1979, to commemorate a century of Roman Catholic celebration in Uganda, the group released Congratulations and Jubilations, both composed by Peter Clive Lwanga.

The Ebonies' rise in popularity coincided with the turbulent years of Idi Amin's oppressive regime, when Ugandans turned to spiritual solace for hope and liberation. The gospel-countryside genre of Jimmy Katumba with the Ebonies resonated deeply with the public, offering both a musical escape and a spiritual counterpoint to the terror of the era. After Amin's fall, the group's influence only grew, eventually becoming synonymous with national revival and celebration.

Drawing heavily on the style of Jim Reeves, several of the group's songs were vernacular adaptations of his hits. For instance, Emitala Eri (There Yonder) borrowed its melody and rhythm from Reeves' Across the Bridge, with lyrics translated into Luganda, while Kinawataka reworked The Wreck of Number Nine. This creative borrowing earned Katumba the affectionate moniker "Black Jim Reeves," a title that found a home in the hearts of fans, many of whom were moved to tears by his performances, often unaware that the songs that touched them so deeply were local adaptations of country music classics. The group's female vocalists also drew acclaim for their versions of songs by Maywood, the Dutch sister duo Aaltje ("Alie") and Doetje ("Edith") de Vries, especially Mother, How Are You Today and Late at Night, which became hugely popular in Uganda in 1980.

In 1982, during their first concert at Makerere University, the audience was so vast that organizers had to move the performance from the

Main Hall to an open-air space at Science Square to accommodate every-one. Nestled among neatly trimmed lawns and mature trees, with paved paths dividing the space into orderly sections, Science Square offered a rare moment of calm within the bustle of campus life. Its quiet symme-try and shaded corners usually lent themselves to study and reflection, but on that day, the square pulsed with excitement. The university vice chancellor, Professor Asavia Wandira, a bespectacled gentleman of quiet authority and composed demeanor, was the guest of honor. There was even talk of awarding Katumba an honorary degree, underscoring just how revered he had become at that time. Other memorable songs from that decade included Give Me Back My Freedom, Tuzaneku (Let's Play), Mwije Mureebe (Come See), Give Me Jesus, Oh God of Faith, Essaala Za Mama Wange (My Mother's Prayers), Malaika (Angel), and Days of Gun Rule, which poignantly recalled the dark legacy of Amin's rule.

Despite the success and fame associated with his name, Jimmy Katumba never owned the group. As an employee of the group, which was owned by John Katende, he grew increasingly disillusioned with its management. In search of a fresh start, he left Uganda for the United Kingdom in 1990. When his style of music failed to gain traction there, he moved to the United States in 1992 to reunite with his wife, Stella Nanteza. Unfortunately, success in the US remained elusive, and by 1995 a disillusioned Katumba returned to Uganda, where he lived in relative obscurity until his death in 2006.

In the years following his departure, the group dropped his name and became known simply as The Ebonies. Evolving from their musical origins, they transformed into a respected drama troupe, staging popular television shows such as That's Life Mwattu (That's Life, Dear) and Bibaawo (It Happens), among other acclaimed dramas. Today, The Ebonies remain one of Uganda's most successful entertainment acts, a lasting legacy of a group that began as a groundbreaking musical group and evolved into a vibrant cultural institution, with its television dramas still highly antici-pated nearly five decades later.

The story of Uganda's syncretic music is inseparable from the nation's broader journey through colonization, independence, dictatorship, and renewal. Musicians adapted, innovated, and endured, shaping sounds that reflected their times while laying the foundation for future generations. They gave voice to the aspirations and struggles of a people seeking their place in a rapidly changing world. Their melodies filled dance halls, echoed through villages, stirred souls in cathedrals and nightclubs alike, and forged a common language across social and ethnic divides. As this chronicle draws to a close, it affirms that Uganda's music is not a relic of the past but a living testament to the power of culture, creativity, and the deep human instinct to respond to life's complexity, its sorrow and its celebration, through music. In the riffs of the guitar, the rhythms of the drum, and the poetry of verse, generations of Ugandans have inscribed their joys, their grief, their resistance, and their dreams. The songs remember what history forgets.

SELECTED BIBLIOGRAPHY

The following list includes the principal books and articles consulted in the preparation of this work. Numerous contemporary newspaper reports were also reviewed.

BOOKS

Aldrick, Judith. The Sultan's Spymaster: Peera Dewjee of Zanzibar. Naivasha, Kenya: Old Africa Books, 2015.

Alexina MacKay Harrison, The Story of the Life of Mackay of Uganda (London: Hodder & Stoughton, 1906), 112.

Allen, Lara Victoria. Pennywhistle Kwela: A Musical, Historical and Socio-Political Analysis. M.Mus. thesis, University of Natal (Durban), 1993.

Ashe, Robert Pickering. Chronicles of Uganda. New York: A.D.F. Randolph & Co., 1895.

Faupel, J. F. African Holocaust: The Story of the Uganda Martyrs. London: Geoffrey Chapman, 1962.

Gale, H. P. Uganda and the Mill Hill Fathers. London: Macmillan, 1959.

Gibbs, Craig Martin. Field Recordings of Black Singers and Musicians: An Annotated Discography of Artists from West Africa, the Caribbean and the Eastern and Southern United States, 1901-1943. Jefferson, NC: McFarland & Company, 2018.

Hall, Mary. A Woman's Trek from the Cape to Cairo. London: Methuen & Co., 1907.

Kagwa, Sir Apollo. Ekitabo kya Basekabaka b'e Buganda: na be Bunyoro, na be Koki, na be Toro, na be Nkole. London: Luzac & Co., 1912.

Kakembo, Robert H. An African Soldier Speaks. London: The Livingstone Press, 1947.

Kasozi, A. B. K., Nakanyike Musisi, and James Mukooza Sejjengo. The Social Origins of Violence in Uganda, 1964-1985. Montreal & Kingston: McGill-Queen's University Press, 1994.

Kintu, Deborah. The Ugandan Morality Crusade: The Brutal Campaign Against Homosexuality and Pornography Under Yoweri Museveni. Jefferson, NC: McFarland & Company, 2017.

Kiwanuka, M. S. The Traditional History of the Buganda Kingdom: With Special Reference to the Historical Writings of Sir Apollo Kaggwa. PhD diss., University of London, 1965.

Maswere, Koliabu M. Keeping the Faith: Autobiography of a 100 Year Old Ugandan. United Kingdom: Lulu Press, Inc., 2017.

Meier, Prita. Swahili Port Cities: The Architecture of Elsewhere. Bloomington: Indiana University Press, 2016.

Moyse-Bartlett, H. The King's African Rifles: A Study in the Military History of East and Central Africa, 1890-1945. Aldershot: Gale & Polden, 1956.

Ranger, Terence O. Dance and Society in Eastern Africa, 1890–1970: The Beni Ngoma. Berkeley: University of California Press, 1975.

Ssempijja, Nicholas. Glocalizing Catholicism Through Musical Performance: Kampala Archdiocesan Post-Primary Schools Music Festivals. PhD diss., University of Bergen, 2012.

Taylor, John Vernon. The Growth of the Church in Buganda: An Attempt at Understanding. London: SCM Press, 1958.

Tucker, Alfred R. 1908. Eighteen Years in Uganda and East Africa. Vol. 1. London: Edward Arnold.

van Oosterhout, Michiel. The Soul of Uganda Through Song: An Alternative History Book. Kampala: The African Studies Bookstore, Uganda Museum, 2021.

Wilson, C. T., and R. W. Felkin. Central Africa: Naked Truths of Naked People: An Account of Expeditions to the Lake Victoria Nyanza and the Makraka Niam-Niam, West of the Bahr-el-Abiad (White Nile). London: Sampson Low, Marston, Searle & Rivington, 1876.

Wilson, C. T., and R. W. Felkin. Uganda and the Egyptian Soudan. Vol. 1. London: Sampson Low, Marston, Searle & Rivington, 1882.

ARTICLES:

Anonymous. A New Enterprise: The Osborn Awards for the Best African Musicians of the Year. Africa: Journal of the International African Institute 28, no. 1 (January 1958): 84–85.

Anonymous. Duncan, J. M. Obituary. The Musical Times 77, no. 1116 (February 1936): 176.

Anonymous. The King's Harp-Player; or, the Story of Mayanja. The Church Missionary Gleaner, September 1, 1904, 139–140.

Anonymous. Uganda: Death of an Archbishop. Time, February 28, 1977.

Blacking, John. Music in Uganda. African Music: Journal of the International Library of African Music 3, no. 4 (1965): 16–20.

Burger, John Steven. Harry Dean's Untold Trip to Uganda in 1905. International Journal of African Historical Studies 48, no. 3 (2015): 501–505.

Carpenter, Frank G. Uganda's Boy King: The Young Ruler and His Country. The Star (Christchurch), June 13, 1908, 1. Reprinted from the Chicago Sunday Tribune

Chislett, W. A. The Fascination of the Talking Drums. African Music 1, no. 1 (1954): 93.

Clayton, Martin. Ethnographic Wax Cylinders at the British Library National Sound Archive: A Brief History and Description of the Collection. British Journal of Ethnomusicology 5, no. 1 (January 1996): 67–92.

Duncan, J. M. Bach in Baganda-Land: An Impression of the Uganda Jubilee. The Musical Times 68, no. 1016 (October 1, 1927): 924–926

Duncan, J. M. Orpheus on the Equator. The Musical Times 76, no. 1110 (August 1935): 733–734.

Duncan, J. M. The First Organ in Central Africa. The Musical Times 73, no. 1071 (May 1, 1932): 440.

Duncan, J. M. Uganda Choral Festival. The Musical Times 76, no. 1114 (December 1935): 1117–1118.

Gould, Loyal N., James Leo Garrett Jr., and James Leo Garrett. Amin's Uganda: Troubled Land of Religious Persecution. Journal of Church and State 19, no. 3 (Autumn 1977): 429–436.

Gowers, William F. Uganda and Its Future. Journal of the Royal African Society 26, no. 102 (January 1927): 85–92.

Haarev, Fleming. East African Shellac Series – History. AfroDisc, May 20, 2013. https://afrodisc.com/east-africa/east-african-shellac-series/east-african-shellac-series-history

Hanna, Judith Lynne, and William John Hanna. Heart Beat of Uganda. African Arts 1, no. 3 (Spring 1968): 42–45, 85.

Hanna, Judith Lynne. "Africa's New Traditional Dance." African Studies Bulletin 7, no. 4 (1965): 27–39.

Henry M. Stanley, Letters of Mr. H. M. Stanley on his Journey to Victoria Nyanza, and Circumnavigation of the Lake, Proceedings of the Royal Geographical Society of London 20 (1875–76): 134–159.

Hoesing, Peter. Kusamira: Singing Rituals of Wellness in Southern Uganda. African Music: Journal of the International Library of African Music 9, no. 2 (2012): 94-127.

Jabbour, A. African Recordings in the Archive of Folk Song. Ethnomusicology 14, no. 1 (1970): 49–55.

Jones, A. M., and F. Giorgetti. AMS Representatives' Notes. The African Music Society Newsletter 1, no. 6 (September 1953): 68–70.

Kasule, Sam. Don't Talk into my Talk: Oral narratives, cultural identity & popular performance in colonial Uganda". African Theatre 9: Histories 1850-1950, edited by Martin Banham, James Gibbs, Femi Osofisan, Yvette Hutchison, Christine Matzke, James Gibbs, Owen Seda, Samuel Ravengai, Sam Kasule, Cristina Boscolo, Marisa Keuris, Steve Nicholson, Jane Plastow and Yvette Hutchison, Boydell and Brewer: Boydell and Brewer, 2010, pp. 72-89

Kisosonkole, Tefiro. On the Slaughter-Place of Namugongo, Uganda. Translated by Ernest Millar. Man 2 (1902): 135–136.

Kubik, Gerhard. Ennanga Music. African Music: Journal of the International Library of African Music 4, no. 1 (1966): 21-24.

Kubik, Gerhard. Neo-Traditional Popular Music in East Africa Since 1945. Popular Music 1 (1981): 83–104.

Martin, Stephen H. Brass Bands and the Beni Phenomenon in Urban East Africa. African Music Journal 7, no. 1 (1991): 72-81.

Mbowa, Rose. Theater and Political Repression in Uganda. Research in African Literatures 27, no. 3 (Autumn 1996): 87–97.

Musisi, Nakanyike B. A Personal Journey into Custom, Identity, Power, and Politics: Researching and Writing the Life and Times of Buganda's Queen Mother Irene Drusilla Namaganda (1896–1957). History in Africa 23 (1996): 369–385.

Nabeta, Tom. The Place of a Music School in Uganda. Journal of the International Folk Music Council 11 (1959): 41–44.

Nyanza Mission: Journals and Letters. The Church Missionary Review 32 (1881): 618.

Rowe, John A. Eyewitness Accounts of Buganda History: The Memoirs of Ham Mukasa and His Generation. Ethnohistory 36, no. 1 (Winter 1989): 61-71.

Rowe, John A. The Western Impact and the African Reaction: Buganda, 1880-1900. The Journal of Developing Areas 1, no. 1 (October 1966): 55-65

Rycroft, David. The Guitar Improvisations of Mwenda Jean Bosco. African Music 2, no. 4 (1961): 81–98.

S. K. Extract from The Uganda Herald: African Opera at Budo. Newsletter (African Music Society) 1, no. 4 (June 1951): 25.

Schleh, Eugene P. A. The Post-War Careers of Ex-Servicemen in Ghana and Uganda. Journal of Modern African Studies 6, no. 2 (June 1968): 203-220.

Schmidt, Cynthia. The Guitar in Africa: Issues and Research. World of Music 36, no. 2 (1994): 3–20.

Sebuliba, Catherine. The Late Ham Mukasa. Uganda Journal 23, no. 2 (September 1959): 184–186.

Serumaga, Robert, and Janet Johnson. Uganda's Experimental Theater. African Arts 3, no. 3 (Spring 1970): 52–55.

Sidiropoulos, George, and Constantine Eliopoulos. The Mountains of the Moon: A Puzzle of the Ptolemaic Geography. ResearchGate, 2013.

Somervelle, D. C. Orpheus on the Equator. The Musical Times 76, no. 1107 (May 1935): 410-411

Stanley, Henry M. The American Christian Tumbles Islamism to the Ground. New York Herald, November 29, 1875.

Strumpf, Mitchel. Early Studies of the Music of East Africa. In Ethnomusicology in East Africa: Perspectives from Uganda and Beyond, edited by Sylvia A. Nannyonga-Tamusuza and Thomas Solomon, 17–36. Kampala: Fountain Publishers, 2012

Thompson, Gardner. Colonialism in Crisis: The Uganda Disturbances of 1945. African Affairs 91, no. 365 (October 1992): 605-624.

Tracey, Hugh. Osborn Awards for the Best Recordings of African Music for the Year 1953. African Music 1, no. 1 (1954): 69–70.

Tracey, Hugh. Recording Tour May to November 1950 East Africa. African Music Society Newsletter 1, no. 4 (1951): 38–51.

Vernon, Paul. Odeon Records: Their 'Ethnic' Output. Musical Traditions, no. 14 (1997). https://www.mustrad.org.uk/articles/odeon.htm.

Wachsmann, K. P. Music. Journal of the Folklore Institute 6, no. 2/3 (Aug.–Dec. 1969): 164–191.

Wachsmann, Klaus. A Century of Change in the Folk Music of an African Tribe. Journal of the International Folk Music Council 10, no. 1 (1958): 52-56.

Weeks, Sheldon. Kampala: Profile of a City. Africa Today 9, no. 8 (October 1962): 6–8.

White, Bob W. Congolese Rumba and Other Cosmopolitanisms (La rumba congolaise et autres cosmopolitismes). Cahiers d'études africaines 42, no. 168 (2002): 663-686.

Williams, J. G.. The Development of Broadcasting in British Africa. Journal of the Royal Society of Arts 103, no. 4942 (7 January 1955): 113-121.

NEWSPAPERS AND PERIODICALS

Munno (1956 – 1979)

Uganda Argus (1955–1972)

Uganda Times (1979-1980)

Taifa (1964 – 1973)

The People 1966–1971

Voice of Uganda (1972–1979)

Index